LIBRARY OF NEW TESTAMENT STUDIES

347

Formerly Journal for the Study of the New Testament Supplement Series

Editor
Mark Goodacre

Editorial Board
John M. G. Barclay, Craig Blomberg, Kathleen E. Corley,
R. Alan Culpepper, James D. G. Dunn, Craig A. Evans, Stephen Fowl, Robert
Fowler, Simon J. Gathercole, John S. Kloppenborg, Michael Labahn,
Robert Wall, Steve Walton, Robert L. Webb, Catrin H. Williams

THE STARS WILL FALL FROM HEAVEN

Cosmic Catastrophe in the New Testament and its World

Edward Adams

t&t clark

Copyright © Edward Adams, 2007

Published by T&T Clark International
A Continuum imprint
The Tower Building, 11 York Road, London SE1 7NX
80 Maiden Lane, Suite 704, New York, NY 10038

www.tandtclark.com

All rights reserved. No part of this publication may be reproduced or transmitted in any form or by any means, electronic or mechanical, including photocopying, recording or any information storage or retrieval system, without permission in writing from the publishers.

The Scripture quotations contained herein are from the New Revised Standard Version Bible: Catholic Edition copyright © 1993 and 1989 by the Division of Christian Education of the National Council of the Churches of Christ in the U.S.A. Used by permission. All rights reserved.

Edward Adams has asserted his right under the Copyright, Designs and Patents Act, 1988, to be identified as the Author of this work.

British Library Cataloguing-in-Publication Data
A catalogue record for this book is available from the British Library

ISBN-10: 0-567-08912-6 (hardback)
ISBN-13: 978-0-567-08912-0 (hardback)

Typeset by Forthcoming Publications Ltd

CONTENTS

Preface		xi
Acknowledgements		xv
Abbreviations		xvii
1	Biblical and Other Ancient Sources	xvii
2	Abbreviations of Periodicals and Series	xix
3	Additional Abbreviations Used	xx
Introduction		1
1	Previous Study	3
2	N. T. Wright, Language of Cosmic Catastrophe and the End of the Space-Time Universe	5
3	Preliminary Evaluative Remarks	10
4	The Aims, Approach and Structure of this Book	16
5	Clarifications and Distinctions	20

Part 1
The Comparative Context

Chapter 1
The Old Testament   25

1.1	The Genesis Flood Story	25
1.2	The Created World Destined to End	28
1.2.1	Genesis 8.22	28
1.2.2	Psalm 46.1-3	29
1.2.3	Psalm 102.25-27	30
1.2.4.	Isaiah 51.6	31
1.3	Other Viewpoints on Creation's Future	32
1.3.1	The Created World an Enduring Structure	32
1.3.2	The Created World to be Transformed and Made New	34
1.4	Language of Global and Cosmic Catastrophe in Prophetic Discourse	35

1.4.1	Global/Cosmic Catastrophe Language in Oracles against Specific Places	36
1.4.2	Global/Cosmic Disaster Language in Oracles that are More Obviously 'Eschatological'	44
1.5	Conclusions	50

Chapter 2
Jewish Apocalyptic and Related Literature — 52

2.1	*1 Enoch*	54
2.1.1	The Book of the Watchers (*1 Enoch* 1–36)	55
2.1.2	The Similitudes of Enoch (*1 Enoch* 37–71)	58
2.1.3	The Astronomical Book (*1 Enoch* 72–82)	59
2.1.4	The Dream Visions (*1 Enoch* 83–90)	61
2.1.5	The Apocalypse of Weeks (*1 Enoch* 93.1-10; 91.11-17)	62
2.1.6	The Epistle of Enoch (*1 Enoch* 91–107)	64
2.2	*Pseudo-Sophocles*, Fragment 2	66
2.3	*Jubilees*	68
2.4	1 QH 11.19-36	69
2.5	*Testament of Moses*	71
2.6	*Testament of Job*	74
2.7	*Biblical Antiquities*	76
2.8	*Fourth Ezra*	78
2.9	*Second Baruch*	84
2.10	*Apocalypse of Zephaniah*	85
2.11	*Second Enoch*	86
2.12	The *Sibylline Oracles*	88
2.12.1	*Sibylline Oracles* Book 3	88
2.12.2	*Sibylline Oracles* Book 4	92
2.12.3	*Sibylline Oracles* Book 5	93
2.12.4	Anti-Cosmic Dualism in the *Sibylline Oracles*?	96
2.13	Conclusions	96
2.13.1	Eschatological Texts Employing Language of Global and Cosmic Catastrophe	96
2.13.2	Texts Envisaging 'Preliminary' Celestial Disturbances	98
2.13.3	Non-Catastrophic Texts Envisaging the End of the Present Created World	98
2.13.4	Texts Envisaging the Non-catastrophic Transformation of the Cosmos	99
2.13.5	The End of the Present Created World in Jewish Apocalyptic and Related Writings	99

Chapter 3
Graeco-Roman Sources — 101

3.1	Cosmic Upheaval in the Mythical Past	101
3.2	The Presocratics and the End of the Cosmos	104
3.3	Plato and Aristotle on the Indestructibility of the Cosmos	107
3.4	The Epicurean View of the End of the Cosmos	109
3.5	The Stoic View of the End of the Cosmos	114
3.5.1	Cosmic Generation	114
3.5.2	Cosmic Conflagration	116
3.5.3	The Cosmic Cycle	118
3.5.4	The Stoic Defence of the Destructibility of the Cosmos	120
3.5.5	Stoic Portrayals of the Cosmic Catastrophe	122
3.6	Belief in the Catastrophic End of the Cosmos in the First Century CE	125
3.7	Conclusions	126

Part 2
New Testament 'Cosmic Catastrophe' Texts

Chapter 4
'The Powers of Heaven Will Be Shaken': Mark 13.24-27 + Parallels — 133

4.1	The 'Eschatological' Discourse of Mark 13	134
4.2	Readings of Mark 13.24-25	137
4.3	Introduction and First Section of the Discourse: Mark 13.1-23(24a)	139
4.4	The Coming of the Son of Man: Mark 13.26-27	147
4.5	The Language of Cosmic Catastrophe in Mark 13.24-25	153
4.5.1	Identifying the Old Testament Influences	154
4.5.2	The Destruction of Jerusalem and the Temple?	155
4.5.3	Illumination by Comparison	158
4.6	The Catastrophic End of the Cosmos? Reading Mark 13.24-25 in Association with 13.31	161
4.7	Timing of the Catastrophe and Consequences of the End of the Cosmos in Mark	164
4.7.1	Timescale	164
4.7.2	Consequences	165
4.7.2.1	Creational Consequences	166
4.7.2.2	Eschatological Consequences	166

4.7.2.3	Practical Consequences	166
4.8	Matthew's Version of the Discourse	166
4.9	Matthew's Parallel to Mark 13.24-25 (Matthew 24.29)	169
4.10	Timing of the Catastrophe and Consequences of the End of the Cosmos in Matthew	171
4.10.1	Timescale	171
4.10.2	Consequences	171
4.10.2.1	Creational Consequences	171
4.10.2.2	Eschatological Consequences	171
4.10.2.3	Practical Consequences	172
4.11	Luke's Version of the Discourse	172
4.12	Luke's Parallel to Mark 13.24-25 (Luke 21.25-26)	175
4.13	Timing of the Catastrophe and Consequences of the End of the Cosmos in Luke	178
4.13.1	Timescale	178
4.13.2	Consequences	179
4.13.2.1	Creational Consequences	179
4.13.2.2	Eschatological Consequences	179
4.13.2.3	Practical Consequences	180
4.14	Conclusions	180

Chapter 5
'I Will Shake Not Only the Earth But Also the Heaven': Hebrews 12.25-29 — 182

5.1	The Citation of Psalm 102.25-27 in Hebrews 1.10-12	183
5.2	The Shaking of Heaven and Earth: Hebrews 12.25-29	185
5.2.1	Hebrews 12.25-29	186
5.2.2	Objections to an 'End of the Cosmos' Interpretation of Hebrews 12.26-27	191
5.3	Timing and Consequences of the Catastrophic End of the Cosmos	194
5.3.1	Timescale	194
5.3.2	Consequences	194
5.3.2.1	Creational Consequences	194
5.3.2.2	Eschatological Consequences	197
5.3.2.3	Practical Consequences	198
5.4	Conclusions	198

Chapter 6	
'The Elements Will Melt with Fire': 2 Peter 3.5-13	200
6.1 The Complaint of the 'Scoffers' in 2 Peter 3.4	202
6.1.1 'Where is the Promise of His Coming?'	203
6.1.2 'Since the Fathers fell asleep'	204
6.1.3 'All things remain'	206
6.1.4 Summary	209
6.2 The Present Heavens and Earth Reserved for Fire: 2 Peter 3.5-7	209
6.2.1 Exegetical Issues	210
6.2.2 The Utilization of Stoic Cosmology	216
6.2.3 The Arguments of 2 Peter 3.5-7	218
6.3 The Fiery Destruction of the Existing Cosmos: 2 Peter 3.10-12	221
6.3.1 'The heavens will pass away with a loud noise'	222
6.3.2 'The elements will be dissolved in the heat'	222
6.3.3 'The earth and the works in it will be found'	224
6.3.4 Recapitulation in 2 Peter 3.11-12	229
6.3.5 Concluding Observations	230
6.4 Timing and Consequences of the Catastrophic End of the Cosmos	230
6.4.1 Timescale	230
6.4.2 Consequences	231
6.4.2.1 Creational Consequences	231
6.4.2.2 Eschatological Consequences	233
6.4.2.3 Practical Consequences	233
6.5 Conclusions	234
Chapter 7	
'Heaven Vanished Like a Scroll Rolled Up': Revelation 6.12-27	236
7.1 The Dissolution and Re-Creation of the World: Revelation 21.1	237
7.2 The Great Day of Wrath: Revelation 6.12-17	239
7.2.1 Old Testament Influences	240
7.2.2 Similar Images Elsewhere in Revelation	241
7.2.3 Comparison with Mark 13.24-25 + Parallels	242
7.2.4 Socio-political Upheaval, Preliminary Woes or Catastrophic Intervention?	243

7.2.5	The Catastrophic End of the Cosmos?	246
7.3	Timing of the Catastrophe and Consequences of the End of the Cosmos	248
7.3.1	Timescale	248
7.3.2	Consequences	248
7.3.2.1	Creational Consequences	248
7.3.2.2	Eschatological Consequences	249
7.3.2.3	Practical Consequences	250
7.4	Conclusions	251

Conclusions 252

1	Summary of Main Findings	252
2	Significance for An Understanding of New Testament Cosmic Eschatology	256
3	Significance for Environmental Ethics	257

Bibliography 260

Index 281

Preface

This book has been some time in gestation, though I began writing it in earnest while on sabbatical leave in the Lent term of 2003. A further period of study leave granted by my university, King's College London, and matched by the Research Leave scheme of the Arts and Humanities Research Council, gave me the freedom to spend six clear months on the project, uninterrupted by normal college duties, as a result of which I was able to bring the work to completion. I am extremely grateful to the AHRC for the funding given.

I became interested in the topic of New Testament language of cosmic catastrophe in my days as a PhD student (I was investigating Paul's cosmological language), when I first encountered Tom Wright's contention that the early Christians, following Old Testament and Jewish apocalyptic convention, used such language for socio-political change. I published an article in 1997, engaging a bit with his interpretation of Mark 13 and trying to show that Mark's association (but not identification) of the fall of the Jerusalem temple and cosmic destruction compares with Lucan's linkage of the collapse of the Roman Republic with the end of the cosmos in his *Civil War*. Over the next few years, I continued to explore the parallels between Mk 13.24-25, etc., and 'cosmic catastrophe' and 'end of the world' texts in Jewish and Graeco-Roman sources, presenting several research papers in this area, while at the same time pursuing other projects. With the encouragement of others, I decided to write a book on the subject.

I have framed this study, to a large extent, as a debate with Wright and a counter-thesis to his claims, but the book is also an attempt to contribute positively to understanding New Testament eschatology, by focusing on an aspect of it which has not received so much research attention.

In Part 1 of the book, which deals with the comparative context, I have cited extensively the relevant primary texts in English translation. I have done so to enable readers to see and assess the evidence for my claims as they go along. I am grateful to Random House, Inc., and Darton, Longman and Todd, for granting me permission to cite from the translations in *The Old Testament Pseudepigrapha*. Biblical citations in my book follow the New Revised Standard Version though in giving English translations of my key texts, Mk 13.24-25, etc., I have modified the NSRV reading slightly to bring out more the Greek wording, on which my analysis is based.

Two books relevant to this study appeared too late to be taken into account. Andrew Angel's *Chaos and the Son of Man: The Hebrew* Chaoskampf *Tradition in the Period 515 BCE to 200 CE* (Library of Second Temple Studies 60; London and New York: T & T Clark International, 2006) deals with Mk 13.24-27 + par., within the course of the investigation (pp. 125–39). Angel comes to a view of this passage similar to my reading of it: that Mark has taken the 'son of man' figure from Dan. 7.13-14 and identified it with the divine warrior, evoking a different scenario from the scene in Dan. 7.9-14 (pp. 126–8; cf. p. 207). As I do, he sees a parallel development in *4 Ezra* 13 (see also my article, 'The Coming of the Son of Man in Mark's Gospel'). We differ, though, in how we interpret the catastrophe language of Mk 13.24-25. Angel sees it as having a historical application and takes the pericope as a whole as referring to Jerusalem's destruction (p. 133). I interpret it cosmologically. Readers may wish to compare our exegeses both of Mk 13.24-27 and other postbiblical Jewish texts employing catastrophe imagery (especially 1QH 11.27-36 and *T. Mos.* 10.1-10).

Harry Hahne's *The Corruption and Redemption of Creation: Nature in Romans 8.19-22 and Jewish Apocalyptic Literature* (Library of New Testament Studies 336; London and New York: T & T Clark, 2006) contains extensive discussion of how the future of the created world is conceived in Jewish apocalyptic writings. He discusses *1* and *2 Enoch*, *4 Ezra*, *2 Baruch*, etc., more fully than I do; indeed over half the book is devoted to this literature (pp. 35–168).

Hahne distinguishes, as others have done, two strands of thought in Jewish apocalyptic literature, one which looks forward to the transformation of the present creation, and another which anticipates a new creation with a new heaven and earth. In this book, I draw a slightly sharper distinction between Jewish texts that envisage the destruction and re-creation of the world and those that look for a non-destructive transformation of the existing creation, and I question whether any of the writers concerned could have expected a new creation in the sense of a brand new *creatio ex nihilo*. Also, I read some texts, such as *4 Ezra* 7.30-32, as destructionist, which Hahne takes as speaking of transformation. Nevertheless, Hahne recognizes that an 'end of the world' expectation is to be found in a significant number of the works in question. Thus, I see his findings on the Jewish apocalyptic evidence as generally supportive of my own claims.

I have had a number of opportunities to deliver my research, both at King's and elsewhere. I cannot acknowledge here every occasion, but I valued the opportunities to present papers, based on my early research, at the Society of Biblical Literature Annual Meeting, Synoptic Gospels Section in 1999 and the Society of Biblical Literature International Meeting, Pastoral and Catholic Epistles Section in 2001. I am also grateful for invitations to present papers at research seminars of the Universities of Exeter (2002), Groningen (2003) and Cambridge (2006), and for the feedback received on these occasions.

Many individuals have contributed to the process that has led to this work, and to them all I am grateful. Special mention must be made of some. I am grateful to all my colleagues in the Department of Theology and Religious Studies at King's for providing a congenial context in which to work. I would like to thank my Biblical Studies colleagues in particular: Judith Lieu, Richard Burridge, Lutz Doering, Deborah Rooke and Diana Lipton. Judith Lieu, my line manager, has been highly supportive and generous with time and advice. I should also thank my former King's New Testament colleagues, Douglas Campbell and Crispin Fletcher-Louis. Although Crispin is one of those with whom I am in dispute in this book, he is also one from whom I have gained much help, both during and since his time at King's, as I have sought to formulate my case. Despite our academic differences, I am glad to say that he remains a good friend. Michael Knibb kindly read and commented on drafts of Chapters 1 and 2. I must also record my thanks to the late Colin Gunton, who always showed an interest in my research, and invited me to give a paper drawn from this work as it was emerging to the King's College Research Institute in Systematic Theology.

Beyond King's, I am grateful to John Barclay for his encouragement of my pursuit of this project and also for writing in support of my AHRC grant application. George Van Kooten has been supportive of my work from the outset and gave me valuable advice to strengthen my reading of 2 Pet. 3.5-13. David Horrell read a draft of this book and offered detailed feedback, which was enormously helpful in writing the final form of the study. Part of the research for the book was carried out at Tyndale House, Cambridge, and I am grateful to the warden, Bruce Winter, and other members of staff at the House for the various ways in which they assisted my work. I must also thank Harold Attridge, John Dillon, Gerald Downing, Andrew Lincoln, Graham Stanton and Stephen Williams. I want, too, to thank the team at T & T Clark for all their work in producing this book.

Since I am in debate with him here, I would like to put on record my indebtedness to Tom Wright, whom I had the pleasure of getting to know during his time as Canon Theologian at Westminster Abbey. I am one of a great many who have been enthused by his lectures and much influenced by his writings. This book is testimony to his agenda-setting scholarship.

I continue to draw inspiration from the encouragement and love of my parents, Edward and Prudence Adams. My greatest debt, though, is owed to my wife, Ruth, who has shared in my struggle to complete this project (in time for the forthcoming Research Assessment Exercise). I am deeply grateful for her patience and I am immensely privileged to have her love.

Edward Adams
February 2007

Acknowledgments

Parts of the following publications are included, in a revised form, in this book. I am grateful for the permission to reproduce them.

'Creation "out of" and "through" Water in 2 Peter 3:4', in G. H. V. Van Kooten (ed.), *The Creation of Heaven and Earth: Re-interpretations of Genesis 1 in the Context of Judaism, Ancient Philosophy, Christianity, and Modern Physics* (Themes in Biblical Narrative 8; Leiden: Brill, 2005): 195–210. Reproduced by kind permission of Brill.

'The Coming of the Son of Man in Mark's Gospel', *TynBul* 56.2 (2005): 39–61. Reproduced by kind permission of *Tyndale Bulletin*.

'"Where is the Promise of his Coming?" The Complaint of the Scoffers in 2 Peter 3.4', *NTS* 51 (2005): 106–22. Reproduced by kind permission of Cambridge University Press.

ABBREVIATIONS

Biblical and Other Ancient Sources

Standard abbreviations are used for biblical, pseudepigraphal and other early Jewish and Christian literature. Note the following abbreviations:

1 Clem.	*1 Clement*
2 Clem.	*2 Clement*
1 En.	*1 (Ethiopic) Enoch*
2 En.	*2 (Slavonic) Enoch*
2 Bar.	*2 (Syriac) Baruch* [= *Apocalypse of Baruch*]
Apoc. Elij.	*Apocalypse of Elijah*
Apoc. Zeph.	*Apocalypse of Zephaniah*
Aristotle	
Cael.	*De Caelo*
Met.	*Metaphysics*
Meteor.	*Meteorologica*
Asc. Isa.	*Ascension of Isaiah*
Barn.	*Barnabas*
Cicero	
Fin.	*De finibus bonorum et malorum*
Nat. de.	*De natura deorum*
Did.	*Didache*
Dio Chrysostom	
Disc.	*Discourses*
Epictetus	
Disc.	*Discourses*
Epicurus	
Ep. Her.	*Epistle to Herodotus*
Ep. Pyth.	*Epistle to Pythocles*
Eusebius of Caesarea	
Ev. Praep.	*Praeparatio evangelica*
HE	*Historia Ecclesiastica*
Gen. Rabb.	*Genesis Rabbah*
Gk. Apoc. Ezra	*Greek Apocalypse of Ezra*
Gos. Thom.	*Gospel of Thomas*
Homer	
Il.	*Iliad*
Irenaeus	
Ad. haer.	*Adversus haereseis*

Josephus
    Ant.   *Antiquities of the Jews*
    War   *Jewish War*
Jub.   *Jubilees*
Justin Martyr
    1 Apol.   *1 Apology*
    2 Apol.   *2 Apology*
    Dial.   *Dialogue with Trypho*
LAB   *Liber Antiquitatum Biblicarum*
LAE   *Life of Adam and Eve*
Lanctantius
    Inst.   *Divine Institutes*
Lucan
    Phars.   *Pharsalia (Civil War)*
Lucretius
    rerum   *De rerum natura*
Malalas
    Chron.   *Chronicle*
Minucius Felix
    Oct.   *Octavius*
Nag Hammadi
    Great Pow.   *Concept of Our Great Power*
    Orig. World   *On the Origin of the World*
Origen
    C. Cels.   *Contra Celsum*
Ovid
    Met.   *Metamorphoses*
Philo
    Aet. Mund.   *De aeternitate mundi*
    Deus Imm.   *Quod Deus sit immutabilis*
    Leg. ad Gaium   *Legatio ad Gaium*
Plato
    Crit.   *Critias*
    Leg.   *Leges (Laws)*
    Rep.   *The Republic*
    Tim.   *Timaeus*
Pliny the Elder
    Nat. His.   *Naturalis Historia*
Plutarch
    Comm.   *De communibus notitiis adversus Stoicos*
    Stoic.   *De Stoicorum repugnantiis*
Ps. Soph.   *Pseudo Sophocles*
Seneca
    Ben.   *De beneficiis*
    Consol. ad Marc.   *De Consolatione ad Marciam*
    Herc. Oet.   *Hercules Oetaeus*
    Nat. quaes.   *Naturales quaestiones*
    Thyes.   *Thyestes*
Sib. Or.   *Sibylline Oracles*
T. Job   *Testament of Job*

T. Levi	Testament of Levi
T. Mos.	Testament of Moses
Targ. Jer.	Targum of Jeremiah
Tacitus	
Ann.	Annals
Hist.	Histories

Abbreviations of Periodicals and Series

AB	Anchor Bible
AC	L'Antiquité Classique
AJP	American Journal of Philology
AnBib	Analecta biblica
ANRW	Hildegard Temporini and Wolfgang Haase (eds), *Aufstieg und Niedergang der römischen Welt: Geschichte und Kultur Roms im Spiegel der neueren Forschung* (Berlin: W. de Gruyter, 1972–)
ANTC	Abingdon New Testament Commentaries
BBR	*Bulletin for Biblical Research*
BETL	Bibliotheca Ephemeridum Theologicarum Lovaniensium
Bib	*Biblica*
BNTC	Black's New Testament Commentaries
BZ	*Biblische Zeitschrift*
CBQ	*Catholic Biblical Quarterly*
CBQMS	Catholic Biblical Quarterly Monograph Series
CGTC	Cambridge Greek Testament Commentary
ConBNT	Coniectanea biblica, New Testament
EKKNT	Evangelisch-Katholischer Kommentar zum Neuen Testament
GCS	Griechische christliche Schriftsteller
HBT	*Horizons in Biblical Theology*
HSM	Harvard Semitic Monographs
HTKNT	Herders theologischer Kommentar zum Neuen Testament
ICC	International Critical Commentary
JBL	*Journal of Biblical Literature*
JJS	*Journal of Jewish Studies*
JNES	*Journal of Near Eastern Studies*
JSJSup	Journal for the Study of Judaism in the Persian, Hellenistic and Roman Period, Supplements
JSNT	*Journal for the Study of the New Testament*
JSNTSup	Journal for the Study of the New Testament, Supplement Series
JSOTSup	Journal for the Study of the Old Testament, Supplement Series
JSPSup	Journal for the Study of the Pseudepigrapha, Supplement Series
KBANT	Kommentare und Beiträge zum Alten und Neuen Testament
NCB	New Century Bible
NIBC	New International Biblical Commentary
NICOT	New International Commentary on the Old Testament
NIGTC	The New International Greek Testament Commentary
NSBT	New Studies in Biblical Theology
NTS	*New Testament Studies*
OTL	Old Testament Library
RB	*Revue Biblique*
RelS	*Religious Studies*

RevExp	Review and Expositor
RGA-E	Reallexikon der Germanischen Altertumskunde – Ergänzungbände
SBLDS	Society of Biblical Literature Dissertation Series
SNTSMS	Society for New Testament Studies Monograph Series
SNTW	Studies of the New Testament and Its World
SP	Sacra Pagina
SVTP	Studia in Veteris Testamenti pseudepigrapha
TynBul	*Tyndale Bulletin*
TNTC	Tyndale New Testament Commentaries
TOTC	Tyndale Old Testament Commentaries
TZ	*Theologische Zeitschrift*
VC	*Vigiliae Christianae*
VT	*Vetus Testamentum*
VTSup	Vetus testamentum, Supplements
WBC	Word Biblical Commentary
WMANT	Wissenschaftliche Monographien zum Alten und Neuen Testament
WTJ	*Westminster Theological Journal*
WUNT	Wissenshaftliche Untersuchungen zum Neuen Testament
ZAW	*Zeitschrift für die alttestamentliche Wissenschaft*
ZNW	*Zeitschrift für die neutestamentliche Wissenschaft*

Additional Abbreviations Used

ASV	American Standard Version
EDNT	Balz, H., and G. Schneider (eds), *Exegetical Dictionary of the New Testament* (3 vols; Edinburgh: T&T Clark, 1990–3).
esp.	especially
KJV	King James Version
KRS	Kirk, G. S., J. E. Raven and M. Schofield, *The Presocratic Philosophers: A Critical History with a Selection of Texts*, usually cited by text number; reference to page numbers is indicated by p./pp.
LS	Long, A. A., and D. N. Sedley, *The Hellenistic Philosophers: Translations of the Principal Sources with Philosophical Commentary*, usually cited by text number; reference to page numbers is indicated by p./pp.
LSJ	Liddell, H., R. Scott, H. S. Jones and R. McKenzie, *A Greek English Lexicon with a Revised Supplement* (Oxford: Clarendon Press, 9th edn, 1996).
LXX	Septuagint
MT	Masoretic Text
NA 27	Nestle, E., K. Aland et al. (eds), *Novum Testamentum Graece*, 27th edition.
NIDNTT	Brown, C. (ed.), *The New International Dictionary of New Testament Theology* (4 vols; Exeter: Paternoster, 1975–8).
NHL	Robinson, J. M. (ed.), *The Nag Hammadi Library in English*.
NRSV	New Revised Standard Version
NTA	Schneemelcher, W. (ed.), *New Testament Apocrypha*, 2 vols.
OTP	Charlesworth, J. H. (ed.), *The Old Testament Pseudepigrapha*, 2 vols.
SVF	Von Armin, H., *Stoicorum Veterum Fragmenta*, 4 vols.
TDNT	Kittel, G., and G. Friedrich (eds), *Theological Dictionary of the New Testament* (10 vols; Grand Rapids: Eerdmans: 1964–76).
Usener	Usener, H., *Epicurea*.

INTRODUCTION

This book is an investigation of language of cosmic catastrophe in the New Testament: talk of sun and moon failing, stars falling from above, heaven and earth being shaken, elements melting, etc., at the coming of the Son of man or the coming judgement. An important set of questions is raised by this material. Did New Testament writers who used such language envisage a 'real' physical catastrophe? If so, did they expect it within their own lifetimes? Did they think that the coming catastrophe would result in the total destruction of the created cosmos?

If these writers (either in the catastrophe texts or elsewhere in their writings) did anticipate the actual end of the cosmos, what were the corollaries of this conviction for them? Did it generate for them a suspicion of, or even contempt for, creation and the material order? Was it connected in their thinking with a purely 'spiritual' and heavenly view of the final state of salvation? Did they reason that since the cosmos is going to be dissolved, perhaps very soon, there is nothing else to be done except to wait passively for the end?

One would expect that these questions have been exhaustively researched in the course of extensive scholarly discussion of New Testament eschatology since the late nineteenth century. To be sure, answers have been given but mostly at a general level; the subject has not received the sustained research attention that it merits.

In recent discussion, one scholar who has recognized the importance of such questions and has sought to address them, though not in the necessary detail, is N. T. Wright.[1] Wright has done much to put the issue of whether Jesus and his first followers looked for 'the end of the space-time universe', as he puts it, back on the scholarly agenda and also to

---

1. See esp. N. T. Wright 1996: 94–8, 202–9, 320–68. For Wright, the question, 'did Jesus, or did he not, expect the end of the world, i.e. of the space-time universe?' is one of the most crucial questions to be addressed in the scholarly quest for the historical Jesus (1996: 94–5). Other scholars who have addressed that question (though not necessarily as Wright frames it) in the recent phase of historical Jesus research (the so-called 'third quest') include: Allison 1998: 152–69; 1999 (in explicit dialogue with Wright); Borg 1984: 201–27; 1987; Harvey 1982: 66–97; Mack 1988: 325–31; Sanders 1993: 169–88, esp. 173–4.

bring it to a wider public audience.[2] Reacting against both a particular scholarly tradition – that of Johannes Weiss and Albert Schweitzer[3] – and a stream of popular Christian eschatology, Wright is adamant that neither Jesus nor the earliest Christians expected the end of the created world.[4] Jesus had nothing or next to nothing to say about the ultimate fate of the cosmos (and many other topics). His future outlook related to the near, not the far distant, future; the immediate future 'contained for him, as a matter of huge concrete and symbolic importance, the destruction of Jerusalem'.[5] Looking back on Jesus' death and resurrection, the early Christians believed that the decisive eschatological event had already happened. They still awaited a consummation, the final outworking of the past pivotal occurrence.[6] The climax that they looked for was indeed cosmic in scope, but, Wright maintains, it consisted in 'the renewal of heaven and earth' or 'the "exodus" of the whole creation', not its coming to an actual end.[7]

According to Wright, language of sun and moon being darkened, stars dropping from the skies and heavenly powers being shaken was standard Old Testament and Jewish metaphorical language for referring to socio-political change.[8] When Jesus used such language, as he is recorded as doing in Mk 13.24-27 (+ par.), he was not, as many have thought, anticipating the end of the world in a cosmological sense. This passage, and the whole discourse of which it is part, is about the fall of Jerusalem.[9] To interpret these verses literally and cosmologically is to misread and do violence to them. Such a reading is quite at odds with Jesus' intention and eschatological beliefs.

    2. He brings it to wider attention through his more popular works, e.g. N. T. Wright 1999b; 2001: 177–88; 2002: 12–24.
    3. N. T. Wright 1992: 285–6; 1996: 94–8. See Schweitzer 2000; Weiss 1971.
    4. N. T. Wright 1996: 321. Whether Wright is correct in his assessment of Weiss, Schweitzer and scholars under their influence has been questioned by Allison (1999: 128–30) and Gathercole (2000). Much depends on the precise nuance given to 'the end of the space-time universe'; on the ambiguity of this phrase as Wright uses it, see further (in the main text) below. Certainly Bultmann (1952: 4) was of the view that the historical Jesus expected a world-ending catastrophe: 'Jesus' message is connected with the hope of other circles which is primarily documented by the *apocalyptic* literature, a hope which awaits salvation not from a miraculous change in historical (i.e. political and social) conditions, but from a cosmic catastrophe which will do away with all conditions of the present world as it is.'
    5. N. T. Wright 1999a: 270.
    6. N. T. Wright 1996: 322.
    7. N. T. Wright 1999a: 270.
    8. N. T. Wright 1996: 362.
    9. N. T. Wright 1999b: 8.

Wright's views will serve as a reference point for this investigation. Against Wright, I will argue that New Testament cosmic catastrophe language cannot be regarded as symbolism for socio-political change; writers who use this language have in view a 'real' catastrophe on a universal scale. It is plausible to interpret Mk 13.24-27 (+ par.) in terms of catastrophic events that lead to the end of the created cosmos. Other catastrophe passages, I will contend, anticipate more clearly the catastrophic end of the cosmos (as envisaged from an ancient cosmological perspective).

1 Previous Study

Surprisingly, there have been few scholarly attempts to study New Testament 'cosmic catastrophe' texts in an integrated fashion.[10] Anton Vögtle discusses the key texts along with other New Testament passages which appear to speak of the cosmic future in his monograph, *Das Neue Testament und die Zukunft des Kosmos*,[11] published in 1970, a work which remains the fullest study of the topic. He does not, though, bring to bear on the catastrophe texts the full range of ancient comparative data. Moreover, his findings as a whole are undermined by the extent to which he reflects the influence of Rudolf Bultmann's conviction that theology is meaningful only as it relates to *human* existence.[12] After a close examination of all the New Testament texts with seemingly 'cosmic' features, Vögtle concludes that the New Testament contains no authoritative statement on the redemption of the wider cosmos.[13] The New Testament message of salvation centres on God's redeeming action toward human beings. The principal interest of New Testament eschatology is the future of the redeemed community. Thus, 'the question of the relative and absolute future of the cosmos the exegete can leave with good conscience to the scientist'.[14]

---

10. There have, of course, been many articles on the individual passages. The texts have also received detailed analysis in the commentaries.
11. Vögtle 1970; see esp. pp. 67–89, 121–42.
12. Bultmann 1960: 69. For Bultmann, 'only such statements about God are legitimate as express the existential relation between God and man. Statements which speak of God's actions as cosmic events are illegitimate.' See further, pp. 14–21, for his rejection of the whole conception of the world presupposed in the New Testament.
13. Vögtle 1970: 233.
14. 'Die Frage nach der relativen und absoluten Zukunft des Kosmos kann der Exeget mit gutem Gewissen dem Naturwissenschaftler überlassen' (Vögtle 1970: 233).

The cultural and academic climate has changed a great deal since the publication of Vögtle's work. Ecological concerns of the past few decades have helped to generate a new interest in biblical teaching about the wider creation, and a willingness to use biblical perspectives on the natural world as resources for contemporary theological and ethical reflection. In terms of what the New Testament has to say about the future of the cosmos, though, attention has tended to focus on passages which speak more positively of creation's liberation or reconciliation, especially Romans 8, rather than on texts which might envisage its catastrophic end.[15] Thus D. M. Russell, in a study of cosmic eschatology in the Bible and in Jewish apocalyptic writings, looks specifically at the theme of the *renewal* of heaven and earth.[16] His discussion of the New Testament in the main chapter of his book is carried out 'with a view toward clarifying the NT understanding of the natural world and its ultimate redemption'.[17] Yet, of the New Testament texts containing language of cosmic catastrophe only 2 Pet. 3.5-13 is dealt with in any detail, and of course here Russell is mainly interested in the promise of 'new heavens and a new earth' (v. 13).[18] An avoidance of 'cosmic catastrophe' texts when relating the Bible to environmental issues is certainly understandable. The possible thought of the present created order being brought to a calamitous end does not seem all that conducive to the development of a positive Christian environmental ethic. After all, if God is going to destroy (indeed incinerate) his world at the end, why bother trying to care for it in the present? However, as Norman Habel has stressed, it is not enough to concentrate on biblical passages that can be used to support the contention that the Bible is environmentally friendly; it is also necessary to engage with biblical texts which less easily serve the environmental

---

15. E.g., Bullmore 1998 (who identifies Rom. 8.18-23 as one of the four most important passages for Christian environmentalism, the others being Psalm 104; Genesis 1–2; Gen. 9.8-17); Byrne 2000; Elsdon 1992: 155–72 (in a more popular-level treatment); Lawson 1994. For Wright (1999b: 11), Rom. 8.18-28 is one of the most central, and certainly one of the clearest, New Testament passages on God's plan for the future of creation.

16. D. M. Russell 1996.

17. D. M. Russell 1996: 7.

18. Mk 13.24-27 gets a passing, parenthetical mention in connection with Rev. 6.12-17, which is in turn discussed only briefly (D. M. Russell 1996: 206–7). There is no discussion at all of Heb. 12.25-29. Other relevant passages (Mk 13.31 + par.; Mt. 5.18 + par.; 1 Cor. 7.31; Heb. 1.10-12) are also neglected. Yet, I do not want to be too critical of this work. As a focused study of the 'new heavens and new earth' motif against its Old Testament and Jewish apocalyptic background, it is nicely conducted and most illuminating.

cause and which may even undermine it.[19] In an essay for the Earth Bible Project, Keith Dyer attempts to grapple with New Testament 'texts of cosmic terror', as he calls them, from an earth-friendly perspective. He endeavours to rescue Mk 13.24-30 from the distorting 'apocalyptic paradigm', but admits that 2 Pet. 3.5-13 'presents irretrievable problems for an ethical response to ecological problems'.[20] The essay is insightful and provocative but too brief to serve as a thorough treatment of the evidence.

Wright himself has concentrated on Mk 13.24-27 when exploring the question of whether Jesus and his first interpreters expected the end of the physical cosmos, though he has commented on other catastrophe texts in other contexts.[21]

The present book seeks to make a positive contribution to a neglected area of research, but one which is of great importance for our historical understanding of New Testament eschatology (especially cosmic eschatology), and which is significant for Christian theology and Christian ecological ethics. The renewed interest in New Testament cosmic catastrophe language generated by the work of Wright makes the contribution a timely one, as does the growing ecological crisis and the continuing need to develop biblically responsible Christian responses to it. The study will be conducted as a historical enquiry, but in my Conclusion I will discuss, albeit briefly, the environmental implications.

Since Wright is my main dialogue partner, it is appropriate at the outset to set out his claims in more detail and to offer a preliminary response to them.

2 N. T. Wright, Language of Cosmic Catastrophe and the End of the Space-Time Universe

Wright observes that the cosmic language of Mk 13.24-25 has its origins in Old Testament prophecy. According to Wright, the prophets deployed 'the language of a dark sun and a quenched moon, of stars falling from the sky'[22] to describe the fall of a political entity. In Isaiah 13, such imagery is applied to the demise of Babylon (the reference to Babylon is made clear in v. 19); in Isaiah 34, it is applied to God's judgement on Edom (cf. vv. 5-7). These are the very passages alluded to in

---

19. Habel 2000a: 30–1.
20. Dyer 2002: 56.
21. He discusses Heb. 12.25-29 in N. T. Wright 2003a: 163–7 and 2003b: 459, and 2 Pet. 3.5-13 in 2003b: 462–3.
22. N.T.Wright 2001: 183.

Mk 13.24-25. In Old Testament prophecy, so he claims, 'language about sun, moon and stars being darkened or shaken has as its primary reference a set of cataclysmic events *within* the space-time universe, not an event which will bring that universe to its utter end'.[23] The firm hope of the Old Testament is for the renewal of the present created order, not its abandonment.[24]

According to Wright, the metaphorical use of cosmic disaster imagery became a linguistic convention in Jewish apocalyptic writing. Wright deals with 'Jewish Apocalyptic' and 'The Hope of Israel' more generally in Chapter 10 of his *The New Testament and the People of God* (this remains his most detailed discussion of the subject). Jewish apocalyptic writers, he claims, used cosmic catastrophe language just as their biblical predecessors had done – as language for describing momentous socio-political happenings. Such language cannot be read 'in a crassly literalistic way' without doing it serious harm.[25] Yet this is precisely how it has been read and expounded by many interpreters since at least the beginning of the twentieth century. This has resulted in a gross misrepresentation and distortion of Jewish apocalyptic hope.

Some Jews, he thinks, may well have expected or witnessed unusual natural occurrences such as earthquakes and meteorites. No doubt these were interpreted as signs and regarded 'as part of the way in which strange socio-political events announced themselves'.[26] But the events that were expected to come as the climax of Israel's restoration remained firmly within 'the this-worldly ambit'.[27] The anticipated redemption had nothing to do with the created world coming to an end, which Wright calls a 'pagan oddity'.[28] Such an idea makes no sense of the basic worldview to which Jewish people adhered. Wright comments,

> the thought of the space-time world coming to an end belongs closely with the radical dualism which brings together, in a quite unJewish way ... the distinction between the creator and the world, the distinction between the physical and the non-physical, and the distinction between good and evil. The result is a dualistic belief in the unredeemableness of the present physical world.[29]

---

23. N. T. Wright 1996: 209.
24. N. T. Wright 2003b: 86.
25. N. T. Wright 1992: 284.
26. N. T. Wright 1992: 285.
27. N. T. Wright 1992: 285.
28. N. T. Wright 1992: 285.
29. N. T. Wright 1992: 285.

Introduction

A radical dualism of this kind has often been imputed to Jewish apocalyptic literature, but the attribution is completely unwarranted by the large majority of the works in question.[30] Wright is insistent that there is no justification for seeing Jewish apocalyptic as envisaging the end of the world in a literal cosmological sense. He writes,

> The great bulk of apocalyptic writing does not suggest that the space-time universe is evil, and does not look for it to come to an end. An end to the *present world order*, yes: only such language, as Jeremiah found, could do justice to the terrible events of his day. The end of the space-time world, no.[31]

In addition to implying a fundamentally 'unJewish' cosmic dualism, the notion of the end of the space-time world conflicts with belief in bodily resurrection, to which most Jews of the period subscribed. Resurrection logically requires the renewal of creation, not its end.[32]

Summarizing Jewish eschatological belief in the time just before and after the rise of the Jesus/early Christian movement, Wright states:

> Within the mainline Jewish writings of this period, covering a wide range of styles, genres, political persuasions and theological perspectives, *there is virtually no evidence that Jews were expecting the end of the space-time universe*. There is abundant evidence that they, like Jeremiah and others before them, knew a good metaphor when they saw one, and used cosmic imagery to bring out the full theological significance of cataclysmic socio-political events. There is almost nothing to suggest that they followed the Stoics into the belief that the world itself would come to an end; and there is almost everything – their stories, their symbols, their praxis, not least their tendency to revolution, and their entire theology – to suggest that they did not.[33]

What, then, were first-century Jews expecting? In the main, they were looking for an end to the present socio-political order, an order in which the pagans held power and they did not.[34] Their hope was for a restored Israel in the context of a renewed creation. The possibility that some Jews believed that the physical world would actually be dissolved, Wright concedes, cannot be ruled out, just as we cannot rule out the possibility that there were some Jews who believed in five gods and held other absurd notions.[35] But such views are marginal to the literature we have

---

30. N. T. Wright 1992: 297.
31. N. T. Wright 1992: 299.
32. N. T. Wright 1992: 332.
33. N. T. Wright 1992: 333.
34. N. T. Wright 1992: 333.
35. N. T. Wright 1992: 333.

from the period and quite alien to the worldview of the vast majority of the people.

Jesus and the early Christians used cosmic disaster language just as their Jewish contemporaries did.[36] Mark 13.24-25 is not about the catastrophic destruction of the physical universe. In the discourse of Mark 13, Jesus is answering a question put to him by his disciples about the destruction of the temple (and by extension Jerusalem as a whole), which he has just prophesied (13.2). The whole of Jesus' speech remains focused on this issue. Only the grandiose language of cosmic catastrophe could convey the awesome theological significance of the occasion – the fall of judgement on a religious and socio-political system opposed to God.[37] The coming of the Son of man of which Jesus then speaks in vv. 26-27 is not his putative 'second coming', though it is commonly interpreted in this way, but his coming into the presence of God after suffering. The 'coming' is his post-mortem enthronement and vindication, manifested on earth precisely in the event of the destruction of Jerusalem, described symbolically in the cosmic language of the preceding verses.

The 'destruction of Jerusalem' interpretation of Mk 13.24-27 is not original to Wright; it has in fact had a long history as a minority line of interpretation.[38] Over the past few decades, it has been championed by R. T. France[39] and recently, it has also been defended by T. R. Hatina.[40]

For Wright, an 'end of the cosmos' (my term) interpretation of Mk 13.24-27 (+ par.) calls into question in a very serious way the credibility of Jesus and his first followers. In Mark 13, Jesus speaks of the fulfilment of 'all these things', which apparently include the events of vv. 24-27, within a generation (cf. v. 30). If Jesus and the early Christians were confidently expecting the end of the space-time universe within their own lifetimes, then historically, 'they were crucially wrong about something they put at the centre of their worldview'. This means that we must 'either abandon any attempt to take them seriously or must construct a hermeneutic which will somehow enable us to salvage something from the wreckage'.[41] In Wright's view, an 'end of the cosmos' reading of Mk 13.24-27 (+ par.) and other passages would also carry serious

---

36. N. T. Wright 1992: 464; 1996: 320–2.
37. N. T. Wright 2001: 184.
38. Advocates of this reading include Carrington 1960: 281–2; Gould 1896: 249–52; J. S. Russell 1887: 76–83. See further Beasley-Murray 1954: 167–71.
39. France 1971: 227–39; 2002: 530–7.
40. Hatina 1996; 2002: 325–73.
41. N. T. Wright 1992: 285.

theological and ethical consequences. If we see the ultimate destruction of the created cosmos as a feature of the eschatological expectation of Jesus and the New Testament writers (and regard this as authoritative), we buy into a worldview which has more affinities with Gnosticism, which treats the physical world as inherently and irredeemably evil, than with Christian orthodoxy.[42] We also buy into what Wright calls an 'escapist salvation', which looks for redemption out of this world and into heavenly, non-material bliss.[43] Such escapism naturally leads to the relinquishing of social, political and environmental responsibility. If, however, the biblical hope is construed in terms of God's aim to renew his creation, there is 'every possible incentive, or at least every Christian incentive, to work for the renewal of God's creation and for justice within God's creation'.[44]

Wright's general approach to biblical language of cosmic catastrophe reflects the influence of G. B. Caird, under whom he (and France) studied. Wright frequently invokes Caird's name when explicating his own views.[45] Caird summarizes his position in two propositions.

1. The biblical writers believed literally that the world had had a beginning in the past and would have an end in the future.
2. They regularly used end-of-the-world language metaphorically to refer to that which they well knew was not the end of the world.[46]

The Old Testament prophets looked to the future, according to Caird, 'with bifocal vision'. With their near sight, they foresaw an imminent historical event. With their long sight, they saw the final end. They imposed one image on the other to produce 'a synthetic picture'.[47] Thus, for Caird, prophetic passages like Isaiah 13 have a double reference, pointing both to a historical crisis on the speaker's immediate horizon and the ultimate end of the world. Wright obviously rejects the second part of Caird's first proposition, though he does not make explicit that he departs from Caird on this point. For Wright, the prophetic metaphor has no basis in any real expectation of the physical world coming to a spectacular end.

Wright's claims have met with approval and support,[48] but also with caution and criticism.[49] His main critic to date (on this issue) has been

---

42. N. T. Wright 1999b: 9.
43. N. T. Wright 1999b: 12.
44. N. T. Wright 1999b: 21.
45. N. T. Wright 1996: 362. See also, pp. 75, 95, 97, 208–9, etc.
46. Caird 1980: 256.
47. Caird 1980: 258.
48. E.g., Fletcher-Louis 1997: 2002.

Dale Allison, who argues for a more literal reading of Mk 13.24-25 and points to 2 Pet. 3.10-13, which, in his view, quite clearly envisions an eschatological scenario involving the catastrophic destruction of the cosmos.[50]

3 *Preliminary Evaluative Remarks*

In bringing the issue of whether Jesus and the early Christians looked for the (catastrophic) end of the cosmos to the forefront of scholarly attention, Wright has performed a valuable service. As stated in my opening comments, the question has not, in my view, received the thorough airing in the scholarly forum that it deserves, and Wright has made this discussion possible.[51] I strongly endorse Wright's view that New Testament language of cosmic catastrophe should be read in its first-century cultural context, though for me this must include the Graeco-Roman context as well as the Jewish one. I can appreciate the appeal of his interpretation of Mk 13.24-27 and his larger reading of the discourse of which these verses are part. It nicely removes any question of Jesus here predicting the collapse of the cosmos within the lifetime of his own contemporaries, and thus being mistaken,[52] but, as I will show later, for various reasons, it is an unsatisfactory line of exegesis.

Wright's thesis that Jesus and his early followers used cosmic catastrophe language in a historical sense, and not in a cosmological and destructionist sense, rests on two main claims relating to the Jewish context: first, that the idea of the created world coming to an actual end was foreign to mainline Jewish thinking; second, that the use of cosmic disaster language for socio-political events was a linguistic convention,

---

49. E.g., Blomberg 1999: 28–9; Eddy 1999: 43–9.
50. Allison 1999.
51. In recent systematic theology, the question of creation's future has received considerable attention from Jürgen Moltmann; see 1979; 1985: 276–96; 1996. Whether the created universe is to be transformed or dissolved and created anew has been a classic topic of Christian theological debate. There was particularly intense discussion of the matter among Lutherans and Calvinists in the seventeenth century. The issue has traditionally been framed in terms of whether heaven and earth are to be transformed or annihilated (i.e. blotted out of existence) and replaced by a brand-new heaven and earth created *ex nihilo* (cf. Berkouwer 1972: 219–25). But it is inappropriate to put the question in this way when dealing with the New Testament evidence. See further §5 below.
52. N. T. Wright 1996: 341. Because it rather too neatly removes this potential embarrassment, Wright's reading arouses Allison's suspicion (1999: 136–7). But it would be a mistake to dismiss it simply on the grounds of its apologetic value.

especially in Jewish apocalyptic writing, rooted in Old Testament prophecy. In my view, Wright has established neither of these claims.

The second claim is founded essentially on a selection of Old Testament 'proof-texts', especially Isaiah 13 and 34. For Wright, such passages show that the Old Testament prophets used cosmic calamity language for events in the socio-political realm. He then maintains that Jewish apocalypticists and other Jewish writers did likewise. But he does not demonstrate the latter point through a careful analysis of the relevant passages in post-biblical apocalyptic and related writings. Indeed, he hardly engages with this material at all.[53] When discussing Jewish apocalyptic, his frame of reference is his own model and generalized account of the phenomenon, rather than the textual data themselves. Wright's failure to substantiate his claim with a body of supporting evidence in post-biblical Jewish sources constitutes a major lacuna in his argument. It is a common view that later apocalyptic writers who took over the cosmic disaster imagery of the biblical prophets used it in a more clearcut final sense than perhaps their biblical forerunners had done.[54] Christopher Rowland, who is rather less inclined than others to draw a sharp distinction between 'prophecy' and 'apocalyptic', at least in terms of eschatology,[55] thinks that, while Old Testament predictions of cosmic disorders were exhausted in historical events of the time, 'in later Jewish eschatology there is sometimes an additional reference to a last assize when God metes out justice to all mankind'.[56] France, who fully agrees with Wright's interpretation of cosmic language in Old Testament prophecy, concedes that in later apocalyptic, 'while such language is relatively uncommon, it has apparently a more "end of the world" reference appropriate to the focus of these works'.[57]

Wright is not necessarily on sure ground in his statements about the original prophetic meaning of this kind of language. The juxtaposition of universal/cosmic and local perspectives in Isaiah 13 and 34 and similar passages is capable of different explanations. Caird, as we have seen, maintained that Isaiah and other prophets really did believe in the actual end of the world, but used 'end of the world' language metaphorically to

---

53. Of the texts that are germane, only *T. Mos.* 10.1-10 figures in the discussion (N. T. Wright 1992: 304–6), and it is dealt with in a cursory fashion.

54. Collins 2000a.

55. Rowland 1982; Rowland rejects the notion of a distinct 'apocalyptic eschatology': see 1982: 23–48.

56. Rowland 1982: 158.

57. France 2002: 533 n. 8. As we will see, the language is not as uncommon as France thinks.

refer to impending historical crises. Thus, these prophecies have a double reference, an immediate historical one and a final-eschatological one. Caird's interpretation is not unproblematic,[58] but in my view it is a more credible account than that offered by his student.[59] As far as Wright is concerned, the cosmic metaphors are effectively grounded on a wholly impossible (and frankly absurd) prospect. But if so, it is difficult to see how these metaphors could be relied upon by the prophets to convey the appropriate level of threat and foreboding that their warnings of impending judgement seem to require. Also, Wright fails to reckon with the apparent development in prophetic usage of this idiom. In later oracles, especially Isaiah 24, global and cosmic catastrophe language does seem to have a more exclusive, final-eschatological reference,[60] which most scholars see as anticipating the application given to it in post-biblical Jewish apocalyptic writings.

Wright's other major claim – that the idea of the created cosmos coming to an end was alien to mainstream Jewish thought – is also not based on an assessment of the literary evidence; rather, it rests on the supposed incongruity of such an idea with other aspects of Jewish eschatology: the common 'this-worldly' view of the future; the hope for the world's 'renewal'; the hope of bodily resurrection. It also, in Wright's view, contradicts Jewish creational monotheism, implying that 'the created order is residually evil'.[61] However, the alleged logical incompatibilities do not stand up to scrutiny.

That Jewish apocalypticists normally envisioned the eschatological state of blessedness in 'this-worldly' terms has been convincingly demonstrated by Rowland.[62] The locus of eschatological blessing in apocalyptic works is often a world very much like the present one, with embodied people, buildings, cities, gardens, etc., but with all the imperfections of the current order erased. However, such a view of the final state of things is not in principle irreconcilable with a genuine expectation that the present created world must come to an end. Rowland does not seem to regard these ideas as mutually exclusive.[63] It is perfectly possible to believe both in the end of the world, in a fully cosmological

---

58. For criticisms, see Geddert 1989: 232–3.
59. Though, as will I suggest in the next chapter, the juxtaposition is best explained in terms of the device of particularization: see pp. 43-4.
60. See further next chapter, pp. 44-50.
61. N. T. Wright 1992: 300.
62. Rowland 1982: 160–76. Cf. Collins 2002: 39–40.
63. E.g., Rowland 1982: 168, recognizing that the eschatological climax in *4 Ezra* involves the return of the world to its primeval condition.

sense, and to have a decidedly 'this-worldly' conception of what follows thereafter. There is hardly any other way of conceiving of a new cosmic reality, which is by definition beyond human experience, than in terms drawn from the present created order. That belief in the destruction of the present cosmos and a fully 'this-worldly' view of the new cosmos can happily co-exist in ancient thinking is shown by the Stoic theory of cosmic conflagration and regeneration. The Stoics expected this present cosmos to be resolved completely into fire and a brand-new cosmos to arise out of the consuming flames. But they believed that the new world would be an exact replica of the current one, and that the whole history of the present cosmos, right down to minute details, would be repeated in the next one.[64] To argue, as Wright does,[65] that the 'this worldly' character of Jewish visions of the new age rules out the possibility of belief in the destruction of the present world is to employ a fallacious line of reasoning.

The expectation of the end of the present created world can also cohere with the expectation of cosmic renewal. It has long been accepted that Jewish apocalyptic writers tend to envisage the final cosmic renewal as either the *re-creation* of the universe or its miraculous *transformation*.[66] Certainly, there can be no thought of a cataclysmic end to the present created order if the expected cosmic renewal is visualized in terms of non-destructive transformation. But if the final renewal is construed as the *remaking* of the heavens and earth, a prior act of *unmaking* would seem to be required. So long as the destruction of the world is followed by an act of cosmic re-creation and this action involves the restoration of the original, even though there may be an enhancement and perfection of it, then world-destruction and world-renewal are not theoretically incompatible. What would be more difficult to square with the concept of cosmic renewal would be the view that the existing world is dissolved into nothing and a completely new world, materially discontinuous with the old, takes its place. But such a conception belongs to later eschatological speculation and not to our period (see further below).

Belief in bodily resurrection, as Wright stresses, does seem to entail a 'worldly' state of final blessedness (an environment for re-embodied

---

64. See further Chapter 3.
65. This line of argument is explicit in 1999a: 265. Wright states: 'we have no reason to suppose that any Jews for whom we have actual evidence expected that the space-time universe was going to come to a stop ... However "cosmic" their language, they clearly envisaged events *after which* there would still be recognizable human life on the recognizable planet, albeit in drastically transformed conditions.'
66. Cf. Aune 1998b: 1116; Volz 1966: 338–40.

people to inhabit), rather than a totally non-material, ethereal state of existence.[67] However, Wright's basic condition could be met in a cosmic-eschatological scheme involving the destruction and re-creation of the world. Resurrection does not in itself rule out the idea of the future dissolution of the existing created order. It rather suggests that a material re-creation should follow the dissolution.

A radical cosmic dualism in which the material world is regarded as inherently evil would certainly fly in the face of the Old Testament view of the natural world as God's good and well-constructed creation. Wright regards this extreme dualism as typical of 'Gnosticism', but recent scholars who work with the sources conventionally labelled 'Gnostic' – principally the Nag Hammadi texts – have stressed the range of cosmological views displayed in them.[68] Certainly, the catastrophic demise of the cosmos is bound up with a negative cosmology in the Nag Hammadi tractate *On the Origin of the World*.[69] In this work, the metaphor of abortion is used to explain the unfortunate circumstances through which this flawed cosmos came into being (*Orig. World* 99).[70] Matter is equated with the afterbirth following the expulsion of the aborted foetus. At the final resolution, the material cosmos is destroyed in cataclysmic fashion by its creator who then turns against and destroys himself (126).[71] In this way, the deficiency is plucked out at its very root (127.3). There is no material re-creation following the destruction; at the final state, it is like creation 'has never been' (127.1).[72] One must not assume, however,

---

67. Though, of course, language of resurrection can be spiritualized, as in the Nag Hammadi literature, on which see N. T. Wright 2003b: 534–51. Paul's defence of resurrection in 1 Corinthians 15 has sometimes been interpreted as implying an ethereal afterlife; for criticisms, see N. T. Wright 2003b: 348–56.

68. The legitimacy of the label 'Gnosticism' for the range of texts and phenomena to which it has been applied is now intensely debated: see King 2003; M. A. Williams 1996. On the variety of cosmological perspectives in the Nag Hammadi literature, see King 2003: 192–201. King (2003: 200) demonstrates that these writings 'do not supply consistent evidence of the extreme anticosmic dualism for which they so often stand as the most famous example in Western history'.

69. The date of the tractate is disputed; it is no earlier than the second half of the second century CE, and may even have been composed in the fourth century (*NHL*, 170).

70. This is a radical re-working of the birth metaphor used from ancient times to explain the origin of the cosmos. Perkins (1980: 37–8) finds here a polemic against Stoic cosmogony in particular. On Stoic cosmogony, see further Chapter 3, pp. 114-16.

71. Again, Perkins (1980: 43–4) finds an anti-Stoic polemic here.

72. MacRae (1983: 323) stresses the complete absence of any new creation in 'Gnostic' eschatology.

that every ancient expression of the idea of the end of the world was bound to an anti-cosmic dualism like this. Stoicism shows that the notion of cosmic dissolution could be held in ancient times within an entirely *monistic* framework of reality, indeed a framework in which the physical cosmos is valued in the highest terms possible (being revered as divine). Caird did not think that belief in the literal end of the world unavoidably entailed a dim view of creation and was happy to attribute the belief to Old Testament writers. Whether the thought of the destruction of the cosmos for Old Testament and Jewish writers who express it implies an anti-cosmic dualism can only be established by looking at what they have to say about creation; it should not be prejudged at the outset.

I will not at this juncture enter into a critique of Wright's reading of Mk 13.24-27 and the discourse as a whole. One point, though, is worth making here. From Wright, one gains the impression that his socio-political interpretation of the cosmic language of vv. 24-25 in terms of the fall of Jerusalem stands over against a consensus 'literal' reading of it in terms of the end of the space-time world.[73] However, vv. 24-25 have been much debated,[74] and many interpreters have stressed that the language should not be read as straightforward 'literal' description.[75] A survey of scholarly opinion shows that a wide variety of views has been expressed on how best to interpret the language (or to understand the metaphors), and, as far as I can tell, there is no clear-cut majority viewpoint. Wright's depiction of the *status quaestionis* with regard to Mk 13.24-25 is thus a little misleading.

As indicated above, Wright has (so far) given much less attention to the other New Testament 'cosmic catastrophe' texts. He rejects the idea that the end of the cosmos is in view in Heb. 12.26-27 and 2 Pet. 3.5-13, but he does acknowledge that a cosmic change is envisaged.[76] It is surprising that he does not defend a socio-political interpretation of the catastrophe language in these two passages. It is not clear (at least to me)

---

73. N. T. Wright 1996: 339–43.
74. See Verheyden 1997: 525–34.
75. Cranfield (1959: 406) calls it 'picture-language' (so also Moule 1965: 107). Hare (1996: 176) states that 'verses 24-25 are poetry, not prose'. Gnilka (1979: 200) comments: 'Ihre Sprache liegt in der Mitte von Metaphorik und Realistik.' Similarly, Hooker (1991: 319) opines that the language is 'more than metaphorical, less than literal'. Hurtado (1989: 222) states: 'the description of the events is not intended as a specific and literal indication of their appearance'. Ladd (1994: 203) thinks that the language 'is poetic and not meant to be taken with strict literalness'. Witherington (2001: 348) states that 'the author is describing cosmic phenomena, but he is not giving an exact or scientific description of the phenomena'.
76. N. T. Wright 2003b: 459, 462–3.

how his approach to these passages squares with his general claim that the early Christians, like their Jewish contemporaries and predecessors, used the imagery of cosmic catastrophe to bring out the full significance of events in the social and political spheres.

4 *The Aims, Approach and Structure of This Book*

This study focuses on New Testament texts employing language of cosmic catastrophe (upheaval, shaking, burning).[77] The passages at the heart of our enquiry are as follows: Mk 13.24-25 and its Matthean and Lukan parallels (Mt. 24.29-31; Lk. 21.25-27); Heb. 12.25-29; 2 Pet. 3.5-13; Rev. 6.12-17.[78] In Mk 13.24-25 + par., Jesus speaks of various cosmic convulsions, including the collapse of the stars, at the coming of the Son of man. In Heb. 12.25-29, the writer warns that God has promised to shake heaven and earth; this cosmic shaking will result in the removal of 'created things'. Second Peter 3.5-13 is a defence of the hope of the Lord's parousia against scoffers who mock God's slowness in fulfilling this alleged promise. The author depicts the day of the Lord as a fiery catastrophe in which 'the heavens will pass away with a loud noise, and the elements will be dissolved in the heat' (v. 10; cf. v. 12). Revelation 6.12-17 envisions cosmic shaking and darkening, stellar collapse and global chaos on the great day of divine wrath.

Other relevant passages will figure heavily in this discussion, most importantly: Mk 13.31 + par., which speaks of heaven and earth passing away; Heb. 1.10-12, a citation of Ps. 102.25-27 affirming that heaven and earth will perish; Rev. 21.1, a visionary declaration of the passing away of the present heaven and earth.

---

77. By 'text' here and generally throughout, I mean a short passage within a written work rather than a written work as a whole.

78. The absence of Pauline texts from this list may seem surprising, but the fact is that we do not find the language of cosmic catastrophe in the Pauline epistles. In his most descriptive passage on the parousia, 1 Thess. 4.15-17, a text which bears some resemblance to Mk 13.24-27 + par., and which may perhaps reflect a knowledge of it (see, e.g., Allison 1999: 135), Paul makes no mention of catastrophic occurrences. The destructive aspect of the parousia is more in view in 2 Thessalonians (1.6-10; 2.7), one of the disputed Pauline epistles, but nothing is said of catastrophic events impacting the natural world.

I do not include Acts 2.19-20, which cites Joel 2.30-31, in this list, because it only contains the motif of the darkening/discolouration of the sun and moon (also found on its own in Rev. 8.12; 9.1-2), which by itself need not betoken a full-blown cosmic catastrophe. I do discuss Acts 2.19-20 but in connection with Lk. 21.25-26 (see p. 177, n. 219).

My primary aim in this study is to try to establish whether the 'cosmic catastrophe' texts have in view an actual catastrophe and, if so, whether that catastrophe results in the total destruction of the created cosmos. I will argue as follows: in all of the catastrophe passages the reference is to an expected 'real' calamity on a universal scale, as the accompaniment of the parousia or the form of the coming judgement. In Heb. 12.25-28 and 2 Pet. 3.5-13, total cosmic destruction is definitely envisaged. It is plausible to regard the catastrophic convulsions of Mk 13.24-27 + par. as resulting in cosmic dissolution. The cosmic occurrences of Rev. 6.12-17 either prefigure or initiate the passing away of the present heaven and earth (cf. Rev. 21.1).

I want to make clear from the outset that it is not my intention to argue for a 'literal' interpretation of New Testament language of cosmic catastrophe over against a metaphorical or figurative one.[79] Right away, I want to side with those who insist that in Mk 13.24-25 we are not dealing with the language of literal or prosaic exactitude. I think it should be obvious that what we have here is linguistic *imagery*, and this will become even clearer on closer inspection. The point I wish to establish in my exegesis is that these writers use language and imagery of universal catastrophe for envisioning precisely that. Since a full-blown cosmic catastrophe (in which the whole solar system is shaken or totally destroyed) is outside human experience, there is no other way of envisioning it than by figure, analogy and imaginative construal.[80]

A secondary aim of this project is to examine the time frame for the anticipated catastrophe in these texts. According to Wright, if we interpret Mk 13.24-27 + par. in 'end of the world' terms, we are forced to conclude that Jesus and his earliest interpreters were mistaken in their eschatology (in a highly embarrassing way). Is the expectation of catastrophic intervention tied to a restricted and delimited timescale for fulfilment, i.e. the lifetime of the first Christians? What signals are given as to the timing of the event?

According to Wright, the very idea of the created cosmos coming to an end has deleterious theological and ethical consequences. A further subsidiary aim is thus to identify or tease out the implications and associations of the notion of the end of the cosmos for the writers. I will do so under the following headings, posing the following questions:

---

79. According to Dyer (2002: 51), the metaphorical/literal distinction betrays 'an underlying modernist duality'.

80. The author of 2 Peter, though, we will see, aims at a more scientifically informed description of the final catastrophe in order to address the objections of his opponents.

- *Creational consequences.* Does the thought of the world's coming to an end engender a disdainful or suspicious attitude toward creation and the material order? Is it linked to a radical cosmological dualism which regards the physical world as congenitally evil?
- *Eschatological consequences.* Is the expectation of cosmic destruction linked with a view of the final eschatological state as one which is purely heavenly and non-material (a perspective the Earth Bible Team has labelled 'heavenism')?[81] Is a material re-creation expected to follow the dissolution of the existing world? If a re-creation is expected, how is the new creation conceived in relation to the present world?
- *Practical consequences.* Does the expectation of the end of the cosmos encourage passivity and stagnation?[82]

It is appropriate to ask these questions of all of our authors, since each of them (it will be seen) expresses belief in the actual end of the present cosmos, if not definitely in the catastrophe texts, then in other passages in their writings. In some cases, only partial answers can be given and, at times, it will be necessary to speculate. But it is important, I think, that the questions are asked and explored.

The approach taken in this study is a historical and exegetical one, conducting a close examination of the key texts in their immediate and wider textual contexts. I will also engage in comparative analysis, using relevant Jewish and even Graeco-Roman comparative material to illuminate the New Testament passages.

What constitutes 'relevant' comparative data needs some explanation. The passages Mk 13.24-25 (+ par.), Heb. 12.26-27 and Rev. 6.12-17 derive their catastrophic imagery from Old Testament prophetic passages such as Isaiah 13 and 34. It is therefore right to look at how such language is used in Old Testament prophetic discourse, and we will take the time to do so. But how the original prophetic writers used this language is not necessarily determinative for New Testament usage. It is more important to have a grasp of how this language, rooted in Old Testament prophecy, was being used and understood in Intertestamental times and

---

81. Earth Bible Team 2002: 3–5. 'Heavenism' is 'the belief that heaven, as God's home, is also the true home of Christians, the place where they are destined to dwell for eternity' (3). The earth is viewed, by contrast, as a temporary and disposable 'stopping place' on the way to heaven (4).

82. Wright does not claim that belief in the end of the space-time universe leads to total passivity, but this has sometimes been seen as a potential corollary of theological belief in the destruction of the world; cf. Elsdon 1992: 190–1.

in the New Testament period. Hence, more attention will be devoted to 'global/cosmic catastrophe' texts in post-biblical Jewish apocalyptic and related writings, and more use will be made of this material in shedding light on the New Testament passages.

Language of cosmic catastrophe was not confined to certain Jewish circles in the world of the first century CE. As Gerald Downing has shown, we also find this imagery in first-century Graeco-Roman,[83] especially Stoic, literature.[84] Indeed, such language, so Downing claims, was shared parlance among Jews, pagans and the early Christians. Though the Graeco-Roman parallels have rarely been taken seriously in discussion of New Testament 'cosmic catastrophe' texts (Downing's articles apart), they form part of the cultural context and must be brought into consideration. The Stoic doctrine of cosmic conflagration, which, as we will see, has exerted an influence on some catastrophe passages in the Jewish *Sibylline Oracles*, is especially relevant to 2 Pet. 3.5-13. Commentators have regularly noted superficial resemblances between this passage and Stoicism but the possibility of Stoic influence is quickly dismissed. I will explore the parallels in some detail and try to show that the writer of 2 Peter has made use of Stoic cosmological teaching in his defence and articulation of the hope of the parousia.

The book divides into two parts. The first sets out the Jewish and Graeco-Roman comparative context. Chapter 1 deals with the Old Testament background. Chapter 2 explores comparative material in Jewish apocalyptic and related writings. Chapter 3 examines language of cosmic disaster and perspectives on the destiny of the cosmos in Graeco-Roman sources.

The second part of the book deals with the New Testament texts. Chapter 4 examines Mk 13.24-27 and its parallels in Matthew and Luke. I should make clear that I am not seeking to determine what Jesus meant by these words if indeed he spoke them or anything like them. My interest lies in the meaning of the catastrophe language for the evangelists. I work on the (generally accepted) understanding that each of the evangelists is not merely a compiler of traditions and sources, but an 'author'

---

83. By 'Graeco-Roman' sources I mean non-Jewish sources from Greek and Roman antiquity. I have chosen not to engage with Persian sources due to the notorious problems in dating this material (cf. Collins 1998: 29–33; see Hultgard 2000 for a more positive assessment). A cosmic conflagration was predicted in the Iranian *Oracle of Hystaspes*, known to Justin Martyr (*1 Apol.* 20.1) and other early church fathers. For discussion and an attempt to reconstruct its contents from passages in Lactantius, see Hinnells 1973.

84. Downing 1995a; 1995b.

and theologian in his own right. I also assume that one can look for a certain level of consistency (not, of course, watertight consistency) in their redactional patterns and proclivities and in their theological perspectives, especially their eschatological outlook. Chapter 5 is concerned with Heb. 12.25-29. In Chapter 6, I discuss 2 Pet. 3.5-13. Chapter 7 treats Rev. 6.12-17.

In the Conclusion, I summarize the key points of the investigation of the New Testament texts and reflect on their significance for a broader historical understanding of New Testament cosmic eschatology. I also discuss the implications for Christian environmental ethics.

5 *Clarifications and Distinctions*

It is important, before we proceed, to clarify what is meant by some of the key terms in this discussion: cosmic catastrophe; global catastrophe; the end/destruction/dissolution of the cosmos.

By 'cosmic catastrophe', I mean a physical disaster that affects both the material heavens (including sun, moon and stars) and the physical earth. The result need not be the total destruction of the material cosmos. Some of the comparative texts we will look at envisage a catastrophe that is cosmic in scope but which does not actually bring about the complete collapse of the cosmos; the earth is devastated and the heavens rocked, but the created world manages to survive. A cosmic catastrophe can either threaten the stability of the cosmos or bring about its dissolution. I will argue that all of the New Testament passages in question have in view a catastrophe that at least destabilizes the cosmic order. Two passages quite definitely envision a catastrophe that ends in cosmic destruction (Heb. 12.25-29; 2 Pet. 3.5-13).

In discussing Old Testament and later Jewish catastrophe texts, I draw a distinction between 'cosmic' and 'global' catastrophe, since some of these passages portray convulsions that affect the whole earth but which do not extend into the realm of the heavens. Again, a global catastrophe need not cause the total destruction of the earth, though in some passages, as we will see, it does seem to do so.

I decline to take up Wright's formulation 'the end of the space-time universe'. This expression is somewhat ambiguous, and in my view Wright himself is not altogether consistent in his employment of it. In one context, he seems to mean by it the final dissolution of the created cosmos and the very extinction of matter itself.[85] In another, he seems to

---

85. N. T. Wright 1996: 286, 300.

have in view a less absolute end, one that does not preclude the creation of another space-time world in material continuity with the old.[86] Generally, I prefer to speak of the 'end', 'destruction', 'dissolution', etc., of the 'cosmos'; such terms are more in keeping with the cosmological terminology of the era. But what did the end or destruction of the cosmos mean in the historical period under discussion? It is essential that we have some precision on this issue. Two points need to be made.

First, there is little to suggest that the *absolute destruction* of the cosmos, involving the annihilation of cosmic matter, was ever seriously contemplated during the period relevant to this study. Philo, in his treatment of philosophical views of the fate of the cosmos, considered this concept nonsense.[87] Ancient Greek and Roman thinkers, from the Milesians to the Stoics, who reckoned with the prospect of the dissolution of the cosmos, did not envisage its total obliteration – its complete reduction to nothing. It was axiomatic for Graeco-Roman cosmology that 'Nothing comes into being out of nothing, and nothing passes away into nothing'.[88] In philosophical discussion of whether the universe endures or passes away, cosmic dissolution meant the reversion of the cosmos to some originating principle, such as fire (as with the Stoics), or its reduction to constituent particles (as with the Atomists and Epicureans). For Old Testament and subsequent Jewish apocalyptic and other writers, the end of the created cosmos meant a going back to the pre-creation chaos.[89] The idea of the absolute destruction of the cosmos, its rendering into nothing, is attested in several of the Nag Hammadi tractates.[90] It was apparently taught by Valentinians of the second century CE,[91] and among the church fathers it was accepted by Tertullian, who also expected a new act of creation *ex nihilo*.[92] But up to and including New Testament times, belief in absolute cosmic dissolution, as far as we can tell, was not a genuine cosmological option.

Second, it also quite clear that the end of the cosmos would not have meant its *absolute end*: 'that beyond which nothing can conceivably happen'.[93] Jewish writers plainly envisaged a state of blessedness after the eschatological finale and often did so, as has been noted, in very

86. When he cites the Stoic belief in cosmic conflagration as an example of it: N. T. Wright 1996: 333.
87. Philo, *Aet. Mund.* 5–6.
88. Furley 1987: 20.
89. Caird 1980: 258.
90. *Orig. World* 126–7; *Great Pow.* 46.
91. Irenaeus, *Ad haer.* 1.7.1.
92. Tertullian, *Against Hermogenes* 34.
93. Caird 1980: 271.

'this-worldly' terms. Greek and Roman thinkers who anticipated the dissolution of the cosmos likewise did not think that it marked an absolute end. For the Epicureans, the cosmic matter into which a cosmos deconstructs when it comes to an end is recycled and goes into the formation of new worlds. In Stoic thought, the conflagration is followed by a regeneration in which a new world appears exactly like the old one. The idea of an end to be followed by nothing at all would have been considered ludicrous, and should not be used as a yardstick for assessing whether ancient Jewish or Christian writers envisaged the end of the cosmos.

Throughout this study, it should be kept in mind that the ancient understanding of the 'cosmos' is quite different from our contemporary awareness of it. People of Graeco-Roman antiquity had little appreciation of the immense scale of the universe which we now take for granted.[94] Our knowledge of the physical universe beyond our own planet has been made possible by advances in ocular and radio astronomy and by direct space exploration. The ancient understanding of the natural world was derived from what could be seen by the naked eye and worked out by mathematical calculation. The model of the cosmos which dominated from the time of Aristotle (and survived until Copernicus) had the earth at the centre, with the sun, moon and planets encircling it, and the sphere of the fixed stars at the periphery.[95] The 'cosmos' was essentially the immediate solar system, perceived from a geocentric perspective.

With these important clarifications and distinction in place, the investigation can now begin. We turn first to the relevant material in the Old Testament.

---

94. This is not to minimize the tremendous advances made by ancient Western cosmologists. For an informative guide to ancient cosmology, see M. R. Wright 1995.

95. Cf. M. R. Wright 1995: 50. Aristarchus of Samos hypothesized that the earth rotates around the sun, but his heliocentric theory was almost unanimously rejected: see M. R. Wright 1995: 28–9.

Part 1

The Comparative Context

Chapter 1

THE OLD TESTAMENT

This chapter explores the Old Testament background. I highlight and discuss Old Testament texts which either imply or affirm that the created universe will eventually be dissolved. I also look at other views expressed in the Old Testament on the cosmic future. I then concentrate on the use of global and cosmic catastrophe language in prophetic discourse,[1] looking first at instances of such language in oracles of local doom (against Babylon, Edom, etc.), then at the use of this language in oracles which have a more 'eschatological' character. I begin, though, by discussing the Genesis flood story. The flood is the biblical archetype of a universal catastrophe unleashed by God for the purpose of judgement, a catastrophe that takes the earth back to the primeval chaos.

1.1 The Genesis Flood Story

The flood story of Genesis 6–9, part of the connected 'primeval history' of Genesis 1–11, is a story of divine judgement in the shape of a universal natural disaster. The account is conventionally regarded as a combination of two originally independent sources, J and P (the 'Yahwist' and the 'Priestly' strands).[2] Despite a certain level of disjointedness, the author/final redactor has nevertheless produced a literary unity with a thematic coherence.[3]

---

1. For the distinction between 'global' and 'cosmic' catastrophe, see the Introduction, p. 20. I use the term 'universal' catastrophe/disaster more loosely, with reference to either a global or cosmic catastrophe.
2. A standard division of the text by source-critics runs as follows. The J source is represented by 6.5-8; 7.1-7, 10, 12, 16b-20, 22-23; 8.2b-3a, 6, 8-12, 13b, 20-22. The P source is manifested in 6.9-22; 7.8-9, 11, 13-16a, 21, 24; 8.1-2a, 3b-5, 7, 13a, 14-19; 9.1-17. Cf. Simkins 1994: 192 n. 7.
3. According to G. J. Wenham (1987: 155–8), Genesis 6–9 exhibits a palistrophic structure (extended chiasm).

The main events of the story are well known. In the face of universal human wickedness and corruption (6.11-12) and the evil in human hearts (6.5), God decides to wipe out his human creation, with the exception of Noah and his family: 'I have determined to make an end of all flesh, for the earth is filled with violence because of them; now I am going to destroy them along with the earth' (6.13). The ensuing cataclysm destroys all animal, bird and human life, but all those inside the ark are spared. The flood paves the way for a fresh start in God's dealings with the world. God makes a new covenant with Noah and all his descendants (9.8-17).

As Gordon Wenham points out, the Genesis narrative brings out links and contrasts between the work of creation and the flood.[4] The list of animals going into the ark (6.7; 7.14, 21; 8.17) echoes the list of created things in Gen. 1.20-26. The flood involves the bursting of the springs of the deep and the opening of the windows of heaven (7.11), reversing the separation of the waters above and below the firmament and the land from the seas in Gen. 1.6-10. The reference to the swelling of the waters on the earth in 7.24 is a reminder of Gen. 1.2 and suggests a partial return to the primordial situation in which 'darkness covered the face of the deep'. These parallels serve to make the narrative point that the flood is an undoing of creation.

A correspondence is also evident between Genesis 1 and the immediate antediluvian situation. The receding of the waters recalls the separation of the waters in Gen. 1.6-10. More particularly, God's first words to Noah after leaving the ark, 'Be fruitful and multiply, and fill the earth' are a clear evocation of Gen. 1.26. The situation after the flood is thus viewed to some extent as a new beginning, with Noah as the new Adam, though the new start is not an ideal state of affairs, since the problem of the evil inclination of the human heart remains (8.21).

The flood, therefore, is a kind of de-creation and re-creation.[5] It is not a complete reversal of the creation process and return to the pre-creation chaos. The waters engulf the earth, but the earth itself does not become 'a formless void' (Gen. 1.2). The high mountains are submerged but they remain intact (7.19; 8.4); they are not levelled or dissolved. The catastrophe is limited to the terrestrial realm ('under the whole heaven', 7.19); the sun, moon and stars are unaffected. The Noachic flood is not then a total collapse and disintegration of creation, though it is interpreted in this way in 2 Pet. 3.6.

---

4. G. J. Wenham 1987: 206–7.
5. Cf. Simkins 1994: 202–5.

In Gen. 8.20-22, Noah builds an altar and sacrifices to the Lord, and God promises: 'I will never again curse the ground because of humankind ... nor will I ever again destroy every living creature as I have done.' The divine promise seems to rule out the prospect of another universal catastrophe.[6] However, as Wenham states, 'It is simply the threat of another flood that is lifted.'[7]

In Gen. 9.1-17, God enters into a covenant with Noah and his descendants and 'every living creature of all flesh' (9.15). The Noachic covenant entails that 'never again shall all flesh be cut off by the waters of a flood, and never again shall there be a flood to destroy the earth' (9.11). Again, this may seem to imply that God will never again afflict the earth with a universal catastrophe, but the assurance of v. 11 is not one of complete immunity from such a disaster. As V. P. Hamilton writes, 'The thrust of this covenant is that the Flood is unique. The possibility of future judgment is not eliminated but that judgment will not be manifested as a flood.'[8]

The story of the flood illustrates the continuing threat of chaos. The work of creation has not eradicated chaos; the ordered world 'is always ready to sink into the abyss of the formless'.[9] As J. D. Levenson states, the present life-bearing world 'exists now only because of God's continuing commitment to the original command. Absent that command, the sinister forces of chaos would surge forth again.'[10] The story also establishes within biblical history (or, if preferred, biblical historicized mythology) the precedent of universal judgement by worldwide natural catastrophe. In later apocalyptic writing, the flood serves as the prototype of the final destructive judgement, a development we find already in Isaiah 24.

---

6. This implication is drawn by some of the rabbis: see Van der Horst 1994: 242.
7. G. J. Wenham 1987: 190.
8. Hamilton 1990: 316. In Isa. 54.9, the divine oath of Gen. 9.11 serves as a model for God's commitment to Israel: 'Just as I swore that the waters of Noah would never again go over the earth, so I have sworn that I will not be angry with you and will not rebuke you.' Yet, the next verse broaches the possibility of a catastrophe in which the mountains (preserved through the flood) disappear ('For the mountains may depart and the hills be removed ...', Isa. 54.10). The judgement oracle of Isaiah 24 envisages a future scenario in which the Noachic covenant is revoked (Isa. 24.5). Humanity's corruption invalidates God's postdiluvian commitment, and 'the windows of heaven are opened' once again. See further, p. 45.
9. Von Rad 1972: 48–9.
10. Levenson 1994: 16.

1.2 The Created World Destined to End

Since the Old Testament displays an interest in the world's origins,[11] it is reasonable to expect that there is some interest in its fate. That the world created by God is destined eventually to come to an end is either implied or stated clearly in several passages.

1.2.1 Genesis 8.22

In Gen. 8.21, as we have seen, God pledges to preserve humankind from another worldwide judgement by flood. In v. 22, he resolves to maintain the seasonal cycles and the alternation of day and night as an expression of his providential care.

> As long as the earth endures,
> seedtime and harvest, cold and heat,
> summer and winter, day and night,
> shall not cease.

The regular patterns of nature are not guaranteed for eternity but 'as long as the earth endures', literally, 'all the days of the earth'.[12] Elsewhere in the book of Genesis, the expression 'all the days' is used of limited human life (e.g. 3.17).[13] Applied here to the earth, the formulation indicates its mortality. The earth has an allotted period of existence like every other created thing. It will not last for ever; as it had a beginning, so it will also have an end.[14] As we will see in the next chapter, the verse is given an eschatological application in subsequent Jewish interpretation.

The thought that the world will eventually cease clearly does not entail a radical cosmological dualism for the author of Genesis, for whom the goodness of God's work of creation is fundamental.[15]

---

11. The creation account of Genesis 1–2 is the most complete in the Old Testament. For vestiges of an older cosmogony, in which creation emerges out of a conflict with chaos, see Pss. 74.12-17; 89.9-10; Isa. 51.9-10. On the conflict model of creation, see Day 1985: 1–61. For an excellent and accessible treatment of the Hebrew view of the natural world, see Simkins 1994.
12. כָּל־יְמֵי הָאָרֶץ.
13. G. J. Wenham 1987: 191.
14. Westermann 1984: 457.
15. Cf. Gen. 1.4, 10, 12, 18, 21, 25, 31.

1.2.2 Psalm 46.1-3

The subject of this psalm is the faithfulness of God to his people in periods of trouble. It consists of three stanzas (vv. 1-3, 4-7 and 8-11). In each, the theme of God as refuge is central (the opening line of v. 1 and the refrain at the end of vv. 7 and 11). Older commentators opined that the origins of the psalm lay in Jerusalem's experience of divine rescue from the hand of Assyria (2 Kgs 18.13-19.36), but there is no obvious reference to this or any another specific event in the psalm. As A. A. Anderson states, 'the language of the Psalm transcends any known historical occasion'.[16]

The first strophe emphasizes divine dependability when all around is chaos.

> though the earth should change,
> though the mountains shake in the heart of the sea;
> though its waters roar and foam,
> though the mountains tremble with its tumult.

The 'change' envisaged is a change of the earth from its present ordered form to its primeval chaotic condition.[17] In the Old Testament, the mountains are connected with the original creative activity of God.[18] They symbolize the constancy and immovability of the created order. Their shaking and trembling thus constitute the destabilizing of creation. The Hebrew verb here rendered 'tremble' (רעש), as B. S. Childs has shown, 'is a technical term within the language used to depict a return, or threatened return, of chaos'.[19] The image of the roaring of the sea also has chaotic overtones.[20] The whole picture is that of reduction to the primeval disorder.

In these verses, the author expresses the conviction that creation, however firmly established and seemingly impregnable, has the potential to revert to its primordial state; the divine work of creation can be undone.[21] As noted above, this belief also underlies the Genesis flood story. But whereas the flood involved a partial return to chaos, the author here imagines a more extensive reversion: now the mountains are drawn into the catastrophe (but there is no mention of the celestial realm). The psalmist does not say that the earth *must* degenerate, but its dissolution is viewed as, at the very least, a genuine geophysical possibility. The precariousness of creation, its capacity to change back to chaos, reinforces

---

16. A. A. Anderson 1972: 355.
17. A. A. Anderson 1972: 356.
18. Pss. 65.7; 90.2; Prov. 8.25; Isa. 40.12; Amos 4.13.
19. Childs 1959: 187.
20. Pss. 65.7; 96.11; 98.7; Isa. 5.30; 17.12; 51.15; Jer. 5.22; 6.23; 50.42; 51.55.
21. Noted by Gunkel in his epochal work on creation and chaos (1895: 100).

the truth that there is only one continuing security, God himself, the unchanging one (v. 1).

In the next strophe, the threat is political rather than geophysical: 'the nations are in an uproar'. But this does not justify a historicizing interpretation of vv. 2-3. Political disorder in this stanza stands in parallel to geophysical chaos in the previous one, but the latter is not a metaphor for the former.

There is no suggestion here that the possible return of the earth to chaos undermines belief in the excellence of creation. It does, though, demonstrate the supremacy of the creator over his creation. The creator is eternal; creation is not. Therefore, he alone is worthy of the total trust of his covenant people.

1.2.3   *Psalm 102.25-27*

The psalm has a somewhat complicated structure and shows features of more than one form, suggesting to some scholars that it was not originally a single piece. Its core form is that of an individual lament (vv. 2-12 and 24-25a). The psalmist calls upon God in a time of great need (illness). But lament turns to praise (vv. 13-23), and the psalm concludes with an expression of confidence and hope in God (25b-29). The climax affirms God's everlastingness. The thought is expressed by means of a contrast with the finiteness of creation.

> 25) Long ago you laid the foundation of the earth,[22]
> and the heavens are the work of your hands,
> 26) They will perish, but you endure;
> they will all wear out like a garment.
> You change them like clothing, and they pass away;
> 27) but you are the same, and your years have no end.

The psalmist marvels at the heavens and earth as wonders of God's creative activity. But the creator is greater than creation because he is immortal and it is not.

These verses express in comparative and poetic language, yet in unmistakable terms, that the present created order will deteriorate and pass away. The heavens and earth must 'perish' and 'wear out'.[23] Like

---

22. The earth is regularly conceived of as having foundations (Pss. 18.15; 82.5; Prov. 8.29; Isa. 24.18; Jer. 31.37; Mic. 6.2) and as resting on pillars (1 Sam. 2.8; Job 9.6; 38.6; Ps. 75.3). The heavens too are seen as resting on pillars (e.g. Job 26.11).

23. The Hebrew verb translated 'wear out' (בלה) means to waste away and is commonly used of garments (e.g. Deut. 8.4; 29.5), bones (Ps. 32.3), wineskins (Job 13.28), etc., i.e. things that perish.

clothing, they have a temporary function; when they have been worn out, they will be discarded. The dissolution will be brought about by God himself; he will cause heaven and earth to be changed and to pass away.

That the author here envisages 'the end of the whole created scheme'[24] is undeniable. Quite obviously the notion of cosmic dissolution as expressed in this psalm does not carry the suggestion that the material creation is inherently bad. The theological point drawn from the perishability of creation is its subordinate status to the eternal God. That the Lord God *made* the physical world *and will ultimately outlast it* demonstrates his power and authority over it. Here, therefore, we have a creational monotheism which actually *requires* the end of the world.

1.2.4 Isaiah 51.6

This verse is a close literary parallel to Ps. 102.25-27. The oracle to which it belongs, Isa. 51.1-8, summons the exiles of Israel to 'listen' (vv. 1, 4 and 7). In vv. 4-6, the reason for harkening is the nearness of divine deliverance (v. 5). In v. 6, the permanence of God's saving action is set against the transitory nature of the physical heaven and earth.

> Lift up your eyes to the heavens,
> and look at the earth beneath;
> for the heavens will vanish like smoke,[25]
> the earth will wear out like a garment,
> and those who live on it will die like gnats;
> but my salvation will be for ever,
> and my deliverance will never be ended.

The transient condition of creation is expressed in two parallel lines, one dealing with the heavens, the other with the earth. The similes of dispersing like smoke[26] and wearing out like a garment make clear that the cosmic structures are ephemeral.[27]

It is true that the main point of this passage is the security and impregnability of God's salvation, rather than the termination of creation,[28] but the prophet expresses the former by means of a contrast with the latter.

---

24. Kidner 1973: 174.

25. The Hebrew particle translated 'for' (כִּי) could also be rendered 'though', which is preferred by Williamson (1999: 107–8).

26. For 'vanish' or 'dissipate' as the correct rendering of נִמְלָחוּ see Williamson 1999: 104–5. Smoke is a standard biblical image for transience: Pss. 37.20; 102.3; Hos. 13.3; Wis. 5.14.

27. Isaiah 54.10 contrasts the impermanence of the mountains with the enduring nature of God's steadfast love.

28. So Brueggemann 1998: 127

The argument advances in three steps: (1) consider the heavens and earth, symbols of permanence and security; (2) even these will perish; (3) but God's salvation is utterly durable. The third and main point rests on points 1 and 2.

The 'creation theology' of the writer/redactor of Isaiah 40–55 is now well recognized.[29] We can be certain that, for him, the prospect of creation's eventual end did not call into question the intrinsic worth of the created order.

1.3 *Other Viewpoints on Creation's Future*

The Old Testament does not offer a singular position on the question of creation's future.[30] Other views also find expression.

1.3.1 *The Created World an Enduring Structure*

Psalm 93.1 declares that the Lord has built the world as an impregnable fortress: 'it shall never be moved' (literally 'will not totter', בַּל־תִּמּוֹט).[31] Several passages speak of heaven or earth as enduring 'for ever'. Psalm 78.69 states that the earth God 'has founded for ever'. Psalm 148.6 indicates that God established the material heavens 'for ever and ever'. Ecclesiastes 1.4 states, 'A generation goes, and a generation comes, but the earth remains for ever' (וְהָאָרֶץ לְעוֹלָם עֹמָדֶת). In these texts, the created order is presented as a permanent and stable physical reality.[32]

The heavenly realm and its monuments serve as standards of comparison in declarations of longevity and perpetuity. Deuteronomy 11.21 articulates the hope that the people remain in the land 'as long as the heavens are above the earth'.[33] In Ps. 72.5-7, the psalmist prays that the king may live 'while the sun endures, and as long as the moon', and that his righteousness and peace flourish 'until the moon is no more'. A similar sentiment is expressed in Ps. 89.29: 'I will establish his line for ever and his throne for as long as the heavens endure' (cf. vv. 36-37).[34] In

---

29. On God's creative activity, see, e.g., Isa. 40.12; 42.5; 45.18; 48.13.
30. This is not surprising given the diversity we find within the Old Testament in many areas of theological thought. On theological diversity in the Old Testament, see Goldingay 1987.
31. Cf. Pss. 96.10; 104.5; 119.90.
32. On this theme, see Houtman 1993: 177–81.
33. Literally, 'as the days of the heavens above the earth', כִּימֵי הַשָּׁמַיִם עַל־הָאָרֶץ.
34. Cf. Ps. 89.29, 36-37. The image of the permanence of the celestial luminaries to express the long rule of the king and his dynasty is found in ancient Near Eastern royal inscriptions: see further Paul 1972.

1 *The Old Testament*

Jer. 31.35-36, the continuance of the nation of Israel is linked to the permanence of the heavenly order.

> 35) Thus says the Lord,
> who gives the sun for light by day
> and the fixed order of the moon and the stars for light by night ...
> 36) If this fixed order were ever to cease
> from my presence, says the Lord,
> then also the offspring of Israel would cease
> to be a nation before me for ever.

In these passages, the celestial realm and its structures serve as symbols representing endurance and long-lasting existence.

This set of passages and the previous set, Gen. 8.22, etc., appear to stand diametrically opposed, but they are not quite as contradictory as they seem. It is doubtful that any of the texts which emphasize the permanence of the created order asserts its *absolute* everlastingness. The Hebrew phrase (לְעוֹלָם) which is normally translated 'for ever' (literally, 'to the age') indicates a very long period of time, but not eternal endurance. When it is stated that earth or heaven has been established or will last 'for ever', the idea is that it 'will last as long as the mind can project into the future'.[35] What is stressed is the longevity and 'onlasting' nature of the world, not its unqualified eternity. Deuteronomy 11.21 and Ps. 89.29 speak literally of the 'days of the heavens',[36] an expression which, as we have seen, suggests a fixed period of existence. And Ps. 72.7 appears to contemplate the actual end of the moon.[37]

Psalm 102.25-27 and Isa. 51.6 pick up the tradition of the permanence of heaven and earth and offer an advance on it. The heavens and earth 'are symbolic of all that is permanent and enduring'.[38] Yet in comparison with God or his salvation, they are like smoke or a cloak which is worn out. We thus see a development in Old Testament cosmological thinking. The conflict between these cosmological perspectives can, to some extent, be resolved in terms of a hierarchy of endurance. As Caird

---

35. Crenshaw 1988: 63. According to Seow (1997: 56), in Eccl. 1.4, the claim is not that the earth is everlasting, but that it stays the same, while generations come and pass away.

36. Ps. 89.29: כִּימֵי שָׁמַיִם.

37. Cf. Ps. 90.9-10: 'all our days pass away'; 'the days of our lives are seventy years'. In Job 14.12, however, the disappearance of the heavens is set forth as an inconceivable idea, since it is equated with returning to life after death, which for Job is an impossibility: cf. Clines 1989: 330.

38. A. A. Anderson 1972: 711.

states, 'In comparison with the transitoriness of human existence, the earth will last till the end of time, but it is not everlasting as God is everlasting.'[39]

1.3.2 *The Created World to be Transformed and Made New*

The author of the late prophetic text, Zechariah 14, looks for a miraculous transformation of the whole created order on the day of the Lord's coming.

> 6) On that day there shall not be either cold or frost. 7) And there shall be continuous day (it is known to the Lord), not day and not night, for at evening time there shall be light. 8) On that day living waters shall flow out from Jerusalem, half of them to the eastern sea and half of them to the western sea; it shall continue in summer as in winter.

This is an enlargement of the long-standing prophetic hope for miraculous changes in the natural environment. Characteristically, the hope is for changes in the terrestrial scene – the land made abundantly fertile (e.g. Amos 9.13-14); violence removed from nature (e.g. Isa. 11.6-9; Hos. 2.18); the wilderness transformed (e.g. Isa. 35.1, 6; 41.19). As it develops, the hope takes on cosmic dimensions (e.g. Isa. 30.26; 60.20).

Isaiah 65.17, which predates Zechariah 14, expresses the promise of 'a new heavens and a new earth' (cf. Isa. 66.22). The promise is clearly intended to recall Gen. 1.1 and the account of creation it introduces (Genesis 1.1–2.4a). The verses that follow (Isa. 65.18-25) describe the blessed future. Jerusalem will be remade as joy and delight, people will live extremely long lives, they will engage in rewarding work, and they will exist in peace and safety.

There has been much debate about whether the promise of a new heavens and earth envisages cosmic renewal through dissolution and re-creation (building on the belief that the present cosmos is to be brought to an end) or renewal by non-destructive transformation.[40] Skinner takes

---

39. Caird 1980: 257.
40. See Gardner 2001. Watts (1987: 354) suggests that the promise refers to 'a new political and social reality under the [Persian] empire'. To facilitate this reading, he renders the Hebrew word אֶרֶץ 'land' rather than 'earth', and understands it as referring to Palestine. On its own, אֶרֶץ often has this sense, but in conjunction with 'the heavens', it must designate the earth as a whole. The phrase 'heaven and earth' is a common formulation for the created order (Gen. 1.1; 2.1, 4; Ps. 113.6; Jer. 10.11; etc.). The allusion to Gen. 1.1 plainly indicates that a renewal of the whole creation is in view, not just a new political situation.

the former view,[41] as does R. N. Whybray, who thinks that the author of this text has taken Isa. 51.6 as a prophecy of the immediate destruction of the heavens and earth and 'has concluded that there is in fact to be a completely new beginning'.[42] Claus Westermann, in contrast, denies that the words imply that heaven and earth are to be destroyed and replaced. Instead, the present world 'is to be miraculously renewed'.[43]

It is difficult to decide between these options. On the one hand, the allusion to Gen. 1.1 seems to point to actual re-creation. On the other hand, there is nothing in the immediate context to indicate that the existing creation is to be undone, and this suggests that what is envisaged is non-catastrophic transformation. The Hebrew word 'new' (חדש) may have a temporal sense, new in time, or a qualitative sense, fresh or pure.[44] The former could support the re-creation interpretation, while the latter would fit with miraculous transformation.[45] The fact that life in the new or transformed creation is very much like life as presently experienced might be thought to indicate transformation. But as emphasized in the Introduction, a 'this-worldly' view of the future blessedness and belief in the end and re-creation of the world are not mutually exclusive. In subsequent Jewish interpretation, as we will see in the next chapter, the promise of Isa. 65.17 is read both in terms of re-creation (*1 En.* 72.1; 91.16) and in terms of non-destructive rejuvenation (*Jub.* 1.29; 4.26). Perhaps, then, it is best to recognize that within its Isaianic context, the hope for a new heavens and new earth lacks clarification and can be developed in either direction.[46]

1.4 *Language of Global and Cosmic Catastrophe in Prophetic Discourse*

Language of global and cosmic catastrophe is employed in a large number of Old Testament prophetic (mainly judgement) oracles.[47] It is

41. Skinner 1929: 240.
42. Whybray 1975: 276, though he takes Isa. 65.17 and 25 as later insertions to the original composition, supplying a cosmic dimension to an otherwise non-cosmic vision.
43. Westermann 1969: 408.
44. Watts 1987: 353.
45. According to D. M. Russell (1996: 75), the word 'new' picks up the theme of newness in the prophecies of Deutero-Isaiah (e.g. Isa. 43.18-19), and so points to 'miraculous transformation'.
46. See further Van Ruitten 1989.
47. My focus here is on prophetic catastrophe language with a global or cosmic dimension, rather than prophecies of local catastrophe in nature (e.g. Ezek. 32.1-16 (esp. v. 7); 38–9).

particularly associated with the themes of God's coming[48] and/or the 'day of the Lord'.[49] The imagery is most frequently found in oracles against specific nations or cities, but it also occurs in oracles of a more general character and that are more clearly 'eschatological'. The latter are generally regarded as later (i.e. as belonging to the post-exilic era, though, as we will see, some treat the global/cosmic element in the earlier oracles as a later addition). We will look first at the usage in 'local' oracles, then at the usage in the more eschatological oracles.[50]

1.4.1 *Global/Cosmic Catastrophe Language in Oracles against Specific Places*

Isaiah 13 belongs to a collection of oracles against foreign nations (Isaiah 13–26). The superscription of 13.1 indicates that the oracle of this chapter is concerned with Babylon, but Babylon is not explicitly mentioned until v. 19. Verses 2-5 portray the gathering of an immense and mighty army. God himself summons the warriors and consecrates them for battle; he is their captain. They are charged to execute his vengeance (vv. 2-3). The vast army assembles from the ends of the earth 'to destroy the whole earth' (v. 5).[51] Verses 6-13 develop the picture of approaching

---

48. God's coming was originally associated with past events in Israel's history: the Exodus (Deut. 33.2; Ps. 68.7-8); the descent to Sinai (Exod. 19.11); the conquest (Judg. 5.4-5). In Psalm 18, God's coming is linked with a personal experience of deliverance in the life of the petitioner. In prophetic discourse (and also in some psalms, e.g. Ps. 96.13), the coming of God lies ahead. Certain images and motifs occur variously in connection with the divine epiphany: clouds (e.g. Isa. 19.1); thunder and lightning (e.g. Pss. 18.13-14; 94.7); fire (e.g. Isa. 66.15-16; Mal. 3.1-4); the angelic host (e.g. Deut. 33.2; Zech. 14.5); the divine glory (Isa. 66.18). God's coming is often styled as a 'theophany', i.e. as attended by upheaval in nature: see further in the main text. On the Old Testament theme of God's coming, see Adams 2006: 3–6; Schnutenhaus 1964.

49. The origins of the concept of the 'day of the Lord' remain disputed. For the view that it originated in 'holy war' tradition, see the classic essay by Von Rad 1959; cf. Cross 1973: 91–111. The earliest reference to the 'day of the Lord' in prophetic literature occurs in Amos 5.18-20. These verses appear to assume that the 'day of the Lord' was already a familiar idea in the prophet's time. Amos warns the people of Israel that the day would be one of darkness not, as they supposed, one of light. In prophetic discourse, the 'day of the Lord' is generally a day of divine judgement. Hoffmann (1981) insists that it is always an eschatological term; for a contrasting view, see Everson 1974.

50. I survey these texts in their canonical, rather than putative chronological, order because of the controversy surrounding their dating.

51. כָּל־הָאָרֶץ could mean 'all the land', but in the light of what follows it should be translated 'all the earth'.

divine judgement in terms of the 'day of the Lord'. Verses 9-13 describe the catastrophic judgement.

> 9) See, the day of the Lord comes,
> cruel, with wrath and fierce anger,
> to make the earth a desolation,
> and to destroy its sinners from it.
> 10) For the stars of the heavens and their constellations
> will not give their light;
> the sun will be dark at its rising,
> and the moon will not shed its light.
> 11) I will punish the world for its evil,
> and the wicked for their iniquity;
> I will put an end to the pride of the arrogant,
> and lay low the insolence of tyrants.
> 12) I will make mortals more rare than fine gold,
> and humans than the gold of Ophir.
> 13) Therefore I will make the heavens tremble,
> and the earth will be shaken out of its place,
> at the wrath of the Lord of hosts
> on the day of his fierce anger.

The judgement is directed at sinful humanity in general (v. 11) and is of cosmic proportions. Sun, moon and stars are darkened (v. 10); heaven and earth quake. Darkness is associated with the 'day of the Lord' in Amos 5.18, 20, the most primitive reference to the topic in the Old Testament (Amos 8.9 prophesies the failure of the sun 'on that day'). As D. Stacey writes, 'What is described here comes close to being an act of universal anti-creation'.[52] But the description is not prosaic; the whole passage follows a rhythmical structure and the style of expression is poetic rather than literal (especially the line, 'the sun will be dark at its rising').

At v. 14, there is a shift from cosmic calamity to national disaster. Verses 15-16 describe the sack of a city. Verse 17 indicates that the Medes are the attackers. Finally, in vv. 19-22, the identity of the devastated city is made clear: Babylon. The city will be destroyed and rendered completely uninhabitable.

Isaiah 34, part of a two-chapter unit contrasting the fortunes of Edom and Zion, begins with a summons addressed to all nations. The prophet announces coming worldwide judgement: 'the Lord is enraged against all the nations ... he has doomed them, has given them over for slaughter' (v. 2). The picture of general human judgement is expanded in v. 4 to include catastrophic events in the celestial realm.

---

52. Stacey 1993: 101.

> All the host of heaven shall rot away,
> and the skies roll up like a scroll.
> All their host shall wither
> like a leaf withering on a vine,
> or fruit withering on a fig tree.

The 'host of heavens' refers to the physical stars and the astral deities thought to be connected with them. The host is to 'rot' (מקק) and 'wither' (נבל) like shrivelling leaves and figs. The image of the heavens being furled up like a scroll picks up the conception of a sky as a tent or cover stretched over the earth. The firmament is rolled back, exposing the earth to unmediated divine judgement.[53]

In the verses that follow in the rest of the chapter (vv. 5-17), the focus narrows to Edom. Verses 5-7 pick up the language of vv. 2-3 and apply it to Edom; the cosmic imagery of v. 4, however, is not taken up.

Jeremiah 4.23-28 forms a distinct unit within a collection of oracles concerning the threat of the 'evil from the north' (4.6). The sequence of oracles runs from 4.5 to 6.30. The deadly foe from the north (Babylon) is coming against Judah and Jerusalem (4.5). Jerusalem is to be besieged (4.16; 6.1-30). Jeremiah 4.6-31 depicts the approaching doom using quasi-mythical imagery. Verses 23-28 describe a scene of widespread disorder and devastation.

> 23) I looked on the earth, and lo, it was waste and void;
> and to the heavens, and they had no light.
> 24) I looked on the mountains, and lo, they were quaking,
> and all the hills moved to and fro.
> 25) I looked, and lo, there was no one at all,
> and all the birds of the air had fled.
> 26) I looked, and lo, the fruitful land was a desert,
> and all its cities were laid in ruins
> before the Lord, before his fierce anger.
> 27) For thus says the Lord: The whole earth shall be a desolation;
> yet I will not make a full end.
> 28) Because of this the earth shall mourn,
> and the heavens above grow black;
> for I have spoken, I have purposed;
> I have not relented nor will I turn back.

The earth has become a formless wasteland; there is no celestial light; there is no sign of human life or birdlife; the fruitful land has been turned into a desert. The reference to the shaking of 'the mountains' and 'all the

---

53. Gardner (2001: 217) points out that the analogy of a scroll being rolled up need not imply that the heavens are destroyed.

hills' points to a global earthquake. The devastation is an act of divine judgement ('his fierce anger') against humanity in general ('there was no one at all').

The description of the disaster is obviously poetic in both structure and style, yet there can be little question that what is being depicted by means of the literary imagery is 'the breakdown of the created order'.[54] Links with the creation narrative of Gen. 1.1–2.4a have often been noted.[55] The clearest connection is the Hebrew phrase translated 'waste and void' in Jer. 4.23 (וְהִנֵּה־תֹהוּ וָבֹהוּ). The collocation occurs only here and in Gen. 1.2, where it refers to the 'formless void' of primeval chaos. The writer seems to be implying that the earth has returned or is in process of returning to its primeval condition. A reversal of the work of creation is further suggested by the references to the absence of light (cf. Gen. 1.3), of human beings (cf. Gen. 1.26) and of birds (cf. Gen. 1.20). The statement, 'the fruitful land was a desert' in v. 26 represents an undoing of the divine command, 'Let the earth put forth vegetation' in Gen. 1.11.

The catastrophe is clearly of global and even cosmic proportions. The cosmic extent of the disaster is evident in Jer. 4.23 with the reference to the lack of light in the heavens (reinforced in v. 28: 'the heavens above grow black').

In vv. 27-28, God speaks.[56] The whole earth is to be made a devastation, 'yet I will not make a complete destruction'.[57] This seems to suggest that the undoing of creation depicted in vv. 23-26 is neither total nor final. Yet, the catastrophe foreseen is inevitable: 'I have not relented nor will I turn back.' After God's pronouncement in vv. 27-28, the focus on the coming invasion by Babylon resumes in v. 29.

The first half of the book of Joel, 1.1–2.27, concerns a locust plague which has just struck or is just about to strike Judah.[58] The prophet interprets the plague in terms of a divine judgement and associates it with the 'day of the Lord' (1.15; 2.1-2, 11). In Joel 2.1-11, the locust invasion is compared to the assault of a mighty army (especially vv. 7-9). In vv. 10-

54. Hayes 2002: 87.
55. Van Ruitten 2005: 27–9.
56. The divine interjection of v. 27 may be a subsequent addition to the poem: Carroll 1986: 170.
57. A more literal translation of וְכָלָה לֹא אֶעֱשֶׂה.
58. Joel 1 seems to deal with a locust plague that has already taken place. In 2.1-11, the invasion of locusts is imminent. The variance has generated numerous interpretations, but it seems unlikely that the prophet is speaking of two different events: see Barton 2001: 68–70. Barton (75) thinks that both chapters are predictive and refer to the same disaster.

12, the threat suddenly takes on universal and cosmic dimensions. The object of divine judgement is now humanity in general (this is implied in the words, 'Who can endure it?').

> 10) The earth quakes before them,
> the heavens tremble.
> The sun and the moon are darkened,
> and the stars withdraw their shining.
> 11) The Lord utters his voice
> at the head of his army;
> how vast is his host!
> Numberless are those who obey his command.
> Truly the day of the Lord is great;
> terrible indeed – who can endure it?

The geophysical and cosmic imagery is here very similar to that in Isa. 13.10, 13. J. L. Crenshaw doubts that Joel is directly dependent on Isaiah 13, but thinks rather that 'the two authors share a common vocabulary and tradition'.[59] The verses that follow (2.12-27) resume the national focus.

The book of Micah, which is set in the eighth century BCE, begins with a warning to all the nations and the inhabitants of the earth (1.2). In v. 3, the prophet announces that God is coming to judge. Verse 4 sets forth the effects of God's coming.

> Then the mountains will melt under him
> and the valleys will burst open,
> like wax near the fire,
> like waters poured down a steep place.[60]

Micah 1.3-4 exhibits the 'theophany' pattern as defined by Jorg Jeremias: God comes from his dwelling place and nature convulses at his presence.[61] The scheme is also found in Old Testament hymns and psalms.[62] The archetypical theophany is the revelation at Sinai, where the effects of God's coming – quaking, smoking, thunder and lightning – are restricted to the immediate vicinity (Exod. 19.16-25).[63] In Mic. 1.3-4, a universal convulsion is in view. This is indicated by the use of plurals with the definite articles ('the mountains'; 'the valleys').[64] The language is figurative and comparative, and the images 'are not altogether

---

59. Crenshaw 1995: 126.
60. Cf. Isa. 64.1; Amos 9.5.
61. Jeremias 1965: 11–15. See also Cross 1973: 162-3.
62. Judg. 5.4-5; Pss. 18.6-19; 68.7-8; 77.16-20; 96.11-13; 97.1-5; 98.7-9
63. In later retellings of the Sinai episode, the impact on nature is of global and even cosmic magnitude. For references, see Chapter 5, p. 188 n. 24.
64. Andersen and Freedman 2000: 165.

consonant'.[65] The general picture seems to be the liquefaction of the earth's surface by means of the dissolving of mountains and, as in the Noachic flood, the release of subterranean waters. The perspective of universal judgement and global geophysical disaster gives way immediately in v. 5 to a narrow focus on Samaria and Jerusalem, and this viewpoint is maintained in the rest of the chapter.

The prophecy of Nahum, which is directed against Nineveh, opens with a hymnic description of the Lord, the divine avenger (1.2-8). The description follows the theophany pattern. In v. 3, the Lord is portrayed as a storm god who comes in clouds. Verses 4-5 describe the effects of his coming on nature.

> 4) He rebukes the sea and makes it dry,
> and he dries up all the rivers;
> Bashan and Carmel wither,
> and the bloom of Lebanon fades.
> 5) The mountains quake before him,
> and the hills melt;
> the earth heaves before him,
> the world and all who live in it.

The references in v. 4 to the rebuking of the sea and the drying up of the rivers reflect the creation mythology of the defeat of the powers of chaos.[66] Verse 5 envisages total global upheaval, through a combination of images of mountains shaking, hills melting and the earth convulsing. The final line of v. 5 focuses on the effects of the upheaval on all the world's inhabitants. From v. 9 onward, the focus is on Nineveh.

The prophecy of Zephaniah (ostensibly set 'in the days of King Josiah', 1.1; 640–609 BCE) begins with an announcement of worldwide judgement.

> 2) I will utterly sweep away everything
> from the face of the earth, says the Lord.
> 3) I will sweep away humans and animals;
> I will sweep away the birds of the air
> and the fish of the sea.
> I will make the wicked stumble.
> I will cut off humanity
> from the face of the earth, says the Lord.

---

65. Andersen and Freedman 2000: 159.
66. Cf. Pss. 18; 77.16-20.

This is a prediction, again in poetic form, of extensive global ruination. All human and animal life is to be destroyed.[67] The universal scope of the catastrophe is reminiscent of the Genesis flood (cf. Gen. 6.7), and seems to exceed it, though it is not a fully cosmic catastrophe since the devastation is restricted to the life-bearing earth. From v. 4, the oracle concentrates on the coming of judgement upon Judah and 'all the inhabitants of Jerusalem',[68] though there is a brief switch back to the global perspective in v. 18.

> in the fire of his passion
> the whole earth shall be consumed;
> for a full, a terrible end
> he will make of all the inhabitants of the earth.

In each of the passages cited above, global and cosmic upheavals are associated with the coming of universal judgement, but in every case the larger context is concerned with judgement against particular cities and nations. How, then, is the global/cosmic catastrophe language functioning in these oracles?

Old Testament scholars are divided on this issue. Some, more or less like Wright, think that the global/cosmic imagery has a narrow socio-political significance. It is being used to describe divine judgement against a particular historical entity. John Barton, for example, writes, 'In Isaiah 13, the "cash value" of the transformation of the sun, moon, and stars is the overthrow of Babylon'.[69] According to H. Wildberger, images of chaos in Isaiah 13 are used 'in order to describe Babylon's demise *as if it were* an event that brought about the return of a chaotic situation' (italics mine). The use of such language 'does not mean that order and the basic functioning of the entire world would grind to a complete halt'.[70] The language is simply being deployed metaphorically for Babylon's fall. There are those who think that the global/cosmic disaster language relates to general eschatological judgement, and who, like Caird, explain the juxtaposition of the universal and the local in terms of the convergence of long-range and short-range prophetic perspectives. For example, E. J. Young comments, with reference to Isaiah 13, that the destruction of Babylon would be 'a type and even a beginning of the

---

67. The order of v. 3a, humans, animals, birds and fish, is the reverse of that of Gen. 1.20-28 (Szeles 1987: 75). The coming disaster is thus portrayed as an overturning of God's work of creation.

68. As Raabe (2002: 669–70) points out, the city's inhabitants are listed in vv. 4b-6 in a manner that mirrors that of the enumeration of earth's inhabitants in v. 3.

69. Barton 2001: 74.

70. Wildberger 1997: 25.

final judgment which was to come over all mankind. Isaiah sees both together.'[71] Some, perhaps most, treat the verses that speak of universal judgement and global or cosmic catastrophe as later additions to the original oracles, giving messages which were first composed with a specific local crisis in mind a universal and eschatological application. Thus, R. E. Clements takes Isa. 13.6-8 and 17-22 as a prophecy relating to the events of 587 BCE, and treats vv. 9-16 as 'a late insertion providing a further, eschatological, interpretation of the Day of the LORD as a coming catastrophe which will embrace all nations'. He assigns the insertion to a late date, 'no earlier than the fourth century BC'.[72]

Old Testament interpreters, therefore, struggle to make sense of the conjunction of global/cosmic disaster and local doom in these oracles, and there is no unanimity on how the catastrophe language should be understood,

In a recent study, Paul Raabe has sought to shed new light on these and other prophetic oracles which combine universal and local perspectives on judgement.[73] He argues that the switch from universal to local, or vice versa, is to be understood in terms of the literary device of 'particularization', which is a well-recognized feature of Hebrew poetry. It involves a move from the general to the particular, in linguistic parlance, from the 'superordinate' to a 'hyponym'.[74] The device manifests itself in two ways.[75] On one pattern, the discourse first envisages judgement on a universal scale then moves to a particular focus. In the other, the discourse first refers to a particular target and then grounds the announcement of local doom in a declaration of universal judgement. For Raabe, the pervasiveness of the device in Old Testament prophecy and its centrality to the line of argument being developed within a given text make it highly unlikely that the universal perspective was a later addition to earlier texts.

In my view, Raabe provides the most convincing explanation of the conjunction of cosmic/universal and local judgement in Isaiah 13, 34, etc. In Isaiah 13, the author first portrays the day of the Lord against the whole world then focuses on the judgement of Babylon: 'The punishment of the whole world is particularized and applied specifically to

---

71. Young 1965: 419.

72. Clements 1980: 135.

73. Raabe 2002. He examines nineteen prophetic texts, including Isaiah 13; 34; Micah 1; Zephaniah 1; Nahum 1.

74. Raabe 2002: 652.

75. Raabe 2002: 672.

Babylon.'[76] The same pattern is exhibited in Isaiah 34; Micah 1; Nahum 1; Zephaniah 1. In Jeremiah 4 and Joel 2, the writer first paints a picture of local doom then relates it to a picture of devastating universal judgement. Every time, the reality of universal climactic judgement is assumed; it is precisely on this basis that the announcement of the 'lesser' local judgement is made.

If Isaiah 13, etc., are read in this way, the language of global and cosmic catastrophe could not be taken as metaphorical for local socio-political upheaval; it would form part of a description of universal judgement, which is subsequently (or was previously) localized within the larger oracle. It would still be possible to take the images of upheaval in nature as metaphorical for human judgement, though on a universal rather than local scale, but it would be more natural to read them as picturing the calamitous, nature-wrenching form that the coming judgement is expected to take.[77]

In the end, we cannot be entirely certain how the writers (or redactors) of these texts meant the language of global and cosmic catastrophe to be understood. In other oracles, though, there is less ambiguity. The expectation of universal judgement is not tempered by talk of a local outpouring of divine judgement. These oracles in their entirety belong to the post-exilic era.

1.4.2 *Global/Cosmic Disaster Language in Oracles that are More Obviously 'Eschatological'*

Isaiah 24 belongs to a collection of oracles (Isaiah 24–27) that has often been called 'the Isaianic Apocalypse'. The designation is questionable since the chapters clearly do not bear the form of an apocalypse by the standard definitions of the literary type. But, certainly, these chapters have emphases and motifs that are more usually found in later apocalyptic writings.

Isaiah 24 is a deeply gloomy oracle of a coming worldwide catastrophe.[78] It begins in v. 1 with the announcement that the Lord is going to empty (בּוֹקֵק) and lay waste (וּבוֹלְקָהּ) the earth (v. 1). He will do so by

---

76. Raabe 2002: 657.

77. This would mean, of course, attributing an expectation of worldwide judgement to pre-exilic prophets, but such an attribution is not as controversial as it used to be; as Collins (1990: 299) states, '*national* eschatology (concern for the future of Israel) and *cosmic* eschatology (concern for the future of the world) cannot be clearly separated, even in the preexilic prophets'.

78. Whether it was originally a unity is debated. Clements (1980: 200) maintains that the basic composition is 24.1-6, to which separate additions have been made.

'twisting' (וְעִוָּה) the surface of the earth, causing those who dwell on it to scatter (v. 1). Verse 2 indicates that the catastrophe will overwhelm all social groups; no one will escape. Verse 3 repeats v. 1, using a more emphatic idiom. Verses 4-13 describe the coming desolation (using the past tense).[79] The earth withers and 'the heavens languish together with the earth' (v. 4).[80] The cause of the global catastrophe is the sinfulness of the world's inhabitants: 'the earth lies polluted' under the transgressions of those who populate it (v. 5). The earth's inhabitants are said to have 'broken the everlasting covenant' (v. 5). It is probable that a reference to the covenant with Noah is meant (Gen. 9.8-17).[81] The violation of this covenant has brought a curse upon the earth (Isa. 24.6), causing God to withdraw his promise to Noah never again to destroy the earth with a flood.[82] Verses 7-9 add to the portrait of gloom by depicting the absence of festivities and occasions for drinking. Verses 10-12 focus on the decimation of the unnamed 'city of chaos' symbolizing human culture opposed to God. That 'the city' has a universal reference is clear from v. 13 – 'for thus it shall be on all the earth and among the nations'.[83] After a brief intermission in vv. 14-16, in v. 17, the theme of coming devastation resumes and intensifies. The reference to the opening of the windows of heaven in v. 18 recalls the flood story (cf. Gen. 7.11; 8.2). The trembling of the earth's foundations similarly suggests a return to the primeval chaos. Isaiah 24.19-20 paints a vivid portrait of the undoing of the earth.

> 19) The earth is utterly broken,
> the earth is torn asunder,
> the earth is violently shaken.
> 20) The earth staggers like a drunkard,
> it sways like a hut;
> its transgression lies heavy upon it,
> and it falls, and will not rise again.

79. The extensive use of the Hebrew perfect tense vv. 4-12 exemplifies the prophetic or visionary perfect, in which the future is described as past: Hayes 2002: 142.

80. The word translated 'heaven' here is מָרוֹם meaning 'height'.

81. This fits with the universal perspective and the allusions to the flood story in vv. 5 and 18. The phrase בְּרִית עוֹלָם occurs in Gen. 9.16, though it also used more widely (e.g. of the covenant with Abraham, Gen. 17.7, 13, 19).

82. Cf. Day 1985: 146.

83. Some have tried to identify the city with a particular city and so link the chapter with a specific historical crisis. Given the complete lack of any national or geographical reference, it seems more likely, as Clements (1980: 202) maintains, that the city is to be understood 'as a pictorial description of the body of organised human society, a type of "vanity fair", which is to be subjected to the divine judgement'.

The images of the breaking and tearing apart of the earth seem to envisage the total dissolution of the earth. In v. 20, the earth is likened to a drunkard who stumbles around and falls under the weight of his own transgression. The last line of the verse seems to say that the earth's demise is final. The concluding section, vv. 21-23, speaks of God's victory over 'the host of heaven' and 'the kings of the earth'. The final verse of the chapter envisages God reigning on Zion (v. 23). Assuming that these verses continue the flow of thought of the chapter, a restoration after the catastrophe is apparently expected (cf. 27.12-13).[84]

In contrast to Isaiah 14, 34, etc., there is no reference in this chapter to any historical city or nation, whether Israel, Judah, Samaria or Jerusalem or some foreign power, such as Babylon or Edom.[85] The doomsday scenario depicted in Isaiah 24 is not restricted to a particular geographical locale. There are clear indications that the author is thinking of universal disaster analogous to the Noachic flood (vv. 5, 18). A worldwide catastrophe, in which the earth is destroyed, is described as plainly as the writer knew how.

The second half of the book of Joel (2.28–3.21) may be regarded as a collection of eschatological oracles 'whose fulfilment lies in a distant or at least undatable future and which give hope more by their assurance that God is ultimately in control ... than by any immediate prospect of fulfillment'.[86] In this part of the book, the 'day of the Lord' is unambiguously a universal, eschatological event. The author envisions a final gathering of the nations of the world against Israel in the valley of Jehoshophat (3.2-17). The 'day of the Lord' is God's awesome intervention against the assembled nations. Joel 2.30-31 speaks of signs which precede the terrifying judgement.

> 30) I will show portents in the heavens and on the earth, blood and fire and columns of smoke.
> 31) The sun shall be turned to darkness, and the moon to blood, before the great and terrible day of the Lord comes.

---

84. There are signals in Isaiah 25–27 of a fairly radical view of the future blessedness, anticipating later eschatological expectation. Isaiah 25.8 predicts a future in which not only sorrow but also death itself will be removed from the scene. Isaiah 26.19 makes reference to the earth giving birth to those long dead. Isaiah 27.1 seems to imagine the complete elimination from the created order of the threat of chaos (in the form of the Leviathan and the dragon).

85. The maverick attempt by D. G. Johnson (1988) to read this oracle as a prophecy of Jerusalem's destruction in 587 BCE, fails to persuade. For criticisms, see Hayes 2002: 138–40.

86. Barton 2001: 92.

The verses which immediately precede (2.28-29) promise blessing in the shape of the pouring out of God's Spirit on all flesh. The transition from salvation to judgement at v. 30 is sudden and unexpected.[87] The 'portents' are divided between heaven and earth. The three earthly signs, blood, fire and smoke, suggest either warfare or geophysical disaster. 'Columns of smoke' may perhaps point to volcanic eruption. The darkening of the sun and moon is linked with the 'day of the Lord' in Isa. 13.10 and Joel 2.10 (cf. Amos 8.9). Here, Joel refers to the reddening of the moon rather than its darkening. In contrast to Isa. 13.10 and Joel 2.10, the celestial events are said here to take place *before* 'the day of the Lord dawns'.[88] They are a prelude to the great day of God rather than part of it. Yet, they serve to raise the 'day of the Lord' to an even greater height of terror since 'the most dreadful cosmic convulsions are no more than preliminary'.[89] A further description of the onset of the 'day of the Lord' is given in 3.14-16.

> 14) Multitudes, multitudes,
> in the valley of decision!
> For the day of the Lord is near
> in the valley of decision.
> 15) The sun and the moon are darkened,
> and the stars withdraw their shining.
> 16) The Lord roars from Zion,
> and utters his voice from Jerusalem,
> and the heavens and the earth shake.
> But the Lord is a refuge for his people,
> a stronghold for the people of Israel.

Verse 15 is a repetition of 2.10b. The shaking of heaven and earth is caused by the *voice* of God, a feature we will encounter in later Jewish 'catastrophic intervention' texts.[90] The cosmic shaking means that the stability of the whole established world is under threat. Yet, the Lord's people are preserved from the destruction. The final lines are reminiscent of Ps. 46.1. In both passages, we find the assurance that God is a refuge to his people when all around is chaos.

The prophecy of Haggai stems from the early post-exilic period, and thus pre-dates Isaiah 24 and Joel 2.28–3.21. In the face of disappointment at the post-exilic temple (in comparison with the grandness of

---

87. Barton (2001: 92–8) treats 2.28-29 and 2.30-32 as two separate oracles.

88. The clause could be taken referentially rather than temporally – *at* the coming of the day of the Lord. A temporal interpretation, though, fits better with the designation of these events as *portents*.

89. Coggins 2000: 52.

90. See next chapter. Cf. Job 26.11; Ps. 46.6.

Solomon's temple), in chapter 2 the prophet announces that God is about to intervene in an awesome way.

> 6) For thus says the Lord of hosts: Once again, in a little while, I will shake the heavens and the earth and the sea and the dry land; 7) and I will shake all the nations, so that the treasure of all nations shall come, and I will fill this house with splendour, says the Lord of hosts.

A comprehensive cosmic quake is envisaged as a means of judgement on the nations. The prophet does not expand on the geophysical and cosmic upheaval, but focuses on the concomitant 'shake-up' of the nations, which is more crucial to the line of thought being developed (vv. 7-9). The nations are to be stripped of their wealth and treasures so that the rebuilt temple can be decked out with riches. The cosmic catastrophe, then, is not a world-ending catastrophe.

The promise that God is going to shake the established cosmos is reiterated in vv. 21b-22.

> 21b) I am about to shake the heavens and the earth, 22) and to overthrow the throne of kingdoms; I am about to destroy the strength of the kingdoms of the nations, and overthrow the chariots and their riders; and the horses and their riders shall fall, every one by the sword of a comrade.

The convulsion of the cosmos is again linked with the general judgement of the nations.

Although the oracles of Haggai 2 relate to specific historical circumstances (the reconstruction of the temple), they do not localize the threat of universal and cosmic judgement. In this respect, they are like Isaiah 24 and Joel 2.28–3.21. Unlike them, though, Haggai's oracles betray a sense of imminence: the prophet seems to view the rebuilding of the temple as the trigger for the final intervention and the new age.

Isaiah 24 and Joel 2.28–3.21 show that in the late Old Testament period, language of global/cosmic upheaval was being used in a more obviously eschatological way. If we assume that the imagery of universal catastrophe belonged to the original oracles of Isaiah 13; 34; etc., and was not a later editorial addition, it is possible to identify a development in the prophetic employment of this language, from an 'original' use in association with pronouncements of impending local doom to a later use in prophecies of a more fully eschatological character, with Haggai 2 perhaps representing a midway stage in the process.[91]

---

91. One might see the theophany vision of Habakkuk 3, with its extensive portrayal of upheaval in nature, as belonging to the later development. Although the main prophecy of Habakkuk appears to have been composed originally just prior to the battle of Carchemish in 605 BCE, chapter 3 has often been regarded as a much

To recognize an eschatological reference in the use of global/cosmic catastrophe language in Isaiah 24, Joel 2.28–3.21 and Haggai 2 is not necessarily to admit that such language genuinely anticipates an actual catastrophe which destroys the earth or shakes the cosmos. One might concede that eschatological, universal judgement is in view and yet claim that imagery of upheaval and turmoil is no more than poetic embellishment. Isaiah 24, though, would be strongly resistant to such an interpretation. The composer of this text conceives of the universal judgement being effected precisely by means of a catastrophe which affects the physical earth as well as the people on it. In this passage, attention is evenly divided between the earth and its inhabitants; it would be doing serious harm to the text to read the statements about the earth as merely embellishing those about humankind.

There are good reasons for assuming that when prophetic writers, such as the author of Isaiah 24, spoke in unambiguous terms of universal judgement by global or cosmic catastrophe, this is what they actually expected. First, as is now widely recognized, the prophetic writers of the Old Testament share a worldview in which humans and the rest of nature are interrelated. As R. Simkins states, 'humans affect the natural world with their actions and are affected by the conditions of nature'.[92] In prophetic thought, human beings are inextricably linked with nature in sin, judgement and redemption. Since human sin has effects on the natural environment, so the judgement of God on human sin has damaging consequences for the environment (crops fail, the land loses its fertility, floods and earthquake wreak havoc). It is perfectly reasonable, given these assumptions, that prophetic writers should expect divine judgement upon humans on a universal scale also to have a devastating universal impact on nature. Second, throughout Israel's 'history', God uses the phenomena of nature as instruments of judgement against human beings, often in dramatic ways.[93] The thought of a comprehensive act of judgement involving the awesome forces of nature and chaos on a massive scale would be consistent with this traditional understanding of God's *modus operandi*. Third, the idea of a universal judgement effected by a worldwide natural catastrophe is firmly established in Israelite tradition in the form of the story of the flood. Even if the flood narratives

---

later addition to the book. In this chapter, the perspective of universal judgement (vv. 6-12) is maintained throughout, suggesting that the vision has an eschatological character.

92. Simkins 1994: 249.

93. E.g., the destruction of Sodom and Gomorrah (Gen. 19.24-25); the plagues on Egypt (Exodus 7–10); the drowning of Pharaoh's army in the Sea of Reeds (Exod. 14.26-31).

are judged to be relatively late, the myth itself is undoubtedly ancient. Thus, within the story of Israel's past, there is a powerful precedent for the notion of judgement by universal catastrophe. As we have seen, clear allusion is made to the flood in Isaiah 24 (vv. 5, 18).

There is broad agreement among Old Testament scholars that Isaiah 24 genuinely envisages the decimation of the earth as part of its scenario of universal judgement. In correlating the flood and coming eschatological judgement this vision paves the way for visions of catastrophic 'final' judgement in post-biblical Jewish apocalyptic and associated writings.

1.5 Conclusions

The notion of divine judgement through universal catastrophe is clearly expressed in the Genesis flood story. In Isaiah 24, this event serves as the type for future judgement.

The idea of the dissolution of the present creation is definitely present in the Old Testament, alongside other perspectives on the cosmic future. The earliest view seems to have been that creation is a permanent structure. The conviction that creation will perish and wear out (especially Ps. 102.25-27 and Isa. 51.6) represents a development of and departure from this cosmological tradition. In late Old Testament prophecy, we find the view that the whole cosmos will be transformed and made 'new', though it is debatable whether Isa. 65.17-25 envisions the destruction and re-creation of the world or a non-destructive renewal of the cosmos. In those passages that imply or express it, the thought of the created universe coming to an actual end does not carry radically 'dualistic' implications of the kind N. T. Wright supposes are bound up with the notion.

Language of global and cosmic catastrophe is found in oracles of local doom, such as Isaiah 13 and 34, and in prophecies which are more obviously 'eschatological', such as Isaiah 24. The usage in Isaiah 13, 34, etc., has been given different explanations by scholars, including that it functions as a metaphor for local socio-political upheaval (the fall of Babylon, Edom, etc.). A more persuasive explanation, in my view, is that such oracles combine the prospect of universal catastrophic judgement and the threat of impending local judgement, presenting the latter as a particularization of the former. However we interpret the sense of the language in 'early' prophetic usage, it is clear that in 'late' Old Testament prophecy, it is given a more eschatological application. Most scholars agree that Isaiah 24 genuinely envisions a world-decimating catastrophe.

It has been instructive to examine the deployment of global and cosmic disaster language in Old Testament prophecy, but, as stressed in the Introduction, Old Testament usage is not necessarily determinative for New Testament usage. For the purpose of clarifying the most natural sense of such language in New Testament times, we must look to instances of it in eschatological contexts in post-biblical Jewish apocalyptic and related writings. To this material, we now turn.

Chapter 2

JEWISH APOCALYPTIC AND RELATED LITERATURE

This chapter deals with comparative material in Jewish apocalyptic and related writings. In this body of literature, language of global and cosmic catastrophe occurs in passages about God's climactic intervention and the final judgement.[1] These passages take up the bulk of our attention. There are also passages that speak of strange celestial events, including the darkening of the sun and moon, as signs of the end or the coming redemption.[2] These texts also merit consideration. The inspiration for the idea of 'preliminary' celestial abnormalities seems to have been Joel 2.30-31. In several texts, celestial disturbances are included among the 'eschatological woes', the disasters and evils that characterize the time of 'tribulation' prior to the end.[3] I also highlight and discuss texts that envisage (or at least imply) the dissolution of the present created order, without using catastrophe language.[4] To provide balance, I note passages which anticipate a cosmic renewal in the form of non-catastrophic transformation (rather than destruction and re-creation),[5] though they are less directly relevant to New Testament 'cosmic catastrophe' texts.

I explore the selected texts on a document-by-document basis (though a couple of our texts belong to fragments rather than documents), rather

---

1. *1 En.* 1.3b-9; 83.2b-5; 102.1-3; *Ps.-Soph.* fr. 2; *T. Mos.* 10.3-6; 1 QH 11.19-36; *2 Bar.* 32.1; 59.3; *Apoc. Zeph.* 12.5-8; *Sib. Or.* 3.80-92; 3.675-681; 4.175-192; 5.155-161; 5.211-213; 5.477-478; 5.512-531.

2. *1 En.* 80.4-8; *LAB* 19.13; *4 Ezra* 5.4b-5; *Sib. Or.* 3.796-804; 5.346-349.

3. On the great tribulation and the eschatological woes, see further Allison 1985: 5–25; Hartman 1966: 28–34; Sim 1996: 42–3.

4. *1 En.* 72.1; 91.16; *T. Job* 33.3-9; *LAB* 3.10; *4 Ezra* 5.50-55; 7.30-42; 14.18; *2 Bar.* 85.10; *2 En.* 65.6-11.

5. *1 En.* 45.4-5; *Jub.* 1.29; 4.26. The expectation of a cosmic renewal is found in 1 QS 4.25 and 4Q225 1.6-7. In the former (on which see Ringgren 1995: 165–6), it is not clear whether the renewal comes by way of de-creation and re-creation or non-catastrophic transformation. The latter text reflects *Jub.* 1.29 (see García Martínez 2005: 65) and presumably points to non-cataclysmic transformation as does *Jubilees*.

than under the distinct categories I have just identified. Some documents contain texts which belong to different categories, and it makes sense to treat these passages together. A document-led approach also makes it easier to discuss the creational/cosmological implications of the idea of the end of the world in those writings in which it is found. I will adopt a categorizing format, though, when presenting the conclusions at the end of the chapter.

Many of the documents to be discussed are conventionally called 'apocalyptic' writings. There has been and continues to be much debate among scholars about how one defines an 'apocalypse' or the 'apocalyptic' genre.[6] Yet, there is general agreement about the particular Jewish works that are in view when the category apocalypse/apocalyptic is invoked.[7] Here, I simply adopt the customary literary label, leaving the troublesome definitional question to the side. Traditionally, scholars have also used the term 'apocalyptic' to denote the worldview or eschatology thought to be embodied in the literary apocalypses.[8] The category 'apocalyptic eschatology', however, has become highly controversial in recent years.[9] In the present discussion, it will be avoided altogether.[10] I want it to be clear when I draw my conclusions at the end, that they have been based on an examination of the *textual* evidence and not on an abstract worldview or eschatological perspective.[11]

---

6. One may contrast the definition formulated by Collins and others in the Society of Biblical Literature Genres Project with the minimalist statement given by Rowland. Collins (1998: 5) describes an apocalypse as '*a genre of revelatory literature with a narrative framework, in which a revelation is mediated by an otherworldly being to a human recipient, disclosing a transcendent reality which is both temporal, insofar as it envisages eschatological salvation, and spatial insofar as it involves another, supernatural world*'. Rowland (1982: 14) defines apocalyptic more generally as 'the direct communication of the heavenly mysteries in all their diversity'.

7. Collins 1998: 3.

8. In addition, the term 'apocalypticism' is used by some for the concrete manifestation of an apocalyptic worldview in social groups: see Collins 1998: 12–14.

9. Rowland has been especially critical. He thinks that the category should be jettisoned from scholarly discussion. What scholars have traditionally called 'apocalyptic eschatology' in his view should rather be termed 'transcendent eschatology'. See the discussion in Rowland 1982: 23–48. For a defence of 'apocalyptic' as eschatology, see Sim 1996: 23–31.

10. This is not a wholesale rejection of 'apocalyptic' as eschatology or worldview; I found the category a useful one in my study of Paul's cosmological language: see Adams 2000: 106–7, etc.

11. Having earlier criticized N. T. Wright for interpreting apocalyptic usage of cosmic catastrophe language in terms of his own generalization of apocalyptic, I do not want to lay myself open to a similar charge.

The writings to be discussed span a wide chronological spectrum, from the third century BCE to the early second century CE. The order of discussion tries to reflect the chronology, insofar as this can be traced with any degree of precision (and in many cases specific dates are elusive). However, I discuss the distinct works that make up *1 Enoch* and the *Sibylline Oracles* (Books 3–5) *en bloc*, even though they stem from different historical periods. To treat the individual compositions that form these compilations at different points in the presentation seems unnecessarily fragmentary. I begin with *1 Enoch*, since it contains what seem to be the earliest of the relevant passages, and end with the *Sibylline Oracles*, Book 5 of which contains what is probably the latest material (80–132 CE).[12] In treating the various works, I offer very little comment on introductory issues relating to them; nor do I elaborate on their general content except as necessary for illuminating and clarifying the key passages and assessing the creational/cosmological implications of belief in the end of the present created order.[13]

2.1 1 Enoch

The composite nature of the work known as *1 Enoch* has long been recognized by critics. The book is a compilation of different writings that span several centuries. The complete collection is preserved only in Ethiopic, though fragments of it survive in Aramaic (from Qumran), Greek and Latin. Five separate works within the Enochic corpus are commonly accepted: the Book of the Watchers (*1 Enoch* 1–36); the Similitudes of Enoch (*1 Enoch* 37–71); the Astronomical Book (*1 Enoch* 72–82); the Book of Dream Visions (*1 Enoch* 83–90, comprising the vision of the flood, chs 83–84, and the so-called Animal Apocalypse, chs 85–90); the Epistle of Enoch (*1 Enoch* 91–105). Embedded in the Epistle is the Apocalypse of Weeks (*1 En.* 93.1-10 and 91.11-17). Passages relevant to our interests are found in all of these discrete compositions.

---

12. Though they contain passages relevant to this enquiry (*T. Levi* 4.1; *Gk. Apoc. Ezra* 3.38; *Apoc. Elij.* 2.1), the *Testaments of the Twelve Patriarchs*, the *Greek Apocalypse of Ezra* and the *Apocalypse of Elijah* will be omitted from consideration because of problems of dating and Christian redaction.

13. A note on translations is in order at this point. For *1 Enoch*, I have followed the translations in Nickelsburg's (2001) commentary, except for the Similitudes and the Astronomical Book, which are not covered in this volume. For 1 QH 11.29-36, I have followed García Martínez 1994; for *Testament of Moses*, I have used Tromp 1993, and for *4 Ezra* I have kept to the translation in the NSRV. All other translations are taken from *OTP*.

2.1.1 The Book of the Watchers (1 Enoch 1–36)

The Book of the Watchers is one of the oldest parts of *1 Enoch*. It is itself a composite work, though the various sources of which it is constituted have been blended together to form an overall unity. The core story of the watchers is told in chs 6–11. Much of the rest of the book (chs 17–36) is given over to Enoch's journeys to Sheol and the limits of the earth. Chapters 1–5 constitute an introduction. George Nickelsburg dates the book as a whole in the middle of the third century BCE.[14]

The opening verse of the book looks ahead to 'the day of tribulation', the time of distress prior to the end.[15] There follows in vv. 3b-9 a dramatic portrayal of God's eschatological coming to save the righteous and chosen ones and to punish all his enemies.

> 3b) The Great Holy One will come forth from his dwelling
> and the eternal God will tread from thence upon Mount Sinai.
> 4) He will appear with his army,
> he will appear with his mighty host from the heaven of heavens.
> 5) All the watchers will fear and quake,
> and those who are hiding in all the ends of the earth will sing;
> All the ends of the earth will be shaken,
> and trembling and great fear will seize them (the watchers) unto the ends of the earth.
> 6) The high mountains will be shaken and fall and break apart,
> and the high hills will be made low
> and melt like wax before the fire;
> 7) The earth will be wholly rent asunder,
> and everything on the earth will perish,
> and there will be judgement on all.
> 8) With the righteous he will make peace,
> and over the chosen there will be protection,
> and upon them will be mercy ...
>
> 9) Behold, he comes with the myriads of his holy ones,
> to execute judgement on all,
> and to destroy all the wicked,
> and to convict all flesh
> for all the wicked deeds that they have done,
> and the proud and hard words that wicked sinners spoke against him.

The vision falls into the standard theophany pattern, familiar from Old Testament passages such as Mic. 1.3-4, in which the divine appearance is attended by convulsions in nature.[16] God descends from his heavenly

---

14. Nickelsburg 2001: 7.
15. Nickelsburg 2001: 136.
16. See VanderKam 1973.

abode to Mount Sinai, with his mighty host (cf. Deut. 33.2; Zech. 14.5), and his coming has a destructive impact on the earth. The reference to Sinai suggests that the writer has in mind an eschatological parallel to the Sinai theophany (cf. Exod. 19.16-25).[17]

The effects of God's coming on the natural order are described in vv. 5-7. The 'ends of the earth' are 'shaken' (v. 5).[18] That the reference is to the ends or extremities (τὰ ἄκρα) of the earth indicates that what is envisaged is *global* seismic activity, not a local earthquake.[19] Mountains and hills shake, are levelled and melt (v. 6). The subject of v. 6a is 'the high mountains'. The Ethiopic text states that they will be shaken; the Greek text adds, 'and will fall and break apart/be dissolved' (καὶ πεσοῦνται καὶ διαλυθήσονται). In v. 6b, the subject is 'the high hills'; they are 'made low'. The wording and thought of this line are taken from Isa. 40.4.[20] The image of hills or mountains[21] melting like wax before the fire in v. 6c is drawn from Mic. 1.3-4, which seems to be the main inspiration behind v. 6. The set of images in v. 6 conveys a portrait of 'the complete destruction of the mountains'.[22] The earth is said to be 'wholly rent asunder' (v. 7). As Nickelsburg points out, in these words, there is an allusion to Isa. 24.19 and its picture of the earth's demise.[23] The Ethiopic text has an alternative reading at this point, 'and the earth will sink',[24] which suggests the return of the earth to chaos. The words 'everything on the earth will perish' (πάντα ὅσα ἐστὶν ἐπὶ τῆς γῆς ἀπολεῖται) in v. 7c allude to the Genesis flood story, picking up the language of Gen. 6.17.[25]

As Nickelsburg states, 'These verses depict the total distortion and disintegration of the earth in the presence of the divine Judge.'[26] The picture is not that of the total dissolution of the whole universe: the scenario is one of complete *global* destruction.

17. Nickelsburg 2001: 145.
18. The line 'All the ends of the earth will be shaken' appears only in the Greek text. The wording may be based on Isa. 41.5; cf. VanderKam 1973: 143.
19. Nickelsburg 2001: 146.
20. VanderKam 1973: 145. The Greek text is again longer here, adding 'so that the mountains will waste away' (τοῦ διαρυῆναι ὄρη).
21. In the Ethiopic, the subject is the hills; in the Greek text, the subject is the mountains.
22. VanderKam 1973: 146.
23. Nickelsburg 2001: 146–7.
24. Knibb 1978: 59.
25. Vanderkam 1973: 146. As noted in the previous chapter, the typological association of eschatological judgement with the flood in Noah's time is already present in Isaiah 24.
26. Nickelsburg 2001: 146.

There can hardly be any doubt that *1 En.* 1.3b-9 refers to a final, eschatological event and not merely a momentous event in ongoing history.[27] God's coming is a supernatural, *history-stopping* intervention. The scope is incontestably universal; God comes to effect judgement on the *whole* of humanity, not a particular nation or state. The universality of God's judgement is underlined by the repeated use of the word 'all' in vv. 3b-9 (11 times in total).[28] The mention of Mount Sinai in v. 4 in no way limits the global horizons. Sinai, as the destination of God's descent, is the epicentre of a quake that extends to the remotest parts of the earth. That the watchers, those responsible for the introduction of sin into the world (*1 Enoch* 6–11), are included in the judgement indicates that the divine intervention is not just about the reversal of Israel's political fortunes, but the total resolution of sin and evil.

That actual global destruction is envisaged is apparent from the allusion to the Genesis flood story. The writer looks for a natural disaster on a global scale like the deluge in Noah's day, but one that is even more destructive in its impact. In depicting the destruction of the earth, he utilizes prophetic language of global upheaval, drawing on specific prophetic texts, especially Mic. 1.3-4 and Isa. 24.19. Obviously, the language should not be taken literally; its function is to evoke a scene of utter global ruination.

A restoration of the earth following its destruction is indicated in *1 En.* 5.7: the righteous and chosen ones are to 'inherit the earth'.[29] The brief description of the future state that follows in vv. 8-9 draws on the account of life on the new earth in Isa. 65.17-25. The pattern of eschatological global destruction followed by renovation is developed further in 10.2–11.1.[30] *Prima facie* 10.2–11.1 is about the judgement and restoration in the time of Noah. But, as most recognize, it also has an eschatological reference:[31] the deluge is a type of the global catastrophe to come and the bliss that follows is a paradigm of the ideal situation in store for the chosen ones.[32] As with *1 En.* 5.8-9, the depiction of the future time of

27. Cf. Hartman 1966: 72.
28. Nickelsburg 2001: 143.
29. Cf. Ps. 37.9, 11, 22, 29.
30. In 10.2, it is stated that 'the whole earth will perish' (ἡ γῆ ἀπόλλυται πᾶσα).
31. Rowland 1982: 161; cf. Nickelsburg (2001: 220): 'deluge and final judgment parallel and coalesce with each other'.
32. The account of the situation after the calamity in 10.16–11.2 goes far beyond what is said in Genesis about the postdiluvian world. According to Gen. 11.10-25, the human lifespan decreased dramatically after the flood (cf. Gen. 6.3). *First Enoch* 10.17, in sharp contrast, looks for a return to the antediluvian longevity. *First Enoch* 10.16–11.2 envisages a world from which sin and evil have been completely

blessing in 10.16–11.2 is partly influenced by the prophecy of the new earth in Isa. 65.17-25.[33]

2.1.2 *The Similitudes of Enoch (*1 Enoch *37–71)*

The Similitudes is the latest of the documents that make up *1 Enoch*.[34] It consists of three extended parables (chs 38–44; 45–57; 58–69) and a twofold epilogue (chs 70 and 71). A major concern of the book is the final judgement and the contrasting fates of the righteous and the wicked. There is also considerable 'messianic' interest.[35] A cosmic renewal is predicted in 45.4-5.

> 4) On that day, I shall cause my Elect One to dwell among them,
> I shall transform heaven and make it a blessing of light forever.
> 5) I shall (also) transform the earth and make it a blessing,
> and cause my Elect One to dwell in her.
> Then those who have committed sin and crime shall not set foot in her.

This passage obviously alludes to Isa. 65.17-25. The language points to a miraculous alteration of the existing creation, rather than a cosmic dissolution and creation anew. There is no indication in the surrounding verses, or indeed anywhere else in the Similitudes, that a destruction of the cosmos precedes the transformation.[36] Taught here is a non-catastrophic cosmic renewal. The transfiguration cleanses the earth of evil (cf. 69.29) and makes it a fit habitation for the righteous.[37]

---

removed. This could hardly apply to the postdiluvian world. *First Enoch* 10.21 depicts the conversion of the nations and their worship of God. This is a feature of Old Testament prophetic expectation, wholly inappropriate to the postdiluvian world of Genesis (cf. Gen. 11.1-9).
33. Nickelsburg 2001: 226–8.
34. Dating the work has proved devilishly tricky. Recent scholarship has tended to favour a date in the early or mid-first century (prior to the Jewish war of 66–70 CE, to which no obvious reference is made). See Suter 1979: 32; Collins 1998: 178. Nickelsburg (2001: 7) dates the work to the first century BCE.
35. The messianic figure is variously called the Messiah (48.10; 52.4), the Righteous One (38.2; 53.6), the Elect One (48.6; 52.6) and Son of Man (46.3, 4; 48.2; etc.).
36. In the allegorical vision of *1 Enoch* 52, metal mountains melt like wax at the presence of the Elect One (v. 6). Micah 1.3-4 seems to lie in the background here. However, within the parameters of the allegory, the melting of metal mountains denotes the general removal of metal at the time of the Elect One, so that no one can make weapons of warfare (*1 En.* 52.7-9).
37. The transformed world is pictured further in 51.4-5, on which see D. M. Russell 1996: 105. Celestial transformation is promised in 58.6.

2.1.3 *The Astronomical Book (*1 Enoch *72–82)*

The Astronomical Book (or Book of the Luminaries) contains very ancient material; according to Nickelsburg, the compilation 'is probably the oldest of the Enochic traditions'.[38] The book is largely concerned with cosmological matters: there is a lengthy account of the movements of the heavenly bodies and the portals of the twelve winds.[39] The opening verse of the book, *1 En.* 72.1, strikes an eschatological chord.

> The Book of the Itinerary of the Luminaries of Heaven ... which Uriel ... showed me – just as he showed me all their treatises and the nature of the years of the world unto eternity, till the new creation which abides forever is created.

These words indicate that the order and regularity of the celestial realm celebrated in the book will not hold for ever, but only 'till the new creation'.[40] The expression 'new creation' almost certainly alludes to the promise of a new heaven and earth in Isa. 65.17 and 66.22. Given the astronomical and pseudo-scientific context, there can be no doubt that the term refers to a new *cosmic* creation.[41]

It is true, as Russell insists, that this verse does not focus on the demise of the present creation.[42] It does, though, strongly imply it. The laws governing the natural order are said to hold *until* the new creation; this presupposes that the advent of the new creation will involve the termination of the current celestial order. Also, the statement that the 'new creation' will 'abide forever' seems to stand in implicit contrast to a view of the present created order as impermanent and mortal. The generation of the new creation thus here entails the de-creation of the existing creation.

A later passage in the book, 80.2-8, predicts that the natural arrangement, which is presently stable and secure, will be distorted in the 'days of sinners'. The years will be cut short; crops will be late; the rain will be withheld; trees will not yield their fruit at the proper times. There will be strange occurrences in the celestial regions.

---

38. Nickelsburg 2001: 8.
39. The empirical observations serve a twofold purpose. On the one hand, they demonstrate the order and harmony of the created cosmos; on the other, they support the solar calendar of 364 days (72.32).
40. The verse has not been preserved among the Aramaic fragments of the Astronomical Book found at Qumran, but its authenticity or pre-Christian date is not in doubt; cf. Black 1976: 13.
41. Black 1976: 15.
42. D. M. Russell 1996: 95.

4) The moon shall alter its order, and will not be seen according to its (normal) cycles. 5) In those days it will appear in the sky and it shall arrive in the evening in the extreme ends of the great lunar path, in the west. And it shall shine (more brightly), exceeding the normal degree of light. 6) Many of the chiefs of the stars shall make errors in respect to the orders given to them; they shall change their courses and functions and not appear during the seasons which have been prescribed for them. 7) All the orders of the stars shall harden (in disposition) against the sinners and the conscience of those that dwell upon the earth. They (the stars) shall err against them (the sinners); and modify all their courses. Then they (the sinners) shall err and take them (the stars) to be gods. 8) All evil things shall be multiplied upon them; and plagues shall come upon them, so as to destroy all.

This is plainly a description of the eschatological woes, the sufferings and disasters expected to occur as the eschatological climax approaches. Since virtually the whole work is devoted to the movements of the heavenly bodies and is of a semi-technical nature, we can be confident that the writer is predicting actual celestial abnormalities. Indeed, here the language of celestial disorder may well be intended rather literally.

Although not an account of the cosmos in its death throes, these verses nevertheless describe the winding-down of the current cosmic order as its terminus draws near. The celestial failures are ominous signs of the impending cosmic dissolution. The exposition picks up on the eschatological proviso of 72.1 – the existing celestial orderliness will only last 'till the new creation'.[43] When the time of the end/new creation comes, the stability of the cosmos will start to break down. Although there is no direct allusion to this verse, it is possible that Gen. 8.22 provides the general inspiration for the line of thought, with its teaching that the patterns of nature continue 'as long as the earth lasts'. As the end of the world approaches, the cycles of nature begin to fail. The cosmic malfunctions described are thus part of a process of cosmic expiration. The winding-down of the cosmic order coincides with an increase of sin and wickedness, and is to some extent brought on by it.

43. VanderKam (1984: 106–7) thinks that 80.2-8 contradicts 72.1. According to VanderKam (107), *1 En.* 72.1 'claims that the laws of nature ... will retain their validity as long as the present creation endures; but 80:2-8, which deal with a time when the old creation still survives, opposes that view. Before the old creation expires, the laws which had governed God's creation are repealed.' He thus concludes that 80.2-8 was a later addition to the Astronomical Book. But VanderKam is applying a degree of exactitude which may never have been intended. The words 'until the new creation' in 72.1 are probably meant to cover the demise of the old creation as well as the advent of the new. *First Enoch* 80.2-8 portrays the time when the present world *begins* to expire, not *before* it does so.

There is no mention of the darkening of the sun and moon, or of the shaking of heavenly bodies, as in Isa. 13.10, 13 and similar Old Testament texts. The thought of the intensifying of the moon's light may be based on Isa. 30.26 ('the light of the moon will be like the light of the sun'). In Isaiah, this is a feature of the coming transformation, rather than an element of cosmic catastrophe. The main emphasis of *1 En.* 80.2-8 is the alteration of the paths of the heavenly bodies; this is in keeping with the subject matter of the book.

The Astronomical Book thus envisages the dissolution of the present created order and its creation anew. It is clear that for the author/editor of this work, the expectation of cosmic dissolution does not entail a radical cosmological dualism. There is no hint of an anti-creational bias in the Astronomical Book; quite the opposite. The extensive discussion of the movements of the luminaries reflects a positive attitude toward the natural world and expresses a sense of wonder at the excellence of the divine ordering of the cosmos.

2.1.4 *The Dream Visions (*1 Enoch *83–90)*

In the first dream vision (83–4), which dates at least from the Maccabean period,[44] Enoch reports the content of a dream he had as a young man while staying in the house of his grandfather Mahalalel.

> 83.3b) I saw in a vision,
> heaven was thrown down and taken away,
> and it fell down upon the earth.
> 4) And when it fell upon the earth,
> I saw how the earth was swallowed up in the great abyss.
> Mountains were suspended upon mountains,
> and hills sank down upon hills;
> Tall trees were cut from their roots,
> and were thrown away and sank into the abyss.
> 5) And then speech fell into my mouth and I lifted up (my voice) to cry
> out and said,
> 'The earth has been destroyed.'

This is incontestably a vision of the collapse of the cosmos (even if the emphasis in v. 5 is on the destruction of the earth). Heaven, pictured in Old Testament terms as a canopy stretching over the earth, falls down onto the world below; the earth and the seemingly immovable features of the terrestrial realm, the mountains and the great trees, sink down into

---

44. Collins 1998: 67. Cf. Nickelsburg 2001: 346–7, 360–1.

the abyss. The world returns to the primordial chaos; creation is unmade.[45]

The references to the mountains and hills may have been inspired generally by Mic. 1.4 and Nah. 1.5. The reference to tall trees seems to allude to Isa. 10.33 ('the tallest trees will be cut down').

Although in its literary context, the vision is understood as a prediction of the Noachic deluge, an eschatological reference is certain. The scale of destruction is cosmic rather than global as in Genesis 6–8, that is, the whole created *universe* reverts to chaos. Also, there is no specific mention of a *flood*. The typological association of flood and final destructive judgement is here so firmly established that a picture of the latter can be superimposed on the former.

The parallel with the Noachic flood rules out the possibility that the language of cosmic destruction is here metaphorical for a local political change within ongoing human history; a world-ending catastrophe, in a fully cosmic sense, is undeniably in view.

The stress on God as creator and sovereign ruler of heaven and earth (83.11; 84.2-3), and the implicit hope that creation will be restored after its catastrophic destruction (by analogy with the restoration after the flood) exclude an extreme cosmic dualism and anti-creational tendency in this work. The First Dream Vision, though, does recognize a theological problem raised by God's destruction of the world. God's decision to dissolve the cosmos thwarts his intention that the world should serve as an everlasting testimony to his glory (84.2). Mahalalel, who confirms that the earth must sink into the abyss and 'be utterly destroyed', nevertheless exhorts Enoch to pray that God 'may not obliterate the whole earth'. Accordingly, Enoch makes supplication that God may not devastate the earth so 'that there be eternal destruction' (84.5). The plea is not that God should go back on his decision to destroy the world; the 'Lord of judgement' (83.11) must carry out the righteous judgement he has decreed. The hope is rather that having turned the world back to the original chaos, he should not leave it to languish for ever in a state of waste but restore it. The problem caused by the divine destruction of the world is thus resolved by the conviction that renewal and restoration follows.

2.1.5 *The Apocalypse of Weeks (1 Enoch 93.1-10; 91.11-17)*

The Apocalypse of Weeks is contained within the Epistle of Enoch, though it is questionable whether it ever circulated independently. Nickelsburg dates the Apocalypse to the first third of the second century

---

45. See Nickelsburg 2001: 349.

BCE.[46] The work consists of a review of history from the beginning of the world to the eschatological consummation. The history of the world is divided into ten weeks.[47] Weeks one to six extend from creation to the destruction of the temple and the exile. The seventh week begins with the Babylonian exile and ends with the election of the chosen ones. The period is dominated by 'a perverse generation'. It is generally agreed that the real author locates himself at the conclusion of this week. Weeks eight to ten mark the time of eschatological fulfilment which is achieved progressively. The eighth week is designated a week of righteousness during which the righteous ones execute vengeance on their enemies (91.12). At the end of it, the righteous take possession of wealth and the eschatological temple is built in great splendour (91.13). The ninth week sees righteousness extend to the whole earth; all humanity is converted to the path of righteousness (91.14). At the close of the tenth week, called its 'seventh part', the judgement of the watchers takes place (91.15). Then, the first heaven passes away and a new heaven appears. After the tenth week, the eternal age ('many weeks without number forever') begins (91.17).

The celestial renewal, the climactic event of the whole scheme, is narrated in 91.16, without elaboration:

> And the first heaven will pass away[48] in it,
> and a new heaven will appear;
> and all the powers of the heavens will shine forever with sevenfold (brightness).

This verse, which picks up the promise of a new heaven in Isa. 65.17,[49] cannot be referring to socio-political change in realization of Jewish national aspirations. The author of the Apocalypse distinguishes three aspects of eschatological fulfilment, national (the restoration of the nation, etc.), universal (the conversion of the Gentiles) and cosmic (the judgement of the watchers and cleansing of the heavens) and allots them to distinct phases of the eschatological programme. National restoration, which happens in the eighth week, is chronologically distinct from the renewal of the heavens, occurring at the very end of the tenth. The celestial renewal is pushed into the distant future.[50]

---

46. Nickelsburg 2001: 440.
47. The division of history into ten segments is also found in the *Sibylline Oracles* (1, 2 and 4).
48. The Ethiopic reads: 'shall depart and pass away'.
49. On the influence and development of Isa. 65.17 here, see Van Ruitten 1989.
50. Nickelsburg 2001: 440.

As Matthew Black states, it is 'undeniable that 1 Enoch is here depicting a totally new cosmic dimension of God's creative work, the newly created heaven at the End of Time'.[51] The wording, especially the distinction between the *first* and a *new* heaven, makes it clear that the author has in view the physical dissolution of the existing heaven and the creation of a new celestial realm. The writer does not expand on the cosmological process involved, but one should not read into his words any thought of the dissolution of existing celestial 'matter' and the creation of brand-new heavenly matter. The new heaven is qualitatively superior to the present heaven: its luminaries shine seven times more brightly (cf. Isa. 30.26, etc.).

Strikingly, there is no reference to the earth in 91.16.[52] From this fact Black deduces that what the author of the Apocalypse of Weeks envisages is a completely heavenly salvation: 'The apparent assumption at 1 En. 91.16 is not that the earth will be transformed with the heavens, but that a new heaven will appear and become the abode of the righteous forever.'[53] Donald Gowan agrees and thinks that this is one of the few passages in Jewish apocalyptic and related literature that look forward to a completely heavenly redemption.[54] But such a conclusion may not be justified. The dissolution of heaven is linked with the judgement of the watchers, who come from heaven. Such is their corruption of the heavenly spheres that only complete destruction and re-creation can cleanse them. The terrestrial realm, from the author's point of view, needs less radical treatment. As Rowland states, 'In the eyes of the apocalypticist removal of the evil from the world by the activities of the righteous was sufficient to make the earth conform to God's eternal purposes.'[55]

2.1.6 *The Epistle of Enoch (1* Enoch *91–107)*

According to 92.1, Enoch's letter is for the benefit of his offspring but especially for 'the last generations'; this clearly gives the work an eschatological horizon. The Epistle fits the format of a testament; like a testament it contains a mixture of woes, exhortations and predictions. The document was apparently composed in the second century BCE.[56]

---

51. Black 1976: 17.
52. The Ethiopic text, though, states that in the ninth week, 'the world will be written down for destruction'.
53. Black 1976: 18.
54. Gowan 1985: 92.
55. Rowland 1982: 165.
56. Nickelsburg 2001: 8, 427–8.

The main section of the Epistle (94.6–104.8) divides into six distinct discourses.[57] The fifth discourse (100.7–102.3) concludes with a description of God's intervention to execute final and universal judgement.

> 102.1) Then, when he hurls against you the flood of the fire of your burning,
> where will you flee and be saved?
> And when he utters his voice against you with a mighty sound,
> will you not be shaken and frightened?
> 2) The heavens and all the luminaries will be shaken with great fear;
> and all the earth will be shaken and will tremble and be thrown into confusion.
> 3) And all the angels will fulfill what was commanded them;
> and all the sons of the earth will seek to hide themselves from the presence of the Great Glory,
> and they will be shaken and tremble.
> And you, sinners, will be cursed forever;
> you will have no peace.[58]

The description conforms to the Old Testament theophany pattern, with nature convulsing as God intervenes. The text recalls the longer account of God's eschatological theophany in 1.3b-9 and is no doubt intended to evoke and reinforce that passage. The devastating impact is caused by God's dramatic action (hurling fire) and the utterance of his voice (cf. Joel 3.16), rather than his appearance, but God's descent from heaven is

---

57. Nickelsburg 2001: 421.
58. The Ethiopic text of 102.1-3 differs from the Greek, and the Greek is somewhat confused. The Ethiopic reads: 'And in those days if he brings a fierce fire upon you, whither will you flee, and where will you be safe? And when he utters his voice against you, will you not be terrified and afraid? And all the lights will shake with great fear, and the whole earth will be terrified and will tremble and quail. And all the angels will carry out their commands and will seek to hide before the one who is great in glory, and the children of the earth will tremble and shake; you sinners (will be) cursed for ever and will not have peace' (Knibb 1978: 237). The Greek text states: 'And when he hurls at you the flood of fire of your burning, where will you run and be saved? And when he utters his voice against you, you will be shaken and terrified with a great sound, and the entire earth will be shaken and will tremble and be troubled. And the angels will fulfil the command given to them, and heaven and the lights will be shaken and tremble; all the sons of the earth and you sinners will be cursed for ever; you will have no peace' (my translation of Black's Greek text, 1970: 41). Nickelsburg's translation, given in the main text basically follows the Ethiopic, with several additions from the Greek, most significantly the reference to the shaking of heaven (which Nickelsburg translates as 'the heavens') and the luminaries, which Nickelsburg places in v. 2, to parallel the reference to the shaking of the earth. For discussion of the textual difficulties and how they may be resolved, see Nickelsburg 2001: 505; Zuntz 1944.

probably presupposed from 1.3b-9. His arrival and presence on earth is indicated in v. 3 ('the presence of the great glory'). As in 1.3b-9, there is a recollection of the Sinai theophany (fire, the voice of God, trembling). Unlike 1.3b-9, the effects of God's climactic intervention extend to the celestial realm: the physical heaven and its light-giving bodies shake and tremble (ὁ οὐρανός καὶ οἱ φωστῆρες σειόμενοι καὶ τρέμοντες), along with the whole earth.

The image of a 'flood of fire' (τὸν κλύδωνα τοῦ πυρός) suggests a fiery repetition of the Noachic flood. The expectation of a fiery catastrophe corresponding to the flood, as we will see, is found in other texts.[59] The 'pagan' idea of recurring destructions by water and fire may be at work here.[60] The writer does not elaborate on the 'flood of fire' theme. Nickelsburg suggests that he may be evoking a more extensive description of the burning deluge such as that in 1 QH 11.28-36 (discussed below).[61]

The overall picture painted in these verses is that of an immense cosmic catastrophe, but the whole cosmos is not destroyed. The fiery flood is hurled at the earth and its sinful inhabitants, but it does not engulf the heavenly region. There can be no question, therefore, of a total cosmic conflagration along Stoic lines.

Once again, it is clear that the occasion in view is a history-stopping, final irruption, and not a turn of events in the progress of history. The evocation of the Noachic flood and the link back to *1 En.* 1.3b-9 strongly suggest that the writer is here conveying the genuine expectation of catastrophic occurrences in nature at the eschatological intervention of God.

2.2 Pseudo-Sophocles, *Fragment 2*

This fragment[62] is part of an extraordinary literary enterprise in the Hellenistic period in which Jewish writers reworked real pieces of Greek poetry and composed their own in the style of the classical poets. These poems circulated in anthologies which served an apologetic purpose – to

---

59. See below on *Ps.-Soph.* fr. 2; 1 QH 11.19-36. Cf. also *LAE* 49.3–50.3; Josephus, *Ant.* 1.70.
60. Plato, *Tim.* 22C–E; Seneca, *Nat. quaes.* 3.29.1; etc. See further next chapter.
61. Nickelbsurg 2001: 509.
62. The fragment with which we are concerned is found in Clement of Alexandria's *Stromata* (5.14, 121-2), which is quoted by Eusebius (*Ev. Praep.* 13.13.48). It is also cited by Pseudo-Justin (*De monarchia* 3), who attributes it to Sophocles (Clement simply introduces it as verses from 'tragedy').

show that Jewish beliefs were in line with the teaching of classical Greek literature.[63] This piece, which may be a revision of original Greek verse, is dated by Harold Attridge to the third or second century BCE.[64] The text runs:

> For there will, there will indeed, come that period of time
> when the gold-faced sky will split apart
> the treasury filled with fire, and the nurtured flame
> will in its rage consume all things on earth
> and in the heavens.
>
> And when the universe gives out,
> the whole wavy deep will be gone;
> and the land will be empty of all dwellings; the air,
> in flames, will not bear winged flocks.
> For we believe there are two paths in Hades,
> one for the just, the other for the impious.
> Then will he preserve all things which previously perished.[65]

Predicted here is a terrible blaze affecting the whole of the cosmos. The reference to 'the treasury (θησαυρός) filled with fire' reflects the Old Testament idea of a treasury of water above the firmament from which God dispenses rain.[66] This in turn suggests an allusion to the Genesis flood, with the author imagining a fiery downpour paralleling (and exceeding) the deluge in Noah's day. That the fiery destruction is for the purpose of divine judgement is clear from the 'two ways' theme and the distinction between the righteous and the wicked. The fire from above consumes everything on earth and also in the material heavens. The scorching causes the waters of the earth to evaporate. The words, 'when the universe gives out' (ἐπὰν δὲ ἐκλίπῃ τὸ πᾶν) may seem to imply that the whole universe is dissolved in the flames, but the earth apparently continues to exist after the fire has died down; it is emptied of all dwellings, but it is still there. What seems to be in mind, as Pieter Van der Horst points out, is a mighty fire that consumes everything on the earth and in the heavens, but not the heavens and the earth themselves.[67] A restoration following the cosmic burn-up is indicated in the final

---

63. Attridge in *OTP* 2: 821.
64. Attridge in *OTP* 2: 821–2.
65. For the Greek text, see Stählin 1906.
66. Deut. 28.12: 'The Lord will open for you his rich storehouse (LXX τὸν θησαυρὸν αὐτοῦ), the heavens, to give the rain of your land in its season and to bless all your undertakings'. Cf. Ps. 135.7; Jer. 10.13; 51.16; Sir. 43.14; *1 En.* 54.7.
67. Cf. Van der Horst 1994: 237.

comment, that he [i.e. God] 'will preserve all things which previously perished' (κἄπειτα σώσει πάντα ἃ πρόσθ[εν] ἀπώλεσσεν).

These verses have sometimes been regarded as an early witness to Jewish appropriation of the Stoic doctrine of *ekpurōsis*.[68] But the scenario envisaged cannot really be equated with the Stoic *ekpurōsis*, since the cosmos itself is not reduced to the element fire.

As an isolated fragment, the passage is context-less and must be read as it stands. It presents itself as a warning of coming judgement in the form of a cosmic (but not world-ending) catastrophe, and there are no internal grounds for treating it as anything other than that.

2.3 Jubilees

The book of *Jubilees* is normally classified among the apocalypses.[69] Certainly it has a revelatory dimension,[70] but it is perhaps more accurately described as 'rewritten Bible'.[71] Its dating has long been the subject of dispute,[72] but it can be related generally to the Maccabean period. The book is introduced as a history of all the years of the world (1.1), though the historical review itself does not get beyond the arrival at Sinai. In 1.29, world history is set between two poles, from the day of creation until 'the day of the new creation',

> when the heaven and the earth and all of their creatures shall be renewed according to the powers of heaven and according to the whole nature of earth, until the sanctuary of the Lord is created in Jerusalem upon Mount Zion. And all of the lights will be renewed for healing and peace and blessing for all of the elect of Israel and in order that it might be thus from that day and unto all the days of the earth.

Envisaged here is a revamped creation, with Jerusalem, and her newly established temple, at its centre.[73] The picture is derived from Isa. 65.17-25.[74] There is no indication that the cosmic renewal is brought about by

---

68. Attridge draws attention to the Stoic notion: *OTP* 2: 826 n. 6.d.
69. Though fragments of the Greek, Syriac and Latin versions survive, the book is preserved in full form only in Ethiopic. The work was originally composed in Hebrew: see Wintermute in *OTP* 2: 41–3.
70. It thus sits quite easily with Rowland's minimalist definition of an apocalypse.
71. It is essentially a re-telling of the pentateuchal history from Genesis 1 to Exodus 24.
72. See the review in VanderKam 1977: 207–13.
73. In the theological geography of *Jubilees*, Zion lies in 'the midst of the navel of the earth' (8.19). See further Scott 2005: 165.
74. Scott 2005: 80–1.

violent means; as in *1 En.* 45.4-5, what seems to be anticipated is a non-destructive transformation of heaven and earth. The eschatological scenario of *Jub.* 1.15-18, 23-29, does not involve a catastrophic intervention. The decisive turning point is rather Israel's repentance (v. 15). This leads to moral transformation and national restoration. The climax of the process is God's descent to earth, not to judge and cause upheaval, but to dwell with his people for ever (v. 26).

A little later in the book, at 4.26, in the context of the birth and career of Enoch, the 'new creation' is spoken of again.

> For the Lord has four (sacred) places upon the earth: the garden of Eden and the mountain of the East and this mountain which you are upon today, Mount Sinai, and Mount Zion, which will be sanctified in the new creation for the sanctification of the earth. On account of this earth will be sanctified from all sin and from pollution throughout eternal generations.

Again, it is clear that the new creation involves a revitalization of the present physical earth rather than its destruction and re-creation. Emphasized is the cleansing of the earth from all sin and corruption. Mount Zion is chiastically linked with the garden of Eden; the correlation indicates that the new creation is a restoration of the world as it was at the beginning.[75]

An account of the future is also given in chapter 23. The author describes in vv. 26-31 a long process of restoration, characterized especially by a gradual increase in the human lifespan (mirroring the decline in human longevity from Adam to Moses). The point that marks the beginning of the restorative process is the return to the law (23.26; cf. 1.15). It is debated whether the author thinks that the decisive turning point lies in the past or is still future.[76]

The book of *Jubilees* thus envisages a protracted era of restoration which culminates in a renewal of the existing natural order. Eschatological fulfilment is 'incrementally accomplished through divine judgment, the regeneration of human hearts to conform with God's law, and the repristinization of the physical world'.[77]

2.4 *1 QH 11.19-36*

This hymn (formerly 1QH 3.19-36) from the Qumran *Hodayot* (Thanksgiving Hymns – an assembly of poetic compositions based on the Old Testament psalms) takes the form of a psalm of gratitude in which the

---

75. Scott 2005: 157–8.
76. Allison (1985: 17–19) thinks it lies in the past.
77. Scott 2005: 140–1.

petitioner praises God for delivering him from peril and bringing him into the community (vv. 19-28a). But midway through the hymn, the psalmist's account of his own experiences becomes an account of a terrifying assault of the power of evil – Belial – on the earth.

> 29) then the torrents of Belial will overflow their high banks
> like a fire which devours all those drawing water (?)
> destroying every tree, green or dry, from its canals.
> 30) He revolves like flames of fire
> until none of those who drink are left.
> He consumes the foundations of clay
> 31) and the tract of dry land;
> the bases of the mountains does he burn
> and converts the roots of flint rock
> into streams of lava.
> It consumes right to the great deep.
> 32) The torrents of Belial burst into Abaddon.
> The schemers of the deep howl with the din
> of those extracting mud.
> 33) The earth cries out at the calamity which overtakes the world,
> and all its schemers scream,
> and all who are upon it go crazy,
> 34) and melt away in the great calamity.
> For God thunders with the thunder of his great strength,
> and his holy residence echoes with the truth of his glory,
> 35) and the host of heaven adds its noise,
> and the eternal foundations melt and shake
> and the battle of heavenly heroes spans the globe,
> 36) and does not return until it has terminated
> the destruction decided forever.
> There is nothing like it.

The writer envisages a flood of fire sweeping through and inundating the whole earth 'caused by the forces of evil'.[78] The swelling fire destroys everything before it, devouring even the great ocean (cf. Amos 7.4) and bursting into Abaddon, the realm of the dead. The inhabitants of the earth melt away in the great calamity. At the height of the terror, God steps in with his heavenly army to do battle with the power of evil. His Zeus-like intervention (thundering with mighty thunder) is marked by geophysical shaking, the characteristic accompaniment of a theophany. The war results in terrible destruction and the defeat of the demonic enemy.[79]

---

78. Knibb 1987: 181.
79. The portrayal is reminiscent of the war between the Olympians and the Titans in Hesiod's *Theogony*. See next chapter, pp. 101-3.

These verses evidently portray an eschatological scenario. The psalmist is not using elaborate language to depict further his own distress and deliverance; there is a clear distinction between the first-person narrative of vv. 19-28 and the impersonal description of vv. 29-36.[80] The author brings his personal battle with suffering into relationship with the final eschatological battle without identifying the two.[81] The scale of the war is universal and cosmic; there is nothing to suggest that a 'local' military event might be in view. The typology of Noachic flood and final judgement seems to be in play, with the fiery flood mirroring the primeval deluge, indicating that an actual global catastrophe is anticipated. Distinctive to this passage is the thought that the flood of fire has a demonic source.

The passage is sometimes cited as evidence of Qumranic belief in the final conflagration of the universe at the end,[82] confirming Hippolytus' attribution of the Stoic doctrine of *ekpurōsis* to the Essenes.[83] But the fire pictured in 1 QH 11.29-36 does not actually extend to the material heavens. The torrents of Belial devastate the earth, penetrate the deep and breach the nether world, but they do not engulf the cosmos as a whole (there is no reference to the setting ablaze of the heavens). The portrait is of global, rather than cosmic burning.[84]

2.5 Testament of Moses

The *Testament of Moses*[85] is not an apocalypse; it presents itself as Moses' farewell speech. The book, or at least the final redaction of it,

---

80. Kittel 1981: 76. From her detailed examination of the hymn, Kittel (79) concludes that the eschatological images are 'drawn from a full-blown dynamic mythology' and are 'not simply ancient metaphors designed to provide superlative language for rescue in the present life'.
81. Knibb 1987: 181.
82. E.g., Collins 1998: 172.
83. Hippolytus, *The Refutation of All Heresies* 9.27; cf. 9.30.
84. This is also the judgement of Van der Horst 1994: 238.
85. The document, known from a single Latin manuscript, edited and published by Antonio Ceriani in 1861, was originally identified as the *Assumption of Moses*, mentioned in early church lists of apocryphal books. In his 1897 edition and translation, R. H. Charles identified it with the *Testament of Moses*, also mentioned in ancient book lists, since the extant work expects a natural death for Moses (1.15; 3.3; 10.12, 14), not an assumption into heaven. Scholarship has generally followed Charles's nomenclature, but a robust defence of Ceriani's original identification with the *Assumption* has been given by Tromp (1993: 115–16). Here, I use the title *Testament*, reflecting the more common designation. I leave open the question of the actual identity of the work in question.

may be dated between 7 and 30 CE.[86] The author writes after the time of Herod, but before any of Herod's heirs rule longer than Herod's reign of 34 years (6.5-6). The work outlines a history of Israel from the conquest to the consummation. Chapter 8 describes a period of unprecedented distress and persecution; this is clearly the end-time tribulation.[87] Chapter 9 concentrates on a particular episode in this period: the faithfulness of Taxo and his seven sons.[88] They fast, withdraw to a cave, and resolve to die rather than transgress God's commandments, assured that God will avenge them. Taxo's faithful death triggers the coming of God and vindication of Israel, the subject of chapter 10.[89]

The prelude to the eschatological deliverance is the priestly consecration of a 'messenger' in heaven (10.2).[90] Tromp has argued convincingly that the messenger is Taxo himself, installed after his death as a mediator in heaven.[91] Exalted in heaven, Taxo announces God's vengeance on Israel's enemies. The coming of God and the redemption of the elect of Israel are described in vv. 3-10. The account of the divine intervention in vv. 3-6 fits the recognizable pattern of the theophany: God goes out from his holy dwelling place, and nature is thrown into turmoil at his advent.[92] He comes in full view to punish the nations (v. 7) and to save his people. The rescue of Israel involves her mounting on the wings of an eagle[93] and being exalted to the stars of heaven, where God himself lives (v. 9). From this vantage point, she looks down on her enemies punished on the earth below (v. 10).

---

86. So Charles 1897: lv–lviii. Charles's dating has generally been accepted. Tromp (1993: 117) places it during the first quarter of the first century CE.

87. Licht 1961: 95. Cf. the allusion to Dan. 12.1 in *T. Mos.* 8.1.

88. Many attempts have been made to identify Taxo historically: see the review in Tromp 1993: 124–8. He is perhaps best seen as a typological figure, symbolizing faithfulness to the law even to the point of death.

89. Licht (1961: 97) states, 'Since Taxo's appearance immediately precedes the final salvation, his acts must somehow be instrumental in forwarding its coming.'

90. 'Then the hands of the messenger, when he will be in heaven, will be filled'. 'Filling (one's) hands' is a technical term for the consecration of priests: see Tromp 1993: 230.

91. Tromp 1993: 230–1.

92. It is not explicitly said that God comes *to earth*, but this is evidently the thought. He arises from his throne, leaves his dwelling place and manifests himself openly (*palam veniet*) to exact vengeance on the nations and to destroy their idols.

93. The motif of mounting on an eagle is drawn from Isa. 40.31. The ancient image of the eagle as a transporter of the soul also seems to be influential here (Bridge 2003: 66–74).

The cataclysmic effects of God's coming are set forth in vv. 4-6. The author describes in turn the effects on the earth (v. 4), the celestial realm (v. 5) and the sea (v. 6).

> 4) And the earth will tremble until its extremes it will be shaken, and the high mountains will be made low, and they will be shaken, and the valleys will sink. 5) The sun will not give its light, and the horns of the moon will turn into darkness, and they will be broken; and (the moon) will entirely be turned into blood, and the orbit of the stars will be upset. 6) And the sea will fall back into the abyss, and the fountains of the waters will defect and the rivers will recoil.

The description is inspired by Old Testament images of global and cosmic catastrophe. Talk of the levelling of the mountains reflects Isa. 40.4. The mention of valleys points to the influence of Mic. 1.4 (though here they sink rather than burst open as in Micah). The celestial imagery of v. 5 is clearly based on Isa. 13.10, Joel 2.10 and 2.31; the idea of the moon turning to blood is especially indebted to Joel 2.31. The language of 'the horns of the moon' (*cornua lunae*),[94] however, is distinctive. The notion of the withdrawal of the sea, springs and rivers probably derives from Nah. 1.4, which envisions the drying up of the sea and the rivers at God's coming.[95]

For N. T. Wright, this passage confirms his interpretation of apocalyptic usage of cosmic disaster language. He states: it is 'clear from the context of this poem that its meaning is not to be found by taking the cosmic imagery "literally". Sun, moon and stars function within a poem like this as deliberate symbols for the great powers of the world'.[96] The language is used 'to express the awesome significance of great political events'. Wright sees *T. Mos.* 10.1-10 as referring to a military triumph of Israel under the leadership of an appointed 'messenger' (10.2),[97] which is interpreted theologically as the coming of God to reign (10.3).

One can readily agree that the language of vv. 4-6 is not meant to be taken literally – a metaphorical dimension is quite obvious (e.g. 'the moon will entirely be turned into blood'). But this does not mean that it has to be taken as symbolism for socio-political events. As far as I can see, there is nothing in the immediate or wider context to indicate that the cosmic language has a socio-political reference. In v. 9, 'stars' means the actual stars, so it would follow that objective stars and other components

---

94. The moon's 'horns' are the extremities of its waxing and waning: so Tromp 1993: 234.
95. Also influential may be Ps. 18.15 with its picture of the sea shrinking back to reveal the foundations of the world.
96. N. T. Wright 1992: 305.
97. N. T. Wright 1992: 306.

of the physical universe are meant in vv. 4-6. The catastrophic occurrences of vv. 4-6 are distinguished from the punishment of the nations (v. 7). I see no reason to interpret the geophysical and cosmic language here any differently than in *1 En.* 1.3b-9, 102.1-3 and 1 QH 11.19-36: as language for envisaging the destructive impact of God's eschatological intervention.

Contra Wright, *T. Mos.* 10.1-10 is about final eschatological events, not changes in the ongoing socio-political order. This is clear from 10.1 which speaks of the appearance of God's kingdom 'throughout his whole creation', the defeat of the devil, and elimination of 'all sadness'. God's intervention has to do with the complete resolution of evil. It does not merely bring about a transformation of socio-political circumstances; it brings the historical process to a definitive end. Wright's interpretation of the chapter in terms of an anticipated military triumph of Israel under the command of an appointed human leader is also at odds with a major thrust of the *Testament*. The example of Taxo teaches that the way to bring in God's kingdom is through *non-violent resistance*, even to the point of death, rather than through military exploits. Non-violent defiance of pagan oppressors will force *God himself* to intervene.[98]

Rowley thinks that what is in view in vv. 4-6 is 'the destruction of the material universe'.[99] This is unlikely, since the earth appears to survive the devastation (v. 10).[100] Even so, it is significant that the earth is not the location of final blessing. The eschatological fulfilment involves 'Israel's exaltation to eternal blessedness in heaven'.[101] The earth becomes a place of punishment. The *Testament of Moses* is one of the few post-biblical Jewish works that looks for a heavenly salvation.

2.6 Testament of Job

The *Testament of Job* is a retelling of the biblical story of Job, depicting the patriarch as an exemplar of perseverance.[102] Current majority opinion

---

98. See Gathercole 2002: 57.
99. Rowley 1947: 94.
100. *in terram.* Charles's suggestion (1897: 88) that 'on earth' should be emended to 'in Gehenna', because the latter seems more appropriate, should be dismissed. Cf. Tromp 1993: 237.
101. Charles 1897: 142. N. T. Wright (2003b: 157) takes v. 10 as an allusion to Dan. 12.3 ('those who are wise shall shine like the brightness of the sky, and those who lead many to righteousness, like the stars for ever and ever'), and thus as indicating bodily resurrection (cf. Dan. 12.2). But I doubt this. *Testament of Moses* 10.10 speaks of living *among* the stars, not being *like* the stars, as in Dan. 12.3.
102. On the theme of Job's perseverance see Haas 1989.

views the work as wholly Jewish and dates it prior to or contemporary with the New Testament era.[103] R. P. Spittler agrees that the document is a Jewish work, written 'probably during the first century B.C. or A.D.', but departs from the consensus in thinking that it may have been worked over by Montanists in the second century CE.[104]

The passage of interest in this book is *T. Job* 33.3-5, which occurs in the context of Job's psalm of affirmation (33.3-9). Eliphas laments the loss of Job's throne, but Job has the assurance of a throne on high.

> 3) My throne is in the upper world, and its splendor and majesty come from the right hand of the Father.
> 4) The whole world shall pass away and its splendor shall fade. And those who heed it shall share in its overthrow.
> 5) But my throne is in the holy land, and its splendor is in the world of the changeless one.

Job asserts that the 'whole world' is destined to pass away (ὁ κόσμος ὅλος παρελεύσεται).[105] This is a clear-cut affirmation of the eventual dissolution of the physical cosmos. The world's passing will be violent; the word translated 'overthrow' is καταστροφή. In v. 8, Job goes on to speak of the passing away of kings and rulers. This is not a cue for reading the cosmological language of v. 4 as metaphorical for the demise of political authorities; the focus narrows from the cosmological to the socio-political, without reducing the former to the latter.

In this document, there is a measure of otherworldliness. In 33.3-5, the physical cosmos is contrasted with 'the upper world' (ὑπέρκοσμος), 'the holy land',[106] 'the world of the changeless one'. Heaven, the divine abode, is obviously in view. The physical cosmos is unstable, changing and destined to be dissolved; the heavenly world is stable, unchanging and eternal (cf. 36.3-6). This leads to a contrast between worldly and heavenly realities (36.3; 38.5; 48.3) and a downgrading of 'worldly things' (τὰ κοσμικά, 49.1; 50.2).[107] There is a thus a relative depreciation of the material cosmos in the *Testament of Job*, but, as H. C. Kee insists, not 'a rejection of the created order or a denial of the goodness of the

---

103. Kee (1974: 55) and Nickelsburg (1981: 247) put the whole document in the first century CE. Van der Horst (1989: 116) dates it to the beginning of the first century CE.
104. Spittler in *OTP* 1: 833-4.
105. In my view, the possibility cannot be totally ruled out that this verse reflects an awareness of 1 Cor. 7.31 and 1 Jn 2.17.
106. The term 'the holy land' is otherwise not used of heaven until Origen (*Contra Celsum* 7.29): so Spittler in *OTP* 1: 855 n. on 33 i.
107. Cf. Tit. 2.12 which speaks of worldly desires (τὰς κοσμικὰς ἐπιθυμίας).

Creator'.[108] The world is viewed from the outset as the craftwork of God (2.4). God is praised as creator (39.12; 47.11; 49.2-3). There is no hint that the world is inherently evil. As Kee states, the otherworldliness of the *Testament of Job* 'cannot be equated with dualistic doctrines – such as those of Gnosticism – which reject the creation and see the goal of existence the escape from enslavement in the material world'.[109] The *Testament* views the ascent of the soul to heaven as the reward for faithfulness on earth,[110] but ultimately, it looks forward to resurrection at 'the consummation of the ages' (συντελεία τοῦ αἰῶνος, 4.6).[111] The reference to resurrection is a tantalizing hint that the author of this work ultimately expects a new 'this-worldly' environment.

2.7 Biblical Antiquities

Pseudo-Philo's Biblical Antiquities (*Liber Antiquitatum Biblicarum*) is a rewriting of parts of the biblical history from Adam to David, interlacing events in the biblical narrative with legendary developments of them. It is generally agreed that the book was written in Palestine in the first century CE.[112] D. J. Harrington thinks that a 'date around the time of Jesus seems most likely'.[113] It is preserved only in Latin, which is thought to be based on a Greek translation of a work originally written in Hebrew. Eschatological elements are woven into the narrative. Interestingly, the author does not develop a nationalistic view of the future; as Harrington notes, he 'does not cast his eschatology in political terms'.[114]

That the created cosmos will be brought to an end is expressed in unmistakable terms in 3.10.

> But when the years appointed for the world have been fulfilled, then the light will cease and the darkness will fade away. And I will bring the dead to life and raise up those who are sleeping from the earth. And hell will pay back its debt, and the place of perdition will return its deposit so that I may render to each according to his works and according to the fruits of his own devices, until I judge between soul and flesh. And the

---

108. Kee 1974: 69.
109. Kee 1974: 68–9.
110. The book ends (chs 52–53) with the ascent of Job's soul into heaven followed by the burial of his body.
111. This is thought by some to be a Christian interpolation. Spittler doubts this because the LXX of Job already teaches a future resurrection. Spittler in *OTP* 1: 841 n. on 4 c.
112. See Feldman's comments in James 1971: xxviii–xxx.
113. Harrington in *OTP* 2: 299.
114. Harrington in *OTP* 2: 301.

world will cease, and death will be abolished, and hell will shut its mouth. And the earth will not be without progeny or sterile for those inhabiting it; and no one who has been pardoned by me will be tainted. And there will be another earth and another heaven, an everlasting dwelling place.

The context is God's assurance to Noah in Gen. 8.21-22 that there will never again be a global flood, and that the cycles of nature will continue 'all the days of the earth'. These verses are cited and elaborated on by the writer. As we saw in the previous chapter, the formulation 'all the days of the earth' in Gen. 8.22 implies that creation has a fixed lifespan.[115] *Pseudo-Philo* plainly understands the Genesis passage as having this meaning, and it is precisely this intimation of the earth's mortality that prompts him to speak of what will happen 'when the years appointed for the world have been fulfilled'.[116] The writer outlines a sequence of eschatological events. First, the celestial cycles will come to a stop. Then, God will raise all the dead and judge them according to their works.[117] Then, the world itself will come to an end, and a new heaven and earth will be created, forming an everlasting and unspoilt habitation for those who enter into it.

In no way can 3.10 be interpreted in terms of Israel's political victory over her enemies. As noted above, political eschatology plays no part in this writer's view of the future. The passage is overtly about the future of the world and the very climax of history. It directly builds on Gen. 8.22. The cessation of the world is linked with other 'final' events – the resurrection of the dead and the last judgement.

The transient nature of the material heavens is underscored later in 19.13: 'But this heaven will be before me a fleeting cloud and passing like yesterday.' The author goes on to speak of astronomical malfunctions as the day of God's visitation approaches.[118]

And when the time draws near to visit the world, I will command the years and order the times and they will be shortened, and the stars will hasten and the light of the sun will hurry to fall and the light of the moon will not remain; for I will hurry to raise up you who are sleeping in order that all who can live may dwell in the place of sanctification I showed you.

---

115. See Chapter 1, p. 28.
116. Murphy 1993: 34.
117. In addition to judgement after the general resurrection, the author envisages a judgement of the soul after death (44.10).
118. The writer seems to regard God's descent at Sinai as a prefiguration of the eschatological visitation. He turns the Sinai theophany into a full-blown cosmic upheaval: 11.5; cf. 23.10; 32.7-8.

These changes to the cycles of the astronomical bodies are not merely portents of the end; as in *1 En.* 82.2-8, they belong to the process of cosmic expiration itself. As stated in connection with *1 Enoch* 82, the belief that natural cycles will go haywire as the end of the world draws near is likely to have been inspired by Gen. 8.22.

In *LAB* 9.3, the writer appears to deny that the cosmos will be dissolved. The context is Pharaoh's decree that every male Hebrew child should be killed.

> It will sooner happen that this age will be ended forever or the world will sink into the immeasurable deep or the heart of the abyss will touch the stars than that the race of the sons of Israel will be ended.

The point, though, is not that the world will never end, but that Israel as a race will be preserved until history and the world reach their terminus. This verse reveals how the author conceives of the end of the world – a return to the primeval chaos, not an obliteration into nothing. It is presumably out of the chaos to which the present heavens and earth are reduced that 'another earth and another heaven' arise.

At a couple of points, the writer speaks of the 'renewal' of the earth/creation.[119] In doing so, he is not necessarily contemplating the non-destructive transformation of the cosmos (as in *1 En.* 45.4-5 and *Jub.* 1.29; 4.26) as opposed to its destruction and re-creation. Language of renewal is perfectly compatible with the unmaking and re-creation of the world so long as material continuity between the old and the new is assumed.

That the author expects a re-creation of the world to follow its end and characterizes the eschatological cosmic change as *renewal* should dispel any thought of the idea of the world's cessation being linked with an anti-creational dualism. God's creation of the world is a *sine qua non* for this author (11.8; 60.2). God's command of nature and his use of it for the purpose of judgement are given special emphasis (10.9; 15.5-6; 16.2-3, 6-7; 26.3-4; 32.13-17). The perspective of the book is decidedly pro-creational.

2.8 Fourth Ezra

The book known as *4 Ezra* (2 Esdras 3–14) was written near the end of the first century CE.[120] Its fictive setting is Babylon, 'in the thirtieth year after the destruction of the city', that is, 30 years after the fall of Jerusalem to

---

119. *LAB* 16.13; 32.17.
120. Stone 1990: 9-10.

2 Jewish Apocalyptic and Related Literature

the Babylonians. The work was probably originally penned in Hebrew and subsequently translated into Greek from which it was then translated into the versions that are extant; of these the Latin version is regarded as the most important. The book addresses the national crisis provoked by Jerusalem's fall to the Romans in 70 CE, though it is also concerned with the broader theological question of the origin and resolution of sin and evil in the world (but still from an Israel-oriented perspective). It falls into seven distinct sections,[121] usually called visions, though the earlier sections are actually dialogues (between Ezra and the angel Uriel).

The book displays an intense interest in eschatology. The passage in which the writer's eschatology is most clearly set out is 7.26-44.[122] Here, we learn that there will be signs (the eschatological woes), then the 'city' (the heavenly Jerusalem) will appear and the land will be disclosed. The messiah will be revealed and he will reign for four hundred years. During this time, those who have survived the horrors of the woes will experience great joy (v. 29). At the end of the messianic bliss, the messiah will himself die along with all other human beings. At this point, the created world itself will come to an end.

> 30) Then the world shall be turned back to primeval silence for seven days, as it was at the first beginnings, so that no one shall be left. 31) After seven days, the world that is not yet awake shall be roused, and that which is corruptible shall perish. 32) The earth shall give up those who are asleep in it and the dust those who rest there in silence; and the chambers shall give up the souls that have been committed to them.

There is some ambiguity attaching to the word *saeculum*, translated 'world'. The term, which is used extensively in *4 Ezra*, can mean 'age' in a temporal sense and 'world' in a spatial sense (reflecting the ambiguity of the underlying Hebrew term עוֹלָם) and it is often difficult to decide which sense applies in a given context.[123] Michael Stone translates it here as 'world', since the passage 'evokes the language and context of creation', though he thinks that it actually means something more like 'world order'.[124] Uncertainty about the precise meaning of *saeculum*, however, should not take away from what is absolutely certain – that the

---

121. 3.1–5.20; 5.21–6.34; 6.35–9.25; 9.26–10.59; 11.1–12.51; 13; 14.

122. There is considerable debate as to whether *4 Ezra* has a consistent eschatological perspective. Stone (1983: 238) argues that the scheme of 7.26-44 is presupposed throughout the book, but that the author uses the term 'the end' (*finis*) rather flexibly 'to denote distinct, different points of the eschatological timetable'. On the eschatology of *4 Ezra*, see esp. Stone 1989.

123. See Stone 1990: 218–19.

124. Stone 1990: 217.

scene depicted in these verses, and also in vv. 39-43, is the dissolution of creation into the primordial chaos.[125] Verse 30 refers to the world's reversion to 'the primeval silence'. This alludes back to *4 Ezra*'s own creation account in 6.38-54, according to which 'darkness and silence embraced everything' (6.39) at the world's beginning.[126] The mention of 'seven days' in vv. 30 and. 31 refers to the seven days of creation and reinforces the idea of de-creation.

After the week of chaos 'the world which is not yet awake' arises. The language implies that the new world already exists (cf. 6.1-6; 7.70; 8.52), probably in the mind of the creator.[127] At this point, resurrection takes place (since corruption has passed away). The wording of v. 32 strongly indicates material continuity from this *saeculum* to the next. As Stone writes, 'there is no suggestion that in the renewal of creation the body or the earth will have lost its material qualities'.[128]

The rest of the passage focuses on the final judgement. The 'day' of judgement corresponds to the week of chaos (v. 43). It is characterized by the abolition of created distinctions.

> 39) a day that has no sun or moon or stars, 40) or cloud or thunder or lightning, or wind or water or air, or darkness or evening or morning, 41) or summer or spring or heat or winter or frost or cold, or hail or rain or dew, 42) or noon or night, but only the splendour of the glory of the Most High, by which all shall see what has been destined.

The description is based on Gen. 8.22 and Zech. 14.6-7. The writer imagines the cessation of the variegated order of the world.[129]

There is no way that creation's eschatological reversion to chaos in *4 Ezra* 7.30-32, 39-42 can be interpreted as a picture of Israel's political salvation. It has long been recognized that, within the eschatological scheme of *4 Ezra*, the temporary messianic kingdom meets the author's immediate political desires – to see Rome defeated and the Davidic kingdom restored. *Fourth Ezra* 7.30-44, as we have seen, looks beyond the reconstituted kingdom, which lasts 400 years, to indubitably 'final' events. The expectation of a new world/age in which corruption and sinful indulgence have passed away satisfies the more general concern for the complete resolution of moral and physical evil.[130]

---

125. Stone 1990: 217.
126. The notion of a primordial silence is also attested in other Jewish texts: *LAB* 60.2; *2 Bar.* 3.7.
127. Box 1912: 117.
128. Stone 1990: 220.
129. *Sib. Or.* 3.88-92, on which see below.
130. Cf. 7.11-13, 113-114.

The idea of the end of the present material world is also conveyed by the theme of the world's senescence in 5.50-55 and 14.17. In 5.50, Ezra enquires, 'Is our mother ... still young? Or is she now approaching old age?' The 'mother' here is mother earth. The issue is the nearness of the end, but the question is framed in terms of the age of the earth. The reply given draws an analogy between the physical degeneration of a woman's progeny and the physical deterioration of successive generations. As children borne by a woman when she is older are inferior (smaller in size) to those borne by her when she is young and in the prime of life, so later generations are inferior to earlier ones. The fact that Ezra's own generation is smaller in size than foregoing generations is a sign that creation is growing old.

> 5.54) Therefore you also should consider that you and your contemporaries are smaller in stature than those who were before you, 55) and those who come after you will be smaller than you, as born of a creation that already is aging and passing the strength of youth.

Involved here is a biological view of the created cosmos. Like any other living creature, it grows, reaches its peak, declines, and then dies. The creation is already well advanced in age, thus nearing the end of its allotted lifespan.[131] The idea of the world's senescence was a feature of Epicurean cosmology, as we will see in the next chapter. Lucretius specifically cites the diminution of the generations as evidence of the world's old age.[132] As Downing suggests, it seems highly likely that the author of *4 Ezra* has inherited his ideas in this passage from this specific Epicurean tradition.[133]

In 14.10, Ezra is told that 'the age has lost its youth'. Here *saeculum* definitely means 'age'. The age is divided into twelve parts, nine and a half of which have passed.[134] Ezra is warned that evils will intensify as the end approaches (v. 16). The reason for this is given in v. 17: 'the weaker the world becomes through old age, the more shall evils be multiplied among its inhabitants'. In this verse, *saeculum* denotes the material world.[135] As in 5.50-55, the thought is of the physical creation declining with age. Here, we have the additional idea that the increasing elderliness of the world brings an increase in evil.[136] This is a combination of the

---

131. *quasi jam senescentis creaturae et fortitudinem juventutis praeterientis.*
132. Lucretius, *rerum* 2.1150-52; cf. Pliny the Elder, *Nat. His.* 7.73.
133. Cf. Downing 1995a: 196.
134. This is the only point in the book where any attempt is made to calculate the duration of the world and nearness of the end.
135. Stone 1990: 423.
136. Stone 1990: 423.

notion of the world's senescence and the expectation of a time of increased distress and evil as the present age reaches its close (the latter is explicit in the next verse). The formulation seems to make the evils of the end a result of the physical deterioration of creation,[137] but, as Stone insists, 'The view must be rejected that it is the material aspect of the earth that in itself is the cause of ... the evils'.[138]

A cosmic transformation at the end of time is indicated in 6.15-16. Ezra is warned that the ground under his feet will shake because 'the foundations of the earth will understand that the speech concerns them. They will tremble and be shaken, for they know that their end must be changed.'[139] As Stone states, the scenario being evoked 'is quite unmistakable. It is the cosmic creation/re-creation with all that this implies.'[140] In the developing narrative, the words point forward to 7.30-32. The shaking of the ground underneath Ezra's feet seems to be a foreshadowing of the cosmic renewal, which might indicate that the author expects the return to chaos to be effected by a violent catastrophe. In 7.75, the author uses the terminology of the renewal of creation (*creaturam renovare*) to describe the end-time cosmic transformation. This does not contradict the scheme of dissolution and re-creation in 7.30-32, 39-43. It reinforces what is in any case clear from 7.30-32, that the end of this world and the advent of the next involve the redemption of creation, not its abandonment.[141]

In 5.1-13, the author outlines a series of turbulent events that precede the dawn of messianic salvation. This is the first of several lists of eschatological woes in the document.[142] In this passage, various disruptions in nature are predicted including fires, seismic activity, the roaming of wild animals in urban areas and abnormal births. In vv. 4b-5, celestial disturbances are included among the portents:

> and the sun shall suddenly begin to shine at night,
> and the moon during the day.

137. That evil intensifies as the natural world reaches the end of its lifespan is taught by Seneca (*Nat. quaes.* 3.30.8): see further p. 122. Elsewhere in *4 Ezra*, the increase of misery that precedes the end is presented as the divine reaction to human sin (8.50).
138. Stone 1990: 153.
139. *quoniam finem eorum oportet commutari*.
140. Stone 1990: 167.
141. *Fourth Ezra* 4.26 and 6.20 refer to the 'passing away' of the *saeculum*. In both instances, it seems likely that *saeculum* means 'age' rather than world.
142. The others are found in 6.20-24; 9.3-12. In *4 Ezra*, the woes that are expected to precede the dawn of salvation can without controversy be called *messianic* woes.

5) Blood shall drip from wood,
and the stone shall utter its voice;
the people shall be troubled,
and the courses of stars shall change.[143]

The thought of the reversal of the roles of the sun and the moon seems to pick up the tradition of the alteration of the solar and lunar cycles (cf. *1 En.* 80.4-8), rather than the specifically Old Testament image of the darkening of the sun and moon.[144] The textual evidence for the last line is extremely confused. The Latin has 'and the course shall change' (*et gressus commutabuntur*) or alternatively 'and the outgoings shall change' (*et egressus commutabuntur*). The Syriac and Arabic have 'the air shall be changed', while the Ethiopic version reads, 'and the stars shall fall'.[145] It is impossible to reconstruct the original with certainty. Box suggests an original reading along the lines of 'the outgoings of the stars shall change',[146] the 'outgoings' referring to the portals through which the stars were thought to proceed. On this reconstruction, the basic idea is that of alterations in the stellar paths, which would comport nicely with the first two lines. Unlike in *1 En.* 80.4-8 and *LAB* 19.13, the shifts in the movement of the astronomical bodies do not signal the collapse of the cosmos; rather they point to the nearness of messianic deliverance.

It is evident from the cryptic nature of some of his predictions in *4 Ezra* 5.1-13 that the writer does not intend his words to be taken with absolute literalness. The predictions that 'blood shall drip from wood' and 'the stone will utter its voice' are certainly not meant to be read factually; the latter was apparently a proverbial expression for a solemn and dreadful omen.[147] But it is also clear that actual fearful events in nature are anticipated.

Is there evidence in *4 Ezra* of a radical anti-cosmic dualism, of the kind N. T. Wright thinks is inherently bound up with the notion of the dissolution of the present space-time world? The author of *4 Ezra* is certainly deeply pessimistic about this age/world; the present world order is for him so bound up with corruption and evil that it must pass away

---

143. The NRSV at this point reads, 'and the stars shall fall' following the Ethiopic reading.
144. The same portent is found in *Asc. Isa.* 4.5, a Christian text. The idea that the stone will speak seems to be based on Hab. 2.11.
145. See Box 1912: 44–5 n. m.
146. Box (1912: 44–5 n. m) suggests that the translators of the Syriac and Arabic versions read ἀστέρες in their Greek text and confused it with ἀέρες, while the Latin versions represents something like ἔξοδοι in the Greek.
147. Stone 1990: 111.

and give way to a new order.[148] Yet, despite the bleakness of his outlook on the world in its present condition, the author does not espouse an anticosmic, anti-creational perspective. He has a robust doctrine of God as creator (e.g. 3.4; 5.42-45; 6.1-6) and includes a narrative on the creation of the world (6.38-55). Though the present created order is destined for dissolution, it remains God's creation: God's ongoing love for his creation, the writer insists, is unsurpassed (8.47). The author makes little attempt, therefore, to distance God from the present world. The dualism of the two ages/worlds is not an absolute dualism: God is the maker of *both* worlds – the present one and the one to come (7.50). The corruption, sorrow and evil which mark the present world are not congenital. It was Adam's transgression that made it a dark place (7.11-12); God did not create it this way. In 14.12, a connection is drawn between the degeneration of creation and the increase of evils prior to the end, but as noted above there is no indication that it is the material aspect of creation that gives rise to these evils. In *4 Ezra,* as Stone insists, there is no hint that materiality as such is the cause of sin.[149] As we have seen (especially in 7.32), the writer looks forward to a material re-creation, following the dissolution of the world. The paradisiacal description of the future age in 8.50-52 seems to indicate that the new world order is a re-establishment of the original goodness of creation.

2.9 Second Baruch

Second Baruch (or the *Syrian Apocalypse of Baruch*) is to be dated after (but not long after) the composition of *4 Ezra*. Like *4 Ezra, 2 Baruch* intermixes a national eschatology and a universal and cosmic one. The national dimension finds its focus in a temporary messianic reign (cf. 30.1; 40.3; 70.3-4).

In 32.1, the eschatological visitation of God is described as 'the time in which the Mighty One shall shake the entire creation'. The formulation seems to be a reworking of Hag. 2.6, 21. A few verses later, the writer speaks of the future time 'when the Mighty One will renew his creation' (*2 Bar.* 32.6). The parallel could suggest a cosmic-eschatological scheme involving cosmic catastrophe followed by an act of cosmic transformation. In 59.3, the author states that 'the heaven will be shaken from its place at that time', referring to the occasion of the

---

148. Cf. *4 Ezra* 4.29, 'if the place where the evil has been sown does not pass away, the field where the good has been sown will not come'. The words 'place' and 'field' here have a double reference: the present world (4.27) and the evil heart (4.30). See Stone 1990: 94; Knibb 1979: 125.

149. Stone 1990: 183.

eschatological visitation. This event is correlated with the shaking (of heaven) at the revelation that took place at Sinai.

That the present created order is finite in nature and is nearing the end of its natural lifespan is indicated in 85.10.

> For the youth of this world has passed away, and the power of creation is already exhausted, and the coming of the times is very near and has passed by.

Expressed in this verse is the conception of the senescence of creation we observed in *4 Ezra*. The writer here imagines that creation is very close to the point of total expiration.[150]

In 3.7, however, the possibility that the ordered universe should return to its primeval condition and go back to the original silence seems to be firmly rejected; it is as inconceivable as God blotting out humanity for ever (3.8). Also, in 19.2, it is said that 'heaven and earth will stay forever'.

Second Baruch does not seem to offer a consistent view of the ultimate cosmic future (or a consistent overall eschatology). The author looks for an eschatological renewal of creation (also at 57.2; cf. 49.3), evidently preceded by a mighty shaking of it, but he gives mixed signals as to whether this will involve the total destruction of the present natural order or its non-catastrophic repristinization.

Like *4 Ezra*, *2 Baruch* has a sharply negative view of the present age/world (cf. 15.8; 21.19; 40.3; 44.9; 51.14), but the writer makes no moves in the direction of an anti-cosmic dualism. There is a strong emphasis throughout the work on God as creator (14.17; 21.4-5; 54.13; 56.3; 78.3; 82.2) and on the world as his creation (14.18; 15.7; 21.24). There is not the slightest suggestion that the material world as such is evil.

2.10 Apocalypse of Zephaniah

The work known as the *Apocalypse of Zephaniah* has survived in a fragmentary state, which makes it difficult to date. It was evidently composed sometime between 100 BCE and 175 CE. Wintermute favours a date before 70 CE.[151] The book is largely an account of Zephaniah's

---

150. The statement, 'everything will pass away which is corruptible' in 44.9 could perhaps be taken as implying the dissolution of the cosmos, as could the reference to 'this passing world' in 48.50, though on the assumption that the underlying Hebrew word for world in 48.50 is עוֹלָם, we cannot be sure that the material world, rather than the temporal age, is in view.

151. Wintermute in *OTP* 1: 500–1.

otherworldly journeys, with scenes from heaven and Hades. At the end, he is told of the coming 'day of the Lord', when 'the Lord almighty rises up in his wrath to destroy the earth and the heavens' (12.5).

> 6) They will see and be disturbed, and they will all cry out, saying, 'All flesh which is ascribed to you we will give to you on the day of the Lord.'
> 7) Who will stand in his presence when he rises in his wrath [to destroy] the earth [and the heaven?] 8) Every tree which grows upon the earth will be plucked up with their roots and fall down. And every high tower and the birds which fly will fall ...[152]

The scenario follows the 'catastrophic intervention' pattern observed in *1 En.* 1.3b-9; 101.1-3, etc. In this instance, God's intervention and theophanic manifestation ('in his presence') result in the destruction of the cosmos, not only the earth, but also the heaven. There are no textual prods to push us in the direction of a socio-political reading of the language. The scene is quite evidently the final judgement, and this is expected to take the form of total world-destruction. The text breaks off precisely at this point, so it is not indicated whether a remaking of the world follows its destruction. There is no particular interest in creation in the surviving fragments, but also there is nothing to suggest a suspicion of it.

2.11 Second Enoch

By general consent, the book known to us as *2 Enoch*, or at least the original composition, is to be dated no later than the first century CE.[153] The provenance is uncertain, but Egypt is thought to be the most likely place of writing.[154] The work survives in two Slavonic recensions, one of which is longer than the other.[155] The book is mainly occupied with Enoch's ascent into heaven through the seven heavenly spheres (chs 3–37) and his return to earth to tell his family what he has seen and to instruct them about the future (chs 38–66).

Second Enoch contains extensive discussion of the structure of the cosmos, and the speculation is conducted in what F. I. Anderson calls a 'quasi-scientific' manner.[156] Chapters 24–33 give a remarkable account of the creation of the cosmos, based on Genesis 1, but also informed by

---

152. For the image of the felling of trees, see Isa. 10.33; cf. *1 En.* 83.4.
153. Collins 1998: 243.
154. Collins 1998: 243.
155. The long and short recensions are commonly identified as J and A respectively.
156. F. I. Andersen in *OTP* 1: 91.

Greek mythological conceptions and natural philosophy. The author tells how God initially created visible things 'from the non-existent, and from the invisible' (24.1).[157] This is not actually an affirmation of creation out of nothing[158] since the writer goes on to indicate that the invisible things existed alongside God before he began to make anything (24.2).[159] He then describes the creative processes by which the differentiated parts of the cosmos were formed.[160] As Andersen points out, the discussion represents one of the earliest attempts to reconcile the Genesis creation account with science. 'It tries to integrate Gk. physics with Gen. 1.'[161]

The work also contains material of eschatological interest. There is particular emphasis on the final judgement (e.g. 50.2, 5; 51.3). In 65.6-10, there is a vision of the end of the world.

> 6) And when the whole of creation, visible and invisible, which the Lord has created, shall come to an end, then each person will go to the Lord's great judgement. 7) [And] then [all] time will perish, and afterwards there will neither be years nor months nor days nor hours. They will be dissipated, and after that they will not be reckoned. 8) But they will constitute a single age. And all the righteous, who escape from the Lord's great judgement, will be collected together into the great age. And the great age will come about for the righteous, and it will be eternal. 9) And after that there will be among them neither weariness [nor sickness] nor affliction nor worry [nor] want nor debilitation nor night nor darkness. 10) But they will have a great light, a great indestructible light, and paradise, great and incorruptible. For everything corruptible will pass away, and the incorruptible will come into being, and will be the shelter of the eternal residences. (J)

Envisaged here is quite evidently the cessation of the present physical cosmos. That the author intends his account to be read 'cosmologically', and not as an extended metaphor for a momentous turn of events in the social and political sphere, is absolutely clear from the sustained and scientifically informed cosmological reflection that has gone before. The passage contains the starkest language we have yet seen on the discontinuity between the present order of creation and the 'great age' to come. The writer seems to imagine the disappearance of time itself. The new age is defined largely in terms of negation: no weariness, sickness,

---

157. Cf. the invisibility of the earth in Gen. 1.2 LXX, ἡ δὲ γῆ ἦν ἀόρατος.
158. *Contra* Gowan 1985: 92.
159. Cf. *OTP* 1: 143. Talk of creation 'from the non-existent' or 'out of non-being' need not give expression to the formal doctrine of *creatio ex nihilo*. See May 1994: 1–38.
160. See F. I. Andersen in *OTP* 1: 142–5.
161. F. I. Andersen in *OTP* 1: 143 n. on 25 a.

affliction, etc. That creation itself will be renewed is not explicitly indicated here, though the reference to 'paradise', with its Edenic connotations, is suggestive of a repristinization of creation.[162]

In *2 Enoch*, there is no question of an anti-cosmic dualism. The material world is viewed positively throughout,[163] and God is praised for his creative wonders (especially 47.3-6).

2.12 *The* Sibylline Oracles

As John Barclay observes, the collection of oracular utterances, written in Epic verse and attributed to a Sibyl, is one of the most remarkable products of Diaspora Judaism in antiquity.[164] It is also remarkable that the Jewish and Christian imitations of the Graeco-Roman Sibylline oracles are the only extended ones to have survived.[165] The Jewish *Sibylline Oracles* (and the later Christian books) are notorious for their predictions of 'doom and gloom'. There are a number of passages that relate to the present discussion, the most striking of which are those that predict the fiery destruction of the cosmos. I will consider relevant material in Books 3, 4 and 5; these are Jewish in origin and relatively free of Christian interpolations.

2.12.1 Sibylline Oracles *Book 3*

Book 3 is generally regarded as the oldest of the Sibylline books. It is a compilation of various oracles. The whole corpus derives from Egyptian Judaism. The main bank of oracles (3.97-161, 162-195, 196-294, 545-656, 657-808) is dated by John Collins to the period 163–45 BCE.[166] The passages in 3.1-96 stem from later periods.

The oracle contained in 3.657-808 attracts our interest. The Sibyl predicts an attack on Jerusalem by the kings of the nations, envious of the great wealth with which the temple is laden (657-662).[167] However, God will intervene with an awesome act of judgement that rocks the earth to its foundations (669-681). The attacking armies will be destroyed in a hail of fire and brimstone (682-701). God's judgement will initiate

---

162. *First Enoch* 31.7 denies that Adam's fall affected the created order.
163. Gowan 1985: 92–4.
164. Barclay 1996: 216.
165. Barclay 1996: 217.
166. Collins in *OTP*1: 355.
167. Cf. Psalm 2; Zechariah 14; on this, see Hartman 1966: 77–101.

an era of blessing when 'he will raise up a kingdom for all' (767). The new order that follows God's intervention, as it is described in lines 741-795, involves a transformed earthly environment, with Jerusalem and its temple at the geographical centre (772-775). The account of the new earthly kingdom (777-795) draws on the familiar prophetic themes of the abundant fruitfulness of the earth, the transformation of topography, everlasting light (cf. Isa. 60.11), the establishment of peace in the animal kingdom and between human beings and animals (cf. Isa. 11.6-8).

The divine intervention for judgement, narrated in lines 669-701, follows the theophany model, but with God's voice, rather than his coming, generating cosmic upheaval. The description draws heavily on Ezek. 38.19-20.[168]

> Fiery swords will fall
> from heaven on the earth. Torches, great gleams,
> will come shining into the midst of men.
> The all-bearing earth will be shaken in those days
> by the hand of the Immortal, and the fish in the sea
> and all the wild beasts of the earth and innumerable tribes of birds,
> all the souls of men and all the sea
> will shudder before the face of the Immortal and there will be a terror.
> He will break the lofty summits of the mountains and the mounds of giants
> and the dark abyss will appear to all. (3.673-681)

The irruption brings the earth to the brink of chaos (the dark abyss is exposed), but the world is not actually destroyed.

This is certainly an oracle about national crisis and deliverance, but the scenario is indisputably eschatological, and the scale of judgement and redemption universal and cosmic. It is not a historical or singular enemy that attacks Israel, but the kings of the earth in general. The occasion is the eschatological world war,[169] with God intervening finally and decisively on behalf of his people and establishing his uncontested dominion on earth. The *Sibylline Oracles* are predictive literature, so there is no doubt that actual catastrophic and transformative events in the natural realm are envisaged, even though the language is metaphorical and colourful.

In lines 796-808, abnormal celestial phenomena are predicted: 'swords are seen at night in starry heaven' (798); 'all the light of the sun / is eclipsed in the middle from heaven, and the rays / of the moon appear

---

168. See Hartman 1966: 91-4.
169. Cf. Joel 3-4; Zech. 14.1-5.

and return to the earth' (801-803). These events are not part of the upheavals caused by God's intervention in judgement; they are signs that precede and announce the final irruption (796). When the faithful see these occurrences in the sky, they will know that final deliverance is at hand.

The brief oracle of 3.75-92 relates to a time when the world is governed 'under the hands of a woman' and 'when a widow reigns'. The woman and the widow are to be identified with Cleopatra, who was widowed several times.[170] Collins thinks that the oracle was written shortly after the battle of Actium (31 BCE) and reflects the pessimism of Cleopatra's defeat.[171] The Sibyl (3.80-92) predicts imminent cosmic destruction as God's judgement on the world:

> then all the elements of the universe
> will be bereft, when God who dwells in the sky
> rolls up the heaven as a scroll is rolled,
> and the whole variegated vault of heaven falls
> on the wondrous earth and ocean. An undying cataract
> of raging fire will flow, and burn earth, burn sea,
> and melt the heavenly vault and days and creation itself
> into one and separate them into clear air.
> There will no longer be twinkling spheres of luminaries,
> no night, no dawn, no numerous days of care,
> no spring, no summer, no winter, no autumn.
> And then indeed the judgement of the great God
> will come into the midst of the great world, when all these things happen.

For the first time we come across a Jewish text in which the final judgement unambiguously takes the form of the total destruction of the cosmos by fire. The fire consumes earth, sea and the fallen heavens, melting them into a single pure substance, not specifically 'air' as the translation above has it; the Greek (εἰς καθαρόν) is better rendered 'into that which is clean/pure'. In *Sibylline Oracles* Book 2, there is a very similar passage: 2.196-213.[172] The description of 2.196-213, though, is somewhat more elaborate and probably represents a later expansion of 3.80-92;[173] it may be an expansion by Christian hands,[174] though as Van der Horst notes, there is nothing specifically 'Christian' in it.

---

170. Collins 1974a: 67–70.
171. Collins 1974a: 64. A more hopeful role for Cleopatra is expressed in 3.350-380, written before the battle of Actium. See Collins 1974a: 57–64.
172. Books 1 and 2 in their existing form are a Christian redaction; see Collins in *OTP* 1: 330–4.
173. It also seems to draw on 5.513-531 with its imagery of colliding and falling astronomical bodies.

2 Jewish Apocalyptic and Related Literature 91

The portrayal of cosmic destruction in 3.80-92 draws on recognizable Old Testament passages. The image of the heavens being rolled up like a scroll is taken from Isa. 34.4. The list of divisions of times and cycles that are to be abolished is based on Gen. 8.22 (there may also be an allusion to Zech. 14.6-7). The idea of a cosmic conflagration is not found in the Old Testament. It could be interpreted as a natural extension of the fiery flood envisaged in *1 En.* 102.1-3, *Ps.-Soph.* fr. 2 and 1 QH 11.29-36, but as Van der Horst states, 'It would seem that here a new step has been taken'.[175] This move is very likely to have been made through contact with the Stoic concept of *ekpurōsis*. A world conflagration figured in Iranian eschatology,[176] but it was well known in the Hellenistic world as a characteristically Stoic teaching. Several features of this passage echo the Stoic conception:[177] first, the reference to the 'elements' (στοιχεῖα) of the cosmos, that is, the basic constituents of earthly matter (air, fire, water and earth);[178] second, the thought that everything will melt 'into one' mass (εἰς ἕν); third, the idea of dissolution into that which is pure. The latter is especially suggestive of the state of purity that exists when the cosmos is resolved into the element par excellence, creative fire. The writer does not adopt the Stoic theory in a thoroughgoing fashion; rather, he incorporates Stoic ideas into his own scheme of eschatological judgement.

As an oracular prediction, we can be certain that 3.75-92 was meant to be read as a forecast of actual and imminent cosmic destruction. The utilization of Stoic motifs gives the expectation a quasi-scientific base.[179]

As Collins points out, 'no indication is given that any renewal lies beyond the eschatological fire'.[180] That the writer says nothing about a future to follow perhaps reflects the deep disillusionment felt by Egyptian Jews after Cleopatra's defeat.[181]

---

174. It is treated as such by U. Treu in *NTA* 2.652-660. Contrast with Van der Horst (1994: 239).

175. Van der Horst 1994: 239.

176. See Pearson 2001. The main literary evidence for Iranian eschatology is relatively late.

177. On the Stoic theory of *ekpurōsis*, see the next chapter, pp. 116-18.

178. In 2.196-213, the elements are defined as 'air, land, sea, light, vault of heaven, days, nights'. The first four correspond to the four material elements, air, earth, water and fire.

179. Though there is no evidence from Stoic sources that the conflagration was an event of the near future; see further next chapter, p. 120.

180. Collins 1974a: 70.

181. Collins in *OTP* 1: 360.

2.12.2 Sibylline Oracles *Book 4*

The Fourth Sibyl is a review of history from the flood to the final world conflagration. The oracle was originally composed shortly after the time of Alexander but was subsequently updated. It is generally accepted that the redacted version was written not long after the last datable event to which reference is made, the eruption of Vesuvius (4.130-135), and therefore dates from around 80 CE.[182] Scholars tend to locate the oracle in Syria or the Jordan Valley.[183] The cosmic conflagration is described in lines 171-178.

> But if you do not obey me ...
> there will be fire throughout the whole world ...
> The whole world will hear a bellowing noise and mighty sound.
> He will burn the whole earth, and will destroy the whole race of men
> and all cities and rivers at once, and the sea.
> He will destroy everything by fire, and it will be smoking dust.

The catastrophe is introduced here as a conditional rather than inexorable event. This is difficult to reconcile with 4.100-101 ('final, but greatest, disaster will come'), and also with the general schema of a fixed and predetermined history.[184] In Collins's view, the assumption that the course of the end is set was the view of the original oracle; the conditional element is part of the later redaction.[185] The idea that the destruction of the world is dependent on human obedience or disobedience is novel and without parallel in the Jewish literature under discussion in this chapter.

The Sibyl goes on to predict resurrection and tribunal judgement after the cosmic incineration. Collins points out that this is 'the only passage in the Jewish sibylline oracles which shows a belief in resurrection or any form of after-life'.[186]

> But when everything is already in dusty ashes,
> and God puts to sleep the unspeakable fire, even as he kindled it,
> God himself will again fashion the bones and ashes of men
> and he will raise up mortals again as they were before.
> And then there will be a judgment over which God himself will preside
> (4.179-183)

---

182. See Collins in *OTP* 1: 382.
183. Collins in *OTP* 1: 382.
184. Collins 1998: 241.
185. Collins 1998: 241.
186. Collins 1974b: 370.

The resurrection is part of a general cosmic renewal after the fire (cf. line 187, 'as many as are pious, they will live *on earth* again'). Material continuity is evident – God will re-fashion 'the bones and ashes of men'. Interesting is the fact that the resurrection involves the raising up of human beings 'as they were before' (ὡς πάρος ἦσαν). This is highly suggestive of the Stoic notion of recurrence. According to the Stoic doctrine, in the new world which is generated after the conflagration, people who once lived would be reconstituted exactly as they were before.[187] Collins agrees that the manner in which the idea of the resurrection of the dead is expressed here 'suggests a rapprochement' with the Stoic theory of recurrence.[188] The cyclical aspect of the Stoic doctrine is of course left out.

2.12.3 Sibylline Oracles *Book 5*

The oracles that comprise Book 5, like those in Book 3, have an Egyptian provenance.[189] The oracles were written at various times, but between the years 80 and 132 CE.[190] The book as a whole reflects a state in which Jews are alienated from Gentiles; it also displays an intense hostility toward Rome.[191] The eschatological adversary is none other than the emperor Nero (5.93-110, 137-154, 214-227, 361-385); the book makes use of current beliefs in Nero's return from the East.[192] The threat of divine judgement by global or cosmic conflagration is a recurring theme of the collection.

In the third oracle, 5.111-178, the Sibyl predicts that a great star will fall from heaven, burn the sea, Babylon, the land of Italy and 'will destroy the whole earth' (5.155-161). Collins thinks that the star from heaven may be a partial allusion to a saviour figure who comes to effect deliverance, as well as to an actual star/comet which is expected to fall on the earth.[193] The portrait in 5.155-161 is of global rather than cosmic conflagration. Noteworthy is the particular focus on Babylon, that is, Rome, and Italy. The doom to fall on Rome is further described in lines 168-178, a passage which Barclay calls 'one of the most politically subversive statements in antiquity'.[194]

---

187. See below, pp. 118–19.
188. Collins 1974a: 103.
189. The six oracles that make up the book are as follows: 1-51; 52-110; 111-178; 179-285; 286-434; 435-531.
190. Collins in *OTP* 1: 391; cf. 1974a: 74.
191. See Barclay 1996: 226–8.
192. See further Collins 1974a: 80–7.
193. Collins 1974a: 89–92.
194. Barclay 1996: 227.

The bulk of the fourth oracle, 5.179-285, consists of prophecies of judgment against the nations. Egypt (179-199), the Gauls (200-205), Ethiopia (206-213) and the city of Corinth (214-219) are targeted. There is a prediction of Nero's return (214-227), followed by a denunciation of the sin of pride (228-237). The oracle concludes with a reflection on the blessings of the Jewish race (238-285). In the context of the prophecy against the Ethiopians, a total cosmic conflagration is announced (211-213).

> There will be a great heavenly conflagration on earth
> and from the battling stars a new nature will emerge,
> so that the whole land of the Ethiopians will perish in fire and groanings.

The account is compressed, but the scenario imagined can be ascertained from the longer account in lines 512-531. Burning and clashing stars fall down to earth causing the earth to be consumed by the fire. The picture is almost certainly derived from Stoic portraits of the cosmic conflagration.[195] The threat of cosmic destruction in lines 211-212 is immediately particularized in line 213: Ethiopia will perish in the fire. Ethiopia functions in this context as the great eschatological enemy of the people of God.[196] The application to Ethiopia in line 213 in no way negates the cosmic scope of the preceding lines.

The statement that a 'new nature' (καινὴ φύσις) will emerge from the cosmic carnage points strongly to a cosmic renewal after the conflagration. The terminology seems to be a variation on the theme of 'new creation' (cf. *1 En.* 72.1; *Jub.* 1.29; 4.26). The words 'until the world is changed' in line 273 also seem to envisage a cosmic renewal. As a whole, 5.238-285 looks forward to an earthly state of future bliss. Lines 249-255 depict a future involving a gloriously reconditioned Jerusalem, and lines 281-283 envisage a restored 'holy land' replenished with the proverbial milk and honey.

The fifth oracle, 5.286-434, consists of prophecies of doom against various places, mainly in Asia, a prediction of Nero's return and a prophecy of a coming saviour figure. Lines 346-352 anticipate a time when the sun and moon will be no more.

> The imperishable flames of the sun itself will no longer be,
> nor will the shining light of the moon be anymore
> in the last time, when God assumes command.
> Everything will be blackened, there will be darkness throughout the earth,
> and blind men, evil wild beasts, and woe.

---

195. So also Collins 1974a: 93. Cf. Seneca, *Consol. ad Marc.* 26.6; *Herc. Oet.* 1102-1117. See further, next chapter, pp. 122-4.

196. Collins 1974a: 80.

> That day will last a long time, so that men
> will take note of God himself, the prince who oversees all from heaven.

The day of darkness is not the end of the world; life in the world seems to carry on, though in the context of a total cosmic blackout. The loss of celestial light is rather a feature of the eschatological woes.

The expected salvation involves the restoration of Jerusalem (5.420-427). The city is to be made 'more brilliant than stars and sun and moon' (420-421). This may indicate that in the era of salvation, the light emanating from Jerusalem will replace the light of celestial bodies.

The sixth and final oracle of the Fifth Sibyl, 5.435-531, is the most pessimistic of the whole book. The long section, 5.447-483, describes a series of terrible woes, leading up to 'the end' (476). The woes include war, famine, a swarm of locusts, and natural disasters—deluge in some places and the drying up of the sea in others. At the end of it, the world returns to the primeval darkness. The Sibyl predicts that the sun will be plunged in the ocean and the light of the moon will be no more (lines 477-480). 'No small mist will cover the folds of the world about, a second time.' Yet, there is a glimmer of hope (482-483): 'But then the light of God will lead the good men, as many as sang out the praise of God.'

In lines 512-531, we have a vivid picture of the final fiery judgement. The chief element in this portrayal is the battle of the stars. God himself instigates the stellar battle – he bids them fight (line 514). The constellations clash with each other, destroying themselves and burning up the whole earth as they fall into the ocean.

> Heaven itself was roused until it shook the fighters.
> In anger it cast them headlong to earth.
> Accordingly, stricken into the baths of ocean,
> they quickly kindled the whole earth. But the sky remained starless.
> (5.528-531)

As Collins points out, the whole description finds its closest parallels in Seneca's descriptions of the cosmic conflagration.[197] As in Seneca's *Consol. ad Marc.* 26.6-7, and *Ben.* 6.22, stellar collisions bring about the conflagration. The portrait of battling constellations may reflect an acquaintance with a passage such as Seneca's *Thyestes* 844-874.

As Collins writes, 'The starless heaven provides a more bleak and dismal closing note than we have found elsewhere in the Sibyllina. It indicates that at this point nothing offered any hope short of the destruction of the universe.'[198]

197. Collins in *OTP* 1: 392.
198. Collins 1974a: 93.

2.12.4 *Anti-Cosmic Dualism in the* Sibylline Oracles?

Is the notion of cosmic destruction in the *Sibylline Oracles* (Books 3–5) bound up with a radical dualism which negates creation? Without doubt, the Jewish *Sibylline Oracles*, especially the Fifth Sibyl, evince a generally pessimistic view of the world. Even so, there is no evidence of an extreme cosmological dualism that regards the created cosmos as inherently evil or a flawed product. It is significant that in the Fifth Sibyl, God is described as 'begetter of all' (328, 406; cf. 285, 360, 478) and 'ruler of all' (277, 499). There is no attempt here to dichotomize God and creation. Nor is there any suggestion in these books that materiality as such is a problem. The longing for cosmic destruction is partly borne out of a sense of social and political alienation, the concrete experience of Egyptian Jews; it is not generated out of a contempt for or suspicion of creation.

2.13 *Conclusions*

Our review of evidence in Jewish apocalyptic and related literature now complete, some general conclusions may be drawn. In presenting these conclusions, I return to the fourfold categorization of the relevant passages with which I began; I then offer some observations and reflections on the expectation of the end of the world as it is found in this range of literature.

2.13.1 *Eschatological Texts Employing Language of Global and Cosmic Catastrophe*

We have considered a total of 16 passages that employ global and/or cosmic catastrophe language in connection with God's coming judgement. In all these texts, more than local socio-political change, that is, the downfall of a city or a nation, is in view; the scenario is one of eschatological, universal judgement. In many cases, the final judgement is envisaged by explicit or implicit analogy with the flood as a universal catastrophic judgement of the past.[199] The evocation of the Noachic flood makes it clear that an *actual* catastrophe of global or cosmic proportions is anticipated.

A significant number of these texts exhibit a pattern that may be called the 'catastrophic intervention' pattern, in which God intervenes for the

---

199. *1 En.* 1.3b-9; 83.3b-5; 102.1-3; *Ps.-Soph.* fr. 2; 1 QH 11.19-36; *Sib. Or.* 4.175-178.

purpose of judgement (though also for salvation), and catastrophe either on a global or cosmic scale ensues.[200] This pattern is essentially the theophany pattern familiar from Micah 1, Nahum 1, etc., except that the disruption is not always caused by God's 'coming' or 'descent', but also by his utterance or dramatic action. A theophanic manifestation (a divine advent) is portrayed in *1 En.* 1.3b-9 and *T. Mos.* 3.3-6 and is implied in *1 En.* 102.1-3 and *Apoc. Zeph.* 12.5-8. A striking feature of all these 'catastrophic intervention' passages is their redeployment of elements of Old Testament prophetic catastrophe texts. Isaiah 13.10, 24.19, Joel 2.10, 31, Mic. 1.3-4, Nah. 1.4-5 and Hag. 2.6, 21 serve as resources for envisioning a world-decimating catastrophe (not merely changes in history). The catastrophic intervention does not result in the total destruction of the cosmos, except in *Apoc. Zeph.* 12.5-8. In *1 En.* 1.3b-9, the earth is destroyed.

Portrayals of the catastrophic destruction of the cosmos are mainly found in the *Sibylline Oracles* (elsewhere only in *1 En.* 83.3b-5 and *Apoc. Zeph.* 12.5-8). In the Sibyllina, the dissolution takes the shape of a cosmic conflagration. This is not a characteristically Jewish idea; the notion of a fiery cosmic destruction is not found at all in the Old Testament.[201] Beyond the Old Testament, the idea of a flood of fire, analogous to the Noachic deluge, is expressed in *1 En.* 102.1-3, the fragment of *Pseudo-Sophocles* and 1 QH 11.29-36.[202] But in these passages, the

200. *1 En.* 1.3b-9; 102.1-3; 1 QH 11.19-36; *T. Mos.* 10.3-6; *2 Bar.* 32.1 (cf. 59.3); *Apoc. Zeph.* 12.5-8; *Sib. Or.* 3.675-681.

201. See the discussion in Van der Horst 1994: 234–6. None of the prophetic catastrophe texts we looked at in Chapter One speaks of heaven and earth being burned up. In Mic. 1.4 and Nah. 1.5, the mountains and hills are said to melt, but this falls short of total cosmic conflagration. Zephaniah 1.18 speaks of the whole earth being consumed 'in the fire of his passion'; here fire is a metaphor for God's wrath (cf. Isa. 30.27; Jer. 40.4, Zeph. 3.8, etc.). Isaiah 34.4 LXX B states that 'all the powers of heaven shall melt' (τακήσονται πᾶσαι αἱ δυνάμεις τῶν οὐρανῶν), which differs from the Hebrew ('all the host of heaven shall rot away'). But this reading is not likely to be original, and may well be based on Mt. 24.29. See further Chapter 4, pp. 154–5. In Old Testament prophetic utterances, fire, as an instrument of God's judgement, is generally directed at wicked or sinful human beings (Isa. 29.6; 30.30; 66.15-16; Ezek. 38.22; Amos 1.4, 7, 10, 12, etc.), and sometimes at the local natural environment (Joel 1.19, 20; 2.3; in Amos 7.4, the shower of fire devours 'the great deep' and the land). Malachi 3.2-3 and 4.1 compare the day of God's coming to a consuming and refining fire.

202. We should also mention in this connection the tradition of Adam's prophecy of twin destructions by flood and fire in *LAE* 49.3–50.3 and Josephus, *Ant.* 1.70. The tradition draws on the 'pagan' belief in recurring natural catastrophes by deluge and fire. In neither passage does the judgement by fire take the form of a total cosmic conflagration.

conflagration is not fully cosmic in scope. While certain Old Testament texts may have paved the way for it, and the idea of a fiery counterpart to Noah's flood smoothed its progress, the notion of the total dissolution of the cosmos by fire most likely entered into the Sibylline tradition by way of Stoic influence.[203] As Van der Horst states,

> Even though biblical passages ... may have facilitated the development of this idea, the concept of a total conflagration of the universe can hardly be assumed to be only an inner-Jewish development in view of the fact that this development took place exactly in the period that Jews had the full possibility to take cognizance of Stoic ideas, which they did. And even though the analogy with the all-encompassing Flood ... may have furthered the acceptance of the idea, we still seem to have here a *metabasis* to a new conception that is not unlikely to have developed also under the influence of Stoic ideas.[204]

2.13.2 *Texts Envisaging 'Preliminary' Celestial Disturbances*

As noted at the beginning of this chapter, the notion of preliminary celestial disturbances probably developed from Joel 2.30-31 with its warning of signs in heaven *before* the awesome 'day of the Lord'. *Biblical Antiquities* 19.13, *Sib. Or.* 3.796-804 and 5.346-349 speak of the darkening/ failure of the sun and moon; *1 En.* 80.5 envisions an increase in the light of the moon; *1 En.* 80.4, 6-8 and *4 Ezra* 5.4b-5 predict alterations in the movements of the heavenly bodies. The Ethiopic version of *4 Ezra* 5.4b-5 refers to falling stars. In *1 En.* 80.4-8 and *4 Ezra* 5.4b-5, the celestial malfunctions are part of a catalogue of eschatological woes. Total cosmic darkening is a feature of the end-time woes in *Sib. Or.* 5.346-352. In *1 En.* 80.2-8 and *LAB* 19.13, the heavenly disorders signify the winding up of the cosmic order. In all cases, actual celestial abnormalities seem to be in view.

2.13.3 *Non-Catastrophic Texts Envisaging the End of the Present Created World*

Various texts envisage or at least imply (in the cases of *4 Ezra* 5.50-55; 14.18 and *2 Bar.* 85.10, which speak of the world's senescence) the end of the present order, without using catastrophic imagery. Especially notable among these passages are *LAB* 3.10 and *4 Ezra* 7.30-32, 39-42, the

---

203. Esp. Mal. 3.2-3 and 4.1, but also Deut. 32.22 ('For a fire is kindled by my anger, and burns to the depths of Sheol; it devours the earth and its increase, and sets on fire the foundations of the mountains').

204. Van der Horst 1994: 239.

latter depicting the reversion of creation to chaos and the emergence of a new world. None of the texts in this category can legitimately be interpreted in socio-political terms. The texts themselves or their wider contexts make clear that the cessation of the existing created order is in view.

2.13.4 *Texts Envisaging the Non-catastrophic Transformation of the Cosmos*

Surprisingly, only a few passages envisage a non-destructive transformation of the created world: *1 En.* 45.4-5; *Jub.* 1.29; 4.26. In apocalyptic and related literature, cosmic renewal more often takes the form of destruction and re-creation.

2.13.5 *The End of the Present Created World in Jewish Apocalyptic and Related Writings*

Contrary to the claims of N. T. Wright, there is much evidence for belief in the ultimate end of the present created world in Jewish apocalyptic and associated literature.[205] The end of the cosmos is integrated into the eschatological schemas of the following works: The Astronomical Book; The Dream Vision of *1 Enoch* 83–84; *Testament of Job*; *Biblical Antiquities*; *4 Ezra*; *Apocalypse of Zephaniah*; *2 Enoch*; *Sib. Or.* 3.75-92; 4; 5.179-285, 435-531. The dissolution of the material heavens is part of the eschatological scheme of the *Apocalypse of Weeks*.

In none of these writings is the thought of the present creation coming to an end connected with an anti-cosmic dualism, suspicious or contemptuous of the work of the creator. As a rule, the writers of these works function with a strong view of God as creator and the world as his creation. The destruction of the present world is normally followed by a cosmic re-creation.[206] In those works that offer any kind of elaboration of the process, cosmic destruction is construed as reversion to chaos (*1 En.* 83.3-5; *LAB* 3.10 (cf. 9.3); *4 Ezra* 7.26-44), resolution into fire (*Sib. Or.* 3.75-92), or reduction to 'dusty ashes' (*Sib. Or.* 4.178-179). There is no explicit evidence for belief in the destruction of the material world into absolutely nothing.

    205. The idea of the end of the world, catastrophic or otherwise, is found in the following passages: *1 En.* 72.1; 83.3b-5; 91.16 (the material heavens); *T. Job* 33.3-9; *LAB* 3.10; *4 Ezra* 7.30-42; *2 En.* 65.6-11; *Sib. Or.* 3.75-92; 5.206-213; 5.513-531 (cf. 476-483); 4.175-192. It is also implied in those texts that speak of the senescence of the created order: *4 Ezra* 5.50-55; 14.10-18; *2 Bar.* 85.10.
    206. Explicitly in *1 En.* 72.1; 91.16; *LAB* 3.10; *4 Ezra* 7.30-32; *Sib. Or.* 5.206-213; 4.175-192.

I would not wish to claim from this evidence that the majority of Jews of the first century CE believed that the present cosmos would someday come to an end. Philo held that the cosmos is destined to last for ever (though it was more his Platonist convictions which drove him to this position than biblical or Jewish teaching on the matter) and it is likely that other Hellenized Jews shared this viewpoint. Some of the rabbis also took this line (but on biblical grounds).[207] The crucial point is this: belief in the end of the existing cosmos is firmly established and very widely attested in a body of literature which most would regard as significant for reconstructing the Jewish context out of which early Christianity emerged. It cannot, then, be regarded as an 'UnJewish' (to take up Wright's formulation) or a marginally Jewish notion unattributable to New Testament writers. An (actual) 'end of the cosmos' reading is therefore a genuine and historically appropriate interpretative option for New Testament 'cosmic catastrophe' texts (and other destructionist passages). But before we turn to the New Testament texts, we must give attention to the non-Jewish, Graeco-Roman comparative evidence.

---

207. 'Thus says the Lord. Just as it is not possible that my covenant which I swore with the day and the night should cease, so is the covenant of the heaven and the earth; I have made them that they should not pass away.' *Targ. Jer.* 33.25 (Hayward 1987: 142). See further Van der Horst 1994: 242.

Chapter 3

GRAECO-ROMAN SOURCES

This chapter deals with language of cosmic catastrophe and views of the end of the cosmos in Greek and Latin literature. The destruction of the cosmos was certainly not an alien concept to Graeco-Roman cosmological discussion: whether the cosmos lasts for ever or is destined to come to a catastrophic end was one of the main cosmological questions considered by Greek and Roman natural philosophers. The issue provoked sharp controversy, especially between Aristotelians and Stoics; an important source of information about the debate is Philo's philosophical treatise *On the Indestructibility of the World* (*De aeternitate mundi*).[1] In Chapter 6, I will argue that the dispute between the author of 2 Peter and his opponents mirrors the cosmological polemics.

I begin by looking at the language of cosmic upheaval in Hesiod's *Theogony*, the earliest example of such language in Greek literature. I next discuss Presocratic 'end of the cosmos' views, before looking at Plato's and Aristotle's influential arguments for cosmic indestructibility. I then focus on the Epicurean and Stoic doctrines of the end of the cosmos, both of which were influential in the first century CE. I give particular attention to the Stoic theory of *ekpurōsis* or cosmic conflagration.

3.1 *Cosmic Upheaval in the Mythical Past*

Hesiod's *Theogony* (*Birth of the Gods*) is a genealogy of the gods of Greece. It represents an attempt by its author to synthesize various archaic myths into a coherent narrative. The poem, composed in Epic style, was written at the end of the eighth century BCE or the beginning of the seventh century BCE.

---

1. Philo's authorship of this work, or the main part of it, was questioned in the past. But there can no longer be any doubt about its authenticity, after Runia's (1981) compelling defence of it. Runia demonstrates that Philo has structured his discussion along the lines of a technical *thesis*.

The poem traces the history of the gods and the world from the appearance of Chaos (116) to the settled and unopposed reign of Zeus. Important for the structure of the narrative is the succession of the three great kings: Heaven, Cronos and Zeus. The first gods, Chaos, Earth, Heaven, Tartarus, etc., are constituents of the material cosmos; thus their emergence corresponds to the formation of the world (116-135). The next gods, the Titans, the Cyclopes and the hundred-handed giants, are anthropomorphic mythical beings; they are all products of the sexual union of Earth and Heaven. The youngest Titan, Cronos, leads a revolt against his father Heaven and takes his throne. The next generation of gods is the offspring of Cronos. The youngest of his children, Zeus, eventually overcomes him to become king.

The reign of Zeus is twice threatened: first, by the war with the Titans; second, by the rebellion of Typhoeus. The war between the Titans and Zeus and his siblings (the Olympian gods) brings the universe to the brink of collapse.

> The boundless sea rang terribly around, and the earth crashed loudly: wide Heaven was shaken and groaned, and high Olympus reeled from its foundation under the charge of the undying gods ... (678-681)

When Zeus enters the fray, hurling his lightning bolts from the sky, a mighty conflagration occurs.

> The life-giving earth crashed around in burning, and the vast wood crackled loud with fire all about. All the land seethed, and Ocean's streams and the unfruitful sea. The hot vapour lapped round the earthborn Titans: flame unspeakable rose to the bright upper air: the flashing glare of the thunderstone and lightning blinded their eyes for all that they were strong. Astounding heat seized Chaos: and to see with eyes and to hear the sound with ears it seemed even as if Earth and wide Heaven above came together; for such a mighty crash would have arisen if Earth were being hurled to ruin, and Heaven from on high were hurling her down; so great a crash was there while the gods were meeting together in strife. (693-705)

Zeus and his allies defeat the Titans, imprisoning them in Tartarus. Later, Zeus faces further opposition in the form of Typhoeus, son of Tartarus and Earth, born after the battle with the Titans. The fearsome deity makes a bid to become the ruler of gods and humankind, but Zeus perceives the threat and acts quickly. As the two gods prepare to do battle, the whole cosmos trembles.

> The whole earth seethed, and sky and sea: and the long waves raged along the beaches round and about, at the rush of the deathless gods: and there arose an endless shaking. (847-852)

Zeus overcomes Typhoeus, hurling him down to the earth. The fiery impact causes a great conflagration.

> A great part of huge earth was scorched by the terrible vapor and melted as tin melts when heated by men's art in channelled crucibles; or as iron, which is hardest of all things, is softened by glowing fire in mountain glens and melts in the divine earth through the strength of Hephaestus. Even so, then, the earth melted in the glow of the blazing fire. (861-868)

The world, however, survives the calamity and cosmic stability is restored. With Typhoeus consigned to Tartarus, all opposition to the rule of Zeus is vanquished. Zeus is acknowledged as the supreme king of the gods.

The imagery of cosmic catastrophe clearly serves a dramatic function in the *Theogony*. The language is contextually appropriate: it is fitting that the clashes of the gods should be played out against the backdrop of a world being rocked to its foundations. It has been suggested that Hesiod must have witnessed the effects of a volcanic eruption to write in this way,[2] but it is quite possible that he is simply drawing on his own imagination.

In the *Theogony*, cosmic upheaval lies firmly in the mythical past. Hesiod gives no indication that such a threat will emerge again. Although at the outset of the poem he is instructed by the muses to tell of things future as well as of things past, the account he gives concentrates on the past: the history of the world goes no further than the establishment of the reign of Zeus. Hesiod does not broach the subject of what lies ahead. The implication of his narrative, however, seems to be that the settled rule of Zeus has brought about *permanent* cosmic stability. The writer appears to believe that the cosmos is of everlasting duration:[3] he ascribes immortality to the gods, and since the first gods are the regions and components of the universe, the ascription implies that the world itself is deathless.[4] Later Stoics, however, cited the passages quoted above as evidence of Hesiod's belief in the periodic destruction of the universe by fire.[5]

---

2. Paley 1883: 244.
3. This is how Philo interprets him: *Aet. Mund.* 17-18.
4. Cf. Furley 1987: 101.
5. One of the characters in Plutarch's dialogue *De defectu oraculorum* (415F) says, 'I observe that the Stoic "Conflagration", just as it feeds on the verses of Heracleitus and Orpheus, is also seizing upon those of Hesiod.'

3.2 *The Presocratics and the End of the Cosmos*

No complete work of any of the Presocratic philosophers has survived. For their teaching, we are dependent on fragments preserved by subsequent ancient writers and later reports and summaries of their thought.[6] A chief topic of interest in Presocratic philosophy was the origin of the physical world. The destiny of the cosmos was also a subject of enquiry, but we are less well informed about Presocratic views on this matter.

According to Aristotle, most of the early philosophers believed that the cosmos is generated and destructible.

> Most of the first philosophers thought that principles in the form of matter were the only principles of all things; for the original source of all existing things, that from which a thing first comes-into-being and into which it is finally destroyed, the substance persisting but changing in its qualities, this they declare is the element and first principle of existing things, and for this reason they consider that there is no absolute coming-to-be or passing away, on the ground that such a nature is always preserved. (*Met.* 983b6-14)[7]

On this scheme, the universe has its origin in an *arche* or a generative principle, to which it returns when it eventually dissolves. The theory involves the eternity of matter; there is no *absolute* generation or destruction.[8]

It is doubtful whether 'most' of Aristotle's predecessors in fact held to this view of the cosmos, but it may be taken as a valid summary of the cosmology of the Milesian philosophers of the sixth century BCE, Thales, Anaximander and Anaximenes, the very first Greek natural philosophers (though Aristotle uses his own terminology and categories to express it). Aristotle identifies Thales as the originator of this kind of cosmology.

The Milesians were hylozoists, viewing matter as a living organism. They explained the emergence of the cosmos in biological terms, as growing to its present state from seed-like beginnings.[9] According to Thales, the originating semen-like substance was water;[10] for Anaximenes,

---

6. Waterfield 2000: xiii.
7. Cited from KRS 85.
8. Furley 1987: 20.
9. Furley 1987: 18. They conceived of this as taking place by spontaneous generation.
10. KRS 85. Thales' view was probably a scientific rationalization of the notion found in Homer that 'ocean' was the begetter of all things, including the gods (*Il.* 14.201, 246). This in turn was probably a development of the ancient Near Eastern mythology of the earth arising from the primeval waters.

it was air.[11] For Anaximander, the seed out of which the cosmos grew was secreted by an undefined mass called 'the boundless'.[12] After a period of growth and maturity, the cosmos goes into decline and at the end of its 'life' it returns to its originating principle.

The Milesians probably did not devote much attention to the circumstances of cosmic destruction. Anaximander apparently taught that the earth is drying up, but it is not clear whether he viewed this as the beginning of the reabsorption of the cosmos into 'the boundless'.[13] A late text preserved by Eusebius and attributed by him (wrongly) to Plutarch[14] suggests that the Milesians, or Anaximander at least, held to a cyclic view of cosmic history, according to which the cosmos is generated, dissolved and regenerated eternally. However, a theory of cosmic cycles cannot be attributed to the Milesians with any degree of confidence.[15]

In the passage from which the citation above is extracted, Aristotle names Heraclitus and Empedocles as advocates of the *arche* cosmology, with the former positing fire as the *arche*, and the latter, the four physical elements. In his treatise, *On the Heavens* (*de caelo*), 1.10, Aristotle ascribes to both thinkers a cyclic cosmological scheme, according to which the world alternates between states of order and dissolution. Later, the Stoics credited Heraclitus with their doctrine of *ekpurōsis*. The fragmentary evidence for Heraclitus,[16] however, indicates that while fire was for him the basic matter of the cosmos, it was not an originating substance as water and air were for Thales and Anaximenes.[17] For Heraclitus, the world itself is an ever-living fire, parts of which are always quenched to form sea and earth. Changes between fire, sea and earth balance out each other, so that cosmic stability is perpetually maintained. Most agree, then, that Aristotle's interpretation of Heraclitus' cosmology is incorrect.[18] In fr. 30, Heraclitus rejects generation and destruction, maintaining

11. KRS 139–41.
12. KRS pp. 105–17.
13. KRS 132; see discussion on pp. 139–40. Xenophanes seems to have believed that the earth had at one time been covered by mud and then had dried out, but was now sliding back into the sea. When the earth returns to mud, humanity perishes. Then the earth starts to dry out again, and life begins afresh. See KRS 184 and discussion on pp. 177–8; cf. Waterfield 2000: 24. The cycles of destruction and regeneration are confined to the terrestrial realm; the cosmos itself is not threatened (KRS p. 178).
14. Eusebius, *Ev. Praep.* 1.7.
15. Furley 1987: 20.
16. KRS 217–220.
17. KRS p. 198.
18. Mansfeld 1979: 140 n. 36.

that the cosmic order 'always was and is and shall be'.[19] Heraclitus thus anticipates Aristotle's eternal 'steady state' view of the cosmos.[20] This fragment also renders invalid the Stoic ascription to Heraclitus of a periodic *ekpurōsis*.[21]

Empedocles presents a more difficult case. Until relatively recently, Empedoclean scholars accepted Aristotle's attribution to Empedocles of a theory of cosmic cycles. On the conventional view, Empedocles saw the whole cosmos as subject to the alternations of the opposing forces of 'love' (attraction) and 'strife' (repulsion).[22] When 'love' is totally dominant, all things are together in a single mass, and the four elements are indistinct. When 'strife' is in absolute control, the four elements are completely separate and occupy distinct layers or spheres in space. An ordered cosmos as we currently experience it is possible at two stages in the cycle, when love is on the rise and when strife is increasing. However, this understanding of Empedocles' cosmology has increasingly been called into question. Some have argued that the cosmic cycle has been imposed on Empedocles by Aristotle, and that Empedocles himself spoke, in the fragments which remain of his works (especially fr. 17, lines 1-13),[23] of cycles at the *micro-cosmic* level, while viewing the cosmos itself as generated but indestructible.[24] The issue is far from being resolved.

Belief in the end of the world, in a fully cosmic sense, can indisputably be attributed to the Atomists. Leucippus and his more famous compatriot Democritus rejected the idea that everything emerged from a single material principle. Rather, atoms form the basis of material reality. Atoms are minute particles of matter, of differing sizes and shape, invisible to the human eye.[25] They move randomly through an infinite expanse of space. They collide with other atoms, interlock and form compounds. The ordered cosmos that we inhabit and of which we are part is a compound of atoms on an immense scale. It was produced, entirely accidentally (no divine hand was involved in its development), when a mass of atoms collected together in an area of space and a vortex or whirlwind

19. KRS 217.
20. Luce 1992: 44.
21. KRS p. 200.
22. See Luce 1992: 62–4.
23. For the texts, see KRS 348.
24. Furley 1987: 101–2; cf. KRS pp. 228–9 n. 1. The conventional interpretation is defended in M. R. Wright 1981.
25. M. R. Wright 1995: 106.

caused them to coalesce.[26] Our cosmos is not alone in infinite space. According to Leucippus and Democritus,

> there are innumerable worlds, which differ in size. In some worlds there is no sun and moon, in others they are larger than in our world, and in others more numerous. The intervals between the worlds are unequal; in some parts there are more worlds, in others fewer; some are increasing, some at their height, some decreasing; in some parts they are arising, in others failing. They are destroyed by collision one with another.[27]

Since all physical compounds are inherently destructible, the present cosmos and all other universes that exist now or will exist in the future are destined to break apart. World-destruction takes place when one world collides with another in space. The image of worlds colliding indicates sudden and violent destruction rather than slow but sure decay and deterioration.

3.3 *Plato and Aristotle on the Indestructibility of the Cosmos*

The destructibility of the ordered cosmos was opposed by Plato. In his cosmological treatise, the *Timaeus,* the most influential of his works in antiquity,[28] he tells how the universe was fashioned by a craftsman-deity, who worked on pre-existing matter to produce a copy of the perfect model. The demiurge has made the best achievable cosmos; it lacks the absolute perfection of the ideal realm, but nevertheless conforms to it as closely as possible (*Tim.* 29A-D). The divine craftsman took steps to make certain that his construction would last for ever. First, he used up all available matter in the making of the cosmos; thus, there is nothing outside of it that can act upon it to cause it harm (33A). Second, he brought the elements into perfect unity, ensuring that the cosmos cannot be undone by disharmony within (32C). The universe, therefore, cannot be affected by external or internal causes of physical destruction. It is entirely secure from age and ailment. Only the demiurge himself is capable of dismantling his handiwork, but we can be sure that he would never do so, since this would be against his nature. A god who is wholly good (cf. 29E–30A) would never wish to destroy what he has made.[29]

Aristotle went a step further than Plato, maintaining that the cosmos is eternal, having neither beginning nor end. His thesis is set forth in *On the*

---

26. KRS pp. 416–21.
27. KRS 565.
28. Cf. Runia 1986: 57.
29. For Plato, god is incapable of change (*Rep.* 378E-383A).

Heavens (*De Caelo*) 1.10-12. He firmly rejects the view that the cosmos is generated and will perish. A once-only generation and destruction is impossible: any creationist must assume a return to a pre-cosmic state, from which generation would begin again.[30] He also dismisses Plato's view that the world is generated but everlasting. It is clear from nature that everything that is generated is also perishable.[31] He is more tolerant, though, of the theory of everlasting alternation which he attributes to Heraclitus and Empedocles (wrongly in the case of the former). On this view, he opines, 'it is not the world that comes into being and perishes, but its dispositions only', and this is not all that different to making the cosmos eternal.[32] His own view is that the cosmos exists in an eternal steady state. Aristotle goes on (in 1.12) to argue for an eternal cosmos on logical grounds, on, as J. Mansfeld puts it, 'the mutual implication of "ungenerated" and "indestructible"'.[33]

Aristotle also defended the thesis of the eternity of the universe in his now lost work, *On Philosophy* (*De Philosophia*). It is generally agreed that Philo has preserved three or perhaps four of the arguments Aristotle advanced in this work (but not the original wording of these arguments), in his treatise, *On the Indestructibility of the World* (§20–44).[34] One of these arguments is a physical argument and is a reworking of Plato's claims (*Aet. Mund.* 20-24). The universe, to be destroyed, must be susceptible to external or internal causes of destruction. Destruction from without is impossible since there is *nothing* beyond the cosmos. Destruction from within is also impossible, for this would entail a part of the cosmos being greater than the whole, which is absurd. Since neither cause is possible for the cosmos, it must be considered eternal. Another of the arguments which Philo hails as 'irrefutable' (*Aet. Mund.* 39) introduces a theological line of reasoning, expanding Plato's point that a good god would have no reason to tear down the world he has constructed (39-44). Aristotle of course denies that the cosmos was formed by a demiurge, so the argument must be seen as hypothetical.[35] Aristotle asks what motive the creator would have for destroying his world. He

30. Long 1985: 17. See *Cael.* 280a23-27.
31. *Cael.* 279b17-280a10.
32. *Cael.* 280a22. In other words, it is not the cosmos as an ordered body that is generated and perishes, but particular states of the cosmic order; thus the eternity of the cosmos is preserved. Cf. Hahm 1977: 191–2.
33. Mansfeld 1979: 141, n. 37. For analysis of the argument, see C. J. F. Williams 1966.
34. Mansfeld 1979: 141–4. Runia (1986: 191–3) thinks that all four of the arguments preserved in *Aet. Mund.* 20-44 come from Aristotle's *On Philosophy*.
35. Mansfeld 1979: 142.

would destroy either to cease from world-making altogether or to make another world. The former is alien to god's nature, which is to bring order out of disorder not disorder out of order. It would also involve god changing his mind. The second motive is also incompatible with divine immutability. If god destroys the world in order to replace it with another world, the new world must be worse than, similar to or better than the present; this is 'a trilemma with three dead ends'.[36]

> For if it is worse its framer is also worse, but the works of God framed with the most consummate skill and knowledge are not liable to censure or condemnation or correction ... If it is a similar world, the craftsman has wasted his toil and differs not a whit from senseless children who often when playing on the beach erect great mounds of sand and then undermine them with their hands and send them tumbling back to the ground. Far better than constructing a similar world would it be neither to take away nor to add ... but to leave where it is what was once originally created. If the work is to be better, the workman also will then be better, consequently less perfect in skill and intelligence when he constructed the first world. And even to harbour such a thought is profane, for God is equal to Himself and like Himself; His power admits neither relaxation to make it worse, nor tension to make it better. (*Aet. Mund.* 41-43)

Both Plato and Aristotle, then, advocated the indestructibility of the cosmos, and this dogma was upheld by their successors in the Academy and the Lyceum. Despite their philosophical differences, Platonists and Peripatetics were united in their opposition to a perishable cosmos.

3.4 *The Epicurean View of the End of the Cosmos*

Epicureanism, along with Stoicism, was one of the two most important philosophical schools of the Hellenistic age. Founded by Epicurus (342–270 BCE) in Athens, the school (known as 'The Garden'), attracted many loyal adherents. It was especially influential in the time of the late Republic. Comparatively little of Epicurus' substantial body of writing has survived.[37] A full account of Epicurean physics is provided by Lucretius (c. 95–55 BCE) in his work, *On Nature* (*De rerum natura*), written to make the philosophical teaching of Epicurus accessible to a Roman public.

36. Mansfeld 1979: 160.
37. Three letters and a set of maxims, known as the *Kyriai Doxai* or 'principal doctrines', have been preserved by Diogenes Laertius. Charred fragments of Epicurus' treatise *On Nature* were discovered in a villa excavated at Herculaneum. Also, a manuscript discovered in the Vatican contains additional maxims attributed to Epicurus. See Luce 1992: 139–40.

The basis of Epicurean physics was the atomic theory of Leucippus and Democritus. The sum of all things is atoms and the void; these are the only absolute realities. Epicurus believed that there are innumerable worlds, some like this world, others unlike it.[38] A world is formed through the chance combination of atoms in the void. To explain the growth of a world, Epicurus drew on a biological model.[39] A world develops by absorbing nourishment. It takes in matter until it reaches the point of maturity and stability.[40] Worlds, like all aggregates, are destined to destruction,[41] and so this world of ours will eventually perish. According to one testimony, 'Epicurus says that the cosmos perishes in very many ways, like a living being or a plant, and in many other ways'.[42] However, he rejected Democritus' view that a world is destroyed when it collides with another world, denying that a world could grow large enough to bump into another one.[43]

Lucretius discusses the destructibility and end of the world in Books 2 (1105-1172) and 5 (91-109, 235-415). In 2.1105-1175, he explains the growth and death of the world on the analogy of a living organism. He outlines three phases in the life of a living creature. The first stage is that of growth to maturity. Every living thing absorbs and gives out particles. As long as the number of particles taken in exceeds those expelled, there is growth and, at the peak of growth, there is equilibrium (2.1118-1119). The second stage is that of gradual decline. During this phase, more particles flow out of the body than are taken in. Also, food consumed is less easily distributed through the body (2.1136). The third stage is that of rapid decline, when the body eventually yields to the blows of the atoms which continually rain down upon it. Weakened by its losses, the body is no longer able to withstand the atomic bombardment, and it disintegrates. So, it is with the world. In its period of growth, it takes in

38. Diogenes Laertius 10.45 (= Epicurus, *Ep. Her.* 45). He suggested that worlds may be of various shapes: some spherical, some oval, others of different shapes (Diogenes Laertius 10.74 (= Epicurus, *Ep. Her.* 74)).
39. See further Solmsen 1953.
40. Diogenes Laertius 10.88-90 (= Epicurus, *Ep. Pyth.* 88-90).
41. Diogenes Laertius 10.73 (= Epicurus, *Ep. Her.* 73). According to Cicero (*Fin.* 1.21; *Nat. de.* 1.67), Epicurus claimed that worlds are forming and perishing at every moment.
42. Usener 305. Cf. Solmsen 1953: 50.
43. Diogenes Laertius 10.90 (= Epicurus, *Ep. Pyth.* 90). Lanctantius states that Epicurus gave no account of how the world would end, or when the end would happen (Lanctantius, *Inst.* 7.1.10 = Usener 304), but Lanctantius may simply be reflecting on the extant evidence, rather than speaking from a knowledge of sources otherwise unknown to us. See W. M. Green 1942: 52.

more particles than it exudes, and earth, sea and sky grow to their limit. Once maturity is reached, equilibrium is followed by decline. Inevitably, the world succumbs to the forces of destruction and breaks up: 'So therefore the walls of the mighty world in like manner shall be stormed all around, and shall collapse into crumbling ruin' (2.1144-1145). The image of the storming of a city points to sudden and violent destruction. For Lucretius, the process of destruction is always quicker than that of formation (1.556). Thus, although the process of decline is a gradual and drawn-out one, the end when it comes will be swift and devastatingly brutal.

Lucretius goes on to claim that the world has already entered its period of decline.[44] Its life-giving and life-bearing power has diminished, and the earth is 'exhausted'. He cites as evidence of the world's terminal decline the smallness of creatures produced by the earth now in comparison to times before (2.1150-1152). He mentions too the complaints of the farmer that the land is less fruitful than in the days of his father and in times past, and the lament of the vine-grower that the vines are less productive than in days gone by (2.1160-1170). What they fail to understand, states Lucretius, is that 'all things gradually decay, and go to the reef of destruction (*ire ad scopulum*)[45] outworn by the ancient lapse of years' (2.1173-1174). Pliny the Elder echoes this line of thought when, writing around 70 CE, he states, 'With the entire human race the stature on the whole is becoming smaller daily, and ... few men are taller than their fathers, as the conflagration that is the crisis towards which the age is now verging is exhausting the fertility of the semen' (*Nat. Hist.* 7. 73).[46] The author of *4 Ezra* also employs this argument (5.50-55), in so doing reflecting Epicurean influence.

In Book 5, Lucretius attacks the Aristotelian thesis of an eternal cosmos and tries to show that the world had a beginning and will have an end (5.65-66).

> observe first of all sea and earth and sky; this threefold nature, these three masses ... these three forms so different, these three textures so interwoven, one day shall consign to destruction; the mighty and complex system of the world, upheld through many years, shall crash into ruins. (92-96)

---

44. According to W. M. Green (1942), the idea that the cosmos is dying was not taught by Epicurus, but was an innovation by Lucretius.
45. Literally, 'go on the rock (in the sea)', as a metaphor for 'go to ruin'. Bailey (1947: 983) prefers the reading *ad capulum*, 'to the grave'.
46. Oddly, Pliny declares his acceptance of the eternity of the cosmos in *Nat. Hist.* 2.1-2. But Pliny does not consistently hold to a philosophy. Cf. *Nat. Hist.* 2.236, discussed below.

The emphatic 'one day' (*una dies*) implies here not a slow process of degeneration, but swift destruction.[47] Remarkably, a few lines later, Lucretius raises the possibility that the disaster could take place within the lifetime of his dedicatee (Gaius Memmius). He comments that 'within some short time (*in parvo tempore*) you will see violent earthquakes arise and all things convulsed with shocks'. Yet, his hope is that fortune will delay the inevitable, and that 'pure reason rather than experience persuade that the world can collapse borne down with a frightful-sounding crash' (104-109).[48] He offers four arguments for the destructibility of the world.

The first argument, and the most complex, 5.235-323, is an argument from the mortality of the four elements. Earth diminishes as it is scorched, trampled down or washed away, water evaporates, air changes and the rays of the sun fall and fade. Since each of the four elemental parts of which the world is composed is mortal, the whole compound must likewise be mortal. Theophrastus had already countered this line of reasoning by insisting that only if the parts of a thing are destroyed together and simultaneously can we argue from the mortality of the parts to the whole.[49]

The second argument, 5.324-350, is an argument based on the belief that the world is subject to periodic natural catastrophes.[50] This belief was expounded by Plato, but undoubtedly it is much older.[51] In *Tim.* 22C–23A, Plato states that great catastrophes occur at long intervals.[52] There have been many such destructions in the past, the worst having been caused by fire and flood. These catastrophes are partial, in that they do not completely decimate the earth and wipe out humanity, yet they are devastating enough to destroy the achievements of human civilization, so that human beings have to start their cultural development all over again. For Plato, these periodic disasters did not call into question the stability and security of the cosmos. Aristotle likewise believed in cyclic catastrophes, by deluge and drought (rather than conflagration).[53] According to

---

47. Bailey 1947: 1335.
48. Again, the image is one of violent destruction (Bailey 1947: 1336).
49. Philo, *Aet. Mund.* 143-144.
50. In the course of this argument, Lucretius opines that 'the world is young and new, and it is not long since its beginning' (330-331), which is notoriously difficult to reconcile with his 'dying world' thesis.
51. We noted above the theory of cyclic transformations, in connection with Xenophanes. See above, n. 13.
52. Cf. *Crit.* 109B; 111A-B; 112A; *Leg.* 677A.
53. See Chroust 1973.

Lucretius, legends of great fires and flood, wiping out cities and cultures prove that the whole cosmos is destructible.

> For when things were assailed by so great afflictions and so great dangers, if then a more serious cause had come upon them, there would have been widespread destruction and a mighty fall. And in no other way are we seen to be mortal than that we see one another fall sick of the same diseases as those whom nature has taken away from life. (345-350)

Aristotle, though, had already insisted that terrestrial damage caused by cyclic catastrophes could never affect the universe as a whole.[54]

Lucretius' third argument (5.351-379) rests on atomic physics. The claim is that the world does not satisfy the conditions of immortality. That which is everlasting must be solid and not liable to penetration (like the atoms), must be insubstantial (like the void), or must have no space around it into which it can be dispersed (like the sum of all things, atoms and void). But none of these conditions applies to the cosmos; therefore it is destructible.

The fourth argument (5.380-415) is based on the strife of the elements. There must some day be an end to the long contest of the four elements. At present, the world is preserved by the evenness of the strife, but one day one of the elements will gain control and bring an end to the ordered world. Partial victories are recorded in legend. The myth of Phaethon[55] bears witness to the one-time prevalence of fire. The story of the flood is testimony to an occasion when water began to triumph. In both instances, the equilibrium was restored, but there will come a time when the balance will not return. Aristotle of course rejected as absurd the notion that the whole world can be undone by one of its parts.

In line with atomic theory, Lucretius, following Epicurus, rejects any notion of absolute destruction: 'no single thing returns to nothing, but all by disruption return to the elements of matter' (1.248-249).[56] He expects the cosmos to end in a calamitous fashion, but not to be reduced to non-being.

Lucretius does not think that the world is wholly good; indeed he teaches that it has many great faults (5.195-234). He seems to connect the world's destructibility with its faultiness.[57] But he does not give expression to an anti-cosmic dualism which regards the world as the bad

---

54. Aristotle, *Meteor.* 351b8-352b18.
55. The story of Phaethon is told by Ovid, *Met.* 2.1-400, a passage replete with images of global and cosmic catastrophe.
56. Cf. Diogenes Laertius 10.39 (= Epicurus, *Ep. Her.* 39).
57. His discussion of the mortality of the cosmos in Book 5 (235-415) follows on directly from his account of the world's faults (195-234).

product of an inferior or malicious creator. Epicurean cosmology is not dualistic, nor does it have any place for divine involvement in cosmic events. The world's formation and its eventual demise are purely naturalistic affairs.

3.5 *The Stoic View of the End of the Cosmos*

Stoicism was founded by Zeno of Citium, who arrived in Athens in 313 BCE and began to teach from about 300 onwards.[58] He was succeeded as head of the school he founded by Cleanthes, who was followed in turn by Chrysippus. The latter wrote extensively and was responsible for the systematization of Stoicism. No complete work of the early Stoics survives; we have only fragments and summaries, yet this material is substantial enough for us to reconstruct their views with some accuracy. Stoicism is usually divided into three periods: early, middle and Roman Stoicism. Zeno, Cleanthes and Chrysippus belonged to the early Stoa. Panaetius and Posidonius are the main figures of middle Stoicism, which spans the second and first centuries BCE. The period of Roman Stoicism ran from the first to the third century CE. The leading Stoics of the first century CE were Seneca, Cornutus, Musonius Rufus and Epictetus.

Like Plato and Aristotle, but unlike the Epicureans, the Stoics regarded the cosmos as a purposeful and well-ordered system deriving its design from a divine intelligence. The Stoics' god, unlike Plato's demiurge, is not external to the material realm, imposing order on it from above; he is utterly conjoined with matter, pervading it as the world's soul. This means that events in the history of the cosmos are at the same time events in the life of the providential deity.[59]

The Stoics believed that cosmic history is cyclic: the ordered world is generated in space or void,[60] continues for a period, ends in an *ekpurōsis* or conflagration, and is recreated anew out of the fire, the sequence repeating itself endlessly.

3.5.1 *Cosmic Generation*

The origin of the world is explained in both physical and biological/ theological terms.[61] On the physical account, the world reaches its present form through elemental change, or, more precisely, through the

---

58. Luce 1992: 132.
59. Long 1985: 15.
60. On the Stoic notion of void, see LS pp. 294–7
61. On Stoic cosmogony, see Hahm 1977: 57–90.

material transformations of the originating element, fire. Chrysippus, in a quotation from his first volume on *Physics* preserved by Plutarch, describes the processes as follows:

> The transformation of fire is like this: by way of air it turns into water (δι' ἀέρος εἰς ὕδωρ τρέπεται); and from this, as earth is precipitated, air evaporates; and, as the air is subtilized, ether is diffused round about, and the stars along with the sun are kindled from the sea.[62]

Diogenes Laertius reports essentially the same scheme:

> The world, they hold, comes into being when its substance (ἡ οὐσία) has first been converted from fire through air into moisture (δι' ἀέρος εἰς ὑγρότητα) and then the coarser part of the moisture has condensed as earth, while that whose particles are fine has been turned into air, and this process of rarefaction goes on increasing till it generates fire. Thereupon out of these elements animals and plants and all other natural kinds are formed by their mixture.[63]

The world arises when the primal fire – the fire of the conflagration – subsides by changing into air and then condenses into water. The watery mass undergoes further changes and eventually produces the four terrestrial elements. The four elements combine in many diverse ways to make the variety of things and life-forms on earth. Through the rarefaction of air, 'ether' is diffused to the periphery of the cosmos. Ether is the fiery substance of the celestial bodies. It is the residue of the originating fire, or 'designing fire', which the Stoics distinguished from the terrestrial element fire, or 'destructive fire'.[64] The former causes growth and preservation; the latter consumes.

In developing this scheme, the Stoics drew on previous cosmological theories, but combined them in a distinctive way. They took from the Milesians of the sixth century BCE, the basic idea that the world developed from a single undifferentiated substance. They drew specifically on Thales' teaching for their view that all things derive most directly from water. From Anaximenes, they borrowed the notion of the growth of the elements from a single root through the twin processes of condensation and rarefaction.[65] The belief that fire is the archetypal form of matter they adapted from Heraclitus.

Viewed in terms of physics, the processes of world-formation appear mechanistic and naturalistic. On the biological/theological model, the

62. Plutarch, *Stoic.* 1053a.
63. Diogenes Laertius 7.142.
64. LS 46D. Cf. Lapidge 1978: 167.
65. KRS pp. 148–50.

changes are brought about by a 'formative, energizing power'[66] active within matter.

> In the beginning he [God] was by himself; he transformed the whole of substance through air into water, and just as in animal generation the seed has a moist vehicle, so in cosmic moisture God, who is the seminal reason of the universe, remains behind in the moisture as such an agent, adapting matter to himself with a view to the next stage of creation. Thereupon he created first of all the four elements, fire, water, air, earth.[67]

At the peak of conflagration, god exists in the form of pure 'designing fire'. At the onset of cosmic generation, the divine fire contracts to become a fiery seed within seminal fluid (the watery mass). As A. A. Long emphasizes, the idea is not that god 'seeds' the world and leaves it to develop independently.[68] He remains within the moisture changing and adapting it until the world is fully formed. Since god is co-extensive with matter, the material processes of creation are self-transformations of god himself. 'His own life-history is co-extensive with that of the world which he creates.'[69] According to Chrysippus, during the conflagration, god exists wholly as soul; when the fire changes to water, it changes into body and soul.[70]

3.5.2 *Cosmic Conflagration*

Like its beginnings, the world's fiery end is given a physical and a biological/theological explanation by the Stoics. As a physical process, the conflagration is the counterphase of cosmic generation: the conversion of the world of four elements back into designing fire, reversing in a flash (though with a gradual build-up) the changes and interchanges that brought about the world's formation.[71] More specifically, the conflagration is the result of the total evaporation of terrestrial moisture by the sun and the other celestial bodies. According to Zeno, everything that burns must have something to burn.[72] The celestial fire of the sun and stars, the Stoics believed, is kindled by the sea and earthly moistures.[73] Eventually,

---

66. Long 1985: 15.
67. Diogenes Laertius 7.136.
68. LS p. 277. An 'orgasmic' account of the conception of the world is given by Dio Chrysostom (*Disc.* 36.56-57).
69. LS p. 277.
70. LS 46F (Plutarch, *Stoic.* 1053b).
71. Long 1985: 20-1.
72. LS 46I.
73. Plutarch, *Stoic.* 1053a (quoted above).

the heavenly fire will dry up the whole earth and consume it. Cicero states: 'when the moisture has been used up neither can the earth be nourished nor will the air continue to flow, being unable to rise upward after it has drunk up all the water; thus nothing will remain but fire'.[74] The sun, as the biggest cosmic burner, has a pivotal role in the process (Zeno states: 'now the sun is a fire and will it not burn what it has?').[75] A fragment of Cleanthes indicates that the sun will draw the other heavenly bodies to itself and consume them in its flames.[76] At the conflagration, the designing fire of the celestial region thus behaves like destructive fire, devouring rather than conserving.[77]

From a biological/theological point of view, the conflagration is caused by the growth of god. In contrast to the Epiruceans, the Stoics emphatically denied that the cosmos experiences death. According to Chrysippus, 'since death is the separation of soul from the body, and the soul of the world is not separated but grows continuously until it has completely used up its matter on itself, the world must not be said to die'.[78] Long explains the thought: 'God, unlike other living beings, does not suffer separation of body from soul. Rather, his soul grows by cannibalising its own body, and so the whole *kosmos* becomes divine soul.'[79] Thus, the present cosmos is dissolved by god's assimilation of all the elements into his own fiery nature. When the conflagration occurs, god 'retires into himself, and is with himself'.[80]

The Stoics apparently called the conflagration a *katharsis*, or purification, in the first instance because, during the state of fire, the universal substance exists in its purest form,[81] but also because the conflagration was understood to have a purging effect: according to one testimony,

74. Cicero, *Nat. de.* 2.118.
75. LS 46I.
76. LS 46L.
77. We may ask whether this does not undermine the very distinction between designing fire and destructive fire that the Stoics were at pains to draw. An excellent discussion of this problem may be found in Mansfeld 1979: 152–6. His conclusion is 'that the effective action of fire is, during cosmogony, wholly benevolent...; that, within the generated and ordered universe itself, its action is for the most part benevolent, but also to a slight extent apparently non-benevolent ... ; and that, in the long run, the latter capacity comes to predominate throughout' (156).
78. LS 46E (= Plutarch, *Stoic.* 1052c).
79. Long 1985: 22.
80. LS 46O.
81. Lapidge 1978: 180. According to Mansfeld (1983: 220), the assumption that the conflagration is a purification is a Christian interpretation, but this witness suggests otherwise. Further testimony to the 'purging' effect of the conflagration can be found in Seneca, *Nat. quaes.* 3.28.7.

when the world is subject to conflagration 'no evil at all remains'.[82] The renewal of the cosmos following the conflagration was apparently called a *palingenesia* or regeneration.[83]

3.5.3 *The Cosmic Cycle*

The cosmos is destroyed and restored in an eternal cycle. Each new world-order is identical to the one which precedes it. When the world is renewed:

> again there will be Socrates and Plato and each one of mankind with the same friends and fellow citizens; they will suffer the same things and they will encounter the same things, and put their hand into the same things, and every city and village and piece of land return in the same way. The periodic return of everything occurs not once but many times; or rather, the same things return infinitely and without end. The gods who are not subject to destruction, from the knowledge of this single period, know from it everything that is going to be in the next periods. For there will be nothing strange in comparison with what occurred previously, but everything will be just the same and indiscernible down to the smallest details.[84]

For their theory of the cosmic cycle, the Stoics drew on earlier ideas. They took up the notion of cyclic terrestrial catastrophes. However, they made *the whole cosmos* subject to periodic destruction. There is no evidence in early or middle Stoic thought for parallel destructions of the cosmos by fire and water,[85] but we do find this idea in Roman Stoicism.

> Both [deluge and conflagration] will occur when it seems best to god for the old things to be ended and better things to begin. Water and fire dominate earthly things. From them is the origin, from them the death. Therefore whenever a renewal for the universe is decided, the sea is sent against us from above, like raging fire, when another form of destruction is decided upon. (Seneca, *Nat. quaes.* 3.28.7)[86]

---

82. LS 46N.
83. Philo, *Aet. Mund.* 47; 76; 85. Cf. *SVF* 2.627.
84. LS 52C. Chrysippus (LS 52B) averred that, 'we too after our death will return again to the shape we now are, after certain periods of time have elapsed'. This enabled later Christian writers to attribute to the Stoics the doctrine of bodily resurrection: see Mansfeld 1983.
85. Mansfeld 1979: 147 n. 52.
86. Cf. Seneca, *Consol. ad Marc.* 26.6. Origen, *C. Cels.* 4.64 ('Providence ... either preserves earthly things, or purges them by means of floods and conflagrations; and effects this, perhaps, not merely with reference to things on earth (οὐ τὰ ἐπὶ γῆς μόνον), but also to the whole universe of things' (τὰ ἐν ὅλῳ τῷ κόσμῳ)).

They also seem to have drawn inspiration from the cyclic theory which Aristotle attributed to Heraclitus and Empedocles. Aristotle did not explicitly reject this thesis, but saw it as a tolerable alternative to his own eternal 'steady state' conception of the cosmos. On the cyclic model, according to Aristotle, it is not the cosmos which is generated and perishes, but its 'dispositions'.[87] Using similar language, the Stoics argued that it is not the *cosmos* in the extended sense of 'god himself ... consisting of all substance' that comes into being and is destroyed, but the *cosmos* in the narrower sense of *diakosmesis* or 'world-order'.[88]

The doctrine of everlasting recurrence – that every man and woman will be born again in the next world-cycle and will repeat their lives exactly – echoes the Pythagorean doctrine of cyclic recurrence,[89] but again the Stoics gave it a cosmic application. Everlasting recurrence was also an inevitable consequence of Stoic views of causation and divine providence. The Stoics, or the early Stoics at least, were strict determinists. Everything that happens in the world, no matter how small an event, is connected in a chain of cause and effect. The course of the world and events in its history are planned in advance by god. Since this world, with all its history, is the best possible, it will be repeated exactly in every cosmic cycle.[90]

The Stoics combined their theory of the cosmic cycle with the notion of the Great Year. The Great Year is the period of time the sun, moon and planets take to complete their revolutions and return together to an

---

Dio Chrysostom (*Disc.* 36.47-49) suggests that the flood is partial compared to the conflagration. But these are distinguished from the complete resolution of all things into one that takes place at conflagration (51-54).

87. Aristotle, *Cael.* 280a11-23.
88. LS 44F. The word *diakosmesis* is the technical Stoic term for the ordered arrangement of the world: Hahm 1977: 242. According to Hahm (190–4), the early Stoics derived the alternation model from the cyclic theory that Aristotle discusses in *Cael.* 1.10. In Hahm's view (193), the Stoic theory of cosmic alternation is 'an exact repetition' of the theory Aristotle considers. Long (1985: 33 n. 31) agrees that the Stoic view is very close to the theory of cosmic cycles that Aristotle reviews, and that the Stoics may well have exploited Aristotle's assessment of it to their advantage, but denies that the Stoic alternation thesis is an exact replica of it.
89. So Hahm 1977: 186.
90. See Long 1985: 25–6. Some Stoics, however, apparently allowed for very slight differences from one world to the next. Thus a man who had moles on his face in one world might no longer have them in another world (LS 52F). Others argued that it is not Socrates himself who will recur but 'someone indiscernible from Socrates' (LS 52G). These modifications are less in tune with strict Stoic determinism.

earlier position in relation to the stars.[91] According to Nemesius, the Stoics taught that the conflagration occurs 'when the planets return to the same celestial sign, in length and breadth, where each was originally when the world was first formed', that is, at the completion of the Great Year.[92] The Great Year is a vast period of time, around 10,000 years or more.[93] There is no indication, though, that Stoics saw themselves as coming to the end of such a period;[94] nor does any Stoic witness suggest that the conflagration is an event of the near future.[95]

3.5.4 *The Stoic Defence of the Destructibility of the Cosmos*

Zeno apparently argued for the destructibility of the present world on empirical grounds: from the unevenness of the earth's surface, the diminution of the sea, the seeming destructibility of each of the four elements, and the recent origin of the arts.[96] At the same time, the Stoics had to defend their view against the physical and theological arguments of Plato and Aristotle. Aristotle insisted that no part of the cosmos can be strong enough to undo the whole. By maintaining that the cosmos will be destroyed by fire, the Stoics were vulnerable to this objection. They countered it by arguing that at the moment of conflagration a part actually *becomes* the whole: 'during total conflagration the whole actually *is* afire'.[97]

The theological argument – that a good creator-deity could have no motive for destroying the world of his making – presented more difficulty. The early Stoics responded to it by representing the conflagration as a wholly positive event, not an act of evil.[98] Chrysippus maintained that at *ekpurōsis*, the cosmos turns into light or brightness (αὐγή);[99] he

91. See M. R. Wright 1995: 138-44.
92. LS 52C. Mansfeld (1979: 146 n. 52) is doubtful of the influence of the Great Year on early Stoic expositions of the doctrine of the conflagration. Seneca (*Nat. quaes.* 3.29.1) cites the Babylonian astrologer Berosus for the view that 'earthly things will burn when all the planets come together in the sign of cancer'. Berosus also spoke of a great deluge when the planets meet in the sign of Capricorn.
93. M. R. Wright 1995: 139.
94. Downing 1995a: 199.
95. Long 1985: 24.
96. Theophrastus, Aristotle's successor as head of the Peripatetic School, and Zeno's contemporary, offered counter-arguments to each of these points. These are preserved in Philo, *Aet. Mund.* 117-150.
97. Mansfeld 1979: 145.
98. Mansfeld 1981: 306.
99. Philo, *Aet. Mund.* 90.

also insisted, as noted above, that the universe does not die; rather god grows to become all in all. The conflagration is a blissful occasion in the life of god; it is not an event to be feared. As Van der Horst puts it, 'The conflagration is – in a sense – not a destruction, it is an act of god in his benevolent providence. It is a blessing, not an evil.'[100] It is worth emphasizing again that the Stoic cosmic conflagration is not part of a negative cosmology;[101] Stoic pantheistic cosmology is eminently positive.

By positing that god destroys the world then re-creates it exactly as it was before, the Stoics were open to Aristotle's criticism that a god who destroys and re-fashions the *same* world has simply wasted his time and is no different to a whimsical child who builds, flattens and rebuilds sandcastles. It is not clear how the early Stoics met this objection.[102] Seneca provides an answer to Aristotle's challenge (though not explicitly) with his statement that god destroys and re-creates because he 'decides to start better things and finish with what is old' (*Nat. quaes.* 3.28.7). Seneca's reasoning can be illuminated by a parallel in Dio. According to Dio, a newly created universe is much more resplendent than it appears today because it is fresh from the creator's hand.[103] By destroying and re-creating the same world, the creator-god thus rejuvenates and re-freshens it. As noted above, the conflagration was thought by some Stoics to clean out evil. This effectively supplies the deity with a moral incentive for discontinuing the present world and starting it

---

100. Van der Horst 1994: 234. Mansfeld (1979: 177) contends that, for the early Stoics, the state of affairs during the conflagration is 'far superior to that of the familiar, ordered universe'. Long (1985: 25) thinks it more likely that the early Stoics 'supposed that whatever state of affairs obtains at any given moment is the best state as viewed from a divine perspective'.

101. I made this point in the Introduction, p. 15.

102. As Mansfeld (1979: 162) points out, they could perhaps have argued that a god who fashions a product which both 'accounts for the phenomena of transitoriness' and ensures the perpetuation of cosmic goodness is not engaged in an act of child's play.

103. Dio Chrysostom, *Disc.* 36.58-60: 'And having performed his task and brought it to completion, he revealed the existent universe as once more a thing of beauty and inconceivable loveliness, much more resplendent, indeed, than it appears to-day ... the entire heaven and universe when first it was completed, having been put in order by the wisest and noblest craft, just released from the hand of the creator, brilliant and translucent and brightly beaming in all its parts ... was fresh and vigorous from the very beginning. At that time, therefore, the Creator and Father of the World, beholding the work of his hands, was not by any means merely pleased, for that is a lowly experience of lowly beings; nay, he rejoiced and was delighted exceedingly.' Cf. Mansfeld 1979: 183 n. 173.

anew.[104] The moral justification for world-destruction and renewal is developed by Seneca in *Nat. quaes.* 3.30.8. By the time the world nears the end of its cycle, human beings will have descended into the savagery of animals. The cataclysm and renewal will halt the moral decline and bring back a period of total innocence: 'Every living created creature will be created anew and the earth will be given men ignorant of sin, and born under better auspices. But their innocence, too, will not last, except as long as they are new.'

In an attempt to escape the theological problem of a benevolent deity destroying the world, some Stoics apparently attributed the conflagration not to god, but to fire,[105] a distinction impossible for 'orthodox' Stoics.

3.5.5 *Stoic Portrayals of the Cosmic Catastrophe*

Seneca and his nephew Lucan attempt to portray the coming cosmic dissolution. In *Nat. quaes.* 3.27, Seneca gives a graphic account of the destruction of the world by flood. In *Consol. ad Marc.* 26.6-7, he describes the terrifying effects of cataclysm and conflagration. Of the fiery destruction of the world he writes,

> stars will clash with stars, and all the fiery matter of the world that now shines in orderly array will blaze up in common conflagration. Then also the souls of the blest, who have partaken of immortality, when it shall seem best to God to create the universe anew – we, too, amid the falling universe, shall be added as a tiny fraction to this mighty destruction, and shall be changed again into our former elements.

A vivid picture of the cosmic conflagration is also drawn in *Ben.* 6.22.

> Let all the heavenly bodies, separated as they are by vast distances and appointed to the task of guarding the universe, leave their posts; let sudden confusion arise, let stars clash with stars, let the harmony of the world be destroyed, and the divine creations totter to destruction; let the heavenly mechanism, moving as it does with the swiftest speed, abandon in the midst of its course the progressions that had been promised for so many ages, and let the heavenly bodies that now, as they alternately advance and retreat, by a timely balancing keep the world at an equable temperature be suddenly consumed by flames, and, with their infinite variations broken up, let them all pass into one condition; let fire claim all things, then let sluggish darkness take its place, and let these many gods be swallowed up in the bottomless abyss.

---

104. Long 1985: 25.
105. Philo, *Aet. Mund.* 8. On the absurdity of making god an agent of destruction, cf. Plutarch, *Comm.* 1075.

The dominant image of these portraits is the clashing of stars, the stellar collisions causing a heavenly inferno. The theme may have been inspired by Cleanthes' statement that at the conflagration the sun assimilates to itself all the other heavenly bodies. A scene of cosmic collapse is depicted by Seneca is in his tragedy, *Thyestes*.

> No more by the rising of his quenchless torch shall the leader of the stars, guiding the procession of the years, mark off the summer and the winter times; no more shall luna ... dispel night's terrors ... Into one abyss shall fall the heaped-up throng of gods. The Zodiac ... falling itself, shall see the fallen constellations; the Ram ... headlong shall plunge into the waves o'er which he had borne the trembling Helle ... Alcides' Lion, with burning heat inflamed, once more shall fall down from the sky; the Virgin shall fall to the earth she once abandoned...and the Wain [the Bear], which was ne'er bathed by the sea, shall be plunged beneath the all-engulfing waves ... Have we of all mankind been deemed deserving that heaven, its poles uptorn, should overwhelm us? In our time has the last day come? ... Greedy indeed for life is he who would not die when the world is perishing in his company. (Seneca, *Thyes.* 835-884)[106]

Here, the fall of the stars is the dominant motif. A similar portrait of the end of the world is found in the tragedy, *Hercules Oetaeus* (1102-1117).

In his epic work, *Civil War* (also known as *Pharsalia*), the poet Lucan re-tells the events of the war between Caesar and Pompey that brought the Roman Republic to an end. At various points in the poem, Lucan alludes or explicitly refers to the destruction of the cosmos. As M. Lapidge states, 'the dissolution of the universe is viewed as parallel to (and, in poetic terms, a result of) the destruction of the state'.[107] The parallel is drawn at the very beginning of the epic: the envious chain of fate that ordained the fall of the Republic has decreed that the universe itself must dissolve.

> when the whole framework of the world is dissolved and the final hour, closing so many ages, reverts to primeval chaos, then [all the constellations will clash in confusion], the fiery stars will drop into the sea, and earth, refusing to spread her shores out flat, will shake off the ocean; the moon will move in opposition to her brother, and claim to rule the day,

---

106. The collapse of the heavens is also imagined in the epic *Octavia* (391-394) which has been preserved among the manuscripts of Seneca's dramatic works, but whose author is unknown (Seneca appears as a character in this tragedy).

107. Lapidge 1979: 359. In my view, Lucan's linkage (but *not equation*) of the fall of the Republic with the dissolution of the cosmos bears comparison with the juxtaposition of local judgement (falling on Babylon and Edom) and global/cosmic judgement in Old Testament prophetic texts such as Isaiah 13 and 34. See further Adams 1997.

> disdaining to drive her chariot along her slanting orbit; and the whole distracted firmament will overthrow its laws. Great things will come crashing down upon themselves – such is the limit of growth ordained by heaven for success. (Lucan, *Phars.* 1.72-81)

Lucan here employs images of clashing and falling stars such as those we find in Seneca's writings. As Lapidge states, he has 'consciously and carefully chosen terminology drawn from and informed by the Stoic cosmological tradition'.[108]

A little later in the narrative, Cato compares the inevitable prospect of civil war with the collapse of the cosmos.

> Who would choose to watch the starry vault falling down and to feel no fear to himself? or to sit with folded hands, when high heaven was crashing down and earth shaking with the confused weight of a collapsing firmament? (Lucan, *Phars.* 2.289-92)

Towards the end of the epic, with the dreadful battle of Pharsalus imminent, Lucan writes that each soldier set aside thoughts of his own fate, regarding instead the fate of Rome and the whole cosmos.

> Who that saw the shore covered by the sea and the waves reaching the mountain-tops, the sky falling down upon the earth and the sun dashed from his place, could regard with selfish fear such wide destruction? (Lucan, *Phars.* 7.135-138)

Such passages in Seneca and Lucan show that the parlance of cosmic calamity was not unique to Jewish tradition in the world that shaped the New Testament. These portraits of the end bear comparison with Old Testament and Jewish 'cosmic catastrophe' texts examined in Chapters 1 and 2. Although the wording is different, there are shared images: the malfunction of the sun and moon; the falling of stars; the collapse of the heavenly vault; the shaking of the earth. The parallels are especially close between the Stoic texts and the relevant passages in the *Sibylline Oracles*. Indeed, authors of the some of the texts in *Sibylline Oracles* Book 5 seem to be familiar with Seneca's pictures of the end, incorporating into their end-time scenarios the more distinctively Stoic images of the heavenly inferno and the clashing of stars. The language of cosmic catastrophe in Seneca and Lucan is clearly language of imaginative portrayal, not that of literal prediction. Just as clearly, it anticipates the actual destruction of the present cosmic order.

---

108. Lapidge 1979: 360.

3.6 Belief in the Catastrophic End of the Cosmos in the First Century CE

Philo's tractate, *On the Indestructibility of the World*, shows that the issue of the fate of the cosmos was very much a 'live' one in Philo's day (c. 30 BCE – 45 CE).[109] Philo himself takes the view that 'the cosmos has been created and should in theory come to an end, but is preserved from destruction by the will and providence of the creator',[110] thus siding with Plato that the world is generated and everlasting, though he reproduces the Aristotelian case. The Aristotelian thesis of the eternity of the cosmos is championed in two other philosophical treatises of the first century CE.[111] That the world is everlasting was probably the predominant view among the philosophically educated.[112] According to Bruce Winter, 'the philosophical concept of a lasting world was reinforced by political propaganda indicating that the commencement of the Empire was, in effect, the beginning of a lasting *Reich*'.[113]

The belief that the present world will come to a definite and catastrophic end continued to be upheld by Epicureans and Stoics. Although it was doubted and even abandoned by some middle Stoics,[114] the doctrine of *ekpurōsis* seems to have been widely accepted in first-century Stoicism.[115] It was supported by three of the four major Stoic figures of the era, Seneca, Cornutus and Epictetus,[116] as well as the Stoic-Cynic philosopher, Dio Chrysostom.[117]

---

109. Diodorus of Sicily, writing at a somewhat earlier time than Philo (between 56 and 36 BCE), also refers to the debate in the opening section of his *History* (1.6.3).

110. Philo, *Aet. Mund.* 132.

111. *De Universi Natura*, attributed (wrongly) to Ocellus of Lucania and *Pseudo-Aristotle*'s *De Mundo*.

112. Winter 2001: 254–5.

113. Winter 2001: 255. This ideological commitment, Winter points out, was replicated in Roman architecture (2001: 255–6). Lucan, in his *Civil War*, was to some extent subverting that ideology.

114. Philo, *Aet. Mund.* 76-77; cf. Mansfeld 1981: 307.

115. Philo (*Aet. Mund.* 8) writes that the doctrine of the destruction of the world is held by 'the great mass of Stoic philosophers'.

116. Lapidge 1989: 1404, 1415 (on Epictetus, *Disc.* 3.13.4). Our knowledge of Musonius Rufus' teaching is confined to fragments of diatribes, which contain little evidence of cosmological interest. Both Epictetus and Dio Chrysostom were students of Musonius and were familiar with Stoic cosmology. As Lapidge (1989: 1413) states, they 'may have derived this familiarity from Musonius, even if the surviving diatribes contain no further evidence to that effect'.

117. Dio Chrysostom, *Disc.* 36.47-49, 51-54.

There is evidence to suggest that Stoic/Epicurean teaching on the catastrophic demise of the world filtered down to the masses. In his first-hand account of the eruption of Vesuvius in 79 CE, Pliny the Younger tells of the panic that ensued as the hot dust and vapours that destroyed Pompeii and Herculaneum reached Misenum:

> You could hear the shrieks of women, the crying of children, and the shouts of men; some were seeking their children, others their parents, others their wives or husbands, and only distinguishing them by their voices; one lamenting his own fate, another that of his family; some praying to die, from the very fear of dying; many lifting their hands to the gods; but the greater part imagining that there were no gods left anywhere, and that the last and eternal night was come upon the world. (Pliny the Younger 6.20)

As Downing notes, 'That sounds like a popular version of Stoic belief, in which all the divine powers, the Gods, are to be absorbed into the one divine fire.'[118] Even Pliny at that moment believed that he 'was perishing with the world itself'. As noted above, Stoics did not see themselves as nearing the end of a cosmic cycle. Perhaps, then, Pliny's account bears witness to a popular fusion of Stoic and Epicurean traditions on the end of the world.[119] It also shows that, 'given a big enough catastrophe' the world-ending disaster could be thought of as happening now.[120]

3.7 Conclusions

Language of cosmic upheaval and destruction was not a wholly Jewish (and early Christian) preserve. Such language is found in the writings of Hesiod, Seneca and Lucan. Certain images and combinations of images are shared between Jewish and 'pagan' sources, and in *Sibylline Oracles* Book 5 a borrowing of more distinctively Stoic imagery (fiery dissolution, clashing stars) seems to have taken place. Stoic catastrophe language is plainly language for envisaging 'real' catastrophe on the cosmic level.

Speculation about the fate of the physical cosmos can be traced back to the very beginnings of Greek natural philosophy, in the sixth century BCE. In the fourth century BCE, Plato and Aristotle maintained that the cosmos is indestructible, and the question of the cosmic future was debated from then on. In the first century CE, both Epicureans and Stoics taught that the physical cosmos, as we know and experience it, would

---

118. Downing 1995a: 200.
119. According to Pliny the Elder (*Nat. Hist.* 2.236), the eruption of a volcano shows that the world is threatened with conflagration.
120. Downing 1995a: 200–1.

come to an actual end. For Epicureans, the cosmos is already in terminal decline, and the final catastrophe may come soon. According to the Stoic doctrine of *ekpurōsis*, the present world will end in a cosmic fireball out of which it will be reconstituted again. While the Platonic and Aristotelian dogma of cosmic indestructibility may have been favoured within educated circles, Epicurean and Stoic teaching about the catastrophic end of the world seems to have exercised some influence at a popular level.

Before moving on, it is perhaps worth highlighting similarities and differences between 'end of the cosmos' views found in Jewish apocalyptic and related writings[121] and Epicurean and Stoic doctrines of the end. Jewish 'end of the cosmos' views, of course, are not uniform, so the shared ideas and differences are not applicable to all the relevant Jewish works.

Jewish and Epicurean Views
Similar Ideas
- The existing created world has a limited life or time-span.
- The created world grows old and declines (*4 Ezra*; *2 Baruch*).
- The end will be catastrophic (especially in the *Sibylline Oracles*).
- The end of the cosmos may happen soon (especially in the *Sibylline Oracles*).
- Cosmic destruction is not destruction into nothing but reversion to pre-cosmic conditions (chaos, randomly moving atoms).
- The end of the cosmos is not part and parcel of an anti-cosmic dualism.

Differences
- In Epicurean thought, the end of the cosmos is tied to a physical theory.
- For Jewish writers, God is responsible for bringing the existing creation to an end, whereas in Epicurean thought the destruction of the cosmos is a wholly naturalistic event, with no divine involvement.
- Jewish writers tend to relate the end of the world to the resolution of God's purposes in history, and *usually* (not always) link it with other consummating events.

---

121. *1 Enoch* 72–82; 83–84; *Testament of Job*; *Biblical Antiquities*; *4 Ezra*; *Apocalypse of Zephaniah*; *2 Enoch*; *Sib. Or.* 3.75-92; 4; 5.179-285, 435-531 (the writings/oracles that specifically envisage the dissolution of the present created world).

- Jewish authors *generally* expect a new creation to follow the end (there are, of course, notable exceptions). Epicureans teach that new worlds will be formed out of the matter of old worlds, but this is very different to the idea of a new creation as found in *1 Enoch* 72–82; *Biblical Antiquities*, etc.

Jewish and Stoic Views
Similar Ideas
- The existing cosmos is intrinsically of limited duration.
- The end will be catastrophic.
- The catastrophe will take the form of a conflagration (only in the *Sibylline Oracles* and only under the direct influence of Stoicism).
- Cosmic destruction is not reduction to nothing but reversion to a pre-cosmic state (chaos, pure fire).
- God/god is responsible for bring the world to an end (though later Stoics apparently try to avoid make god the agent of the world's destruction).
- After the end of this cosmos, a new world in continuity with the old arises.
- The destruction of the cosmos is not part of an anti-cosmic dualism.
- The period leading up to the end is marked by moral decline (among Stoics, this idea is only found in Seneca).

Differences
- In Stoicism, the end of the cosmos is tied to a scientific, physical theory (there is, though, some allusion to Stoic 'science' in *Sibylline Oracles* 3).
- Stoic writers do not conceive of the world's end as an event of the near future.
- Stoics recognize a problem in the thought of the creator destroying the world he has created and respond to it. Jewish writers rarely see a problem here.[122] The idea of God destroying what he has made can be more easily accommodated within Old Testament/Jewish understandings of God's freedom and omnipotence.
- Stoics expect the regenerated world, following conflagration, to be exactly the same as what went before. Jewish writers who

---

122. Only the writer of *1 Enoch* 83–84 seems to deal with it.

look for a new creation generally look for a transformed world (which is nevertheless continuous with the present world).
- Stoics expect the world to be destroyed and renewed in endless cycles.

In the past three chapters we have set out the comparative context, both Jewish and Graeco-Roman, for assessing the historical meaning of New Testament 'cosmic catastrophe' language and the likelihood of New Testament writers expressing belief in the catastrophic end of the cosmos (within ancient cosmological parameters). Having completed this important exercise, we now turn to examine the New Testament texts.

Part 2

New Testament 'Cosmic Catastrophe' Texts

Chapter 4

'THE POWERS OF HEAVEN WILL BE SHAKEN':
MARK 13.24-27 + PARALLELS

This chapter deals with the first and most controversial of our New Testament 'cosmic catastrophe' texts: Mk 13.24-27. One can hardly discuss these verses in isolation from the larger discourse to which they belong, one of the most debated and heavily commented on stretches of text in the New Testament. I thus begin with a brief outline of its contents and some general remarks on the critical issues surrounding its interpretation. I then briefly review ways in which the cosmic references of vv. 24-25 have been read. I next examine vv. 1-23 and vv. 26-27 in closer detail, engaging with the claims of N. T. Wright and R. T. France that nothing beyond the destruction of Jerusalem is envisaged in them. I defend the view that 'the Son of man coming in clouds' in v. 26 refers to Jesus' parousia, which is here a 'Christologization' of the eschatological hope of the coming of God. I then focus specifically on vv. 24-25, first looking at the terminology and motifs and identifying the Old Testament source texts from which they are drawn, before discussing how these verses are best interpreted. Drawing illumination from the Jewish comparative material, I show that Mk 13.24-27 reflects the 'catastrophic intervention' pattern observed in Chapter Two. I argue that the catastrophe language refers to actual catastrophic events expected to attend the eschatological coming of the Son of man. Turning to v. 31, I show that the declaration of the passing away of heaven and earth is a clear-cut affirmation of the eschatological dissolution of the created cosmos. When vv. 24-25 are read in the light of v. 31, it is plausible to regard the upheavals as initiating the cosmic end. I then explore the timescale attaching to the coming of the Son of man and assess the creational, eschatological and practical consequences of the expectation of the end of the created cosmos in Mark. The interpretation given to Mk 13.24-27, I try to show, also holds for the parallels in Matthew and Luke (Mt. 24.29-31; Lk. 21.25-27). I consider the timescale and consequences involved for these evangelists too.

It is generally agreed that Mark is the earliest of the Synoptic Gospels and that it was used as a source by Matthew and, to a lesser extent, Luke. I operate on the (well-founded) assumption that Mark's version of the eschatological discourse is the earliest form of it and that Matthew's and Luke's versions are primarily redactions of Mark.[1]

Mark's Gospel is usually dated between 65 CE and 75 CE,[2] with opinion sharply divided as to whether it was written before or after the destruction of Jerusalem in 70 CE.[3] Precisely how long after Mark the Gospels of Matthew and Luke were written is debated, though most agree they post-date Jerusalem's fall.

4.1 *The 'Eschatological' Discourse of Mark 13*

The discourse of Mark 13 is the largest block of uninterrupted teaching delivered by Jesus in the whole of Mark's Gospel.[4] It is given privately to four disciples in response to questions provoked by Jesus' prophecy of the temple's destruction, though it ends with an exhortation addressed to all (v. 37).

The discourse falls into four distinct sections: vv. 5-23, 24-27, 28-31 and 32-37. In the first section, vv. 5-23, Jesus predicts various coming woes. Verses 24-27 focus on the glorious coming of the Son of man and accompanying events. Verses 28-31 constitute a brief paragraph consisting of a lesson based on the sign of the fig tree and the twin affirmations: 'this generation will not pass away until all these things have taken place' (v. 30) and 'heaven and earth will pass away, but my words will not pass away' (v. 31). In the final section, vv. 32-37, Jesus emphasizes the unknown time of 'that day' and the consequent need for constant vigilance. At its centre is a parable of a householder who goes away on a journey, leaving his servants in charge (vv. 34-36). The disciples must stay awake because they do not know when the master of the house will

---

1. D. Wenham's thesis (1984) that each of the Synoptic evangelists drew independently upon a larger pre-synoptic version of the discourse has failed to win acceptance. For criticisms, see Beasley-Murray 1993: 298–303.

2. Crossley has recently made a case for placing Mark 'between the mid to late thirties and mid-forties' (2004: 209). It remains to be seen whether his arguments will force a major rethink of the date of the Gospel within Markan scholarship.

3. One of the key issues is whether the prediction of the temple's destruction in 13.2 has been shaped by knowledge of an event that has already happened. Theissen (1992: 259) thinks so, but Crossley (2004: 41–3) is doubtful.

4. The next longest discourse of Jesus within Mark is 4.1-34, which is broken at 4.10 with the change of audience and the enquiry of the disciples.

come back. The paragraph and the discourse as a whole conclude with a reiteration of the call to 'keep awake' (v. 37).

Mark 13.5-37 has generated a truly immense amount of critical discussion.[5] It has often been described as the 'Eschatological Discourse' or more controversially, the 'Little Apocalypse'. The latter designation stems from T. Colani's highly influential view that the discourse was a short apocalypse written by a Jewish-Christian author. It is increasingly being recognized, however, that it is inappropriate to call the discourse an 'apocalypse', at least in terms of its literary shape,[6] since it does not meet the standard definitions of the genre (e.g. it is not cast as the revelation of a heavenly mystery). It has also been likened to a 'testament' or 'farewell speech'.[7] However, it lacks the formal narrative setting that such speeches are normally given; moreover, Jesus does not explicitly refer to his upcoming death in it.[8]

A great deal of the scholarly discussion surrounding Mark 13 has focused on the questions of the source or sources underlying the discourse, the historical context/s out of which this material arose, and the editorial activity of Mark himself.[9] Colani held that Mark's source was a singular one, a preformed apocalyptic tract, which was simply slotted into the narrative.[10] Others have maintained that the discourse is the result of the weaving together of various traditions which originally circulated independently.[11] Attempts have been made to delineate distinct stages in the formation of the discourse from its historical origins to its present state and position in Mark's Gospel.[12] How much of the discourse may be traced back to Jesus himself has been vigorously debated. On Colani's theory, Mark 13 contains the eschatology of Jewish-Christians, not at all the teaching of the historical Jesus. Some scholars maintain that the discourse contains a mixture of authentic and inauthentic material, while

---

5. For the history of scholarly discussion see Beasley-Murray 1993.
6. Rowland (1982: 43) writes: 'the present form of the chapter makes it difficult to justify the description of it as apocalyptic'.
7. E.g., Hooker 1991: 297.
8. Cf. C. A. Evans 2001: 290.
9. See Beasley-Murray 1993; Dyer 1998.
10. For an outline of Colani's theory, see Beasley-Murray 1993: 13–20.
11. E.g., Beasley-Murray 1993: 355–65. Beasley-Murray thinks that Mark himself was responsible for turning the varied traditions behind Mark 13 into a unitary discourse (362–3).
12. One of the earliest and most impressive is Lars Hartman's 1966 study. At the heart of Mark 13, Hartman contends, lies an original 'midrash' of passages in Daniel which grew by a process of accretion into the form in which we now find it in Mark's Gospel. Hartman delineates six stages in the compositional development.

others, including N. T. Wright, think that the whole substantially derives from Jesus.[13] For the purpose of the present exercise, it is not necessary to pursue such questions. The starting point for us is the discourse as it presently stands within Mark's Gospel; issues relating to its pre-Markan history can be conveniently left to the side.

As to the subject-matter of the discourse, while a few think that the speech essentially looks beyond the destruction of Jerusalem in 70 CE to a future time and the consummation of history,[14] the majority conclude that it deals *both* with events of the time *and* the parousia of Jesus and the final end. Of this majority, most assume that the discourse reflects or anticipates (depending on the extent to which it is regarded as prophecy *ex eventu*) the events of 66–70 CE in particular,[15] but some argue that it more strongly echoes the Caligula crisis of 40–1 CE[16] and its aftermath.[17] Whether the parousia is expected within the time frame of the 'generation' mentioned in v. 30 is debated. The view of Mark 13 taken by Wright, though not without pedigree,[18] stands apart from the consensus approach. For him, the entire discourse, from beginning to end, is about the destruction of Jerusalem and its temple;[19] it has nothing to do with the second coming of Jesus or the putative end of the world. Wright calls the speech 'Jesus' Temple-discourse'.[20] As noted above, Wright takes Mark 13 as an authentic prophetic speech by Jesus; this prophecy stands as fulfilled. It does not match exactly what happened in 66–70 CE, but Jesus was not making literal predictions. Rather, he was using the metaphorical and

---

13. In a recent contribution to the discussion, S. E. Porter (2000: 210–37) has argued on text-linguistic grounds that the discourse of Mark 13 is a cohesive unit which the evangelist has incorporated without much change into his Gospel and which is 'possibly authentic Jesus tradition' (235).

14. In recent scholarship this position has been taken by C. A. Evans (2001: 292) who writes: 'Jesus words primarily have in view the end of the sinful age that would eventually and finally give way to the kingdom of God.'

15. For an exposition of this view, see esp. Hengel 1985: 1–45; Marcus 1992.

16. The Caligula crisis is the crisis occasioned by Gaius Caligula's threat to install a statue of himself in the temple at Jerusalem (Philo, *Leg. ad Gaium* 197-337; Josephus, *War* 2.184-203; *Ant.* 18.256-309). See further, Theissen 1992: 137–51.

17. Crossley 2004: 19–43; N. H. Taylor 1996; Theissen 1992: 125–65. Theissen thinks that Mark 13 originated during the Caligula crisis, but that it was given its present shape after the fall of the temple in 70 CE. For Crossley, the parallels between Mark 13 and events of the late thirties and early forties point toward a dating of the Gospel around that time.

18. In an earlier generation of scholarship, it was advocated by Gould (1896: 240–55).

19. N. T. Wright 1996: 515. So also Hatina 1996; 2002: 325–73.

20. N. T. Wright 1996: 515.

symbolic language of Old Testament prophecy and Jewish apocalyptic to speak of events which he saw as coming upon Israel.[21] France, who also believes that the discourse accurately recalls the teaching of Jesus, agrees with Wright that the bulk of the speech relates to events leading up to and including the fall of Jerusalem, but he thinks that the subject changes to the parousia at v. 32, with the mention of 'that day and that hour'.[22]

4.2 *Readings of Mark 13.24-25*

The meaning of the language of cosmic catastrophe in Mk 13.24-25 has been much discussed. Some see it as referring to the collapse of the cosmos. Lenski takes the language quite literally; he writes: 'The whole siderial world shall collapse ... All that holds the heavenly bodies in their orbits and enables sun, moon, and starts to light the earth, shall give way. Thus the sun's light will be extinguished, the moon's radiance will disappear in the same instant, and the stars will come tumbling from their places.'[23] Others take it as referring to the end of the cosmos, but in more figurative terms. Thus D. E. Nineham states that the language is 'quasi-literal' but nevertheless refers to 'the general break-up of the universe'.[24] According to F. Moloney, the language of Mk 13.24-25 is 'common apocalyptic symbolism to indicate that the world as we know it is coming to an end'. What the language points to is 'very real – the end of the world as we know it'.[25] Downing argues that the imagery of Mk 13.24-25 would have been familiar to ancient Jewish and non-Jewish readers as language for referring to the end of the cosmos, and this is how Mark's Gentile readers would have understood it.[26]

Others maintain that the cosmic phenomena of Mk 13.24-25 are cosmic/celestial 'signs' or 'portents',[27] a designation that suggests they have premonitory rather than world-ending significance. For H. Anderson, though, they are 'cosmic signs' which indicate 'the winding up of the universe'.[28]

21. N. T. Wright 1996: 340.
22. France 2002: 500. Dyer 1998: 273, 276–7; 2002: 53–5.
23. Lenski 1961: 584. So also Hahn 1975: 265–6; Tödt 1963: 34.
24. Nineham 1968: 357. Similarly Tuckett (2001: 914) thinks that the picture is that of 'the total break-up of the present cosmic order', but that the description is 'intended as a mixture of "myth" and reality'.
25. Moloney 2002: 266.
26. Downing 1995a: 202.
27. E.g., Donahue and Harrington 2002: 374; Juel 1991: 182; Taylor 1952: 517, adding, 'it seems probable that objective phenomena are meant' (518).
28. H. Anderson 1976: 298. Painter (1997: 177) states that the cosmic portents are concurrent with the end itself.

R. H. Gundry denies that the cosmic phenomena are signs; rather they are 'celestial disasters' which attend the coming of the Son of man. These disasters, though, do not constitute the end of the cosmos; Mark gives no indication that the new creation is in view. Gundry, while recognizing that it has a figurative application in the Old Testament texts from which it is borrowed, Isa. 13.10 and 34.4, is inclined to take the cosmic language more literally here. He also suggests that the sun, moon and stars are viewed here not only as celestial objects but also as astrological powers.[29] Allison opines that Mk 13.24-25 forecasts an 'astronomical disaster'. He thinks that the motif of falling stars could be referring to 'meteor showers', a phenomenon with which the ancients were quite familiar.[30]

H. B. Swete thinks that Mk 13.24-25 is primarily about 'dynastic and social revolutions' in the period between the fall of Jerusalem and the parousia,[31] a view also taken by Cole.[32]

George Beasley-Murray maintains that the language of cosmic convulsions in Mk 13.24-25 is 'theophany' language. He writes: 'the function of this ancient mythological language is purely to highlight the glory of that event [the parousia of Jesus] and set it in its proper category: it represents the divine intervention for judgment and salvation'.[33] It tells us nothing about the physical nature of Christ's expected return.

All these views are based on the understanding that the coming of the Son of man in Mk 13.26 is the parousia of Jesus, which is questioned by Wright, France and others. But not all who reject a reference to Jesus' eschatological return in v. 26 take the view that vv. 24-25 are about the destruction of Jerusalem. Dyer agrees with Wright and France that v. 26 refers to Jesus' vindication and exaltation in heaven,[34] and that vv. 24-25 refer to political upheavals in Mark's day, but he thinks that the political turmoil in view is 'the realignment of temporal powers in the East after the fall of Jerusalem'.[35] Bas Van Iersel interprets Mk 13.26-27, as do Wright and France, as a picture of Jesus' heavenly enthronement, but he argues that Mark's original readers would have understood vv. 24-25 as

29. Gundry 1993: 783.
30. Allison 1999: 131.
31. Swete 1909: 311. Yet, at the same time, he states, 'they do not exclude, perhaps they even suggest, a collapse of the present order of Nature immediately before the παρουσία'.
32. Cole 1989: 280.
33. Beasley-Murray 1993: 425. This comment is cited favourably by C. A. Evans (2001: 329). See also Vögtle 1970: 70–1.
34. Dyer 2002: 52.
35. Dyer 2002: 52; cf. 1998: 230–1.

referring to 'the dethronement of the pagan idols',[36] and in particular to the eclipse of the deities *Sol* and *Luna*, divinities which were especially popular in Rome.[37] For C. S. Mann, Mk 13.26 points to Jesus' passion, rather than his ascension and enthronement.[38] The celestial phenomena of vv. 24-25 are 'of one piece with Mark's understanding of the Passion',[39] though it is not possible, in Mann's opinion, to determine whether the evangelist intended us to understand actual astronomical activity.[40] Peter Bolt also thinks that Mk 13.26 relates to Jesus' death on the cross; Bolt sees the prediction of cosmic darkening in v. 24 as fulfilled in the darkness that came over the land when Jesus was being crucified (Mk 15.33).[41]

A wide range of views have been articulated on the meaning of the cosmic language of Mk 13.24-25. Most favour a non-literal reading, but there is no clear consensus on to what the language actually refers. In what follows, I will engage particularly with the 'destruction of Jerusalem' interpretation, while arguing for my preferred 'real' catastrophe reading.

4.3 *Introduction and First Section of the Discourse: Mark 13.1-23(24a)*

Mark 13 begins with Jesus' departure from the temple precincts, the consistent location of his teaching and controversies in the Markan narrative since 11.27. The disciples' comment about the splendour of the temple buildings (v. 1) provokes Jesus' prediction of the temple's destruction: 'Do you see these great buildings? Not one stone will be left here upon another; all will be thrown down' (v. 2). The scene switches to the Mount of Olives (v. 3), overlooking the city and its temple.[42] Jesus is seated, the normal posture of a Jewish teacher. The four disciples, Peter,

---

36. Van Iersel 1996: 90.
37. Van Iersel 1996: 89–90. In his reader-response commentary on Mark (1998), he seems to revert to a traditional parousia interpretation of v. 26 (see p. 408), while retaining his interpretation of vv. 24-25 as referring to the overthrow of pagan divinities.
38. Mann 1986: 532.
39. Mann 1986: 530.
40. Mann 1986: 531.
41. Bolt 2004: 125–6; cf. 85–115.
42. The site has eschatological associations. According to Zech. 14.4-5, when God 'comes' with all his holy ones, he will stand on the Mount of Olives. Allusion is made to Zech. 14.5 in Mk 8.38. See further below in the main text.

James, John and Andrew (the first disciples called, cf. 1.16-20), pose Jesus a question arising from his prophetic word.[43]

The question of v. 4 is actually two questions (linked in Greek by the connective καί): 'When will these things be, and what will be the sign that all these things are about to be accomplished?' (πότε ταῦτα ἔσται καὶ τί τὸ σημεῖον ὅταν μέλλῃ ταῦτα συντελεῖσθαι πάντα;) The first question plainly refers back to Jesus' prediction that the temple buildings will be torn down (v. 2). The plural 'these things' (ταῦτα) recognizes that the temple's fall would not be a solitary event but part of a larger crisis; there would at least be an offensive against the city as a whole.[44] According to Wright and France, the second question also refers to the fall of the temple:[45] the disciples not only want to know when the temple will be destroyed but also what sign will prepare them for it.[46] Yet, most commentators agree that this question looks forward to something more 'final' than the temple's destruction. France thinks that the eschatological interpretation of the second question is dependent on the assumption that the verb συντελέω is an eschatologically loaded word. The verb συντελέω, he points out, simply means 'to accomplish' or 'to bring to completion'; it need not have any eschatological connotations (cf. Lk. 4.2, 13; Acts 21.27). In the context of Mk 13.1-4, it simply refers to the completion of the process of the temple's destruction.[47] However, the eschatological sense of the second question emerges not from the word συντελέω alone, but from the larger formulation of which it is part: ταῦτα συντελεῖσθαι πάντα, 'all these things to be accomplished'. As many have recognized, we have here a very clear allusion to Dan. 12.6-7 LXX.[48] In this passage, Daniel asks how long it would be until 'the end', and the angel replies, 'when the shattering of the power of the holy people comes to an end, *all these things would be accomplished*' (καὶ συντελεσθήσεται πάντα ταῦτα, Dan. 12.7). In Dan. 12.6-7 'all these things' refers to the unprecedented 'time of anguish' referred to in 12.1; 'the end' is the end of this time of affliction and the arrival of deliverance. It is clear from the *Testament of Moses* that in the first century CE, Daniel 12 was being read in terms of the final time of trouble that

---

43. This is a recurring pattern in Mark's Gospel: 4.10; 7.17; 9.28; 10.10.
44. C. A. Evans 2001: 304.
45. N. T. Wright 2001: 178; France 2002: 506–7.
46. France 2002: 506.
47. France 2002: 508.
48. See esp. Hartman 1966: 145. France (2002: 507–8), in discussing Mk 13.4, does not indicate any awareness of this well-recognized allusion. Hatina (2002: 348–9) also seems to miss it.

marks the transition between the present age and the age of blessedness.[49] In most examples of the schema which predate or are close in time to Mark, the end-time tribulation or period of woes is followed by an unmistakably 'final' event.[50] It is natural then to see the disciples' second question as looking ahead to the eschatological climax.

The disciples, as Mark portrays them, thus relate Jesus' prediction of the temple's fall to the eschatological woes. What they are asking for in their second question is a sign that will indicate that the woes have ended and that the final divine intervention is at hand. The double question of v. 4 thus sets up the expectation that the ensuing discourse will (1) discuss the timing of the temple's demise; (2) refer to the eschatological finale.[51] Mark's Jesus does not disappoint.

The first section of the discourse, vv. 5-23, consists of predictions, warnings and exhortations. Notable in this section is the frequent use of the second person plural form:[52] most of the things about which Jesus speaks here are things that his contemporary followers – represented by the four immediate hearers – will see, hear about or endure.

On France's reading, an eschatological dimension does not come into the discourse until v. 32. However, there can be very little doubt that what Jesus describes from v. 5 to v. 23 is the final tribulation, the eschatological woes.[53] France thinks that this reading of vv. 5-23 places too much weight on the word 'birthpangs' (or 'woes').[54] However, the 'tribulation' interpretation of this section is not based on the appearance of the word 'birthpangs' alone. The whole pattern of these verses is suggestive of the scheme: wars, natural disasters including earthquakes

49. Cf. the allusion to Dan. 12.1 in *T. Mos.* 8.1.
50. God's eschatological advent (*1 En.* 90.15-19; 91.7; *T. Mos.* 10.1-7) or his awesome intervention (*Sib. Or.* 3.669-701); the day of judgement (*1 En.* 100.4); the destruction and re-creation of the cosmos (*1 En.* 80.2-8; cf. 72.1). In *4 Ezra* and *2 Baruch*, the tribulation precedes the coming of the messiah: *4 Ezra* 5.1-13; 6.13-25; etc; *2 Bar.* 26-30; 70. If Allison (1985: 17–19) is correct in his interpretation of *Jub.* 23.13-23, this text would be unique in depicting the tribulation as past.
51. Geddert (1989: 203–6) tries to argue that 13.1-4 does not set the agenda for the discourse that follows, but this is a rather strained attempt to deny the obvious and to render Mark even more esoteric than he is already.
52. βλέπετε (v. 5); ἀκούσητε, μὴ θροεῖσθε (v. 7), βλέπετε, δαρήσεσθε, σταθήσεσθε (v. 9); μὴ προμεριμνᾶτε τί λαλήσητε, λαλεῖτε, ἐστε (v. 11); ἔσεσθε (v. 13); ἴδητε (v. 14); προσεύχεσθε (v. 18); μὴ πιστεύετε (v. 21); βλέπετε (v. 23).
53. Rowland 1982: 43. N. T. Wright is happy to see these verses as about the 'birthpangs of the age to come' (1996: 346), though for him, the climax to which the traditional scheme heads is a turning point in history, rather than the actual end of history (cf. 1996: 208).
54. France 2002: 508–9, 521–3.

and famines, the persecution of the faithful, and betrayal within families and among friends, are typical of descriptions of the final time of trouble.[55] Moreover, and decisively, Jesus explicitly speaks of 'tribulation' (θλῖψις) in v. 19 in terms which plainly allude to Dan. 12.1.[56] That the section is largely couched in terms of what the disciples will actually witness and experience during their lifetime does not in any way undermine this interpretation, since Jewish descriptions of the final tribulation normally incorporate recent, current and soon expected events.[57]

The discourse itself begins with a warning: 'Beware that no one leads you astray' (v. 5). Deceivers will come (v. 6), saying 'I am he' (v. 6) and deluding many. It seems likely that messianic claimants (broadly understood) are in view (cf. vv. 22-23). Between the death of Jesus and the destruction of Jerusalem, various individuals, such as the prophet Theudas,[58] emerged, presenting themselves as agents of divine deliverance. Leading figures in the Jewish War itself apparently had 'messianic' pretensions.[59] Mark's Jesus then speaks of wars and international conflicts, and of earthquakes and famines (vv. 7-8).[60] Conflicts, earthquakes and famines are documented for the years 30–70 CE (though the period was not marked by a unique intensity of such occurrences).[61]

---

55. Sim 1996: 42–3.
56. France (2002: 527) recognizes a similarity with Dan. 12.1, but thinks it is 'unwise to press too closely any specific link with the Daniel text here'.
57. *Contra* France 1971: 231.
58. Josephus, *Ant.* 20.97-98.
59. See France 2002: 510. In the Jewish War, Menachem, the son of Judas the Galilean (Josephus, *War* 2.433-434) and Simon bar Giora (Josephus, *War* 7. 29-31) seem to have viewed themselves as 'messianic' figures; cf. Marcus 1992: 458–9.
60. The language of the first half of v. 8 is based on Isa. 19.2 ('I will stir up Egyptians against Egyptians, and they will fight, one against the other, neighbour against neighbour, city against city, kingdom against kingdom.') Cf. *4 Ezra* 13.31; 15.15.
61. These years saw several conflicts in the ancient Near East: the war between Rome and Parthia (Josephus, *Ant.* 18.96-104; Tacitus, *Ann.* 6.31-44); civil war in Parthia (Tacitus, *Ann.* 6.31-37); the war between Herod Antipas and Aretas, king of Nabatea (Josephus, *Ant.* 18.109-119); the Jewish War of 66–70 CE itself and the various stirrings in Palestine in the years leading up to it. The empire was threatened with civil war in the brief but massively turbulent period that followed the death of Nero in 68 CE. There were earthquakes at Antioch in 37 CE (Malalas, *Chron.* 243.10), Laodicea in 61 CE (Pliny, *Nat. Hist.* 2.84), Pompeii in 62 CE and Jerusalem in 67 CE (Josephus, *War* 4.286-287). There was a serious famine during the reign of Claudius (cf. Josephus, *Ant.* 3.320; 20.101; Acts 11.28); see further Winter 2001: 220–2. Food shortages were quite common in the Roman world.

These things must take place, but the 'end', which in the context must mean the final eschatological denouement, is not about to happen yet. All these events have a preliminary character; they are the 'the beginning of the birthpangs' (v. 8).

The next paragraph (vv. 9-13) focuses on what is to happen to the disciples. They will be handed over to courts, beaten in synagogues and brought before governors and kings. We read of events like this in the book of Acts.[62] The disciples will experience persecution and universal hatred because of their allegiance to Jesus (v. 13). Interrupting the flow of these verses is the affirmation of v. 10 that the gospel must first be preached to all nations;[63] significantly this is not specifically said to be something that the disciples will live to see fulfilled.[64] The family betrayal that Jesus predicts in v. 12 (using the language of Mic. 7.6) may be part of the hostility that the disciples themselves are to endure or,[65] more generally, a mark of the end-time societal decline.[66]

Verses 14-18 concentrate on events in Judaea; a great crisis is predicted. Jesus speaks in v. 14 of 'the abomination of desolation' standing where it (or he) ought not to be. When it (or he) appears, it is time to flee; those in Judaea must run to the hills. The note of urgency continues in vv. 15-16: there is no time to rescue one's possessions; one must simply run. Since haste is essential, women who are pregnant or have small children in tow will have little chance of escape (v. 17). If the flight takes place in winter, the refugees will struggle to survive (v. 18).

The 'abomination of desolation' is mentioned three times in the book of Daniel (9.27; 11.31; 12.11).[67] The exact expression, τὸ βδέλυγμα τῆς

62. Acts 16.23; 17.1-5; 24-26; all with reference to Paul. Acts 12.1-2 states that Herod Agrippa (whom Luke calls 'king') 'laid violent hands upon some who belonged to the church' and had James, the brother of John, killed. In Acts 22.19, Paul confesses his earlier harsh treatment of the believers: 'Lord ... in every synagogue I imprisoned and beat those who believed in you.'

63. This is sometimes seen as Mark's editorial addition to his source material. The adverb 'first' almost certainly means 'before the end' (cf. vv. 7, 13) rather than 'before you are handed over' (to trial).

64. The statement is expressed in the third person. For Rowland (2002: 290) this indicates that for Mark, 'there was still a significant period of time which had to elapse before Christ would vindicate the elect'. It is perhaps worth noting, though, that in Col. 1.23, the proclamation of the gospel to all creatures is regarded as having been achieved, most probably in a representative way (cf. Rom. 15.19, 23).

65. Luke (21.16) has: '*You* will be betrayed even by parents and brothers, by relatives and friends; and they will put some of you to death.'

66. Cf. *1 En.* 100.1-2; *Jub.* 23.19; *4 Ezra* 6.24.

67. In Matthew's account, the Danielic origins of the phrase are made explicit: Mt. 24.15.

ἐρημώσεως, used in Mk 13.14 occurs in Dan. 12.11 LXX. In Daniel, it refers to the blasphemous object set up in the Jerusalem temple by Antiochus Epiphanes in 167 BCE,[68] which was probably a pagan altar.[69] Mark 13.14 takes up the Danielic tradition; Jesus prophesies a future desecration of the temple, reminiscent of Antiochus' action. Though βδέλυγμα is neuter, the related participle, ἑστηκότα, 'standing', is masculine. This seems to suggest that the temple violation envisaged in v. 14 is some kind of desecrating *personal* presence within the temple (or an idolatrous manifestation in the temple, such as the erection of a statue of the emperor or a Roman god). The word ἐρημώσις suggests physical ruination and destruction; in the LXX, it is often used for the desolation of the land and the destruction of the holy city.[70] Given this connotation, and given the Markan frame of the discourse, relating the speech to the prophecy against the temple, it seems very likely that τὸ βδέλυγμα τῆς ἐρημώσεως, as it is used here, has the nuance, 'the (temple) abomination that *leads to/results in* (the) desolation (of the temple and the holy city)'.[71] In other words, the expression itself, within this context, conveys a linkage between the occurrence/appearance of the 'abomination' and the temple's anticipated destruction. Here, then, Jesus provides an answer to the disciples' first question: 'When will these things (the destruction of the temple and city) be?' Mark's Jesus effectively replies: 'The moment you see the desecrating abomination standing in the sanctuary. This will be the signal that the temple and the city's destruction is close at hand.'[72]

The parenthetical remark in v. 14, 'let the reader understand', which looks like Mark's own interjection into Jesus' speech, seems to indicate that the event had already occurred at the time of writing, though its 'true' significance may not have been obvious to the readers.

Establishing the historical reference of v. 14 has proved very difficult. Of the three main historical candidates, perhaps the best is the Zealots' occupation of the temple as their base of operations in the middle of the

---

68. Cf. 1 Macc. 1.54.
69. The exact nature of Antiochus' temple violation is disputed. For discussion of the options, see Collins 1993: 357–8, who takes it to be an altar (cf. 1 Macc. 1.59).
70. Lev. 26.34, 35; Jer. 4.7; 7.34; 22.5; 25.18; 44.6, 22; Dan. 8.13; 9.18; 1 Esd. 1.58; Jdt. 8.22.
71. Cf. Beasley-Murray 1993: 416; Dyer 1998: 223. In Dan. 9.26-27, the destruction of the temple and its sanctuary precedes the appearance of the abomination. Mark reverses this sequence.
72. Cf. N. T. Wright 2001: 182.

Jewish War, and their installation of a false high priest.[73] The Zealots' temple action took place in the winter of 67–8,[74] before the main Roman assault in the summer of 68 which left the city isolated; it would thus have allowed the necessary time for flight.[75] The masculine participle could refer to the Zealot leader or, as Ben Witherington thinks, the mock-priest Phanni.[76]

Verses 19-20 describe a period of unprecedented and unparalleled tribulation. The repetition of the words 'those days' from v. 17 may seem to indicate that vv. 19-20 are a continuation of the description of the calamity in Judaea, but as Craig Evans states, 'the warning that the period of tribulation will be so severe that unless shortened it will extinguish human life argues that the prophecy portends more than the Jewish war'.[77] These verses should probably be read, therefore, as

---

73. The others are (1) Caligula's command that a statue of himself should be set up inside the temple and (2) Titus' entry into the temple (right into the holy place) and the subsequent installation of Roman standards in the temple area (Josephus, *War* 6.316). Assuming that the Gospel was written between 65 and 75 CE, as is generally thought, the gap between the Caligula incident (40 CE) and the temple's destruction would be too great. Also, Mark would have known that Caligula's order was not carried out. Caligula's plan to erect the image of himself may well, however, have been the reference in an earlier pre-Markan form of the discourse. Titus' walk through the temple took place after the sanctuary had already been set on fire. It could not, therefore, have been interpreted as a precursor of imminent destruction. Also, by this time it was too late for anyone to flee; the war was effectively over. Moloney (2002: 261) thinks that the reference to the abomination in v. 14a and the call to flee in v. 14c refer to two different stages in the Jewish War which Mark has mistakenly conflated. But if, as Moloney thinks, Mark is writing not long after these events, it is difficult to see how the evangelist could get them so badly confused. Dyer (1998: 223–9) makes the interesting suggestion that the abomination refers to freshly minted coins carrying the image of the new emperor Vespasian which circulated in Judaea in advance of Titus' army, but the connection seems rather tenuous.

74. Josephus, *War* 4.150-157. So Marcus 1992. The problem with this view is that the Danielic expression 'abomination of desolation' more obviously suggests a *pagan* desecration of the temple rather than a Jewish one.

75. I leave aside the vexed question of the historicity of the tradition of a flight to Pella (Eusebius, *HE* 3.5.3).

76. So Witherington 2001: 345.

77. C. A. Evans 2001: 322. The term 'elect' more naturally refers to the whole true people of God, rather than the elect ones in Jerusalem and Judaea. The general idiom 'never has been ... nor will be again' (expressed in various ways) is a standard biblical one for a great disaster: Exod. 10.14; 11.6; Joel 2.2. According to France, the phrase καὶ οὐ μὴ γένηται ('and never will be'), 'sits very uncomfortably with any interpretation which understands these words to be describing the end of history'

referring to the end-time tribulation in general. Mark's Jesus does not say how long the tribulation is destined to last, only that God has shortened the days.

Verses 21-22 reiterate the warning of v. 6 about deceivers who are now specified as 'false messiahs' and 'false prophets'. In v. 23, Jesus repeats his call to be on the alert, with which he began the discourse. As Moloney states, 'The section 13:5-23 is thus carefully constructed around an elegant inclusion',[78] with vv. 5-6 mirroring vv. 21-23. Jesus has told his followers 'all things' (πάντα) in advance so that they will not be taken by surprise when they happen. The statement does not necessarily mean that the disciples have been given an exhaustive account of the end-time woes; rather they have been told everything that is directly relevant to them.

Verse 24 introduces a new section. The events described in these verses are distinguished from those previously narrated. Jesus is now dealing with what is to take place 'after that tribulation' (μετὰ τὴν θλῖψιν ἐκείνην, v. 24). There is no indication of a temporal gap between the close of the tribulation and what is about to be described. The events of vv. 24-27, it must be presumed, *directly* follow the time of distress.

According to France, the question of v. 4 requires Jesus to make specific mention of the temple's destruction within the discourse. Since he has not done so up to this point, having mentioned only its profanation (v. 14), we must presume that he comes to it now in vv. 24-27.[79] But there is nothing in the question of v. 4 that necessitates a further description of the fall of the temple beyond what Jesus has already said in v. 2. The disciples ask Jesus about the *timing* of the temple's demise; they do not press him to supply a further, more dramatic, account of the demolition. The event of the temple's destruction is in any case implicit in v. 14, if, as argued above, the expression 'the abomination of desolation' refers to a blasphemous event which leads to or brings about the crushing of the temple.

What takes place 'after that tribulation' can only be the eschatological climax. As noted above, in Jewish eschatology, the drama of the end-time woes normally culminates in a 'final' event, and this is what we should expect in vv. 24-27. It is significant that the second person plural form is not used in vv. 24-27. Thus, Jesus does not explicitly say that his hearers will be around to see these things happen.

(2002: 527). It seems to me to be quite consistent with the idea of a tribulation which is the greatest and *last* of history.

78. Moloney 2002: 249.
79. France 2002: 530; cf. 1971: 233.

4.4 *The Coming of the Son of Man: Mark 13.26-27*

In vv. 26-27, Jesus speaks of the coming of the Son of man. This is the peak-point of the whole development. These verses read:

> 26) Then they will see 'the Son of man coming in clouds' with great power and glory. 27) Then he will send out the angels, and gather his elect from the four winds, from the ends of the earth to the ends of heaven.

The conventional interpretation of vv. 26-27 understands them as about Jesus' parousia, or second coming,[80] but this reading is rejected by Wright and France. In their view, v. 26 alludes to the vision of Dan 7.9-14 and vv. 13-14 in particular. Daniel's vision is set in a throne-room or courtroom. The Ancient One, God himself, takes his throne, and myriads of angels attend him (vv. 9-10). The four great beasts, representing successive world empires (cf. vv. 1-8) receive their judgement (vv. 11-12). Then 'one like a son of man' comes into the presence of the Ancient One and is presented before him; the humanlike one is given authority, glory and an indestructible kingdom (vv. 13-14).[81] Wright and France maintain that Mk 13.26 and Gospel language of the coming of the Son in general evoke this visionary scene. In Daniel's vision, it is claimed, the 'coming' is not a downward movement from heaven to earth, but an upward movement from earth to heaven. It is not a return to earth, after a period in heaven, but an ascent into heaven.[82] Applied to Jesus, the image of 'the Son of man coming in clouds' most naturally refers to his post-mortem ascension and vindication, which is manifested precisely in the fall of divine judgement on the city of Jerusalem, described symbolically in vv. 24-25 (and in the world-wide growth of the church, expressed by the imagery of v. 27).[83]

Others have sought to defend a mainstream parousia reading of vv. 26-27, against the claims of Wright, partly on the basis of the parallels between these verses and 1 Thess. 4.13-18, a passage which without dubiety refers to Jesus' parousia.[84] For Wright, this kind of approach

---

80. The parousia of Jesus may be defined as 'the coming of the exalted Jesus from heaven to earth', an event associated with the judgement of God and the winding up of human history (Marshall 1992: 194).

81. It is not explicitly said that the humanlike one is enthroned, but this is the logical inference. As Collins (1993: 301) states, he 'is a given a kingdom, so it is reasonable to assume that he is enthroned'.

82. N. T. Wright 2002: 122. Actually, in Daniel, it is not clear that the movement is upward: see Collins 1993: 311–12.

83. France 2002: 536–7; Wright 1996: 363.

84. Allison 1999: 135; Crossley 2004: 24.

merely demonstrates that the notion of Jesus' parousia cannot be derived from Mk 13.26-27; it has to be brought into it from elsewhere.[85] However, a reference to Jesus' parousia can be securely established from Mark alone.[86]

Mark's Jesus has already spoken of the coming of the Son of man, earlier in the Gospel, at 8.38. In this saying, Jesus issues a warning: 'Those who are ashamed of me and of my words in this adulterous and sinful generation, of them the Son of man will also be ashamed when he comes in the glory of his Father with the holy angels.' France thinks that Dan. 7.9-14 controls the picture here, but this judgement can hardly stand.[87]

Talk of a coming Son of man in this verse is obviously drawn from Dan. 7.13. The references to 'glory' and 'angels' also seem to echo details of the wider vision (vv. 9-14).[88] But there are notable differences between this saying and Daniel's vision precisely at the points of apparent similarity. First, in Mk 8.38, 'coming' is for the purpose of judgement.[89] A coming for judgement is logically required by the preceding verses and by the first half of v. 38 itself. In vv. 34-38, Jesus sets out two alternatives: allegiance to him or denial of him. The consequence of present defection is future 'shaming'. The word 'ashamed' (ἐπαισχύνομαι), as Marcus observes, 'carries a nuance of eschatological judgment, as in the Septuagint'.[90] But in Dan. 7.9-14, the 'one like a son of man' comes to take up his throne. He arrives on the scene *after* judgement has taken place; he does not himself do any judging.[91] Second, in Mk 8.38, the Son of man *comes with* an angelic entourage (μετὰ τῶν ἀγγέλων

---

85. See his response to Allison in N. T. Wright 1999a: 266–7.

86. In Rev. 1.7, Dan. 7.13 is unquestionably applied to Jesus' return; the 'coming with the clouds' is from heaven to earth, not toward God. This shows that within the New Testament itself, Dan 7.13 can be given the sense that Wright wishes to exclude for Mk 13.26.

87. France 2002: 341–3.

88. So France 2002: 342.

89. In Matthew's version of the saying, the judgement is universal in scope (Mt. 16.27).

90. Marcus 1993: 166.

91. N. T. Wright (1996: 514 n. 138) disputes that the humanlike one has no juridical function. He points out that 'the whole scene is precisely forensic' and claims that the humanlike one is installed as 'the executive officer of the central Judge'. But while the right to judge may well be implied in the authority given to him at his installation, his forensic capacity is not developed in any way in the Danielic passage. The fact remains that the 'one like a son of man' does not engage in any juridical activity (this is stressed by VanderKam 1992: 188).

τῶν ἁγίων); angels accompany him in his very act of coming.[92] But in Daniel's vision, the humanlike figure *arrives into* the presence of angels. Third, in Mk 8.38, the Son of man comes *in* or *with* glory (ἐν τῇ δόξῃ), but in Dan. 7.13, glory is *given* to the 'one like a son of man' *following* his coming and his presentation before the Ancient One. In Mark, the glory with which he comes is said to be that of 'his Father' (τοῦ πατρὸς αὐτοῦ) and this is without parallel in Daniel. In 8.38, therefore, Mark is quite evidently *not* trying to reproduce the entire picture of Dan. 7.9-14. The only concrete connection with the passage in Daniel is the image of a coming Son of man.[93]

Daniel 7.13 is not the only Old Testament text on which Mk 8.38 draws; there is also a clear allusion to Zech. 14.5: 'Then the Lord my God will come, and all the holy ones with him.'[94] Both France and Wright acknowledge this echo but make nothing of it.[95] Zechariah 14 envisions God's end-time coming from heaven to earth with his angelic forces to rescue his people from their enemies. The scene is thoroughly eschatological; as J. L. McKenzie states, the main event 'is as clearly final as the author could make it'.[96]

The allusion to Zech. 14.5 illumines the connection between 'coming' and judgement which Mk 8.38 presumes. Self-evidently, it clarifies the reference to coming 'with' (μετά) angels. The influence of Zech. 14.5 also sheds light on the unusual designation of God as 'his Father'. Zechariah uses the personal possessive when speaking of God in his coming: 'the Lord my God'. The desire to establish the personal relationship between God and the Son of man, resulting in the fusion of the normally distinct categories of Son of God and Son of man, could well have arisen from the prophet's wording.[97] There is no mention of 'glory' in Zech. 14.5 or its surrounding context. The manifestation of 'glory', however, figures in other Old Testament descriptions of the coming of God.[98]

---

92. There is an alternative form of the saying of Mk 8.38 (+ par.) in Lk. 12.8 (= Mt. 10.32). In this saying, which does not involve the idea of the Son of man's coming, an angelic court, rather than an angelic entourage, seems to be in view.

93. France (2002: 343) claims that in Mk 8.38 Jesus 'looks forward' to receiving his sovereign authority at his exaltation. But in Mark's story, the Son of man is invested with sovereign authority *from the outset of his ministry* (2.10, 28).

94. The LXX reads: καὶ ἥξει κύριος ὁ θεός μου καὶ πάντες οἱ ἅγιοι μετ' αὐτοῦ. The MT has וּבָא יְהוָה אֱלֹהַי כָּל־קְדֹשִׁים עִמָּךְ.

95. France 2002: 342; N. T. Wright 2001: 111.

96. McKenzie 1974: 305.

97. The thought of Jesus as God's Son occurs at strategic points in the Gospel: 1.11; 3.11; 5.7; 9.7; 15.39.

98. See n. 107 below.

Mark 8.38 thus combines Dan. 7.13 with Zech. 14.5 on the basis of the link verb 'to come'.[99] The Danielic 'son of man' is identified with Jesus. His 'coming' is no longer a coming to God, but a coming as God's agent, *from heaven to earth*, for the purpose of eschatological judgement. It is unlikely that the whole prophecy of Zechariah 14 is being evoked in all its details; what the Markan text takes from Zechariah is the basic idea of God's eschatological coming to earth in judgement.[100] The divine function is transferred to Jesus, the Son of man.

As Richard Bauckham points out, 'much early Christian thinking about the Parousia did not derive from applying Old Testament messianic texts to Jesus but from the direct use of Old Testament texts about the coming of God'.[101] The New Testament expectation of Jesus' parousia is to a large extent a Christological specification of the Old Testament and Jewish expectation of God's end-time coming/descent to earth.[102] Mark 8.38 reflects this pattern of transferring the hope of God's advent to the exalted Jesus and in so doing expresses the essential concept of Jesus' parousia.

It is highly likely that the evangelist would wish his readers to understand the reference to the coming of the Son of man in 13.26 in the light of the previous mention of it in 8.38. In 13.36, there is a more extensive borrowing from Dan. 7.13 – 'the Son of man coming *in clouds*' – but this makes all the more striking the omission of the notion of coming *to* the Ancient One to receive a kingdom. This feature seems to have been deliberately excluded precisely to make clear that what is envisaged is a coming for judgement, as in 8.38, not an enthronement scene. Although the referent of 'they will see' is not made explicit, it does suggest an earthly vantage-point, and thus a descent to earth, not an ascent into heaven.

---

99. In the LXX of Zech. 14.5, the verb ἥκω is used, rather than ἔρχομαι. Generally in the LXX, ἥκω is the preferred word for expressing the idea of God's coming: e.g. Deut. 33.2; Ps. 97.9 LXX; Isa. 19.1; 35.4; 59.19-20. But ἔρχομαι is also used: Ps. 95.13 LXX; Isa. 30.27; 40.10; 66.18. According to Mundle ('ἔρχομαι', *NIDNTT* 1.320-4, esp. 320), the use of ἔρχομαι and ἥκω in the LXX and the New Testament 'passes over into each other'.

100. Zechariah 14.5 is applied to the parousia of Jesus in Mt. 25.31; 1 Thess. 3.13; 2 Thess. 1.7-8; *Did.* 16.7; cf. Jude 14-15.

101. Bauckham 1983: 97. As we have seen, God's advent is clearly envisioned as the final intervention and is associated with the last judgement (e.g. *1 En.* 1.3-9; 91.7; 100.4; *T. Mos.* 10.1-10), the appearance of the kingdom (*T. Mos.* 10.1-10), the resurrection of the dead (*LAB* 19.12-13) and the transformation of creation (*Jub.* 1.27-29).

102. As Matthew Black (1973: 194) notes 'It is within this theophanic tradition that the New Testament Parousia expectation belongs.'

The imagery employed in vv. 26-27 in the scenario of the Son of man's coming is entirely consistent with a picture of the coming of God:
- *Coming in clouds*: generally, in the Old Testament, it is God who travels with clouds.[103] Daniel's portrayal of the 'one like a son of man' as the cloud-rider is a re-working of the traditional image of Yahweh.[104] It is likely that the cloud reference in Dan 7.13 is taken up precisely because it is a recognizable element of portraits of God's advent.[105] When God rides with/in clouds, the direction of movement is from heaven to earth.[106]
- *Coming with power and glory*: in the Old Testament, God's coming often issues in a revelation of his 'glory'.[107] 'Power' is not immediately connected with the advent of God in the Old Testament, but it is a commonly mentioned attribute of Yahweh, especially in salvific contexts.[108]
- *Coming with angels*: God comes with an angelic entourage in Zech. 14.5, *1 En.* 1.9 and other texts.[109] Here, they are given the role of gathering up the elect.
- *Coming to gather an international people*: the gathering together of the dispersed people of Israel and Judah is a prominent element of Old Testament hope.[110] The wording of v. 27 echoes several Old Testament texts that envision that gathering of the Jewish exiles out of their far-flung places of banishment: Deut. 13.7; 30.4; Zech. 2.6. However, in this context, the language of universality functions to indicate that the redeemed company is *made up* of people from all nations (cf. 13.10). The thought here, especially in view of the mention of 'glory' in v. 26, is very close to Isa. 66.18, in which the Lord declares: 'I am coming to

---

103. Exod. 19.9; 34.5; Num. 11.25; 12.5; 2 Sam. 22.12; Pss. 18.11-12; 97.2; Isa. 19.1; Nah. 1.3.

104. Clouds figure in some of the most vivid Old Testament descriptions of God's coming, involving 'shaking' in nature: Judg. 5.4-5; 2 Sam. 22.8-20; Pss. 18.7-19; 97.2-5; Nah. 1.3-5.

105. Mark's ἐν νεφέλαις differs from Daniel's ἐπὶ τῶν νεφελῶν τοῦ οὐρανοῦ (LXX). ἐν νεφέλαις is used in Ps. 18.11 (LXX 17.12).

106. Cf. *Gen. Rabb.* 13.11: 'R. Johanan said: Clouds come from above, as it is written, *And, behold, with clouds of heaven* (Dan. 7.13)', noted by Crossley (2004: 25).

107. Isa. 59.19; 66.18; Hab. 3.3.

108. E.g., Pss. 21.13; 46.1; 59.16; 66.3.

109. In addition to Zech. 14.5, see Deut. 33.2; Ps. 68.17; Zech. 9.14-15.

110. Isa. 11.11; 27.12-13; 43.6; 60.1-9, etc.

gather all nations and tongues; and they shall come and shall see my glory'.[111]

Mark 13.26-27 thus builds on and reinforces the fusion of the Danielic image of a coming Son of man with Zechariah's image of God's coming to earth in judgement in 8.38, by adding other Old Testament 'coming of God' images and applying them to Jesus.[112] As we will see, the cosmic references of vv. 24-25 strengthen the picture of God's coming. Without employing the term παρουσία these verses nevertheless convey the thought of Jesus' eschatological coming as God's agent of final deliverance and judgement.[113]

The internal Markan evidence for a reference to Jesus' parousia in 13.26-27 is thus compelling. The conventional parousia interpretation of the coming of the Son of man in 13.26 coheres with Mark's previous reference to the Son of man's coming in 8.38, which is a coming *to earth* for judgement;[114] it is consistent with all the images and details of 13.26-27; also, it fits the literary context, which requires a final, history-consummating event at this point. To this evidence, sufficiently persuasive in itself, we may add the widespread New Testament testimony to early Christian belief in the return of Jesus, an event, which as Maurice Casey emphasizes, is often referred to as his 'coming'.[115] In the light of this testimony, it is extremely difficult to believe that an early Christian audience would not have heard a reference to Jesus' 'second coming' in these verses. There are parallels to Mark's combination of the Danielic 'son of man' figure with 'coming of God' imagery in the first-century

---

111. Cf Westermann 1969: 424.

112. It is hard to see how the imagery would fit a reference to Jesus' crucifixion; *contra* Bolt; Mann.

113. Hatina (1996: 62) agrees that the picture is that of God's coming to dispense judgement and vindicate the righteous, but he does not think that this imagery necessarily implies a reference to the final judgement in history. However, in post-biblical Jewish eschatological texts, God's coming is very clearly the *final* intervention and is associated with other final events. See above, n. 101.

114. There is one more reference to the future coming of the Son of man in the Gospel, at 14.62, where Jesus says to the High Priest, 'you will see the Son of man sitting at the right hand of the power and coming with clouds of heaven'. Jesus' asseveration combines Dan. 7.13 with Ps. 110.1. France (2002: 612) again thinks that the heavenly exaltation of Jesus is in view, 'sitting' and 'coming' referring to the one concept, that of 'sovereign authority'. However, it is more natural to see a distinction between sitting and the coming, the former referring to Jesus' heavenly session, the latter to his eschatological coming, as indicated in Mk 8.38.

115. Casey 1979: 176.

Jewish writings, *1 Enoch* 37-71 and *4 Ezra* (ch. 13).[116] By contrast, as Wright himself acknowledges, there is *nothing* in the historical Jewish sources remotely approaching a parallel to the alleged application of the motif of the coming of the Son of man to the temple's destruction.[117] As Crossley states, 'The return of Jesus ... would have been the only way this text could have been taken by the Markan audience, and indeed any first-century Christian audience, on the basis of the available evidence.'[118]

The view of Wright and France that the cosmic language of 13.24-25 concerns the fall of Jerusalem is dependent on their reading of v. 26 in terms of Jesus' post-mortem vindication. In showing that the parousia interpretation is really the only legitimate interpretation of the first-century historical meaning of vv. 26-27, their reading of vv. 24-25 has already been dealt a decisive blow. This also applies to other explanations of vv. 24-25 which are linked to a non-parousia understanding of v. 26.[119]

4.5 *The Language of Cosmic Catastrophe in Mark 13.24-25*

We come then to Mk 13.24-25. As the layout given below (following NA 27) shows, Mk 13.24b-25 is poetic in style, reflecting traditional Hebrew parallelism.

the sun will be darkened,
and the moon will not give its light,
and the stars will be falling from heaven,
and the powers in the heavens will be shaken.

ὁ ἥλιος σκοτισθήσεται,
καὶ ἡ σελήνη οὐ δώσει τὸ φέγγος αὐτῆς,
καὶ οἱ ἀστέρες ἔσονται ἐκ τοῦ οὐρανοῦ πίπτοντες,
καὶ αἱ δυνάμεις αἱ ἐν τοῖς οὐρανοῖς σαλευθήσονται.

The first two 'lines' stand in obvious parallel, linked by the common pairing of sun and moon and also by the thought of darkening. The reference to heaven/the heavens links the third and fourth lines. The language is clearly derived from Old Testament prophetic passages.[120] Let us examine the Old Testament influences.

---

116. See further Adams 2005b: 44–8. This present section (4.4) on the coming of the Son of man in 13.26-27 is an abridged version of pp. 48–59 of that article.
117. N. T. Wright 1996: 519.
118. Crossley 2004: 25.
119. I.e., the views of Bolt, Dyer, Mann and Van Iersel.
120. The fullest discussion of the Old Testament background to vv. 24-25 is to be found in Verheyden 1997: 534–40. But see also Dyer 1998: 110–13; Hatina 2002: 326–31; D. Wenham 1984: 309–11.

4.5.1 Identifying the Old Testament Influences

The principal Old Testament texts on which these verses draw are Isa. 13.10 and 34.4 LXX. Joel 2.10 and 4.15-16 LXX also seem to have exerted some influence.[121]

The first line, ὁ ἥλιος σκοτισθήσεται, takes its vocabulary from Isa. 13.10 LXX (ὁ ἥλιος and the future passive σκοτισθήσεται). Isaiah 13.10 LXX reads καὶ σκοτισθήσεται τοῦ ἡλίου ἀνατέλλοντος, 'and it shall be dark at sunrise'. Mark (or his source) does not appropriate the reference to the sun's rising. The second line, καὶ ἡ σελήνη οὐ δώσει τὸ φέγγος αὐτῆς, closely reflects Isa. 13.10 LXX (καὶ ἡ σελήνη οὐ δώσει τὸ φῶς αὐτῆς).[122] The only difference is that Mark has φέγγος for φῶς, which may derive from Joel 2.10 or 4.15.[123] The third line, καὶ οἱ ἀστέρες ἔσονται ἐκ τοῦ οὐρανοῦ πίπτοντες, is based on Isa. 34.4. The LXX of Isa. 34.4 has πάντα τὰ ἄστρα πεσεῖται ('all the stars shall fall').[124] Mark's addition of τοῦ οὐρανοῦ, 'from heaven', may be picking up the opening words of the LXX of Isa. 13.10: οἱ γὰρ ἀστέρες τοῦ οὐρανοῦ ('the stars of heaven').[125] Mark does not take up Isaiah's comparison of the fall of the stars to the dropping of leaves from a vine and leaves from a fig tree. The fourth line, καὶ αἱ δυνάμεις αἱ ἐν τοῖς οὐρανοῖς σαλευθήσονται, resembles the opening clause of the variant of Isa. 34.4 in LXX B and Theodotion: καὶ τακήσονται πᾶσαι αἱ δυνάμεις τῶν οὐρανῶν ('and all the powers of the heavens shall melt'). This is a rendering of the Hebrew, 'all the host of heaven shall rot away'. The clause is omitted altogether in the Alexandrian tradition, and in Isa. 34.4 LXX B, it is evidently an interpolation.[126] It is possible that Mark's noun phrase, αἱ δυνάμεις αἱ ἐν τοῖς οὐρανοῖς, is derived from an early Greek translation of Isa. 34.4a

---

121. Isaiah 13.10 refers to the stars, sun and moon, but Mark's sequence is sun, moon and stars, which corresponds to the order in which they are mentioned in Joel 2.10 and 4.15.

122. The LXX of Ezek. 32.7 (καὶ σελήνη οὐ μὴ φάνῃ τὸ φῶς αὐτῆς), though a clear parallel, is less close to the wording.

123. Though in Joel, it occurs in connection with the stars.

124. In contrast to the simple future tense of πεσεῖται in Isa. 34.4, Mark has the periphrastic construction, ἔσονται ... πίπτοντες.

125. Van Iersel (1996: 88–9) suggests that v. 25a echoes Isa. 14.12-15 ('How you are fallen from heaven, O Day Star, son of Dawn!', Isa. 14.12a; the LXX reads: πῶς ἐξέπεσεν ἐκ τοῦ οὐρανοῦ ὁ ἑωσφόρος ὁ πρωὶ ἀνατέλλων). N. T. Wright (1996: 355) also thinks Isa. 14.12-15 is influential. A secondary echo of Isa. 14.12 cannot be ruled out, but the primary influence is plainly Isa. 34.14; cf. Verheyden 1997: 535 n. 43.

126. Verheyden 1997: 538.

which has been preserved in the variant reading of LXX B.[127] But it is also possible that the reading of LXX B is based on Mk 13.25 (or more likely Mt. 24.29). In my view, the phrase is best explained as Mark's reworking of the LXX expression, ἡ δύναμις τοῦ οὐρανοῦ ('the power of heaven') which translates 'host of heaven' on several occasions (but not of course in Isa. 34.4).[128] Mark uses the plural form, αἱ δυνάμεις, to take up the subjects of the previous lines (sun, moon and stars).[129] The motif of shaking is found in Isa. 13.13, Joel 2.10 and 4.16, but the verb used in the LXX of each of these passages is σείω rather than σαλεύω as in Mk 13.25. J. Verheyden points out that in the LXX, σαλεύω is used more frequently in Old Testament theophany texts (Isa. 64.1-2; Mic. 1.4; Nah. 1.5-6; Hab. 3.6),[130] and that the only instance in which it occurs with the heavens as its subject is in a theophany context (Sir. 16.18). He suggests that this verb has been chosen precisely in order to depict the coming of the Son of man in vv. 26-27 as a theophany.

As Verheyden notes, these lines of Mk 13.24b-25 do not 'merely reproduce the text of the LXX'.[131] They are a creative reworking of the passages on which they depend. What we have in Mk 13.24-25 are not Old Testament quotations as such, but as Verheyden puts it, 'a freely formulated ... conflation of related OT texts'.[132] The result of the conflation is 'a quite different text' to any of its sources.[133] How, then, should the language be interpreted? Let us deal first with the view that it is a symbolic description of the fall of the Jerusalem and the temple.

4.5.2 *The Destruction of Jerusalem and the Temple?*

Wright's (and France's) view that 13.24-25 refers to the destruction of Jerusalem and its temple is related to a larger claim that the whole discourse (or the major part of it according to France) is entirely conditioned by the prophecy of the temple's demolition in v. 2 and does not look beyond this event. But I have argued against this claim. The question of v. 4 links the prophesied temple destruction to the climax of all history, and Mark's Jesus deals with both in the discourse that

---

127. Hatina 2002: 330; Verheyden 1997: 538.
128. 2 Kings 17.16; 21.3, 5; 23.4, 5; 2 Chron. 18.18 (but without the article).
129. The grammatical structure, αἱ δυνάμεις αἱ ἐν τοῖς οὐρανοῖς seems to reflect Mark's own style; cf. 11.25, ὁ πατὴρ ὑμῶν ὁ ἐν τοῖς οὐρανοῖς.
130. Verheyden 1997: 546.
131. Verheyden 1997: 534.
132. Verheyden 1997: 540.
133. Verheyden 1997: 540.

follows. The climactic event is his own eschatological coming, as God's agent of final deliverance (vv. 26-27).

Linguistically, Wright's 'destruction of Jerusalem' interpretation of vv. 24-25 is based on his contentions that the cosmic language we find in these verses was regularly used by Old Testament prophets to describe local socio-political upheavals and that subsequent Jewish writers, especially the apocalyptists, continued to use the language in this way. Wright may be right about the use of global/cosmic catastrophe language in Old Testament passages such as Isaiah 13 and 34, but the usage (as we saw in Chapter 1) is much debated, and in my view it is best explained in terms of a strategy of particularization which grounds the announcement of impending local judgement in the genuine expectation of ultimate universal judgement by global or cosmic catastrophe. Also, in later Old Testament prophetic oracles, such as Isaiah 24, global/cosmic disaster language has a more exclusively eschatological reference. Crucially, Wright is incorrect about the subsequent usage of catastrophe language in post-biblical Jewish apocalyptic and related sources. In none of the relevant post-biblical texts examined in Chapter 2 is the reference to the downfall of city or nation. The evidence of the parallel material in Jewish apocalyptic and associated writings *strongly counts against* his reading of Mk 13.24-25. France, as we have previously noted,[134] acknowledges that later Jewish apocalyptic writers employed this kind of language with a more 'end of the world' sense, and even recognizes that it sometimes refers to universal judgement in Old Testament prophecy, but insists that the more regular prophetic style of usage, for judgement against specific places, as in Isaiah 13, 34, etc., is determinative for Mk 13.24-25.[135] However, even if the originally intended meaning of the catastrophe language in Isaiah 13; 34, etc., could be established with absolute certainty, subsequent post-biblical Jewish usage of this kind of language (from the third century BCE to the end of the first century CE) has to be regarded as more important for interpreting Mk 13.24-25,[136] and the fact remains that this evidence does not support a narrow socio-political reading of these verses.

Hatina defends the 'destruction of Jerusalem' interpretation of Mk 13.24-25 on intertextual rather than linguistic grounds.[137] He argues that

---

134. Introduction, p. 11.
135. France 2002: 532–3.
136. On the priority of synchrony over diachrony in determining linguistic meaning, see Cotterell and Turner 1989: 25–6, 131–5.
137. Hatina (2002: 363) acknowledges that in Jewish pseudepigraphal literature, images of cosmic disaster 'express a sense of finality' (though he doubts that they imply an actual universal catastrophe).

the allusions to Isa. 13.10 and 34.4 are meant to call to mind the larger oracles of which they are part (Isaiah 13 and 34 as whole prophecies) and the fact these oracles are principally concerned with judgement on Babylon and Edom respectively.[138] When Mk 13.24-25 is read with the fuller contexts of Isa. 13.10 and 34.4 in view, it becomes clear that what is being predicted is the doom of a city. Within Mark 13, that city is Jerusalem. However, it is not evident that the full oracles of Isaiah 13 and 34 are being evoked in Mk 13.24-25. The Markan verses, as we have seen, draw on the imagery and language of Isa. 13.10 and 34.4, along with other Old Testament passages – one of which is in fact part of an oracle exclusively concerned with universal judgement (Joel 3.15) – but in such a way as to form a text which is actually rather different to any of its sources. This is not to say that Mark or his source selected material from Isa. 13.10 and 34.4 with blatant disregard for the literary contexts of these verses, but it was probably the *immediate* context of the prophetic verses, the connection with worldwide judgement, rather than the wider context and the subsequent targeting of a city, which prompted the use of them. There is no indication in Mk 13.24-27 or anywhere else within the discourse that the fate of Babylon and Edom is being recalled. The fact that Mark's Jesus, having spoken of cosmic upheaval utilizing the language of Isa. 13.10 and 34.4, does *not* go on to localize and particularize it, by referring to a specific place, more obviously suggests that the universal and cosmic perspective of Isa. 13.6-13 and 34.1-4 is the *exclusive* focus of interest. A universal event is certainly in view in v. 27.

The 'destruction of Jerusalem' interpretation of Mk 13.24-25 should, therefore, be discounted; it is contextually inappropriate and it is at odds with (what seems to have been) contemporary Jewish usage of the language.[139] The relevant parallel data militates against *any* historicizing interpretation of these verses, including Dyer's view that they refer to political turmoil after Jerusalem's fall and Swete's and Cole's view that the reference is to 'dynastic and social revolutions' during the whole period between 70 CE and the return of Christ.

138. Hatina 2002: 358–9, 363–4.
139. It is worth making the point here that the 'destruction of Jerusalem' interpretation of Mk 13.24-27 is very difficult to sustain on the view that Mark's Gospel was written after 70 CE. The final section of Mark 13 emphasizes the need for constant watchfulness and ends with a call issued to the readers as a whole to 'keep awake' (v. 37). This would be superfluous had the prophecy been fulfilled at the time of writing. One could perhaps argue, as France does, that 13.31-37 leaves the topic of Jerusalem's fall behind, and deals with the parousia, but this imposes a change in subject-matter which is not signalled in the text.

4.5.3 *Illumination by Comparison*

It makes good exegetical sense to use the comparative material, explored in the first part of this study, to illuminate Mk 13.24-25. As we saw in Chapter 3, cosmic shaking, the failure of the sun and the moon and the falling of stars figure in Stoic portrayals of the coming cosmic conflagration.[140] As Downing has suggested, Mark's Gentile readers, might well have recognized the commonalities and, on that basis, have taken the language in 'end of the cosmos' terms. However, since the terminology and motifs in Mk 13.24-25 are so very clearly derived from the Old Testament, and definitely not from Stoic sources, we cannot be certain that Mark was aware of the Stoic parallels and wanted to evoke them.

For the purpose of clarifying the meaning which Mark himself wanted to convey, the Jewish comparative data are key. In Jewish apocalyptic and related writings, as we have seen, there are texts which speak of 'preliminary' celestial abnormalities as well as texts envisioning a global/cosmic catastrophe. We will consider first the potential relevance of the former.

The darkening of the sun and moon or the disruption of their normal cycles is a 'portent' of the end/deliverance or a feature of the end-time woes in a number of texts.[141] The fall of stars functions as sign and messianic woe in the Ethiopic version of *4 Ezra* 5.4b-5. As 'preliminary' events, these celestial disturbances are not in themselves world-ending, though in *1 En.* 80.4-8 and *LAB* 19.13, they belong to the drawn-out process of cosmic expiration.

The cosmic occurrences of Mk 13.24-25 are firmly distinguished from the 'tribulation' (v. 24a); thus they are not presented as eschatological woes. Even so, they do seem to function as portents. The cosmic events obviously herald the coming of the Son of man and, in this sense, they are signs of it. Indeed, they appear to constitute the conclusive 'sign' requested by the disciples that the tribulation is over and redemption is nigh (v. 2). But, as Hooker states, insofar as they are signs of the coming of the Son of man they are signs that are 'part of the event itself', leaving no time for preparations.[142] The narrative sequence indicates that the cosmic occurrences precede the coming of the Son of man, but there is no indication of a gap in time between them.[143] The celestial upheavals

140. See pp. 122–64.
141. *1 En.* 80.4-8; *LAB* 19.13; *4 Ezra* 5.4b-5; *Sib. Or.* 3.796-804; 5.346-349.
142. Hooker 1991: 301–2.
143. In v. 26 (and also in v. 27) τότε probably means 'then' in the sense of 'at that time' rather than 'then' in the sense of 'next in order of occurrence'. Cf. Gundry 1993: 783.

evidently continue *as* the Son of man comes. They both *announce* and *accompany* the eschatological coming. They are not, then, really equivalent to the preliminary celestial malfunctions of *1 En.* 80.4-8; *LAB* 19.13, etc. While the darkening of the sun and moon, and even falling stars, could be interpreted as ominous portents, and events that fall short of full-blown cosmic disaster, the image of cosmic shaking is more readily suggestive of a world-threatening catastrophe.

Jewish texts that envisage a global/cosmic catastrophe are more obviously relevant to Mk 13.24-27. Of these, the passages that exhibit the 'catastrophic intervention' pattern stand closest to it.[144]

The coming of the Son of man, as we have seen, is depicted in vv. 26-27 in terms of the coming of God. The cosmic phenomena of vv. 24-25 add to that picture by making it a theophanic manifestation. It is true that none of the Old Testament texts on which Mk 13.24-25 draws is a theophany text; rather they are, in their original contexts, descriptions of the 'day of the Lord'. But, as noted above, the idea of a theophany is conveyed by the verb σαλεύω, which is a characteristic term in Septuagintal theophany descriptions, and which is not derived from Isa. 13.10; 34.4; Joel 2.10, 31.[145] Also, as we have seen, the distinct notion of the 'day of the Lord' is to a large extent fused with the idea of God's coming or the eschatological theophany in Jewish apocalyptic and associated writings.

Mark 13.24-27 invites comparison with the depictions of God's coming in *1 En.* 1.3b-9, 102.1-3 and *T. Mos.* 10. In *1 En.* 1.3b-9, God comes down from heaven with his angelic host to execute judgement and to preserve his elect. The catastrophic convulsions, though, are confined to the earth. In *1 En.* 102.2, which presupposes the portrait of *1 En.* 1.3b-9, 'the heavens and all the luminaries' are 'shaken with great fear' at the eschatological theophany. This is quite close to Mark's 'the powers in the heavens will be shaken'.[146] *Testament of Moses* 10.5 speaks of the darkening of the sun and moon, the reddening of the moon, and the deflection of the stars in their orbits. The pattern of solar, lunar and

---

144. *1 En.* 1.3b-9; 102.1-3; 1 QH 11.19-36; *T. Mos.* 10.3-6; *2 Bar.* 32.1; *Apoc. Zeph.* 12.5-8; *Sib. Or.* 3.675-681.

145. Beasley-Murray 1993: 424; Verheyden 1997: 544–6. The verb σαλεύω occurs in the LXX of Judg. 5.5; Pss. 17.8 (= MT 18.7); 76.19 (= 77.18); 95.9 (= 96.9); 96.4 (= 97.4); 97.7 (= 98.7) 113.7 (= 114.7); Job 9.6; Amos 9.5; Nah. 1.5; Hab. 3.6; Jdt. 16.15; Sir. 16.18; 43.16. It should be remembered that the theophany texts, Micah 1, Nahum 1 and Habukkuk 3, are as much concerned with judgement as 'day of the Lord' texts. Verheyden's otherwise excellent (1997) study of the cosmic language of Mk 13.24-25 is marred by the false dichotomy he draws between theophany as salvation-event and 'day of the Lord' as judgement.

146. In *1 Enoch* 1, however, the verb is σείω.

stellar disruptions (in that order) is similar to Mk 13.24b-25a. Like Mk 13.24-25, this text utilizes Isa. 13.10 and Joel 2.10, though Joel 2.31 is more influential on the wording. The larger eschatological scenario of *Testament of Moses* 7-10 is also very close to Mk 13.5-27: after a time of tribulation the like of which has never been seen since creation began (*T. Mos.* 8.1; cf. Mk 13.19, 24a), God descends from his heavenly habitation, and global and cosmic havoc ensues; he comes in full view of human onlookers (*T. Mos.* 10.7; cf. Mk 13.26, 'they will see') to execute vengeance on his enemies and to rescue his chosen people (10.8-10; cf. Mk 13.27). Now, I am not suggesting that Mark is literarily dependent on any of these passages; the point is that Mk 13.24-27 conforms to a well-established and probably well-known Jewish eschatological pattern.

Jewish 'catastrophic intervention' texts employ traditional prophetic images of cosmic turmoil and large-scale catastrophe. Old Testament prophetic texts such as Isa. 13.10, 24.19 and Joel 2.10 serve as resources for envisioning the coming divine irruption. Mark 13.24-27 exhibits a similar redeployment of Old Testament texts and images in connection with the eschatological coming of the Son of man.

Since the Jewish catastrophe texts anticipate actual catastrophic happenings, it would seem likely that Mk 13.24-27 does so too. Is there anything in Mark 13 itself that would point to such an interpretation? The prediction of 'earthquakes' (σεισμοί) in Mk 13.8 very plainly looks for real earthquakes (few would dispute this). From this, the inference may be drawn that objective cosmic 'shaking' and other upheavals are expected in vv. 24-25. This is not, of course, to say that the language of vv. 24-25 is meant 'literally'. My claim is that like the writers of *1 Enoch* 1, etc., the evangelist very probably expects the stereotypical images of catastrophe to translate into actual cosmological events of a calamitous nature.

But does Mk 13.24-27 envisage the catastrophic end of the cosmos? In Jewish apocalyptic and related writings, God's catastrophic intervention does not usually result in the destruction of the cosmos, at least not explicitly; it does so only in *Apoc. Zeph.* 12.5-8. One might argue that since the earth still seems to be in existence in v. 27, the upheavals of vv. 24-25 cannot be world-ending. But the scene being evoked could be that of the cosmos in *process* of collapse. From Mk 13.24-27 alone, it is not possible to determine whether the convulsions occasion cosmic dissolution. However, an 'end of the cosmos' reading is suggested when these verses are read alongside v. 31.

4.6 The Catastrophic End of the Cosmos? Reading Mark 13.24-25 in Association with 13.31

In Mk 13.31, Jesus asserts, 'heaven and earth will pass away, but my words will not pass away' (ὁ οὐρανὸς καὶ ἡ γῆ παρελεύσονται, οἱ δὲ λόγοι μου οὐ μὴ παρελεύσονται).[147] This statement seldom figures in discussion of the interpretation of vv. 24-25. Yet, in view of the close contextual proximity of this verse to vv. 24-25 and the fact that both employ language of cosmic instability and insecurity, it seems natural to bring them into association. Wright comments on v. 31 that Jesus' statement must not be taken 'as an indication that the discourse has after all been about the end of the space-time universe'.[148] But as Crispin Fletcher-Louis states, 'it is difficult to imagine that the language of 13:31 should not refer specifically to what has preceded'.[149]

The statement of 13.31 seems to be modelled structurally on Isa. 40.8 ('The grass withers, the flower fades; but the word of our God will stand forever'), even though there are no explicit verbal allusions to that verse. The first half of Mk 13.31 reads as an unequivocal statement of the ultimate cessation of the created universe, and most commentators take it as such, though it is often stressed that the emphasis falls on the permanence of Jesus' words.[150] Wright, though, denies that it speaks of the end of the created cosmos. In his view, the reference to heaven and earth passing away is a 'typical Jewish metaphor' meaning *'even though* heaven and earth ... should pass away' (italics mine).[151] It is 'a way of drawing attention to the unshakeableness ... of the prophetic word, much as in Isa 40.8'.[152] It is, he states, 'like saying "Truly, truly, I say to you", only magnified to the furthest degree'.[153] The formulation is simply an emphatic way of affirming the authority of Jesus' words. According to France, in Mk 13.31, Jesus is appealing to the order of creation as 'a guarantee of permanence', in the manner of Isa. 51.6, 54.9-10, Jer. 31.35-36 and 33.20-21. He comments, 'This verse is not therefore

---

147. In context, it serves to support the preceding affirmation (v. 30, to which it is linked by the verb 'pass away', παρέρχομαι). But it also functions by extension to endorse the validity and durability of all of Jesus' teaching in the discourse.

148. N. T. Wright 1996: 364.

149. Fletcher-Louis 1997: 148.

150. E.g., H. Anderson 1976: 300; C. A. Evans 2001: 335; Gould 1896: 235; Hooker 1991: 31; Moloney 2002: 269; Witherington 2001: 349.

151. Cf. Nineham 1968: 360: 'The idiom is Hebrew and the meaning "though heaven and earth should pass away, my word will not pass away".'

152. N. T. Wright 1996: 364 n. 168.

153. N. T. Wright 1996: 365. Cf. Beasley-Murray 1993: 451.

speaking of a future passing away of heaven and earth as something which may be contemplated, still less as part of what Jesus is predicting, but rather, as in Isaiah and Jeremiah, using the unthinkableness of such an event as a guarantee for the truth of what Jesus has declared.'[154]

I do not dispute that the emphasis of this verse lies on the durability of Jesus' words. Yet, the saying expresses the permanence of Jesus' teaching *by means* of a contrast with the impermanence of the cosmos. As David Sim puts it, 'it is precisely the ephemeral nature of the present order which gives point to the christological statement'.[155] In Lk. 16.17, the passing away of heaven and earth is expressed in more conditional terms ('But it is easier for heaven and earth to pass away'),[156] but the saying of Mk 13.31 cannot be taken in this way. There is no element of conditionality; the grammar does not permit the sense that Wright wants to give it ('even though ... '). Grammatically, the verse presents two equally valid, yet contrasting (as indicated by the adversative δέ), truths – creation will be dissolved; Jesus' words will endure. As Fletcher-Louis points out, Wright's appeal to Isa. 40.8 actually counts against his reading, since Isaiah obviously 'believes that the grass and flowers do *literally* expire'.[157]

France confuses Old Testament teachings about creation's future. It is true, as we saw in Chapter 1, that the order of creation often serves in the Old Testament as a guarantee of permanence. In Jer. 31.35-36 and 33.20-21, the permanence and fixity of the created order assure God's faithfulness to Israel. But the point of Isa. 51.6 is rather different. Like Ps. 102.25-27, Isa. 51.6 affirms that the seemingly permanent realities of heaven and earth will be outlasted by God and his salvation.[158] Mark 13.31 stands in the tradition of Ps. 102.25-27 and Isa. 51.6, not that of Jer. 31.35-36 and 33.20-21 (Isa. 54.9-10 refers to the mountains and hills). It is an unequivocal statement that heaven and earth will be dissolved. Not only is the end of heaven and earth contemplated, but it is also set forth as a definite and certain prospect. As Sim states, 'A more clear expression of the end of the present cosmic order would be difficult to find.'[159]

Fletcher-Louis agrees on the unequivocal nature of Mk 13.31. In his view, though, it expresses not the thought of the collapse of the cosmos, but that of the end of the Jewish temple. He argues that Mk 13.31 reflects

---

154. France 2002: 540.
155. Sim 1993: 8.
156. On this form of the saying, see below n. 221.
157. Fletcher-Louis 2002: 120.
158. See pp. 31–2. The MT of Isa. 54.10 seems to contemplate the end of the mountains.
159. Sim 1993: 8.

the Jewish belief that the Jerusalem temple is a microcosm of heaven and earth.[160] Language of heaven and earth 'passing away' is thus metaphorical for the demise of the temple, prophesied at the beginning of the chapter (13.2).[161]

Fletcher-Louis's interpretation of v. 31 is dependent on a temple-focused reading of vv. 5-31 as a whole, and vv. 24-25 in particular, a reading which, as I have endeavoured to show, is not really sustainable. That an analogy was frequently drawn in Jewish writings between the temple and the cosmos is clear.[162] What is far less clear is whether the mere mention of 'heaven and earth' would have been sufficient to activate the symbolism. After all, the phrase 'heaven and earth' is ubiquitous in the Old Testament and in Jewish literature and occurs all over the place without any explicit temple associations. In Mk 13.27, 'heaven' and 'earth' unquestionably refer to the physical heaven and earth. That the terms suddenly become metaphorical for the temple in v. 31 does not seem very likely. Nowhere else in Mark are the terms 'heaven' and 'earth' connected with the temple.

Mark 13.31a most obviously reads as an unambiguous affirmation of the ultimate cessation of the created order, and in my view there are no legitimate textual grounds for taking it in any other way. The idea of creation coming to an end is not at all foreign to Jewish theology and eschatology. The cessation of the present creation is both implied and explicitly taught in the Old Testament, and, as was demonstrated in Chapter 2, it is a well-attested conviction in Jewish apocalyptic and related writings. It is thus entirely plausible, within a Jewish context, that the evangelist (or even Jesus himself) should express it.

If we assume that Mark 13 is an internally coherent discourse, presenting a consistent eschatological scheme, and not merely a pastiche of traditions, it seems reasonable to connect the passing away of heaven and earth in v. 31 with the cosmic upheavals of vv. 24-25.

Now one could maintain that the 13.24-27 and 13.31a relate to two different events in Mark's eschatological programme, the parousia of Jesus and the ultimate passing away of heaven and earth (prior to its re-creation), events separated by an intermediate phase of eschatological fulfilment, characterized by Christ's reign on earth. This would be to read the eschatological scheme of Mark 13 in terms of a 'premillennial' interpretation of the eschatological denouement of Rev. 19.11–22.5.[163]

160. Fletcher-Louis 1997: 156–62.
161. Fletcher-Louis 1997: 162
162. See the evidence collated in Fletcher-Louis 1997: 156–62.
163. See further Chapter 7, p. 247.

Craig Blomberg seems to take this line.[164] However, there is no indication in Mark 13 or anywhere else in the Gospel that a temporary messianic reign is expected to intervene between the parousia and the ultimate end. Mark appears to operate with a straightforward and uncomplicated division between this age and the age of blessedness to come (10.30).

The saying on the passing away of heaven and earth in v. 31 is not a direct comment on vv. 24-27, so we cannot be certain that Mark intended his readers to view the latter in the light of the former. But given the shared language of 'cosmic fragility',[165] it is not unreasonable to take the announcement that 'heaven and earth will pass away' as expressing the outcome of the catastrophe envisaged in vv. 24-25.[166]

4.7 Timing of the Catastrophe and Consequences of the End of the Cosmos in Mark

We must now deal with the issues of timing and consequences. We will take up first the question of the timescale linked with the catastrophic intervention of 13.24-27.

4.7.1 Timescale

Is the coming of the Son of man set within a restricted time frame? Many have thought that it is, on the basis of the declaration made by Jesus in 13.30: 'this generation will not pass away until all these things have taken place'. It is virtually certain that 'this generation' means the generation living at the time of utterance.[167] The time frame in this verse is thus the lifetime of Jesus' own contemporaries. The key question, though, is, what is meant by 'all these things', ταῦτα πάντα? Does it include the coming of the Son of man, and the catastrophe that accompanies it?

Verse 30 should be read in close connection with vv. 28-29. In v. 28, Jesus advises his hearers to learn from the fig tree. As leaves on the tree show that summer is near, 'So also, when you see these things (ταῦτα) taking place, you know that it/he is near (ἐγγύς ἐστίν), at the very gates.'

---

164. Blomberg 1999: 28–9.
165. Fletcher-Louis 2002: 122.
166. Cosmic darkness is connected with the end of the cosmos in *4 Ezra* 7.39; *Sib. Or.* 3.80-92; 5.477-480; the fall of the stars is a prominent feature of the 'end of the cosmos' scene in *Sib. Or.* 5.512-531.
167. This is the sense of the word elsewhere in Mark (8.12, 38; 9.19). A generation covers roughly a period of 40 years.

The words ἐγγύς ἐστίν refer either to the coming of the Son of man, that is, the parousia, or the Son of man in his coming. The ταῦτα of v. 29 cannot include the parousia with its attendant upheavals; it would be illogical to say that the parousia demonstrates that the parousia is approaching. The ταῦτα of v. 29 are evidently to be identified with the dramatic events of vv. 5-23, not the tribulation as a whole, whose temporal length is undefined (vv. 19-20), but the specific things which Jesus has told his hearers they will see, hear about or experience (cf. 'when you see', v. 29)[168] – deceivers (v. 5), wars and natural disasters (v. 7-8); arrest, trial and hostility from outsiders (vv. 9, 11, 13); the abomination of desolation (v. 14); false messiahs (vv. 21-22). It makes sense to see ταῦτα in v. 29 as the antecedent of ταῦτα πάντα in v. 30. The addition of πάντα does not widen the embrace of ταῦτα now to include the events of vv. 24-27; it simply emphasizes that every one of 'these things', that is, the things of vv. 5-23, must take place. The πάντα of v. 30 matches the πάντα of v. 23 ('I have already told you *all things*'). On this understanding, then, the catastrophic intervention that is the coming of the Son of man is not among the events that are expected to take place within a generation. To be sure, the cosmic convulsions and the parousia are said to follow on 'after that tribulation' (v. 24a), but Mark leaves room for the continuation of the time of distress beyond the existing generation.[169]

Mark does not, then, set a deadline for the parousia. Indeed, Mark's Jesus insists that the day and the hour are unknown (v. 32).[170] Yet, readers of the Gospel must remain in constant readiness for the day of Jesus' return, since it may come sooner rather than later (vv. 33-37; cf. v. 29).

4.7.2 *Consequences*

Mark 13.31a shows that Mark *does* envisage the end of the present created cosmos, whether or not he connects this with the cosmic upheavals of 13.24-25. On this basis, it is appropriate to consider what consequences he draws from this expectation for creation, the final state and 'Christian' praxis.

168. The second person plural form is used, as in vv. 5-23.
169. Thus, a distinction may be drawn between 'these things'/'all these things' in vv. 29-30 and the tribulation as a whole.
170. It is debated whether Jesus' statement in v. 32, 'about that day or hour no one knows, neither the angels in heaven, nor the Son, but only the Father', asserts absolute or relative ignorance about the date of the parousia. For defence of the interpretation in terms of absolute ignorance, see Beasley-Murray 1993: 459-61.

4.7.2.1 Creational Consequences

Does the thought of the cosmos coming to an end generate any sense of a negative assessment of creation? There is not the slightest hint of such an outlook in Mark's Gospel. Indeed, within the eschatological discourse itself there is a very strong affirmation of God's creation of the world: 'from the beginning of the creation that God created' (13.19; cf. 10.6).[171] The impermanence of creation, as we have seen from elsewhere, does not make it a flawed product; it simply shows that creation was not formed to be everlasting. In Genesis, the mortality of creation does not undermine its declared goodness. There is no reason to suppose that Mark thinks differently.

4.7.2.2 Eschatological Consequences

Does Mark look for a purely heavenly and non-material final state? The evangelist gives little indication as to the nature of the final eschatological state. Mark's Jesus speaks of 'the age to come', in which eternal life will be realized (10.30), but it is not explicitly indicated that the new age will take the form of a new creation. The affirmation of resurrection in 12.25, though, seems to point in this direction.[172]

4.7.2.3 Practical Consequences

No practical implications are drawn directly from the affirmation in 13.31 that heaven and earth will pass away, but any thought of passive waiting is ruled out in vv. 32-37. Here, Mark's Jesus makes clear that the unknown timing of 'that day' must not be an excuse for inertia. Rather, it should promote faithful activity and a strong sense of ethical responsibility (vv. 32-37). The call to 'keep awake' in vv. 35 and 37 is a call to diligent service and fulfilment of one's designated task. As Dyer states, it is 'a positive call to faithful discipleship and mission ... not despair over the evils of the world and a longing to escape from them'.[173]

4.8 Matthew's Version of the Discourse

We turn now to the parallel material in Matthew's Gospel. Matthew's eschatological discourse is substantially longer than Mark's, extending from Mt. 24.4 to 25.46. The first and main portion, 24.4-36, more or less parallels Mk 13.5-31, and is dependent on it. The second, 24.37-44,

---

171. ἀπ' ἀρχῆς κτίσεως ἣν ἔκτισεν ὁ θεός.
172. Assuming he thinks of resurrection along traditional lines. Resurrection and cosmic re-creation are connected in *4 Ezra* 7.30-32; *LAB* 3.10; *Sib. Or.* 4.179-182.
173. Dyer 1998: 271.

comprises illustrations of the suddenness of the Son of man's coming and exhortations to be watchful and ready. The third, 24.45–25.30, consists of three parables relating to the time of waiting (for the coming of the Son of man). The final section, 25.31-46, focuses on the final judgement, with the extended analogy of the shepherd separating the sheep from the goats.

As in Mark, Jesus' prediction of the temple's overthrow (24.2) prompts the further enquiry of the disciples (v. 3),[174] which in turn initiates the discourse. In Matthew's handling, the eschatological orientation of the disciples' second question is made crystal clear: 'Tell us, when will these things be, *and what will be the sign of your parousia and of the end of the age*?' (πότε ταῦτα ἔσται καὶ τί τὸ σημεῖον τῆς σῆς παρουσίας καὶ συντελείας τοῦ αἰῶνος;).[175] Wright denies that παρουσία here has an eschatological sense. He points out that the word simply means 'presence' as opposed to 'absence'.[176] It sometimes denotes a 'royal' visit, and this is its sense in the present context. The disciples are not asking Jesus about his second coming, but 'his actual enthronement as king'.[177] Wright is correct about the basic meaning of παρουσία, but by Matthew's time the word had become a standard term in early Christian vocabulary for the second coming of Jesus or the eschatological intervention.[178] In the discourse itself, παρουσία is used interchangeably with the verb ἔρχομαι with reference to the coming of the Son of man (παρουσία in vv. 27, 37 and 39; ἔρχομαι in vv. 30, 44; 25.31).[179] Wright argues that the 'end of the age', συντελεία τοῦ αἰῶνος, is not the end of the world and history, but 'the end of Israel's period of mourning and exile'.[180] This part of the disciples' question, he maintains, must be read to mean: 'When will the evil age, symbolized by the present Jerusalem regime, be over?'[181] But this interpretation is quite unsustainable. The phrase συντελεία τοῦ αἰῶνος is found several times in Matthew's Gospel, and very clearly it refers to the close of human history, coinciding with the final judgement (13.39, 40, 49). The Gospel ends

174. In Matthew, the disciples as a whole, rather than Mark's group of four, pose the query.
175. The single Greek article governing both the parousia and the end of the age indicates the 'conceptual unity' of the two: so Hagner 1995: 688.
176. N. T. Wright 1996: 341.
177. N. T. Wright 1996: 346.
178. France 2002: 501. The word is found 24 times in the New Testament. Only 7 cases are non-eschatological (1 Cor. 16.17; 2 Cor. 7.6, 7; 10.10; Phil. 1.26; 2.12).
179. On the advent of the Son of man in Matthew's Gospel, see Sim 1996: 96–9.
180. N. T. Wright 1996: 346.
181. N. T. Wright 1996: 346.

with Jesus' promise, 'I am with you always, to the end of the age' (28.20). This hardly means that Jesus' spiritual presence among his followers extends only to the fall of the existing Jerusalem regime (which was probably a past event by the time Matthew wrote)!

The account of the eschatological birthpangs (Mt. 24.4-28) follows Mk 13.3-23 quite closely: Jesus warns of deceivers who will lead many astray (v. 5); wars and conflicts on the international stage (vv. 6-7); earthquakes and famines (v. 7); the persecution of the disciples (v. 9);[182] trouble in Judaea (vv. 15-20); great tribulation (vv. 21-22); false-messiahs and false-prophets (vv. 23-24). As in Mark, the mention of the abomination of desolation standing in the temple (v. 15)[183] provides an answer to the disciples' first question, 'When will these things be?', referring to the timing of the temple's demolition. Its appearance will be the signal that the temple and the city are soon to fall.

Verses 26-28 are Matthean additions;[184] the central theme is the unambiguous nature of the coming of the parousia of the Son of man (v. 27). There will be no doubt about the event when it happens: it will be as unmistakable as lightning flashing across the sky.

Verses 29-31 are Matthew's equivalent to Mk 13.24-27. Matthew indicates that the cosmic occurrences take place 'immediately' (εὐθέως) after the tribulation. Since Mark does not envisage a temporal gap between the end of the tribulation and the eschatological intervention, Matthew only makes explicit what Mark implies. The most significant addition to the pericope of Mk 13.24-27 is the reference to 'the sign of the Son of man in heaven' (τὸ σημεῖον τοῦ υἱοῦ τοῦ ἀνθρώπου ἐν οὐρανῷ, Mt. 24.30), which causes those on earth to mourn.[185] This sign appears along with the cosmic phenomena and together they herald the Son of man's manifestation. There has been much debate as to the precise nature of the 'sign', but most likely it is some kind of battle standard or ensign.[186] The mention of a sign announcing the arrival of the

---

182. Matthew has already used Mk 13.9-13 in Mt. 10.17-21; in 24.9-14, he summarizes the Markan pericope, supplementing it with other themes: the falling away of many; the rise of false prophets; the increase of lawlessness and diminution of love (vv. 10-12). Matthew makes clear that the universal proclamation of the gospel must precede *the end* (v. 14).

183. Matthew indicates the Danielic origin of the phrase 'abomination of desolation' and specifies that it will be seen standing 'in the holy place', i.e. in the temple.

184. Reflecting the same traditions used in Lk. 17.23-24, 37.

185. The words 'all the tribes of the earth will mourn' are drawn from Zech. 12.10-14. Daniel 7.13 and Zech. 12.10-14 are also combined in Rev. 1.7.

186. Sim 1996: 104. Sim (99–108) emphasizes the militaristic nature of Matthew's scenario of the coming of the Son of man.

Son of man provides a clear link back to the disciples' request for a sign of the parousia and the end of the age. But the sign is so closely related to the coming that it hardly serves as an advance warning. Like the cosmic occurrences, it is a feature of the whole consummating event. As in Mk 13.24-27, the total event of the coming of the Son of man is portrayed in terms of the eschatological coming of God. Matthew adds the detail that the Son of man will dispatch his angels with a 'loud trumpet call', which is most likely a call to battle (cf. Zech. 9.14).[187] Bearing in mind that the 'sign of the Son of man' probably also has a military function, Matthew seems to present the coming of the Son of man as the coming of God to war.[188]

4.9 *Matthew's Parallel to Mark 13.24-25 (Matthew 24.29)*

Matthew 24.29 parallels Mk 13.24-25. Matthew makes two very slight alterations to Mark's text. In the third line, Matthew changes Mark's periphrastic 'the stars will be falling from heaven' to the simple future, 'the stars will fall from heaven' (οἱ ἀστέρες πεσοῦνται ἀπὸ τοῦ οὐρανοῦ).[189] In the fourth line, the evangelist adjusts Mark's 'the powers in the heavens' to 'the powers of the heavens' (αἱ δυνάμεις τῶν οὐρανῶν).[190] These amendments make no difference to the sense.

The interpretation offered for Mk 13.24-25 works equally well for Mt. 24.29. Depicted are full-scale cataclysmic occurrences announcing and attending the arrival of the Son of man for eschatological judgement and redemption. Like Mk 13.24-27, Mt. 24.29-31 fits the 'catastrophic-intervention' pattern observed in Chapter 2. Since the parallel Jewish texts envisage an actual catastrophic scenario, it seems likely that Matthew does too. Matthew's own linguistic patterns point to objective events. Elsewhere in Matthew, the words 'sun' (ἥλιος) and 'star' (ἀστήρ) denote actual celestial bodies (2.2, 7, 9, 10; 5.45; 13.6, 43; 17.2). The darkening of the sky at the crucifixion (27.45) is for Matthew an objective, physical event. Quakes are concrete (and spectacular) occurrences when they are narrated at other places in Matthew's narrative (8.24; 27.54; 28.2; cf. the earthquakes of 24.7). This is not to say that Matthew

---

187. See further Plevnik 1997: 57–8. The trumpet is a feature of the parousia portrait of 1 Thess. 4.15-17; cf. 1 Cor. 15.52.
188. In Zech. 9.14-15 and 14.1-5, God's future coming is a supernatural military intervention.
189. This is more in line with Isa. 34.4 LXX.
190. This fits with the LXX B reading of Isa. 34.4, but it is perfectly explicable as a simplification of Mark's cumbersome αἱ δυνάμεις αἱ ἐν τοῖς οὐρανοῖς.

intends the cosmic images of v. 29 to be taken literally, but that he expects them to cash out into real cosmic disasters. In 24.38-39, the parousia of the Son of man is compared to the judgement at the flood. The explicit point of comparison is the suddenness with which the event overtook an unsuspecting people, but the underlying assumption seems to be that the flood and the parousia are parallel universal catastrophes, affecting the natural world as well as humankind.

Matthew 24.32-36 reproduces Mk 13.28-32. Matthew's version of the saying in Mk 13.31, 'Heaven and earth will pass away … ' (Mt. 24.35) is almost exactly the same as that in Mark. There is a slight variation in the grammatical structure, but this has no effect on the meaning.[191] As in Mark, the saying indicates that the existing cosmos will be dissolved at the eschaton.[192] When we read v. 29 in conjunction with v. 35, it is legitimate to conclude, as Sim does, that the cataclysmic events of v. 29 are 'the beginning of the breakdown of the existing cosmic order'.[193]

---

191. Matthew has the singular παρελεύσεται in the first clause and the plural aorist subjunctive παρέλθωσιν in the second clause (though there are textual variants); Matthew thus takes ὁ οὐρανὸς καὶ ἡ γῆ as a singular entity.

192. Davies and Allison 1997: 368.

193. Sim 1996: 104. Matthew has another saying on the passing away of the heaven and earth: 'until heaven and earth pass away, not one letter, not one stroke of a letter, will pass from the law until all is accomplished' (5.18). Luz (1989: 266) thinks that the wording, ἕως ἂν παρέλθῃ ὁ οὐρανὸς καὶ ἡ γῆ, means 'never'; thus the point is the law will remain in force forever. But this is not likely. The clause stands in parallel to the words, ἕως ἂν πάντα γένηται, 'until all is accomplished', which point to a definite consummation (cf. 24.34, ἕως ἂν πάντα ταῦτα γένηται). The addition of these words, as Davies and Allison (1988: 495) state, 'eliminates the possibility of interpreting "until heaven and earth pass away" as being the rhetorical equivalent of "never": rather is a definite end to the law set forth'. J. P. Meier (1976: 57–65) argues the passing away of heaven and earth in 5.18 refers to the death and resurrection of Jesus as '*die Wende der Zeit*, the turning point between the old and the new aeon' (p. 64; cf. pp. 30–40). But Matthew, unlike Paul, does not have a doctrine of the overlap of the ages; the end of the age for Matthew is, as noted above in the main text, the final judgement (13.39, 40, 49). For further criticisms of Meier, see Sim 1993: 9–11. Both Luz (1989: 265) and Meier (1976: 61) agree that the passing of heaven and earth in 24.35 refers to the catastrophic end of the cosmos. Fletcher-Louis (1997) maintains that Mt. 5.18 refers to the destruction of the temple, but such a reference is no more plausible here than in Mk 13.31 + par.

When Mt. 24.35 and 5.18 are read in conjunction, there is a hierarchical distinction between the law and Jesus' words. The words of Jesus, unlike the law, will endure for ever. The fixed duration of heaven and earth is the standard by which their continuity is measured.

4.10 *Timing of the Catastrophe and Consequences of the End of the Cosmos in Matthew*

Does Matthew assign a restricted time frame to the expectation of the final intervention? Does he draw troublesome consequences from the notion of cosmic dissolution?

4.10.1 *Timescale*

Matthew retains in 24.34 the affirmation that 'this generation will not pass away until all these things have taken place'. The interpretation given to Mk 13.30 is just as valid for the statement in Matthew. The words πάντα ταῦτα in Mt. 24.34 refer back to the same phrase (not just ταῦτα) in the previous verse. In v. 33, the expression πάντα ταῦτα embraces the specific events of vv. 4-25, but patently does not include the parousia of the Son of man. The catastrophic coming of the Son of man is not, therefore, tied to the time frame of a generation. The fulfilment of 'all these things' brings the parousia near, indeed 'at the very gates'. Yet, 'about that day and hour no one knows' (v. 36). Like Mark, Matthew treads a line between the nearness and the complete unknowableness of the end. The three parables of 24.45–25.30 envisage a period of waiting and apparent delay (24.48; 25.5).

4.10.2 *Consequences*

Like Mark, Matthew affirms that heaven and earth must pass away (24.35), and it seems likely that this is the outcome of the catastrophe envisaged in 24.29. Does this expectation have awkward theological and ethical entailments for the evangelist?

4.10.2.1 *Creational Consequences*
There is nothing to suggest that the thought of the world's coming to an end generates a negative view of creation for Matthew. The world is God's foundation (24.21; 25.34); God is Lord of heaven and earth (11.25). The natural world reflects God's good design and is a source of ethical instruction (5.45; 6.25-33). There is no question of heaven and earth being dissolved because they are inherently evil.

4.10.2.2 *Eschatological Consequences*
'Heaven' is an important category for Matthew. Matthew's Jesus advises his hearers to store up 'treasures in heaven' (6.20). The beatitude of Mt.

5.5, however, anticipates a state of earthly future blessedness. In Mt. 19.28, Matthew's Jesus speaks of 'the regeneration (παλιγγενεσία), when the Son of Man is seated on the throne of his glory'. Some scholars are content to see in παλιγγενεσία a reference only to the age to come,[194] which is simply construed as a temporal reality, but the word itself suggest more than this.[195] The term was used by Stoics for the regeneration of the physical cosmos after its conflagration.[196] As Sim has argued at length, in Mt. 19.28, παλιγγενεσία more probably means 'not just the new age but the total re-creation of the cosmos which accompanies the new age'.[197] Taking 24.35 and 19.28 together, we get a scheme of destruction and re-creation.

4.10.2.3 *Practical Consequences*
Like Mark, Matthew does not draw any practical implications directly from the declaration that heaven and earth are to pass away. It is clear from the parables of 24.45–25.30, though, that there is no place for inertia. The time of waiting for the parousia, which may be quite lengthy, is to be marked by faithful service, a state of readiness and productive activity. Indeed, Matthew's Jesus warns that indolence will incur very severe judgement (25.26-30). Matthew seems to be aware that the expectation of the potentially imminent parousia could lead to torpor but is at pains to ensure that his readers do not jump to this conclusion.

4.11 *Luke's Version of the Discourse*

We come now to Luke's Gospel.[198] Luke's version of Jesus' eschatological discourse (21.5-38) differs from Mark 13 in certain significant

---

194. E.g., Burnett 1983.
195. Had Matthew only wanted to refer to the coming age, he could have used the formulation ἐν τῷ αἰῶνι τῷ ἐρχομένῳ as in Mk 10.30; cf. Mt. 12.32.
196. See above p. 118.
197. Sim 1993 (here p. 11); Russell 1996: 156–9. Despite the Stoic associations of the term *palingenesia,* there is nothing to suggest that Matthew expects the world to end in a conflagration. As Sim points out (1993: 11), the references to eschatological fire in the Gospel have in view the fiery torments of Gehenna, the place where the wicked are punished (3.12; 5.22; 7.19, etc.), not the destruction of the cosmos.
198. One can hardly enter into a discussion of any aspect of Luke's eschatology without mentioning Hans Conzelmann's controversial theory that Luke has replaced the expectation of an imminent end with a concept of 'salvation history'. According to Conzelmann (1960), Luke has divided up the history of salvation into three periods: the Old Testament period, the ministry of Jesus; the era of the church. The ecclesial era, for Luke, extends into the far distant future, so there is no prospect of

respects.[199] It seems clear that Luke has used Mark 13 as his literary source,[200] but he has edited it much more freely than Matthew has done, and has apparently made use of other traditions.

As in Mark, the discourse responds to a twofold question elicited by Jesus' prediction of the flattening of the temple (Lk. 21.6).[201] But the enquiry (v. 7) concerns only the demise of the temple: 'Teacher, when will these things be, and what will be the sign that these things are about to take place?'[202] Unlike in Mark and Matthew, the second part of the question has no obvious eschatological connotations. No link is assumed between the destruction of the temple and the close of the age. As John Nolland writes, 'In the Lukan question, nothing appears beyond the destruction of the temple'.[203]

Verses 8-24 are equivalent to Mk 13.5-24a. Luke covers the same subject matter in the same sequence (deceivers; wars and conflicts; natural disasters; the persecution of the disciples; crisis in Judaea), though he does not reproduce the warning about false messiahs and false prophets in Mk 13.21-23. Despite the broad convergence, there are several important differences from Mark's account, as well as numerous minor ones. Of the latter, the most interesting to us is the expansion of the natural disasters in Lk. 21.11 to include 'dreadful portents and great signs from heaven'. It is perhaps significant that celestial abnormalities

---

Jesus returning any time soon. Taken together, Luke's Gospel and the book of Acts do seem to present a threefold schematization of history with the ascension of Jesus and coming of the Spirit as the boundary between the era of Jesus and the epoch of the church (the boundary between the first and second periods is less clear). At the same time, Luke also reflects a twofold division between the era of promise and that of fulfilment, the latter beginning with the mission of Jesus and *continuing* into the church (cf. Acts 1.1), and this division of time may perhaps be more fundamental for him: so Tuckett 1996: 48. There is evidence, not least in Luke 21 itself, that Luke has reworked the eschatological material he has taken over, but, as we will see, he has not simply consigned the parousia to a far-away future.

199. Luke's Jesus has already given eschatological teaching in 12.35-48 and 17.20-37.

200. The wording of Mark 13 is followed fairly closely in Lk. 21.5-11, 21a, 23, 27, 29-33.

201. In Luke, there is no shift in scene from the temple to the Mount of Olives between Jesus' temple prediction and the raising of the question which educes the discourse. The discourse is apparently given within the temple precincts (cf. vv. 37-38).

202. The question is asked by an unidentified group (cf. v. 5). As Marshall (1978: 762) points out, the title 'teacher' is generally used by non-disciples in Luke's Gospel (e.g. 8.49; 9.38; 10.25; 11.45).

203. Nolland 1993: 990.

were believed to have occurred before the fall of Jerusalem to the Romans.[204] The major divergences are as follows. First, Luke avoids those aspects of Mark's account which overtly characterize these evils as the end-time woes: he omits the comment, 'this is but the beginning of the birthpangs'; he drops entirely Mk 13.19-20, which defines the period under description as the eschatological tribulation; and he does not reproduce the opening words of Mk 13.24, 'but in those days, after that tribulation'. First-century Jewish readers of Luke's Gospel would have had little trouble recognizing the well-known eschatological scheme, but the evangelist tries to tone down as much as possible the resonances of the traditional drama in an effort (so it would seem) to de-eschatologize these events, to show that these phenomena 'are *not* apocalyptic signs of the End'.[205] Second, Luke drops Mark's enigmatic reference to the abomination of desolation standing in the temple. In its place, he has, 'When you see Jerusalem surrounded by armies, then know that its desolation has come near' (Lk 21.20).[206] Luke's Jesus then speaks candidly about Jerusalem's fall, having already prophesied its destruction earlier in the narrative (19.41-44): the city will be desolated and trampled down, and its inhabitants will be slain or taken away as captives (vv. 20, 24). Luke's version of this paragraph more closely matches actual historical events; the language, though, is firmly based on the Old Testament.[207] The devastation of Jerusalem is viewed as a divine judgement: 'these are days of vengeance, as a fulfilment of all that is written' (v. 22).[208] Third, Luke's Jesus talks about Jerusalem being trampled down by the Gentiles until the completion of 'the times of the Gentiles' (v. 24). This is obviously a period of Gentile domination of the city, but otherwise, as Judith Lieu states, it has no 'distinguishing characteristics'.[209] A fixed period is evidently in view, but no indication of its length is given.

In vv. 25-28, the topic shifts to the eschatological intervention. As noted above, the theme is not raised in Luke's form of the opening question. In Luke's discourse, the switch in subject depends on a natural link between the judgement on Jerusalem and the final judgement at the coming of the Son of man. Luke's Jesus has already spoken in some

204. Josephus, *War* 6.288-316; cf. Tacitus, *Hist.* 5.13.
205. Marshall 1978: 766.
206. Luke 21.20-24 is obviously a revision of Mk 13.14-18; the evangelist reproduces Mk 13.14b and 17 almost exactly. Yet in rewriting Mark, Luke has probably used traditional material (so Marshall 1978: 771).
207. Ezra 9.7; Isa. 63.18; Jer. 20.4-6; Ezek. 32.9, 20; Dan. 8.13; Zech. 12.2-3; 14.2.
208. There may be a specific allusion here to Isa. 61.2.
209. Lieu 1997: 170.

4 *'The Powers Of Heaven Will Be Shaken'* 175

detail about the coming of the Son of man in 17.20-37, so Luke's readers are not unprepared for the topic.

Luke reproduces Mk 13.26 but changes Mark's 'coming in clouds' (ἐν νεφέλαις) to 'coming in a cloud' (ἐν νεφέλῃ), objectifying the Danielic image. The reference to a singular cloud provides a link with Acts 1.9-11, were Jesus ascends into heaven on a cloud, and it is promised that he will return in exactly the same way. Luke omits Mark's reference to the gathering of the elect. Instead, Luke's Jesus says that 'when these things begin to take place ... redemption is drawing near' (v. 28). The phrase 'these things', it would seem, refers to the events of vv. 25-26, beginning with the celestial portents.[210]

Luke 21.29-33 follows Mk 13.28-31 quite closely. Luke's ending to the discourse, vv. 34-36, is different from Mark's,[211] but there is a similar call to vigilance ('Be on your guard', v. 34; 'Be alert', v. 36). 'That day' will arrive suddenly and will be like a snare that catches its victims unawares; it will come upon all the world's inhabitants (v. 35).[212] Here, Luke's text alludes to Isa. 24.17,[213] which of course envisions a coming world-judgement analogous to the Noachic flood. The expression 'that day' points back to vv. 25-28.

4.12 *Luke's Parallel to Mark 13.24-25 (Luke 21.25-26)*

We focus now on Lk. 21.25-26 which is the Lukan counterpart to Mk 13.24-25. The text reads as follows:

> 25) There will be signs in the sun, the moon, and the stars, and on the earth distress among nations confused by the roaring of the sea and the waves. 26) People will faint from fear and foreboding of what is coming upon the world, for the powers of the heavens will be shaken.
>
> 25) Καὶ ἔσονται σημεῖα ἐν ἡλίῳ καὶ σελήνῃ καὶ ἄστροις, καὶ ἐπὶ τῆς γῆς συνοχὴ ἐθνῶν ἐν ἀπορίᾳ ἤχους θαλάσσης καὶ σάλου, 26) ἀποψυχόντων ἀνθρώπων ἀπὸ φόβου καὶ προσδοκίας τῶν ἐπερχομένων τῇ οἰκουμένῃ, αἱ γὰρ δυνάμεις τῶν οὐρανῶν σαλευθήσονται.

Like Mark, Luke mentions in order the sun, moon and stars. Luke also reproduces Mk 13.25b, changing, as Matthew has done, Mark's 'the

---

210. Marshall 1978: 777.
211. Luke has partial parallels to Mark's ending to the discourse (Mk 13.33-37) at 19.12-13 (Mk 13.34) and 12.38 (Mk 13.36).
212. The text presents difficulties at this point. For discussion see C. F. Evans 1990: 763.
213. φόβος καὶ βόθυνος καὶ παγὶς ἐφ᾽ ὑμᾶς τοὺς ἐνοικοῦντας ἐπὶ τῆς γῆς, 'terror, and the pit, and the snare are upon you that dwell on the earth'.

powers in the heavens' to 'the powers of the heavens' (αἱ δυνάμεις τῶν οὐρανῶν). But there are obvious differences. First, whereas Mark's Jesus talks of sun and moon being darkened and of the stars falling from heaven, Luke simply refers to 'signs' (σημεῖα) in the sun, moon and stars. Second, Luke introduces material (vv. 25b-26a) which has no parallel in Mark. Third, in contrast to Mark's poetic style, Luke's account is somewhat more prosaic.[214] This is not to say, though, that Luke's version lacks structure; it exhibits a nicely balanced chiastic arrangement. Celestial occurrences are mentioned first and last; in between, events on earth are narrated. Most commentators think that Lk. 21.25-26 is a fairly free adaptation of Mk 13.24-25, but it is also possible that Luke is dependent on another tradition for vv. 25-26a (and then returns to Mark for the final clause).

The reference to signs in the sun, moon and stars could simply be an abridgement of Mk 13.24-25a, but it could also be a summary conflation of Joel 3.3 LXX (2.30 MT) ('I will give portents in the heavens and on the earth', καὶ δώσω τέρατα ἐν τῷ οὐρανῷ καὶ ἐπὶ τῆς γῆς) and 2.10 LXX ('the sun and moon will be darkened, and the stars shall withdraw their light', ὁ ἥλιος καὶ ἡ σελήνη συσκοτάσουσιν καὶ τὰ ἄστρα δύσουσιν τὸ φέγγος αὐτῶν).[215] Significantly, Joel 2.28-32 is cited in full in Acts 2.17-21. The mention of the roaring of the seas and the waves picks up Old Testament chaos imagery.[216] The thunderous roaring of the sea is part of the reaction of nature to the coming of God for universal judgement in Pss. 96.11-13 and 98.7-9. The image of people fainting from terror at the judgement falling upon the world could have been inspired by Isa. 24.17-18, to which, as we have seen, allusion is made in v. 35.

Within the literary context, these verses cannot be read as a symbolic account of Jerusalem's destruction. Luke clearly distinguishes the events of vv. 25-28 from those of Jerusalem's fall, inserting the indefinite period of the 'times of the Gentiles' between them. The universal nature of what is pictured here ('on the earth ... among nations'; 'upon the world') contrasts with the localized perspective of vv. 20-24.[217]

Verses 25-26 depict the onset of worldwide judgement. There seems to be an escalation from v. 25a to v. 26b; there is, as Nolland states, 'a

---

214. C. F. Evans 1990: 753. This judgement is based on the Greek style.
215. So Hartman 1966: 232.
216. For references, see Chapter 1, p. 29 n. 20.
217. In v. 23, ἀνάγκη μεγάλη ἐπὶ τῆς γῆς evidently means 'great distress *on the land*' and not 'on the earth' as the NRSV translates. The word γῆ refers to Judaea (cf. Marshall 1978: 773).

developing pattern of disasters'.[218] The 'signs in the sun, the moon, and the stars' signal the beginning of the development. In Joel 2.30-31, celestial portents are the prelude to the full revelation of judgement (the 'day of the Lord') and they seem to have that function here as well. The 'roaring of the sea and the waves' represents an intensification of the gathering doom – the release of the devastating forces of chaos on earth, a swell hitherto held in check by God. The shaking of 'the powers of the heavens' raises the terror to an even higher level; now the whole cosmos is destabilized. The cosmic shaking seems to be the immediate precursor of the advent of the Son of man. The escalation, though, is not gradual. What is presented here is a rapidly accelerating crisis, not a drawn-out period of woes.

The pattern of vv. 25-27 is consistent with the 'catastrophic intervention' scheme observed in various Jewish eschatological texts. The combination of celestial disturbances and aquatic chaos is paralleled in *T. Mos.* 10.4-6. Luke places emphasis on the fearful reaction of the world's inhabitants to the gathering catastrophe. There is a similar theme in *1 En.* 102.1-3 and *Apoc. Zeph.* 12.5-8.

Again, the extent to which Lk. 21.25-27 conforms to the recognizable 'catastrophic intervention' pattern suggests that actual physical catastrophe is expected. Actual physical events are definitely in view in v. 11, with the mention of 'earthquakes' and 'dreadful portents and great signs from heaven'. It follows that actual quaking and cosmic 'signs', though on a much grander scale, are anticipated in vv. 25-26.[219]

---

218. Nolland 1993: 1006. The thought of an observable escalation of disasters is somewhat difficult to reconcile with vv. 34-35, which emphasize that 'the day' will come suddenly and unexpectedly. Perhaps the idea of vv. 34-35 is that some may become so embroiled in dissipation, indulgence and worldly concerns and dulled in their senses, that they fail to appreciate the significance of what is coming upon the world.

219. In Acts 2.16-21, Joel 2.28-32 is cited with the introductory formula, 'this is what was spoken through the prophet Joel'. It is clear that the first part of Joel's prophecy, relating to the outpouring of God's Spirit, is viewed as being fulfilled at Pentecost. Does Luke mean his readers to think that the heavenly portents also happened then, in some non-cosmological sense? It seems likely that Luke interprets Joel's phrase 'the last days' (Acts 2.17) in terms of the whole period from Jesus' exaltation/ascension to the parousia. As Barrett (1994: lxxxii) states, 'They are initiated by the gift of the Spirit, described by Luke before the text is quoted, and their end will be heralded by cosmic phenomena ... which have manifestly not yet happened'. So also Haenchen 1971: 186; Witherington 1998: 143. The celestial signs of Acts 2.19-20 are thus to be equated with the 'signs in the sun, the moon, and the stars' in Lk. 21.25.

The reference to the passing away of heaven and earth in v. 33, mirroring Mk 13.31,[220] suggests that the terrible events of vv. 25-26, and the heavenly shake-up in particular, result in the collapse of the cosmos.[221]

4.13 Timing of the Catastrophe and Consequences of the End of the Cosmos in Luke

It can thus be concluded that Luke, like Mark and Matthew, expects a full-blown universal catastrophe at the parousia of Jesus. This can plausibly be equated with the dissolution of heaven and earth spoken of in 21.33. What indications does he give as to the timing of the parousia?

4.13.1 *Timescale*

Despite his attempt to separate off the destruction of Jerusalem from the final intervention and judgement, Luke retains the saying about fulfilment within a generation: 'Truly I tell you, this generation will not pass away until all things have taken place' (21.32). As in Mark and Matthew, it is extremely unlikely that anything else is meant other than Jesus' own generation.

Luke makes one small but telling change to Mark: he has πάντα rather than ταῦτα πάντα. This makes the saying less precise than Mk 13.30, and a little less construable as a prediction of the end of the world within the present generation. As it stands it could simply convey the general point that all that God has determined for this generation will come to pass. It is reasonable to suppose, though, that πάντα relates to some aspect of the preceding discourse. The formulation of v. 32 recalls that of v. 22: 'a fulfilment of all (πάντα) that is written'. Verses 20-22 refer quite specifically to the events surrounding Jerusalem's destruction. It seems likely, therefore, that these events are in mind in v. 32.

220. Luke 21.33 follows Mark's wording exactly.
221. Luke also has a form of the saying found in Mt. 5.18. Luke 16.17 reads: 'But it is easier for heaven and earth to pass away, than for one stroke of a letter in the law to be dropped' (εὐκοπώτερον δέ ἐστιν τὸν οὐρανὸν καὶ τὴν γῆν παρελθεῖν ἢ τοῦ νόμου μίαν κεραίαν πεσεῖν). Luke's wording seems to imply that the dissolution of the physical cosmos is hardly possible, and that the passing away of the law is even less so. This would seem to run against the clear-cut affirmation of ultimate cosmic dissolution in 21.33. Yet, the formulation of 16.17 does not indicate that cosmic dissolution is totally impossible (the same formulation is used in 18.25, of that which is hardly conceivable by human reckoning but entirely possible with God). The tension between 16.17 and 21.33 (like that between Mt. 5.18 and 24.35) can be resolved in terms of an ascending scale of endurance: the law lasts longer than heaven and earth, but Jesus' words outlast both creation and the law.

Like Mark and Matthew, Luke stresses the need for vigilance (21.34-36; cf. 12.39-40, 42-46). The potential nearness of the final intervention is implicit in 21.36, the concluding exhortation of the discourse: 'Be alert at all times, praying that you may have the strength to escape all these things that will take place'. Luke does not reproduce Jesus' declaration of ignorance as to the timing of the final intervention in Mk 13.31. However, the unknown timing of the consummation is underlined in Acts 1.7.[222]

4.13.2 *Consequences*

Whether or not the catastrophic occurrences of 21.25-26 are judged to be cosmos-ending, that Luke expects the eschatological dissolution of heaven and earth is evident from 21.33. What repercussions does this have for creation, the final state and 'Christian' activity?

4.13.2.1 *Creational Consequences*
There is nothing to suggest that the notion of the present creation coming to an end entails a radical dualism for Luke. There is not the slightest trace in Luke's Gospel of a bleak view of the natural order. Luke's Jesus draws various analogies from the natural world in his teaching (6.43; 9.58; 12.6, 34-37; 13.6-9, 19, 34; 17.6). He declares that God is the Lord of heaven and earth (10.21) and speaks of the world as his foundation (11.50). God's creation and providential ordering of the world receive more attention in Luke's second volume, the book of Acts (4.24; 14.15-17; 17.22-31).

4.13.2.2 *Eschatological Consequences*
There are a few glimpses of a post-mortem afterlife in Luke (16.19-31; 23.43; cf. Acts 7.56), but these probably relate to an intermediate stage rather than the final eschatological state.[223] Within Luke's Gospel, there is no explicit indication that a new creation is to follow the passing away of the present created order. However, in the book of Acts, we read of the 'restoration of all things', ἀποκαταστάσεως πάντων, which Jesus will inaugurate when he returns (Acts 3.21). The restoration is universal,

---

222. The nearness of the end is hardly if at all evident in Acts (perhaps at 3.19-21). The opening scene, that of Jesus' ascension, contains a solemn promise that Jesus will return (1.11). But the possibility that Jesus might come back soon plays no role in motivating the mission of the disciples.

223. Cf. Tuckett 1996: 40.

and probably cosmic in scope.[224] What seems to be anticipated is a 'restoration of the original order of creation'.[225]

4.13.2.3 *Practical Consequences*
The eschatological vigilance required by Luke's Jesus of his hearers involves steadfast continuance along the path of discipleship so that they may stand secure in the presence of the Son of man at his coming (v. 36). Passive waiting is, therefore, totally out of the question.

4.14 *Conclusions*

This chapter has given detailed attention to Mk 13.24-27, the most debated of the New Testament 'cosmic catastrophe' texts. According to Wright and France, vv. 24-25 are about the fall of Jerusalem and its temple as the earthly manifestation of Jesus' heavenly vindication (v. 26), but close analysis reveals the implausibility of such an interpretation. The main section of the discourse, vv. 5-27, concerns the traditional scheme of the eschatological woes, a drama which normally culminates in an ultimate, history-consummating event, such as the final intervention, and not a socio-political crisis in a rolling historical process. In Mark 13, the climactic intervention takes the form of the coming of the Son of man, which cannot be construed as Jesus' post-mortem heavenly enthronement. Mark has already identified the coming of the Son of man with the eschatological coming of God for judgement and salvation (8.38, linking Dan. 7.14 with Zech. 14.5). In 13.24-27, that identification is consolidated with further allusions to and gestures toward the tradition of the coming of God. The coming of the Son of man in vv. 26-27 is thus correctly understood as Jesus' parousia, which is essentially a 'Christologization' of the hope of God's eschatological manifestation. The cosmic upheavals of vv. 24-25 are part of the event of the coming of the Son of man, not only heralding it but also accompanying it.[226]

---

224. Haenchen 1971: 208. Witherington (1998: 187), however, thinks that the restoration of all Israel is in view. But the wording clearly goes beyond the nationalistic outlook of Acts 1.6. D. M. Russell (1996: 159) notes that ἀποκαταστάσεως πάντων is Luke's equivalent to Matthew's παλιγγενεσία.
225. Haenchen 1971: 208.
226. Mark 13 does establish a connection between the fall of Jerusalem and the end of the age, but it does so without equating the two or placing them in immediate chronological succession. There is a striking parallel between Mark's association of the destruction of Jerusalem and the eschatological resolution and Lucan's linkage of the collapse of the Roman Republic and the collapse of the cosmos in his *Civil War* (on which see Chapter 3, pp. 123–4). See further Adams 1997.

4 *'The Powers Of Heaven Will Be Shaken'* 181

I have argued that Mk 13.24-25 should be read in relation to parallel texts in Jewish apocalyptic and related writings. These passages show how language of celestial failures and cosmic upheavals, drawn from the Old Testament, was being used prior to and during the first century CE. This data, as we saw in Chapter 2, contradicts Wright's claim that such language was characteristically used of localized crises in the political sphere. Comparison with relevant post-biblical Jewish texts shows that Mk 13.24-27 conforms to the 'catastrophic intervention' pattern identified in Chapter 2. Since these passages envision actual upheaval on a universal scale, it seems likely that Mk 13.24-27 does so as well. This reading can be supported internally from Mark 13.

When vv. 24-27 are read in association with v. 31, it is plausible to interpret the upheavals of vv. 24-25 as the catastrophic beginning of the end of the present cosmic order. A similar line of interpretation can also be sustained for the parallel passages in Matthew and Luke.

None of the Synoptic evangelists, on the exegesis of Mark 13 + par., I have offered in this chapter, ties the catastrophic intervention to a fixed time frame for fulfilment. They were not proved wrong, therefore, when a supposed deadline for its occurrence came and went. Certainly, the parousia is regarded as near; yet, at the same time, its absolute timing is known only to God.

For none of the evangelists does the expectation of the end of the cosmos, as articulated in Mk 13.31 + par., entail a radical dualism that denigrates God's work of creation. Nor is it necessarily linked with a totally heavenly and non-material final state. In Jewish eschatological thought, the dissolution of creation is normally the prelude to its remaking, and we would expect this to be the case for the Synoptists, even if it is not explicitly indicated. Matthew (in 19.28) and Luke (in Acts 3.21) do seem to indicate that they look for a restoration of the created order. Each of the Synoptic evangelists is clear that the time of waiting for the final intervention is to be marked by active service and mission.

Chapter 5

'I WILL SHAKE NOT ONLY THE EARTH BUT ALSO THE HEAVEN': HEBREWS 12.25-29

The letter to the Hebrews is one of the richest theological documents in the New Testament, but it is notoriously enigmatic. Neither author nor addressees are named,[1] and the exact historical situation which prompted its writing is unclear. Whether the document is best described as a letter is open to dispute, since it does not begin like one.[2] Dating the work with any degree of precision has proved enormously difficult; 'interpreters may have to be content with the less than satisfactory conclusion that Hebrews might have been written at any time between the mid-60s and 90 CE'.[3] The pastoral purpose of the composition, though, is not in doubt: the author writes to remind and reassure his readers of the supremacy of Jesus and the sufficiency of his saving work. The doctrinal exposition, much of which (especially chs 8–10) relates to the cult of Israel, is interspersed with moral admonitions. Evidently some of the addressees had been tempted to drift away or turn back from their original confession (2.1-4; 3.7–4.14; 6.1-8; 10.26-31; 12.14-17; 12.25-29).[4] The author urges them to hold firm (3.14; 4.14) and persevere in Christ (10.36; 12.1; 13.13), and warns them of the perilous consequences of apostasy (6.4-6; 10.26-31).

 1. The title, 'To the Hebrews', is not part of the original letter but was added at a later point. The greeting from 'those from Italy' in 13.24 would seem to suggest an Italian destination, presumably Rome or its environs.
 2. It does, though, end like one (13.18-25). Many argue that Hebrews is really a sermon (a 'word of exhortation', 13.22; cf. Acts 13.15) in written form: e.g. Lane 1991a: lxix–lxxxvii; Lincoln 2006: 10–14. However, the ancient epistolary genre was a highly flexible one. Letters were written for a range of purposes, including philosophical exposition and moral exhortation: see Gamble 1995: 36–7.
 3. Lincoln 2006: 40. Hebrews is certainly known to *1 Clement*, a work which is usually dated in the mid 90s CE.
 4. The writer does not make explicit to what they were being drawn back. The traditional view posits that the readers were Jewish Christians and that they were turning back to 'Judaism'. For a defence of this reading, see Lincoln 2006: 52–68.

The passage of interest to us in this letter is Heb. 12.25-29, and specifically vv. 26-27, on the shaking and 'removal' of heaven and earth. Before turning to these verses, I will look at the quotation of Ps. 102.25-27 in Heb. 1.10-12, which makes clear at the outset of the letter that the author expects the present physical cosmos to be dissolved.

5.1 *The Citation of Psalm 102.25-27 in Hebrews 1.10-12*

Hebrews 1.5-13 is a chain of seven scriptural citations, mainly from the Psalms, designed to show that Jesus is greater than the angels (cf. v. 4).[5] The use of the same introductory formula ('to which of the angels did/has God ever say/said ... ?') at the beginning and end of the catena (vv. 5, 13) binds the quotations together. Psalm 102.25-27 is cited as proof that Christ, unlike the angels, is immutable and eternal.[6]

> 10) In the beginning, Lord, you founded the earth,
> and the heavens are the work of your hands;
> 11) they will perish, but you remain;
> they will all wear out like clothing;
> 12) like a cloak you will roll them up,
> and like clothing they will be changed.
> But you are the same,
> and your years will never end.

The quotation broadly follows the LXX (Ps. 101.26-28), which differs slightly from the MT (Ps. 102.25-27). In the psalm itself, these words are of course applied to God, but the writer of Hebrews treats them as God's address to the Son (cf. v. 5). This reading is facilitated by the LXX, which mistranslates the Hebrew עִנָּה 'he afflicted' in v. 23 (LXX 101.24) as ἀπεκρίθη, 'he answered', suggesting that vv. 25-27 are God's words, rather than the petitioner's. The writer reinforces his interpretation of these psalmic verses as a dialogue between God and the Son by adding the word 'you' (σύ) to the first line. In agreement with some LXX witnesses, the author has 'you will roll ... up' (ἑλίξεις) instead of 'you will change' (ἀλλάξεις), which is the major LXX reading.[7] The image of rolling up recalls Isa. 34.4 ('the heaven will be rolled up like a scroll', ἑλιγήσεται ὁ οὐρανὸς ὡς βιβλίον). The phrase 'like clothing' (ὡς ἱμάτιον) in Heb. 1.11 is repeated in the second line of v. 12. There is no

---

5. Psalm 2.7; 2 Sam. 7.14; Deut. 32.43 (conflated with Ps. 97.7); Pss. 104.4; 45.6-7; 102.25-27; 110.1

6. The mutability of the angels is deduced by the writer from Ps. 104.4: 'He makes his angels winds, and his servants flames of fire' (Heb. 1.7).

7. Ellingworth 1993: 128–9.

Septuagintal evidence for this reading; it is probably the writer's own addition (the repetition of 'like clothing' is not in the MT).

Psalm 102.25-27, as we saw in Chapter 1, expresses the sovereignty of God over the material universe; he created it and will outlast it. Verses 26-27 draw a contrast between the impermanence of creation and the endurance and changelessness of the creator. The author applies the contrast to Christ as 'Lord'.

The eventual dissolution of creation is affirmed in v. 11a, 'they will perish/be destroyed', αὐτοὶ ἀπολοῦνται, referring to the aforementioned 'earth' and 'heavens'. This idea is then developed through the clothing imagery of vv. 11b-12b. The clothing comparison is applied in a slightly different way in each of the three clauses. First, like a garment (ὡς ἱμάτιον), heaven and earth will grow old/wear out (παλαιωθήσονται). Hebrews 8.13 speaks of the old covenant as having grown old, employing the same verb, παλαιόω. There, the author states that what has grown old will soon be destroyed or disappear,[8] plainly associating ageing with perishability and destructibility.[9] Second, like a cloak (ὡσεὶ περιβόλαιον), heaven and earth are destined to be 'rolled up' and put away. Third, 'like clothing' (ὡς ἱμάτιον), heaven and earth will be changed. The author's addition of the phrase ὡς ἱμάτιον enables him to retain the imagery of attire which the psalmist drops at this point. The word ἀλλαγήσονται, 'they will be changed', should not be taken as indicating that creation will be transformed rather than dissolved (which would be at odds with vv. 11a-12a); as Thompson notes, that it is not the intent of the verb ἀλλάσσω here, where the thought is of a change of clothes.[10] As Attridge points out, by adding ὡς ἱμάτιον to this line, the author makes clear that 'the heavens will be not simply changed, but "removed"'.[11]

The statements of vv. 11a-12b express, as much as they do in their original psalmic context, the destructibility of the natural world. Heaven and earth had a beginning, they will grow old and they will eventually be dissolved. The cosmic order is viewed as 'naturally' perishable: it deteriorates with age. It was not created to be everlasting, but with the propensity to decay. When the time comes, the creator himself (in this context, the Son) will dissolve the works of his hands; he will actively 'roll them up'.[12]

---

8. The Greek reads: ἐγγὺς ἀφανισμοῦ.
9. Ellingworth 1993: 128.
10. Thompson 1982: 136.
11. Attridge 1989: 61. Cf. Koester 2001: 196.
12. In this text, therefore, Christ is made responsible for the ultimate destruction of the cosmos. Cf. Lane 1991a: 30.

Obviously Ps. 102.25-27 has been included in the catena of scriptures because it supports the idea of the enduring and unchanging nature of the Son. In the contrasting statements of vv. 11-12 (Ps. 102.26-27), it is clear where the author's emphasis lies: 'but you remain (σὺ δὲ διαμένεις) ... you are the same (σὺ δὲ ὁ αὐτὸς εἶ)'. However, the Lord's (i.e. the Son's) eternity and changelessness are expressed precisely by means of the contrast with the perishability and mutability of the existing cosmic order. There are no grounds for assuming that the writer accepts the former, while rejecting or remaining agnostic about the latter. Since the author cites these verses with approval, we must take it that he is in *full* agreement with their *entire* content. He obviously endorses the view of Ps. 102.25 that the world had a created beginning (cf. Heb. 1.2; 2.10; 3.4; 4.3-4; 11.3); it follows that he also supports the view of Ps. 102.26-27 that it will have an end. Hebrews 1.10-12 thus indicates that the writer of this epistle, in contrast to Philo with whom he is often compared, believes that the world is 'both created and destined to final destruction'.[13]

5.2 *The Shaking of Heaven and Earth: Hebrews 12.25-29*

Hebrews 12.25-29 is the main eschatological passage of the epistle.[14] It belongs to the larger section, 12.18-29, which W. L. Lane describes as 'the pastoral and theological climax' of the letter.[15] Hebrews 12.18-29 exhibits the pattern of exposition followed by exhortation that is characteristic of the epistle.

In the first part, vv. 18-24, the writer establishes a comparison between Mount Sinai (although the mountain is not named) and Mount Zion, which is the heavenly Jerusalem. He compares the two in order to illustrate the difference between the covenants with which they are associated. The structure of vv. 18-24 (one long sentence in the Greek) is determined by the contrast, 'You have not come ... but you have come ... ' (vv. 18, 22).[16] Israel's experience at Sinai is contrasted with the Christians'

---

13. Stewart 1965–6: 203; the contrasting approaches of Philo and Hebrews to creation and materiality are nicely brought out by Stewart.
14. Thompson 1982: 42–3.
15. Lane 1991b: 489.
16. According to Thompson (1982: 45–7), 'You have not come to something that can be touched' (οὐ γὰρ προσεληλύθατε ψηλαφωμένῳ) in v. 18, reflects an alleged Platonic disparagement of material reality over against the intangible ideal, but this is reading too much into the text. It rather reflects the fact that readers' access to the heavenly Jerusalem is experienced now by faith, the conviction of things not yet seen (cf. 11.1). Cf. Lane 1991b: 461.

approach to Zion, God's city. As Lane notes, there is a resumption here of 'the theme of the distance that separated worshippers from God under the old covenant' in contrast to the unhindered access to God that marks the new covenant.[17] The Sinai revelation is characterized in terms of the phenomena accompanying it: 'a blazing fire, and darkness, and gloom, and a tempest, and the sound of a trumpet' (cf. Exod. 19.16; Deut. 4.11-12; 5.22-26). The author also refers to the divine voice (cf. Deut. 5.22-26), a feature he picks up again in v. 26. He emphasizes the excluding nature of the Sinai event by recalling the ban placed on any person or animal touching the mountain on pain of death (v. 20; cf. Exod. 19.12-13). Only Moses was allowed to venture near the divine presence, and even he did so, according to the writer, with fear and trembling.[18] In contrast to the Israelites who had no direct access to God, believers in Christ have been admitted to 'Mount Zion ... the city of the living God' (v. 22). They are said to have come to the heavenly Jerusalem, to an assembly of God's people and angels, to God, the judge of all, and to Jesus (vv. 23-24). This access to God's city has been made possible by the blood of Jesus, the mediator of the new covenant (v. 24).

In the second part, vv. 25-29, the author draws a comparison between the Sinai theophany and the final intervention, and issues a solemn warning on the basis of the coming judgement.

5.2.1 *Hebrews 12.25-29*

The shift from exposition to moral appeal at the beginning of v. 25 is abrupt: 'See that you do not refuse the one who is speaking'. The warning is supported by an *a fortiori* argument: 'for if they did not escape when they refused the one who warned them on earth, how much less will we escape if we reject the one who warns from heaven!'[19] Those who 'did not escape' are the Israelites whom Moses led out of Egypt. In 3.16, the author describes the wilderness generation as those 'who heard and yet were rebellious' (cf. 3.18, 'those who were disobedient'). The writer's argument assumes that the new covenant entails obligations just as the old covenant did, and that those who stand under the new covenant are held accountable for disregarding these obligations, as the Israelites were held responsible for their disobedience under the old dispensation.

---

17. Lane 1991b: 489; cf. Heb. 9.1-14; 10.1-10.
18. Here, the writer goes beyond Old Testament accounts of the Sinai theophany. The theme of Moses' fear seems to be drawn from the golden calf incident (cf. Deut. 9.19).
19. This mode of argumentation is also employed in 9.13-14; 10.28-29; 12.9.

5 'I Will Shake Not Only the Earth But Also the Heaven'

Since believers have been granted much greater privileges than Israel (vv. 18-24), they are liable to a more severe judgement. The author appears to draw a distinction between 'the one who warned them on earth' and 'the one who warns from heaven', but, as recent commentators agree, a single speaker, God himself, is in view in both clauses.[20] The contrast is rather between 'two distinct events of speaking',[21] and their different points of origin: on earth (the sphere of the Sinai revelation); from heaven (the source of the new covenant revelation). Here (and in v. 23), 'heaven' is the uncreated abode of God, not the visible heavens as in 1.10.[22]

In vv. 26-27, the geophysical shaking that took place at Sinai is compared with a forthcoming and final shaking of both heaven and earth.

> 26) At that time his voice shook the earth; but now he has promised, 'Yet once more I will shake not only the earth but also the heaven.' 27) This phrase, 'Yet once more,' indicates the removal of what is shaken – that is, created things – so that what cannot be shaken may remain.
>
> 26) οὗ ἡ φωνὴ τὴν γῆν ἐσάλευσεν τότε, νῦν δὲ ἐπήγγελται λέγων· ἔτι ἅπαξ ἐγὼ σείσω οὐ μόνον τὴν γῆν ἀλλὰ καὶ τὸν οὐρανόν. 27) τὸ δὲ ἔτι ἅπαξ δηλοῖ [τὴν] τῶν σαλευομένων μετάθεσιν ὡς πεποιημένων, ἵνα μείνῃ τὰ μὴ σαλευόμενα.

In the brief account of the phenomena accompanying God's manifestation at Sinai in vv. 18-19, no mention was made of the shaking of the mountain (cf. Exod. 19.18). The writer now takes up and focuses on this feature of the event, making it a direct effect of the awesome voice of God (cf. vv. 19b-20). He recasts the Sinai quake as a *global* earthquake: 'his voice shook the earth'.[23] In *Pseudo-Philo's Biblical Antiquities*, *4 Ezra* and *2 Baruch*, the Sinai earthquake is transformed into a

---

20. So Attridge 1989: 379–80; Ellingworth 1993: 683–4; Lane 1991b: 476. An older reading finds a contrast between Moses and Christ (e.g. Moffatt 1924: 270), but there is little justification for that view. Elsewhere in Hebrews the verb 'to warn' (χρηματίζω) has God as its subject (8.5; 11.7). The 'voice' of v. 26 is obviously God's voice. God is the implied subject of 'he has promised' in v. 26, and what follows are clearly his words. God is explicitly mentioned in vv. 28-29. It is therefore natural to see him as the implied referent in v. 25bc.

21. Lane 1991b: 475.

22. The author of Hebrews uses the word 'heaven' (οὐρανός) with reference both to the visible heaven (1.10; 4.14; 7.26; 11.12) and the dwelling place of God beyond the physical heaven (e.g. 9.24).

23. It is possible that the writer is picking up the theme of the shaking of the earth in Old Testament hymnic representations of the Exodus and conquest, which exhibit the theophany pattern (Judg. 5.4; Pss. 68.8; 77.18).

cosmic upheaval;[24] the writer of Hebrews moves in this universalizing direction, but he limits the impact of the quake to the terrestrial domain.[25] The shaking of heaven and earth is spoken of as something that God 'has promised now', νῦν δὲ ἐπήγγελται. The perfect tense of the verb ἐπαγγέλλομαι indicates that though the promise was made in the past, it remains active. The word νῦν seems to imply that the time of its fulfilment is drawing near. The promise referred to is Hag. 2.6. The author's citation is a somewhat free rendering of the LXX of Hag. 2.6 as can be seen from the comparison below:

> Yet once more I will shake not only the earth but also the heaven. ἔτι ἅπαξ ἐγὼ σείσω οὐ μόνον τὴν γῆν ἀλλὰ καὶ τὸν οὐρανόν. (Heb. 12.26)
>
> Yet once more I will shake the heaven and the earth, and the sea and the dry land. ἔτι ἅπαξ ἐγὼ σείσω τόν οὐρανὸν καὶ τὴν γῆν, καὶ τὴν θάλασσαν καὶ τὴν ξηράν. (Hag. 2.6 LXX)

The writer does not take up the references to the sea and the dry land, so as to concentrate on heaven and earth. Also, he transposes the order of Haggai, mentioning the earth first, then the heaven. More significantly, he adds the construction, 'not only ... but' (οὐ μόνον ... ἀλλά), thus emphasizing the difference between Sinai and the coming intervention; the latter will be far more extensive. Here 'heaven' denotes the created heaven, not the uncreated realm of God.[26] 'Earth' and 'heaven' together designate the whole created order (as 'earth' and 'heavens' in 1.10).

As we saw in Chapter 1, Haggai's prophecy is set within the historical context of the rebuilding of the temple in the latter half of the sixth century BCE. In an oracle aimed at encouraging the post-exilic community (Hag. 2.1-9), the prophet announces that God is about to shake the established cosmos and shake the nations. Envisaged is a worldwide catastrophe, though not a world-ending one. As a result of the great shaking, Haggai declares, the wealth of the nations will come to Israel, and the temple will be filled with a splendour that will put the Solomonic temple in the shade (Hag. 2.7-9). The writer of Hebrews avoids the reference to the temple, as he studiously avoids any mention of the tem-

---

24. *LAB* 11.5; 23.10; 32.7-8; *4 Ezra* 3.18; *2 Bar.* 59.3.

25. By making it a cosmic quake, he would of course undermine the contrast with the eschatological theophany.

26. Lane (1991b: 480) interprets it as a reference to the divine abode in line with the previous mention of the word in v. 25. However, 'heaven' is indisputably the visible heaven in the writer's source text, Hag. 2.6 LXX. The 'heaven' is subject to a shaking which entails its removal; this could hardly be said of the realm of God.

ple in the letter (focusing instead in the cultic arguments of chs 8–10 on the wilderness tabernacle). He declines entirely to take up the 'national' aspects of Haggai's prophecy. He treats it simply as a promise of a universal final shaking.[27]

Hebrews' deployment of Hag. 2.6 fits the 'catastrophic intervention' pattern evident in post-biblical Jewish eschatological texts. The writer of *2 Baruch* is particularly indebted to Hag. 2.6, 21 for his conception of the cataclysmic intrusion: 'the Mighty One shall shake the entire creation' (32.1); 'the heaven will be shaken from its place at that time' (59.3). In several pseudepigraphal texts, the catastrophic intervention is depicted as the eschatological counterpart of the Sinai theophany: *1 En.* 1.3-9; 102.1-3; *2 Bar.* 59.3. *First Enoch* 102.1-3 bears particular comparison with Heb. 12.26 because of its stress on the shaking of 'the heavens and all the luminaries' as well as 'all the earth'.

The shaking of the created cosmos promised in Heb. 12.26 must be interpreted in relation to the Sinai event to which it is compared. The Sinai theophany is plainly understood by the writer as a divine intervention in history accompanied by terrifying and disruptive *physical* phenomena, including a global earthquake (vv. 18-21, 26a). He obviously believes these things actually happened. It follows that he anticipates actual cosmic convulsions at the final intervention. The language of shaking is not, then, for our author just a 'powerful metaphor' for coming judgement, as Lane argues;[28] in line with the consistent pattern of usage of this kind of language in comparable Jewish catastrophe texts, it expresses the awesome and dramatic form the coming judgement will take.

In v. 27, the author gives his own interpretative comment on Haggai's prophecy.[29] His explanation focuses on the phrase 'yet once more' (ἔτι ἅπαξ). The author, in accord with his own particular use of the word ἅπαξ (9.26, 27, 28; 10.2), understands the phrase as entailing finality: 'once again and *finally*'. He contends that the expression points to 'the removal of what is shaken – as created things' ([τὴν] τῶν σαλευομένων μετάθεσιν ὡς πεποιημένων).[30] The standard meaning of the word

---

27. He drops Haggai's language of imminence 'in a little while' (which is missing in the LXX of Hag. 2.6), but the thought that the event lies in the near future is implicit in the context ('has promised *now*').

28. Lane 1991b: 480. So also Vögtle 1970: 88.

29. According to Lane (1991b: 481), the writer's exposition of Hag. 2.6 'is an example of parenetic midrash'.

30. In his explanation of Hag. 2.6 in Heb. 12.27, the author substitutes the verb σαλεύω for σείω. As we noted in connection with Mk 13.24-25, the verb σαλεύω frequently occurs in theophany contexts in the LXX. It may be that the writer opts for

μετάθεσις is 'removal' in a spatial sense, but in some contexts it can have the sense 'change'/'alteration'. The term has been employed twice before in the letter. In Heb. 7.12, it is used for the 'change' of the law after the replacement of the order of priesthood. But what is in view is a change that entails a removal, since the law is not simply altered but taken out of the way.[31] In 11.5, the word is used of Enoch's translation to heaven, and plainly means 'removal' in a spatial sense. In 12.27, it is generally agreed, the sense 'removal' is required by the immediate context, which sets up a contrast between that which is shakeable and subject to μετάθεσις and that which is unshakable and destined to 'remain'.[32] What is liable to removal are the 'shakeable things' (τὰ σαλευομένα), referring to the previously mentioned heaven and earth. The shakeable things are then defined as 'created things', πεποιημένα.[33] By defining heaven and earth in terms of their createdness,[34] the writer is calling attention to their transient character.[35] Through his citation of Ps. 102.25-27 at 1.10-12, the author has made clear that the material cosmos was not created to be everlasting; it decays, grows old, and will ultimately be dissolved. The setting of heaven and earth in contrast to that which 'remains' in vv. 26-27 suggests that the writer is referring back to the earlier text (cf. 'they will perish, but you *remain*', 1.11).[36] The designation πεποιημένα thus serves to remind readers that the cosmos is created *and destructible*.

The author of Hebrews thus envisions in this passage a cosmic catastrophe that results in the dissolution of the cosmos. By declaring that heaven and earth, as created things, are destined for 'removal', is he indicating that they are to be annihilated, that is, reduced to nothing? This

---

this verb because of its traditional theophanic connotations. Another factor influencing his preference for this word is the fact that σαλεύω with the negative is a Septuagintal idiom for unshakeableness (esp. in the Psalms): e.g. Pss. 9.27 LXX; 14.5 LXX; 15.8 LXX; 20.8 LXX; 29.7 LXX. Vanhoye (1964: 250–1) argues that the source of the verb is Ps. 95.10 LXX, but this is far too specific.

31. Ellingworth 1993: 688.

32. So Attridge 1989: 380–1; Ellingworth 1993: 688; Koester 2001: 547; Lane 1991b: 482.

33. The comparative particle ὡς, as Ellingworth (1993: 688) notes, signifies here a real property (cf. 3.5, 6), not a comparison. Lincoln (2006: 99) thinks a comparison is being drawn, but the translation he offers on the basis of it ('the removal of what is shaken, as created things are shaken') seems to involve a tautology.

34. The verb ποιέω is used of God's creation of the world in 1.2

35 There are no grounds for seeing in the word πεποιημένων an allusion to a metaphysical dualism which regards materiality as inerently problematic: *contra* Attridge 1989: 381.

36. In 1.11, the verb is διαμένω, rather than μένω.

seems unlikely since such a thought probably lay beyond his horizon.[37] Most likely, he means that they will be reduced to their pre-created, *material* condition.[38]

The present heaven and earth are to be removed 'so that what cannot be shaken may remain' (ἵνα μείνῃ τὰ μὴ σαλευόμενα). The writer does not spell out what it is that remains. In the course of the letter, he has identified various things that 'remain' (using the verb μένω): Melchizedek (7.3); Christ (7.24 cf. 1.10); the better possessions (10.34); brotherly love (13.1); the city to come (13.14). But in view of what follows in the next sentence, he is almost certainly thinking specifically of the 'kingdom'. In 12.28, he writes: 'Therefore, since we are receiving a kingdom that cannot be shaken, let us give thanks, by which we offer to God an acceptable worship with reverence and awe'. The kingdom is defined here as 'unshakeable', thus as something that is not liable to the mighty convulsion.

In v. 29, the writer concludes his argument with the ominous words, 'for indeed our God is a consuming fire', thus ending on the note of threat with which he began the subsection in v. 25. Is this perhaps an allusion to the Stoic idea of cosmic conflagration, with God as the fire that consumes the cosmos? This is very unlikely. Verse 29 is an explicit allusion to (almost a direct citation of) Deut. 4.24 ('For the Lord your God is a devouring fire'), where fire is a metaphor for God's zeal and wrath.[39]

5.2.2 Objections to an 'End of the Cosmos' Interpretation of Hebrews 12.26-27

Hebrews 12.26-27 predicts the catastrophic end of the cosmos, and most interpreters seem to understand the passage in this way.[40] Some, however, maintain that the actual destruction of the world is not anticipated here.

---

37. Cf. Ellingworth 1993: 688.
38. In 11.3, the writer indicates that the world was created out of 'things that are not visible' (μὴ ... φαινομένων). This is not an assertion of *creatio ex nihilo* (so rightly, Koester 2001: 474). The author seems to mean that the world was formed out of invisible matter (cf. *2 En.* 24.1).
39. In 6.7-8, the writer speaks of γῆ whose 'end is to be burned' (ἧς τὸ τέλος εἰς καῦσιν). Here γῆ means 'ground' and the thought is of a plot of land being burned over to wipe out damaging growth ('thorns and thistles'); cf. Koester 2001: 316. This is not a reference to the fiery end of the created earth.
40. E.g., Bruce 1964: 383–4; Ellingworth 1993: 688; Hughes 1977: 558; Koester 2001: 547–8 (though he thinks that, 'There is both transformation as well as annihilation'); Moffatt 1924: 221; Wilson 1987: 234–5.

Vögtle argues that it is not the writer's intention to develop a cosmological thesis; the shaking of heaven and earth is simply a metaphor for judgement.[41] Lane (as noted above) agrees that the shaking of earth and heaven is metaphorical for judgement.[42] It signifies neither the transformation nor the destruction of the cosmos, but rather the divine reckoning of human beings. The clause, 'so that what cannot be shaken will remain' in v. 27, in Lane's opinion, indicates that the judgement will have a discriminating function; it will remove some, but allow others – the faithful members of the community – to endure. It is true that the author is talking about divine judgement in this passage, but it is a judgement that takes the shape of a cosmic catastrophe. There is no warrant in the text for reducing the writer's cosmological perspective to an anthropological one. The author's own interpretation of Hag. 2.6 makes clear that he interprets the cosmological language of his source text in solidly cosmological terms. Also, the 'shaking' is not, as Lane contends, discriminating in nature. The wording is unequivocal: whatever is shaken is removed. That which remains does so not because it manages to survive or resist the cosmic shaking but precisely because it is *not subject* to this process.

Wright agrees that a cosmological prospect is in view in vv. 26-27 (which is itself noteworthy since we might have expected him to argue for a socio-political interpretation of the catastrophe language). But he thinks that the prospect anticipated is 'radical change' in heaven and earth rather than cosmic destruction. He writes,

> Heaven and earth alike must be 'shaken' in such a way that everything transient, temporary, secondary and second-rate may fall away. Then that which is of the new creation ... will shine out the more brightly.[43]

In a similar way, Andrew Lincoln thinks that Heb. 12.26-27 is about the transformation of the cosmos, not its destruction.[44] All creation is 'capable of being shaken in a final judgement, but those created things that have been purified must be part of what remains and take their place in the unshakeable kingdom'.[45] But the wording does not permit a distinction to be drawn between transient and intransient, purified and impure, redeemed and irredeemable aspects, of the present material order. Both Wright and Lincoln assume that the shaking is a discriminatory and sifting process, but, as I have emphasized, this is not the case. The

41. Vögtle 1970: 88–9.
42. Lane 1991a: 480.
43. N. T. Wright 2003a: 165.
44. Lincoln 2006: 97–9.
45. Lincoln 2006: 99.

shaking, as the author understands and explains it, is a wholly destructive divine action, resulting in complete undoing. The word πεποιημένα designates the *whole* created order, and the writer is quite clear that πεποιημένα are to be shaken and removed.

Attridge agrees that vv. 26-27 reflect the apocalyptic scenario of the destruction of heaven and earth but suggests that 'our author may have understood the decisive "shaking" promised by Haggai as something other than a literal cosmic cataclysm'.[46] He thinks that the death of Christ may be in view, noting that seismic activity takes place at Jesus' crucifixion in Matthew's Gospel.[47] Such a referent, though, is quite unlikely: the shaking of vv. 26-27 lies in the future from the author's temporal viewpoint, which surely rules out any reference to the death and resurrection of Jesus.[48] The futurity of the event from the writer's perspective is not in any way compromised by the fact that believers are said in v. 28 to be 'receiving' the kingdom, a formulation (the present participle, παραλαμβάνοντες) indicating not, as Attridge thinks, that the kingdom is something the readers 'already possess',[49] but that it is something they are in process of receiving, the process to be completed in the eschaton.[50]

Randall Gleason argues that the shaking of heaven and earth is meant to be understood 'as a symbolic description of the destruction of the Jerusalem Temple'[51] (this is the kind of position we might have expected Wright to take). However, such a reference is not very likely. The author has assiduously kept the temple out of the picture till this point. Why would he suddenly introduce it now and in such an oblique and unprepared for way? It is true that the Jewish temple was often viewed as a microcosm of heaven and earth, but we cannot assume from this, as Gleason seems to do, that the combination 'heaven' and 'earth', without any qualification, could serve in a context like this to designate the temple.[52] Gleason points to the fact that the temple is mentioned in Hag. 2.7, but, as we noted above, the author of Hebrews shows no interest in this part of Haggai's prophecy. In any case, Hag. 2.7 refers to the eschatological embellishment of the rebuilt temple, not to the temple's

---

46. Attridge 1989: 382.
47. Mt. 27.51, 'The earth shook, and the rocks were split.'
48. It should also be noted that in Mt. 27.51, there is no shaking of the heaven, which for the author of Hebrews is precisely the feature that distinguishes the coming intervention from the Sinai theophany.
49. Attridge 1989: 382.
50. Lane 1991b: 484.
51. Gleason 2002: 111.
52. The same criticism was made of Fletcher-Louis's reading of Mk 13.31. See pp. 162–3.

destruction. It would be hard to maintain a reference to the fall of the temple in 12.26-27 if the composition of Hebrews post-dates the tumultuous events of 70 CE, since (as stated above) the author speaks of the shaking of heaven and earth as a still future event.

I see little in these alternative interpretations, therefore, to dissuade us from reading Heb. 12.25-29, and vv. 26-27 specifically, in 'end of the cosmos' terms. The author warns of a coming catastrophic intervention of cosmic magnitude, a catastrophe which will bring about the dissolution of the established cosmos.

5.3 *Timing and Consequences of the Catastrophic End of the Cosmos*

What position does the author of Hebrews take on the timing of the coming catastrophe and what implications does he derive from the expectation of the world's ending?

5.3.1 *Timescale*

A note of imminence may be detected in 12.26, when the author declares that God 'now ... has promised' to shake the heaven as well as the earth. A sense of nearness is evident as elsewhere in the letter. Believers should be 'eagerly waiting' for Christ to appear a second time (9.28). The 'day' is said to be 'approaching' (10.25). With a quotation which conflates and modifies Isa. 26.20 and Hab. 2.3b, the author assures his readers that Jesus will appear soon: 'in a very little while, the one who is coming will come and will not delay' (10.37).[53] The author thus engenders a sense of anticipation for the eschatological climax. Crucially, though, he does not set the cataclysmic intervention within a definite and limited time frame.

5.3.2 *Consequences*

Does the expectation of the end of the cosmos entail an anti-creational dualism, a non-material conception of the final state and ethical passivity in the present?

5.3.2.1 *Creational Consequences*
Hebrews's teaching on the transience and end of heaven and earth is sometimes related to a 'Platonic' dualism which is negatively inclined

---

53. This text may indicate that there was a waning of belief in the imminent parousia and judgement of the world in the community addressed.

toward the material creation (especially James Thompson).[54] There is a touch of irony here because Plato himself (as we have seen) insisted that the physical cosmos is indestructible and this remained the 'orthodox' Platonic position.[55] Plato's cosmology, as expressed in the *Timaeus*, is in many respects a world-affirming one. Espousal of a 'Platonic' worldview is not necessarily indicative of a disparaging view of creation and the cosmos.[56] That the author of Hebrews operates with a Platonic cosmology, however, is in any case extremely doubtful. In his discussion of the relationship between the earthly tabernacle and the heavenly sanctuary in chs 8–9, the author uses Platonic-like language. He speaks, for example, of the earthly sanctuary as a ὑπόδειγμα and σκιά of the heavenly one (8.5), recalling Plato's distinction between 'shadow' and 'reality' for the components of the material world and the eternal forms on which they are based. Whether the writer is actually evoking Platonic categories is much debated.[57] But even if he is, he limits their application to the tabernacle–heaven relationship. At no point in these chapters, or anywhere else in the letter, does the author suggest that the transcendent heaven is a κόσμος νοητός, an 'intelligible world' on which our material world of shadows is modelled.

The attitude which Hebrews displays towards the created order is a positive one. At the very outset of the letter, the author speaks of God's fashioning of the world, identifying Christ as God's agent in creation and his means of sustaining it (1.2), and he refers to God/the Son as creator at various points in what follows (1.10; 2.10; 3.4; 4.3-4, 10; 11.3). Belief in

54. Thompson 1982: 48–52, 135–9.
55. Thompson (1982: 137) recognizes that 'Plato never argued that the earth will be destroyed'.
56. Philo's acceptance of Plato's cosmology did not lead him to disparage the created cosmos. Philo views the cosmos as indestructible and, in several places, he accords it a semi-divine status (*Deus Imm.* 31; *Aet. Mund.* 10, 20). On Philo's cosmology, see Adams 2000: 58–64. Plato's cosmology was developed in different ways by his successors, and more radical versions of it did emerge, esp. in Neo-Pythagoreanism: see further, Dillon 1996.
57. Hurst (1990) is doubtful. He points out (13–17) that the term ὑπόδειγμα is normally used of that which is copied (example, sketch, outline) rather than 'copy'. He argues that the contrast the author is drawing in chs 8–9 is not between the earthly tabernacle and its eternal archetype in heaven, but between the Mosaic tabernacle and the eschatological temple of Jewish apocalyptic thought. The earthly tabernacle is not the *copy* of the greater sanctuary, but rather its *prototype*. The point is that Moses' tabernacle *foreshadows* the eschatological temple. Attridge (1989: 219) grants that in 10.1, when the law is spoken of as a 'shadow' (σκιά) of what was to come, the idea is of foreshadowing. However, he is persuaded that the Platonic-like language of chs 8–9 (8.5; 9.11, 23-24) fits into a 'Platonic pattern'.

God as creator and the world as his creation is absolutely fundamental to the theology of the epistle. We have no reason to doubt that our author disagrees with the verdict of the Genesis creation narrative that all God made was good. The contrast between the destructibility of heaven and earth and the eternity of God/the Son and the enduring nature of God's kingdom is derived from the Old Testament (Ps. 102.25-27; Isa. 51.6); it is not an expression of an anti-material dualism.[58]

According to Thompson, the author of Hebrews exhibits an 'anti-worldliness';[59] this comes out, especially in chapter 11, in the treatment of the theme of faith. Here, Thompson claims, the writer develops a view of faith as involving 'a distrust of this creation' and an orientation toward the invisible reality.[60] In 11.7 and 38, the author uses the word κόσμος in a distinctly negative manner. Noah, by heeding God's warning and building the ark, is said to have 'condemned the world' (κατέκρινεν τὸν κόσμον); the fathers of faith are described as those 'of whom the world was not worthy' (ὧν οὐκ ἦν ἄξιος ὁ κόσμος). In 11.13, the patriarchs are depicted as 'strangers and foreigners on the earth' in 11.13. And in 11.16, it is said that they sought a homeland and 'a better country', not in this world, but in a 'heavenly' realm. In Thompson's view, the chapter as a whole teaches that the created physical word is illusory and deceptive and is an obstacle to be overcome in the pilgrimage of faith.[61] However, Thompson is reading this cosmic dualism into the author's exposition of faith, rather than discerning it from the text. In 11.7 and 28, κόσμος refers to the human world, not the physical cosmos. In 11.13-16, the 'heavenly' homeland is clearly valued more highly than the 'earth', the place of sojourn, but the distinction is hierarchical ('better') not oppositional. The earth is not a bad, inhospitable environment, but a temporary host country.[62] The 'faith' commended by the writer in this chapter is not conditioned by an anti-material bias, but by eschatological hope (11.1, 39-40).

The writer is aware that the wider social world which his readers inhabit is or can be a hostile environment,[63] but this must not be confused with an anti-cosmic dualism. That is an altogether different kind of thing.

58. *Contra* Thompson 1982: 135–9. Since Heb. 1.10-12 is wholly a citation of Ps. 102.25-27, it completely escapes me how Thompson is able to detect Platonic metaphysics in these verses.
59. Thompson 1982: 76.
60. Thompson 1982: 76.
61. Thompson 1982: 75.
62. For a more 'earth-friendly' reading of Hebrews 11, see Cadwallader 2002.
63. Heb. 10.32-4; 11.26, 32-37; 12.4-12; 13.13.

5.3.2.2 Eschatological Consequences
The writer of Hebrews does not explicitly indicate that there is to be a material re-creation following the dissolution of heaven and earth. Some interpreters think such an expectation would be incompatible with his alleged, anti-material dualism.[64]

There is certainly evidence that might suggest that the writer looks for a purely 'heavenly' salvation. The future hope of believers is often placed in the heavenly sphere. The writer speaks of their 'heavenly calling' (3.1) and their 'heavenly gift' (6.4). Faith is directed toward a 'heavenly' country (11.16) and 'the heavenly Jerusalem' (12.22). But there are also solid indications of a more 'temporal' eschatology: the eschatological dualism of the two ages (2.5; 6.4; 9.9, 26); the writer's talk of things 'to come' (2.5; 6.5; 10.1; 13.14); above all, the expectation of an eschatological intervention (expressed in terms of Christ's future coming in 9.28 and 10.37) and judgement at the end of history (especially, 12.25-29).

Although the author does not speak overtly of a new creation, there are some tantalizing indications that this is what he anticipates:

- The writer expresses his belief in the resurrection of the dead (6.2; 11.35; cf. 13.20), a belief which in Jewish eschatology is often bound up with the renewal of creation.
- In 9.11, the writer speaks of 'this creation' (ταύτης τῆς κτίσεως); the formulation could suggest that he anticipates *another* creation.
- The 'heavenly Jerusalem' in 12.22 is undoubtedly to be equated with 'the city that is to come' in 13.14. The phrase in 13.14 has a definite temporal future. This seems to indicate that the city which presently exists as a transcendent, heavenly reality will also be revealed in the future. It would be natural to presume that the future manifestation takes place in an earthly (i.e. *new-earthly*) context (cf. *4 Ezra* 7.26; 13.36; Rev. 21.9–22.5).[65]
- The writer intensifies the imagery of Ps. 102.25-27, by emphasizing that heaven and earth will be changed 'like clothing'. Since a *change* of clothes normally involves the *exchange* of one set of clothes for another, the author could be hinting that when the present creation is brought to an end, having served its purpose, it will be succeeded by a new cosmic creation.
- Talk of the Son's cosmic inheritance in 1.2 and of God's intention to subject all things to Christ in 2.7-8 (interpreting Ps. 8.4-6)

64. Thompson 1982: 50. So also Ellingworth 1993: 688.
65. Cf. Hurst 1990: 40–1.

appears to indicate a consummation involving a restored/ perfected created order.

- In 2.6-8, the author indicates that the universal subjection envisioned in Ps. 8.6 is to be realized in ἡ οἰκουμένη ἡ μέλλουσα. The expression has tended to be taken as a reference either to the heavenly realm which Christ entered at the time of his exaltation or the new 'age' he inaugurated at that time.[66] But given that the word οἰκουμένη normally means 'earth', 'inhabited world',[67] the expression ἡ οἰκουμένη ἡ μέλλουσα would more naturally refer to a future earthly environment. If the present earth is to be destroyed, the writer is presumably thinking about a new earth which God will create.

None of these indicators constitutes decisive proof of the expectation of the re-making of the material creation, but cumulatively, they present, I think, persuasive evidence. If this reading of the clues is correct, we should infer that the unshakeable kingdom which believers are in the process of receiving will ultimately be manifested in a new creation consequent on the dissolution of creation in its present form.

5.3.2.3 Practical Consequences

The writer uses the expectation of the coming shaking of heaven and earth to warn against apostasy. In the immediate exhortatory context, the aspect of divine judgement is to the fore. The reminder of God's promised shaking of the existing cosmic order is aimed at shaking recalcitrant and disaffected members of the community out of their state of disobedience and complacency (as the writer sees it). In this sense, God's promise to shake heaven and earth is more of a threat than a promise! There can be no question, then, of the expectation of the cataclysmic end of the world encouraging passivity and docility; rather, as the author handles it, it promotes perseverance and Christian commitment.

5.4 Conclusions

An unforced exegesis of the passage shows that Heb. 12.25-29 envisages a cosmic catastrophe that brings about the end of the cosmos. The author makes clear with his own explanatory remarks that the divine promise to shake heaven and earth, derived from Hag. 2.6, is to be taken in both a

---

66. E.g., Bruce 1964: 33; Lane 1991a: 45.
67. LSJ 1025. This is its sense elsewhere in the New Testament outside Hebrews: Mt. 24.14; Lk. 2.1; 4.5; 21.26; etc.

cosmological and a destructionist sense. The future and final shaking of heaven and earth will result in their 'removal', that is, dissolution. The writer has already indicated though his citation of Ps. 102.25-27 in 1.10-12, that the created cosmos is destined to be dissolved. He interprets Hag. 2.6 as referring to the preordained destruction.

The final intervention is expected soon, but is not tied to a specific timescale for fulfilment. The belief that the created cosmos will come to a drastic end does not entail for the writer a repudiation of God's work of creation. The transient created order is subordinated to the eternal God and his unshakeable kingdom, but it is not thereby negated. There is nothing to suggest that it is valued as anything less than good. Although the writer does not explicitly speak of a material re-creation to follow the end of the present cosmos, there is, in my view, good reason to assume that this is what he expects. The coming cosmic shake-up is not a cause for passivity and stagnation, but a spur to action and steadfast continuance.

Chapter 6

'THE ELEMENTS WILL MELT WITH FIRE':
2 PETER 3.5-13

Of all the New Testament passages examined in the present study, 2 Pet. 3.5-13 is the text that most ostensibly expresses the expectation of the catastrophic end of the cosmos. The author envisages a cosmic conflagration on the day of the Lord and the emergence of 'new heavens and a new earth'. This is the only place in the New Testament, and indeed the whole Bible, where it is explicitly taught that the cosmos will undergo a conflagration.[1] Allison is in no doubt that this passage speaks of the dissolution of the present universe. He writes: 'Here, it seems to me, is exactly the sort of expectation Wright wants to emphasize did not exist or at least was rare. But here it is in the New Testament.'[2] Wright calls 2 Pet. 3.5-13, 'a difficult and obscure text'. He does not try to defend a socio-political interpretation of the catastrophe language, as one might perhaps have expected him to do, given his general claim about how Jesus and the early Christians used cosmic catastrophe language.[3] He recognizes that the passage is about the destiny of creation but denies that it envisions the end of the cosmos. He argues that the critical point in the passage is v. 10. Were this verse to end 'the earth and the works that are therein shall be burned up', as some translations (e.g., KJV, ASV) have it, it would indeed, he concedes, seem to teach that creation is to be destroyed and be replaced with a new world. But the best manuscripts

---

1. This is disputed by Thiede (1986: 81) who thinks that quite a number of New Testament passages express the notion, including Mt. 3.11; 1 Cor. 3.13; 2 Thess. 1.8; Heb. 6.8. Such passages do speak of a fiery judgement, but not of the fiery dissolution of heaven and earth. A cosmic conflagration figures in the eschatological teaching of some early patristic writers: Justin, *1 Apol.* 20.1-4; 60.8-9; *2 Apol.* 7.2-3; Minucius Felix, *Oct.* 11.1, 34; Theophilus, *Ad Autolycum* 2.37-38.

2. Allison 1999: 139-40.

3. J. S. Russell (1887: 319-26) has argued for a 'destruction of Jerusalem' interpretation of 2 Pet. 3.5-13, as part of his general thesis that the parousia expectation of the New Testament was wholly fulfilled in the events of 70 CE.

have 'will be found' rather than 'will be burned up', which indicates the survival of the earth. The teaching of 2 Pet. 3.5-13 is that creation is to undergo a purging process in which the new world and its inhabitants will emerge tried, tested and purified.[4] In support of this reading Wright appeals to the case made by Al Wolters in an important and influential article.[5] We will consider Wolters' arguments in due course.

Second Peter is generally regarded as a pseudonymous composition of the late first or perhaps even early second century.[6] Some think it may be the latest work in the New Testament. Its form is obviously that of an epistle, yet it also has features associated with the 'testamentary' genre.[7] The situation envisaged in the letter is one in which 'false teachers' are active in the churches addressed, undermining and attacking accepted apostolic teaching.[8] The main target of their attack is the expectation of the parousia and coming judgement (1.15-21; 3.4-10). The author denounces his opponents in the strongest terms; the whole of chapter 2 is an extended polemic against them. In 2.1 and 3.3, the writer speaks of these dangerous agitators as a phenomenon of the future, but it is clear from the rest of the letter that they are around and causing trouble at the time of writing. As Bauckham states, 'It is hardly possible to read 2 Peter without supposing the false teachers to be contemporaries of the author with whom he is already in debate'.[9]

Second Peter 3.5-13 is a passage with a particularly high concentration of exegetical difficulties. It is not necessary to deal with all the exegetical problems in detail; I will concentrate on aspects of the text and issues of interpretation that bear directly on our topic, focusing especially on vv. 5-7 and 10-12.

---

4. N. T. Wright 2003b: 463.
5. Wolters 1987.
6. See Bauckham 1983: 157–8. Bauckham himself favours a date in the decade 80–90 CE. One of the main bases for the view that 2 Peter is to be dated toward the end of the first century at the earliest is the assumption that the decease of the apostolic generation is reflected in 3.4, but this is an assumption which will be challenged below. For a defence of an earlier dating and Petrine authorship, see Ellis 1999: 293–303.
7. See Bauckham 1983: 131–5. The occasion of writing, as the text presents it, is Peter's impending death (1.14-15). Like testaments, 2 Peter contains both ethical exhortation and prediction.
8. The false teachers are not infiltrators from outside the churches addressed, but are apparently members of these churches who have developed 'heretical' views (2.1). They are still involved in the Christian community, participating in its meals (2.13). They evidently carry some influence within the congregations (2.2).
9. Bauckham 1997: 924.

The section 2 Pet. 3.5-13 is the writer's response to his opponents' objections to the eschatological coming of God/Christ as 'voiced' in v. 4, and I begin by examining this verse.[10] I try to demonstrate that one of the grounds on which they object to the parousia is the indestructibility of the cosmos. I then explore the author's answer to this objection in vv. 5-7, before analysing his description of the coming catastrophe in vv. 10-12. In discussing vv. 5-7 and 10-12, I highlight the points at which the author is, in my view, indebted to Stoic cosmology. Concluding that the writer does indeed teach that the present cosmos is to be destroyed in a fiery catastrophe, I assess the consequences of this expectation for him.

6.1 *The Complaint of the 'Scoffers' in 2 Peter 3.4*

In 3.3, the writer states that 'in the last days scoffers will come'. Evidently, he identifies the time in which he is living with the last days. The 'scoffers' are plainly to be equated with the false teachers mentioned in 2.1, who were the subject of the extended polemic of that chapter.[11] In v. 4, the author reports their protest: 'Where is the promise of his coming? For ever since the fathers fell asleep, all things remain as they were from the beginning of creation!' (ποῦ ἐστιν ἡ ἐπαγγελία τῆς παρουσίας αὐτοῦ; ἀφ' ἧς γὰρ οἱ πατέρες ἐκοιμήθησαν, πάντα οὕτως διαμένει ἀπ' ἀρχῆς κτίσεως.)[12] The citation falls into two parts; the first consists of a complaint in the form of a rhetorical question. The implied answer to the question is clearly: 'The promise is nowhere; it has failed to materialise.' The second part supplies argumentation to support the complaint.

---

10. I will spend some time on v. 4, since I depart from the current consensus on its interpretation and this divergence requires some defending. The line taken up, though, is a modified version of a reading found in older commentaries, esp. Bigg 1910: 291–2.

11. It is generally agreed that the author makes of use of the letter of Jude or something like it throughout chapter 2 and up to 3.3: e.g. Bauckham 1983: 141–3; Horrell 1998: 140–62.

12. Whether or not the writer is reporting the actual words, the *ipsissima verba*, of his opponents, it is highly probable that the citation is an accurate representation of the claims they were making, giving us the *ipsissima vox* (the very voice) of the opponents. To be sure, we ought to be sceptical about the historical accuracy of much of the polemical portrait of the opponents in chapter 2, with its accusations of immorality, underhand tactics and impure motives, but when the writer gives explicit information about the content of their teaching as in 3.4, I think we can treat his account with some confidence. Barclay's (1987: 76) rule of thumb for mirror-reading a New Testament polemical letter is applicable here: 'statements about the character and motivation of... opponents should be taken with a very large pinch of salt', but 'the letter is likely to reflect fairly accurately what [the author] saw to be the main points at issue'.

6.1.1 'Where is the Promise of His Coming?'

The words, ποῦ ἐστιν ἡ ἐπαγγελία τῆς παρουσίας αὐτοῦ, are normally interpreted as a straightforward reference to Jesus' expected return. Most modern commentators think that the 'promise' is Jesus' own promise of his return (or the promise imputed to him) in Gospel passages such as Mk 13.24-30. However, in the light of the dominant pattern of New Testament usage, the word 'promise' (ἐπαγγελία) would more naturally refer to a pledge or pledges made by God in the Old Testament.[13] That the author interprets the promise spoken of by the scoffers as an undertaking made by God emerges fairly clearly from v. 9, in which the author states that 'the Lord is not slow about his promise' (οὐ βραδύνει κύριος τῆς ἐπαγγελίας) referring back to the promise of v. 4. The 'Lord' is God, not Jesus, as the continuation of the verse shows ('but is patient with you, not wanting any to perish, but all to come to repentance'). Also, in v. 13, 'his promise' (τὸ ἐπάγγελμα αὐτοῦ) of a new heaven and new earth is plainly a reference to *God*'s promise of a new creation in Isa. 65.17 and 66.22.

The formulation 'the promise of his coming' thus indicates that the target of the opponents' ridicule, as reported here, is not so much the parousia of Jesus but Old Testament promises relating to it.[14] The specific 'promise' giving rise to their scorn is very likely to have been the Old Testament prophetic expectation of God's coming,[15] together perhaps with that of the 'day of the Lord'[16] (specifically mentioned in

---

13. E.g., Lk. 24.49; Acts 1.4; 2.33, 39; 7.17; 13.23; Rom. 4.13, 14, 16, 20; Gal. 3.14, 16, 17, 18, 21, 22, 29; Heb. 4.1; 6.12. References to Jesus' own promises are in fact extremely uncommon in early Christian literature. For a rare reference, see *2 Clem.* 5.5. Bauckham (1983: 179) thinks that Christ's promises are in mind in 2 Pet. 1.4. But 'the precious and very great promises' are much more likely to be Old Testament promises (cf. 3.13), which (in the writer's view) have now been imparted to Christians.

14. This fits well with 1.20-22. The apologetic section, 1.16-22, makes clear that the validity of belief in Jesus' parousia is the main issue in the debate reflected in 2 Peter (esp. 1.16). These verses also reveal that the opponents attack not only the notion of Jesus' return but also Old Testament prophecy associated with it. In vv. 20-22, the author replies to an accusation by his opponents that the prophecies which the apostles used in support of the expectation of Jesus' return were not divinely inspired, but were merely human products. In response, the writer affirms the divine origin of Old Testament prophecy. It may be suggested, therefore, that 3.4 picks up the prophetic aspect of the debate reflected in 1.20-22, rather than the specifically Christological aspect of it (which is to the fore in 1.16-18).

15. E.g., Mic. 1.2-4; Nah. 1.3-5; Hab. 3.3-15.

16. Isa. 13.9-13; 34.8-17; Joel 1.15; 2.1-2; 2.20-31; 3.14; Amos 5.18-20; Zeph. 1.7-18; etc.

3.10 and 12). As we have seen with respect to Mk 8.38 and 13.26-27, Old Testament prophecies concerning the coming of God played an important role in the development of the notion of Jesus' parousia.[17] That the 'promise' being derided is the expectation of God's eschatological coming which Christians transferred to Jesus – is consistent with a rather curious feature of 3.4-13: the absence of any clear reference to Christ in the whole passage.[18] Significantly, in 3.12, the writer speaks of 'the coming of the day of *God*', τὴν παρουσίαν τῆς τοῦ θεοῦ ἡμέρας. This unique phrase combines the term παρουσία with the notion of the 'day of the Lord' and unambiguously connects both with God. As we will see, what the writer defends in 3.5-13 is the expectation of a final divine intervention, with world-ending consequences; the Christological dimension of that hope is not the focus of attention.

6.1.2 *'Since the Fathers fell asleep'*

The opponents advance two objections against the parousia promise. The first and main objection concerns the problem of non-fulfilment. The issue of delay is implicit in the initial question. The taunt/question indicates that the promise is unfulfilled at the time of writing and insinuates that it is surely going to remain so.

The mention of the fathers' decease serves as a time note which is meant to add weight to the problem of frustrated expectation. On the majority view, the 'fathers' are the apostles and their generation, and their death is the deadline for the promise's fulfilment, a deadline which has been exceeded, rendering the promise a failure.[19] But there are difficulties with this interpretation.

First, the words οἱ πατέρες would more readily refer to the Old Testament fathers. As Bauckham concedes, 'In early Christian literature, continuing Jewish usage ... οἱ πατέρες ... means the OT "fathers", i.e. the patriarchs or, more generally, the righteous men of OT times'.[20] The two passages which are sometimes adduced as parallels to the alleged sense, *1 Clem.* 23.3 and *2 Clem.* 11.2, both citing an otherwise unknown 'scripture', do not exemplify the desired usage, but rather speak of '*our*

17. See further Adams 2006.
18. The lack of Christological reference was noted by Käsemann (1964). In Käsemann's view, the writer of 2 Peter defends 'a non-christologically oriented eschatology' (183).
19. Bauckham 1983: 291.
20. Bauckham 1983: 290. E.g. Mt. 23.30, 32; Lk. 1.55, 72; 6.23; Jn 4.20; 6.31; Acts 3.13, 25; Rom. 9.5; Heb. 1.1; 3.9. In Lk. 1.17 and 1 Jn 2.14, 'fathers' means actual physical fathers.

fathers'. In both texts, the fathers are the physical fathers of the speakers. If the author of 2 Peter is using 'fathers' as an honorific term for the apostles or the first Christian generation, he is exhibiting a usage for which there is no parallel in Christian writing of the first two centuries CE.[21]

Second, that the death of the fathers is intended to denote a time limit for the promise is grammatically doubtful. The Greek wording (ἀφ' ἧς)[22] indicates that the emphasis is on what has happened, or more exactly, not happened, *since* the fathers' decease.[23] The fathers' death functions as a chronological point from which the extent of the delay can be judged; it does not designate a point beyond which there can be no fulfilment.[24] The point of the temporal objection is not that the fathers' decease itself has rendered belief in the parousia unsustainable, but that the time that has passed *since* their death makes it untenable. In vv. 8-9, where the author responds to the scoffers' temporal objection, he does not address the supposedly key issue that a deadline has passed. In his reply, he makes no mention of a 'generation' or any specific time frame for fulfilment. This renders it unlikely that the scoffers' objection had anything to do with the lapse of a time limit.

The temporal argument of the scoffers is best interpreted as an argument based on the excessively long period of time that has passed since the promise of the eschatological intervention was first announced. The mention of a thousand years in v. 8 seems to presuppose a very lengthy time of waiting, over many generations. Implicit in the objection is the assumption that the original prophecies of God's coming did not envisage such an extensive time frame for fulfilment. The prophets, of course, seemed to speak of God's coming as a near rather than distant event.[25] Thus, the extreme delay in fulfilment, for the scoffers, shows that the promise is ineffectual.[26]

---

21. The issue here, it should be stressed, is not the novelty of the proposed meaning (this is not in itself a problem), but rather its isolated nature.

22. The expression is an idiomatic form of ἀφ' ἡμέρας ἧ, 'from the day on which'.

23. Bauckham (1983: 291) recognizes this but persists with his contention that the objection is really about the missing of a deadline.

24. If the latter were the thought, the wording is more likely to have been: 'the fathers *have* fallen asleep *and yet/but* all things remain as they were from the beginning of creation' (οἱ πατέρες κεκοίμηται, καὶ (or ἀλλα) πάντα οὕτως διαμένει ἀπ' ἀρχῆς κτίσεως).

25. Isa. 40.10; Mic. 1.2-4; Nah. 1.3-5; Hab 2.3 (LXX). The latter is alluded to in 2 Pet. 3.9. The 'day of the Lord' is portrayed as near in Joel 2.1; 3.15; and Zeph. 1.7, 14.

26. The identification of 'the fathers' as the Old Testament fathers has been criticized by Bauckham (1983: 290). On such an interpretation, he contends, the scoffers' objection would be a general one based on the non-fulfilment of Old

6.1.3 *'All things remain'*

The second objection relates to the continuance of 'all things'. This clause extends the temporal objection by providing the proof that the promise has not been fulfilled: we know that the prophecy is unrealized because the world remains as before. Yet, at the same time, it expresses an additional objection to the promise of the parousia.

The standard view in recent discussion is that the statement constitutes a principled rejection of the possibility of divine intervention. The scoffers' point is that the world carries on as it always has done, without divine interference. Influential here has been the work of Jerome Neyrey setting 2 Peter against an Epicurean background.[27] Accepting Neyrey's reconstruction, Bauckham states, 'The scoffers assumed that God does not intervene in the world'; they were influenced 'by a rationalist skepticism ... to which the Epicurean denial of providence seems the closest pagan parallel'.[28] But this explanation is unsatisfactory. There is little textual warrant for assuming that the issue is whether or not God can get involved in the world. First, the scoffers make reference to the *continuous duration* (διαμένει) of the cosmos as an unaltered (οὕτως) physical structure from the day of its creation, not to its closed nature, or its freedom from divine activity. Second, as it stands, the statement is perfectly compatible with belief in divine action in the ongoing history of the world; the words neither deny it nor affirm it.[29] Third, if the scoffers'

Testament prophecy over many centuries. He points out that, 'Early Christianity constantly argued that OT prophecies, after remaining unfulfilled for centuries, had quite recently been fulfilled in the history of Jesus.' In such a climate, he argues, it does not seem very relevant for the scoffers to object that Old Testament prophecy remains unfulfilled since Old Testament times. But, 2 Pet. 1.20-21 indicates that the opponents did not have a high regard for Old Testament prophecy; thus, they may well have dissented from the supposedly shared Christian assumption that scriptural prophecy had begun to be fulfilled with the historical appearance of Jesus. In any case, the scoffers' objection is not just that prophecy has lain dormant since Old Testament times, but more precisely that the specific prediction of a *soon-approaching* (and world-stopping) event has remained unfulfilled. It is because oracles of God's coming present the ultimate event as *temporally near* that they are falsified by the increasing passage of time.

27. Neyrey 1980.
28. Bauckham 1983: 294. Also: Horrell 1998: 139, 176; Knight 1995: 67; Kraftchick 2002: 152–3. Craddock (1995: 119), M. Green (1987: 138–9), Meier (1988: 255–7) and Vögtle (1994: 221) assume that the objection stems from a view that the world is closed to divine intervention, but do not specifically connect it with Epicureanism.
29. Cf. Meier 1988: 255.

objection is that God does not/cannot intervene in the human and natural world, especially for the purpose of judgement, it is very strange that in his reply to it in vv. 5-7 the author does not recite other biblical examples of God's dramatic interventions for judgement, beyond the flood. He could have mentioned the destruction of Sodom and Gomorrah, the plagues on Egypt, the destruction of the Egyptians in the sea of reeds, the fall of Jericho and so on.[30] He concentrates *exclusively* on the flood story and his reason for doing so is clear; it is the one biblical example of God intervening to *destroy* the world. This shows that the writer does not see the point at stake as whether or not God can intervene to judge. Rather, for him, the question is whether the cosmos is subject to destruction.

That the cosmological assertion of the scoffers reflects Epicurean thought is highly unlikely. The scoffers affirm the *created* nature of the universe (κτίσις); Epicureans, of course, totally repudiated the notion of the divine creation of the cosmos. Also, the scoffers maintain that the world has endured without disturbance or change. But as we saw in Chapter 3, according to Lucretius, the world has experienced many great disturbances and has undergone very considerable change during the course of its life; 'nothing remains as it was: all things move, all are changed by nature and compelled to alter' (*rerum* 5.828-30). Epicureans, of course, taught that this cosmos and all the cosmoi are inherently destructible.[31] It is very hard to see how the affirmation 'all things remain just as they were from the beginning of creation' could in any way be informed by an Epicurean view of physical reality.

Earlier commentators, most notably Charles Bigg, saw in the scoffers' cosmological claim an expression of belief in the imperishability of the cosmos, reflecting the Platonic and Aristotelian doctrine of cosmic indestructibility.[32] On this understanding, the scoffers reject the expectation of the divine parousia because it is thought to involve the dissolution of the cosmos. Rarely in post-biblical 'catastrophic intervention' texts (and not all in the Old Testament) does God's coming or intervention result in

---

30. In 2.3-10, the author does cite past examples of judgement (the judgement upon the sinful angels, the flood and the destruction of Sodom and Gomorrah). He does so, however, not to defend the principle of divine intervention, but to affirm the certainty of future judgement (2.3, 9). In 3.4-7, 10-13, the point at issue is not the fact of coming judgement, but the particular *form* that future judgement will take, namely, total cosmic destruction.

31. Neyrey (1993: 231) appears to attribute belief in the eternity of the cosmos in an Aristotelian sense to Epicurus, which would be erroneous. Epicurus believed in the eternity of matter, but this is very different from Aristotle's view that the ordered cosmos is ungenerated and indestructible.

32. Bigg 1910: 292. Cf. Sidebottom 1967: 119.

the total destruction of the cosmos (only in *Apoc. Zeph.* 12.5-8), but this is easily an inference that could be drawn from these texts.

Bauckham doubts that the assertion of the opponents amounts to an affirmation of the Platonic/Aristotelian doctrine of cosmic indestructibility. According to Bauckham, while the scoffers point out that everything continues as it always has been, 'There is no assertion that the nature of the universe is such that everything *must* go on as it has always done.'[33] But, in using the world's freedom from major catastrophe during the period from creation to the present moment as *an argument against the parousia*, the opponents evidently assume that the world's unswerving continuity from past to present ensures its future constancy: the stability which the cosmos has evinced up till now serves as a guarantee of its stability in the time ahead. That this is a stable, immutable world is their premise. That it will remain so – ruling out the parousia – is their conclusion.[34] It should be noted that the present tense of the verb διαμέμω carries the idea of permanent and unending duration. The present tense clearly functions in this way in Heb. 1.10-12, and it would seem likely that it does so here too. Had the thought been of the continuity of the world only up to the moment of speaking, the perfect tense would surely have been used.[35] Both in terms of its argumentative logic and linguistic formulation, therefore, the cosmological statement of 3.4 is best taken as affirmation of cosmic indestructibility.

The scoffers' argument may be compared to an argument advanced by Critolaus, the head of the Peripatetic school in the second century CE. In a fragment preserved by Philo (*Aet. Mund.* 61), Critolaus defends the eternity of the cosmos on empirical grounds.[36]

> Has the earth too grown so old that it may be thought to have been sterilised by length of time? On the contrary it remains as it was ever young (ἀλλ' ἐν ὁμοίῳ μένει νεάζουσα ἀεί), because it is the fourth part of the All and is bound to remain undecayed in order to conserve the sum of things, just as also its sister elements, water, air and fire, continue to defy old age.

Critolaus offers as proof of the world's immutability the perpetual fruitfulness of the earth (*Aet. Mund.* 62-65). Far from displaying the signs of age and decay, it remains in its ever-youthful condition. Its long

---

33. Bauckham 1983: 293.
34. Cf. M. Green 1987: 140.
35. Cf. Lk. 22.28.
36. Theophrastus, of course, also used empirical arguments in defence of Aristotle's thesis of an eternal cosmos: Philo, *Aet. Mund.* 117-49.

continuity in the same stable condition indicates that it will endure for ever. A similar line of reasoning is apparent in 2 Pet. 3.4, though from a creationist perspective.

6.1.4 *Summary*

To sum up, then, the 'promise of his coming' rejected by the author's opponents is the expectation of God's eschatological advent which Christians applied to Jesus, generating the specifically 'Christian' notion of the parousia/second coming of Jesus. The opponents deny the validity of the hope of God's coming on two grounds: first, the very long stretch of time that has passed since the promise of God's advent was originally made; second, the philosophically based conviction that the cosmos is unchanging and indestructible.

The claims reported in v. 4 set the agenda for what follows in vv. 5-10. The author tackles their cosmological objection first, in vv. 5-7. In vv. 8-9, he responds to the opponents' temporal argument. In v. 10, he asserts the certainty of the coming of the Lord, and describes its catastrophic outcome.

6.2 *The Present Heavens and Earth Reserved for Fire:*
2 Peter 3.5-7

In vv. 5-7, the writer delivers his response to the opponents' assertion that 'all things remain just as they were from the beginning of creation'.

> 5) They deliberately ignore this fact: that long ago there were heavens and an earth formed out of water and through water by the word of God, 6) through which the world of that time was deluged with water and destroyed. 7) But by the same word the present heavens and earth have been reserved for fire, being kept until the day of judgement and destruction of the godless.

> 5) Λανθάνει γὰρ αὐτοὺς τοῦτο θέλοντας ὅτι οὐρανοὶ ἦσαν ἔκπαλαι καὶ γῆ ἐξ ὕδατος καὶ δι' ὕδατος συνεστῶσα τῷ τοῦ θεοῦ λόγῳ, 6) δι' ὧν ὁ τότε κόσμος ὕδατι κατακλυσθεὶς ἀπώλετο· 7) οἱ δὲ νῦν οὐρανοὶ καὶ ἡ γῆ τῷ αὐτῷ λόγῳ τεθησαυρισμένοι εἰσὶν πυρὶ τηρούμενοι εἰς ἡμέραν κρίσεως καὶ ἀπωλείας τῶν ἀσεβῶν ἀνθρώπων.

He brings into association (1) the creation of the world, conceived in biblical terms as creation by divine word, (2) the flood in the time of Noah and (3) the future judgement by fire. This short section, as Kelly states, 'is beset with grammatical, exegetical and syntactical difficulties which make its analysis in detail tantalizing'.[37] Before elucidating the author's argumentation, it is necessary to deal with the exegetical issues arising from the text.

6.2.1 *Exegetical Issues*

The first of these issues confronts us in the opening words; the Greek clause, λανθάνει γὰρ αὐτοὺς τοῦτο θέλοντας ὅτι, could either be translated (as above) as, (1) 'They deliberately ignore this fact ... ',[38] or as (2) 'in maintaining this, they overlook the fact that ... '[39] On the latter rendering, the opponents accidentally neglect or forget a truth; on the former, they deliberately disregard it. Either is possible. The position of the word τοῦτο immediately next to θέλοντας favours the second option,[40] though this rendering involves giving θέλοντας an unusual (but not unparalleled) sense ('maintaining, 'asserting'). But option (1) is more consistent with the author's presentation of his adversaries as deceivers and twisters of the truth (2.3; 3.16) and for this reason is to be preferred.[41] What they wilfully ignore, as the writer depicts them, is not the fact of the world's creation, which on the basis of the report in 3.4 they clearly accept, but the event of the Noachic flood and the character of that event as a reversal of creation.

Does the Greek participle συνεστῶσα, 'formed' refer to both οὐρανοί and γῆ or only to the latter? Grammatically, it belongs just with γῆ, but since the writer obviously believes that the heavens, as well as the earth, were created by God, it ought to be taken with both.[42]

The formulation ἐξ ὕδατος καὶ δι' ὕδατος presents particular difficulty. The first phrase, ἐξ ὕδατος, is taken by most modern commentators as an allusion to the emergence of the heavens and earth from the pre-existent waters of chaos as described in Genesis 1.[43] The mention of 'heavens and earth' and the reference to 'the word of God' certainly echo

37. Kelly 1969: 357. Bauckham (1983: 302) states, 'This passage is perhaps the most difficult of several passages in 2 Peter'.
38. Taking τοῦτο with λανθάει giving the sense, 'this escapes their notice wilfully'.
39. Taking τοῦτο with θέοντας giving the sense, 'it escapes their notice maintaining this'.
40. So Bauckham 1983: 297, following Kelly 1969: 356–7.
41. Kraftchick 2002: 155.
42. So, e.g., Bauckham 1983: 296. Its feminine singular form is to be explained by attraction to the gender and number of the closest antecedent.
43. The notion of a primeval sea is a generic feature of ancient Near Eastern mythological cosmogony: KRS pp. 11–17.

the Genesis creation narrative. The thought expressed by the writer's wording, if taken literally, goes beyond the description in Genesis, but the phrase ἐξ ὕδατος is at least, as Kelly puts it, 'an understandable gloss' on it.[44] The complementary phrase, δι' ὕδατος, in contrast, is very difficult to explain purely in terms of Genesis 1, and none of the mainline attempts to make sense of it fully satisfy.

An older explanation is that the writer is using the Greek preposition διά with the genitive in a local sense meaning 'in the midst of' or 'between', rather than 'through'.[45] However, the use of διά + genitive with this meaning, though not unprecedented, is extremely unusual.[46]

Another suggestion is that δι' ὕδατος has an instrumental sense and refers to the means by which the earth was sustained, that is, rain (cf. Gen. 2.5).[47] But the reference in 2 Pet. 3.5 is clearly to the *formation* of the world not to the sustenance of life upon it.[48]

The standard approach among commentators is to take δι' ὕδατος instrumentally, with the sense, 'by means of water', and to see it as a rather nebulous reference to God's separation of the waters. Thus Bauckham writes, 'the writer means that water was, in a loose sense, the instrument of creation, since it was by separating and gathering the waters that God created the world'.[49] But this is a very strained attempt to make the language fit Genesis 1.

The difficulty commentators have in making sense of δι' ὕδατος against the background of the Genesis creation narrative raises the question of whether the author in his coupling of the phrases ἐξ ὕδατος and δι' ὕδατος is dependent on another creation tradition, alongside the biblical one.

Tord Fornberg, in his landmark study of 2 Peter in its Hellenistic context, points out that the verb translated 'formed', συνιστάναι, is a technical creation term in Greek and Hellenistic authors.[50] Used in connection with the preposition ἐκ, it normally indicates the material out

---

44. Kelly 1969: 358.
45. E.g., Mayor 1907: 151; Chaine 1937: 210 n. 3.
46. Cf. Kelly 1969: 358-9. Significantly, the LXX of Gen. 1.6 uses the constructions ἐν μέσῳ and ἀνὰ μέσον to relate the creation of the sky 'in the midst of' and 'between' the waters. γενηθήτω στερέωμα ἐν μέσῳ τοῦ ὕδατος καὶ ἔστω διαχωρίζον ἀνὰ μέσον ὕδατος καὶ ὕδατος καὶ ἐγένετο οὕτως.
47. E.g., Bigg 1910: 293; M. Green 1987: 141.
48. The verb συνιστάναι can mean 'subsist', as in Col. 1.17, but here the sense is plainly 'put together', 'form'.
49. Bauckham 1983: 297.
50. Fornberg 1977: 67.

of which the cosmos was made.[51] With the construction ἐξ ὕδατος ... συνεστῶσα, therefore, the author seems to be saying that water was the very stuff out of which the cosmos was created. Such a notion, of course, exceeds the teaching of Genesis 1. Bauckham thinks that the scientific sense of the language should not be pressed; the author means to convey no more than the mythological concept found in Genesis 1, that the world emerged from a primeval sea.[52] But given the level of acculturation displayed by the writer, the choice of words is surely significant. The author of 2 Peter is culturally sophisticated[53] and philosophically informed (see further below). It is highly likely that he is well aware of the scientific implications of his wording and that he is deliberately evoking them.

In 2 Pet. 3.5, therefore, as well as calling to mind Genesis 1, the writer appears to be alluding to a particular Greek or Hellenistic cosmological tradition, one in which water is specifically identified as the substance out of which the world was made. That tradition would give clarity to the enigmatic δι' ὕδατος.

Thales taught that water is the primal element out of which everything else has emerged.[54] Kelly thinks that the author of 2 Peter is interpreting Genesis 1 in the light of Thales' doctrine.[55] However, it is not obvious why the writer would set so much store by Thales' opinion. Thales' views on cosmic origins were certainly treated with respect but hardly represented the cutting edge of scientific thinking in the late first or early second century CE. Also, from what we know about Thales' teaching, there is nothing in it that would illuminate the phrase δι' ὕδατος. A modified version of Thales' notion, though, was adopted by the early Stoics and, as we saw in Chapter 3, formed part of their cosmogony.

The double prepositional construction, 'out of water and through water', in fact makes very good sense against the background of Stoic cosmogony, as outlined in Chapter 3. On the basis of the Stoic account of cosmic origins, it would be quite correct to say that the cosmos was formed 'out of' water, since water, though not the archetypal element, was nevertheless the immediate substance out of which the cosmos was made, the malleable, corporeal stuff which the divine craftsman shaped

---

51. See references in Fornberg 1977: 67 n. 12.
52. Bauckham 1983: 297.
53. He writes in a style of Greek known as 'Asiatic Greek' which was still fashionable at the time he was writing: see Reicke 1964: 146–7.
54. See Chapter 3, p. 104.
55. Kelly 1969: 358.

and adapted into an ordered world.[56] It would be equally correct to say that the heavens and the earth were formed 'through' water, since water was not the original state of things but one of the material alterations experienced by the universe on its way to becoming a fully formed structure. On this understanding, διά + genitive does not have the instrumental sense 'by means of', which most commentators ascribe to it, but has the sense of 'through the medium of', denoting a temporary material state.[57]

If the author, then, is alluding to the Stoic view of world-formation, he is implying that the watery pre-cosmic state of Gen. 1.2 was preceded by a more primal state of things – a state of pure fire.

The prepositional phrase δι' ὧν in 2 Pet. 3.6 is plural, and there is debate about its antecedents,[58] but, most naturally, it picks up the two previously mentioned entities, water and word. There is thus 'a neat parallelism' in all three verses:[59] by water and word God created the world (v. 5); by water and word he destroyed it (v. 6); by fire and word he will destroy it again (v. 7).

---

56. In Stoic cosmogonal thought, the change to water is properly *the beginning of our world*. It is the moment of the world's conception: this is clear from the comparison of the cosmic water to male reproductive fluid and is vividly expressed in Dio's 'orgasmic' depiction of the Stoic cosmogonal scheme (*Disc.* 36.56-57). Although, within the Stoic scheme, the transition to air precedes that to water, it is connected more with the abatement of the conflagration than with the emergence of a new world. Little is made of it in the biological explanation of how the world began. That the shift to water constitutes the point at which a new cosmos starts to materialize is confirmed by Seneca (*Nat. quaes.* 3.13); he writes: 'I will add, as Thales says, "Water is the most powerful element." He thinks it was the first element, and all things arose from it. We Stoics are also of this opinion, or close to it. For we say that it is fire which takes possession of the universe and changes all things into itself; it becomes feeble, fades, and sinks, and when fire is extinguished nothing is left in nature except moisture, in which lies the hope of the universe to come. Thus, fire is the end of the world, moisture the beginning.'

57. That this would give διά + genitive a different sense from its use in the very next verse (δι' ὧν, 'by means of which') is not a strong objection. In 1.4, the writer use ἐν + dative twice in back-to-back phrases to express two different meanings: ἐν τῷ κόσμῳ ἐν ἐπιθυμίᾳ. In the first phrase ἐν is locative, 'in the world'; in the second, the preposition is causal, 'because of desire'. The phrase δι' ὕδατος, admittedly, is not attested in the sources cited above with reference to the transformation to water, so there is no exact verbal parallel to it in the Stoic tradition. Yet, the words δι' ἀέρος in Diogenes 7.136, 142 serve as a close comparison, indicating as they do a transitional step in the process that leads from fire to life-sustaining cosmos.

58. For the possibilities, see Bauckham 1983: 298.

59. Bauckham 1983: 298; cf. D. M. Russell 1996: 188.

The phrase ὁ τότε κόσμος, 'the world of that time' could be interpreted as referring either to the world of human beings, or the physical cosmos. In 2.5, in connection with the Noachic flood, the writer speaks of 'the ancient world' (ἀρχαίου κόσμου) and the 'world of the ungodly' (κόσμῳ ἀσεβῶν). In that verse, the word κόσμος in both instances seems to refer primarily to the human inhabitants of the world.[60] However, the present context definitely favours the physical universe. The prior references to the heavens and earth in 3.5 and the apparent parallelism between ὁ τότε κόσμος and οἱ δὲ νῦν οὐρανοὶ καὶ ἡ γῆ, 'the present heavens and earth' in vv. 6-7 would indicate that the sense is cosmological.

The depiction of the Noachic flood in v. 6 obviously recalls Gen. 7.17-24. The term κατακλυσθείς, 'deluged', which occurs only here in the New Testament, is not found in the Genesis flood story, though it does appear in Wis. 10.4 with reference to the Noachic flood. The addition of 'with water' (ὕδατι) is not strictly necessary (especially if 'through which' effectively means 'through water and word'), but it lays emphasis on the watery nature of the destruction and reinforces the parallel with creation. The writer goes further than Genesis in presenting the Noachic flood as a *cosmic* cataclysm, resulting in cosmic destruction: 'the world (i.e., cosmos) of that time ... was destroyed' (ἀπώλετο). The parallel with creation in v. 5 indicates that the writer views the flood as a return to the pre-creation watery state of things at the beginning. It is often pointed out that *1 En.* 83.3-5 portrays the flood as a cosmic catastrophe, and the deduction is then made that the author of 2 Peter must have been dependent on a Jewish tradition like this.[61] However, *1 En.* 83.3-5 does not actually depict a cosmic *flood*. The passage says nothing about the opening of the windows of heaven or the bursting out of the fountains of the deep (cf. Gen. 7.11). Rather, heaven collapses onto the earth and the earth sinks back into the abyss. The picture is really that of the final world-ending catastrophe which the author has imposed on the flood.[62] The closest parallel to what is imagined in 2 Pet. 3.6 is the Roman Stoic notion of a cosmic deluge, corresponding to the cosmic conflagration.[63] Assuming the author's dependence on Stoic teaching for his cosmogony in v. 5 (and his expectation of a cosmic conflagration in vv. 7, 10-12), indebtedness to Stoicism for the thought of a *cosmic* flood seems likely.

In v. 7, the writer speaks of the present heaven and earth (οἱ δὲ νῦν οὐρανοὶ καὶ ἡ γῆ) being 'reserved' for fire. The choice of verb,

---

60. Bauckham 1983: 250.
61. E.g., Bauckham 1983: 299; Kelly 1969: 359; Kraftchick 2002: 157; etc.
62. See pp. 61–2.
63. Seneca, *Nat. quaes.* 3.28.7. See p. 118.

θησαυρίζω, which more literally means 'to store up' (treasure) is, as Bauckham states, somewhat surprising, but reflects the use of this image in other (Jewish and New Testament) writings for the idea of 'preservation until the Day of Judgment'.[64] It is quite clear from the context that what the writer means by 'reserved for fire' is *reserved for fiery destruction*. He anticipates a judgement by fire which parallels the earlier judgement by flood, which had *destroyed* (ἀπώλετο) the world of that time.

The source of the author's expectation of a cosmic conflagration is the subject of much controversy. Most reject the possibility of Stoic influence, preferring to see an Old Testament and Jewish background to the thought. But as emphasized in Chapter 2, the idea of the total destruction of the cosmos by fire is not found in the Old Testament. Bauckham thinks that it was 'a fairly widespread conception' in post-biblical Jewish texts, but as the investigation of Chapter 2 showed, in Jewish apocalyptic and similar writings, the notion is in fact very rare; indeed the only certain instances of it are passages in *Sibylline Oracles* in which Stoic influence is at work.[65] In the author's time, the expectation of a cosmic conflagration was commonly viewed as a characteristically Stoic conception. It seems entirely reasonable to conclude that it was from Stoicism that he derived it.[66] The scriptural catalyst for our author's embracing of the Stoic notion may well have been Mal. 3.1 and 4.1.

The fact that the section ends with reference to 'the day of judgment and destruction of the godless' has been used to downplay the author's apparent interest in cosmological matters, especially the question of the fate of the cosmos.[67] Thus S. J. Kraftchick writes, 'the author is not interested in cosmology *per se*, but in proving that there is a future judgment for human sin'. According to Kraftchick, the writer uses elements of cosmology 'to convey the idea of universal divine judgment, not to propose a theory of cosmology'.[68] The final clause shows that the author is not concerned with cosmic destruction, but the punishment of the wicked.[69] I have to disagree. On linguistic content alone, cosmology is *self-evidently* the main interest of these verses. The shift to the thought of

64. Bauckham 1983: 299; cf. Rom. 2.5; Jas 5.3; Cf. *Ps. Sol.* 9.5; *4 Ezra* 7.77, 83-84.
65. See pp. 90–91, 92–3, 94–5.
66. Pearson (2001) argues for the influence of Persian traditions of fiery judgement as well as Stoicism. This conjecture faces the problem of the relatively late date of the main sources for Iranian eschatology.
67. Vögtle 1970: 136.
68. Kraftchick 2002: 158.
69. Kraftchick 2002: 159.

the judgement of the ungodly does not in the least negate, undermine or relativize the previous cosmological statements. As I will show below, the author is presenting a concentrated argument for cosmic destructibility; the theme of judgement, as we will see, is introduced *in support of* that case, supplying a reason for God's destruction of the world.

That the writer envisages in v. 7 the *actual* destruction of the cosmos should, I hope, be abundantly clear. The comparison with the Noachic flood, which the writer interprets as a cosmic catastrophe which takes the created world back to pre-created conditions, in itself is sufficient to establish this point.[70]

6.2.2 *The Utilization of Stoic Cosmology*

In the foregoing exegetical discussion, I identified three features of the argument of vv. 5-7 which seem to be dependent on Stoic cosmology:

- the assertion that the heavens and earth were 'formed out of water and through water', which evokes the distinctively Stoic account of world origins;
- the portrayal of the Genesis flood as a cosmic deluge, reflecting the (Roman) Stoic belief that the cosmos is subject to destruction by water as well as by fire;
- the claim that the present cosmos is destined for fire, reflecting the Stoic theory of cosmic conflagration.

The writer focuses on three great moments in the biblical history of the world, creation, flood and the coming fiery judgement, and matches these with key events in a Stoic view of cosmic history – the watery emergence of the world, the cosmic cataclysm and the great conflagration.

A resemblance between the writer's teaching on the world's fiery demise and the Stoic doctrine of *ekpurōsis* is generally recognized. Most commentators, though, point out that the author displays major differences from Stoic cosmology, and on this basis conclude that he owes little if anything in this section to Stoicism.[71]

---

70. So rightly Bauckham (1983: 294), who also points out that the judgement of Sodom and Gomorrah (2.6) is plainly conceived of by the writer as a physical destruction.

71. E.g., Bauckham 1993: 301; M. Green 1987: 143; Horrell 1998: 178; Kelly 1969: 361; Vögtle 1994: 228. This approach goes back to Justin, who notes the apparent similarity of the 'Christian' expectation of cosmic conflagration to the Stoic *ekpurōsis* but denies any dependence on it: *1 Apol.* 20.1-4; 60.8-9; *2 Apol.* 7.2-3; cf.

That the writer's outlook differs in fundamental ways from Stoicism is readily apparent. His creational monotheism and linear eschatology stand in sharp contrast to Stoic pantheism and cyclic eschatology. Other alleged differences are perhaps not so pronounced,[72] but, to be sure, the author's overall worldview is definitely not a Stoic one. However, this does not rule out or render implausible an indebtedness to Stoicism for the ideas highlighted above, and the expectation of cosmic conflagration in particular. The Jewish writers of the *Sibylline Oracles* incorporated features of the Stoic doctrine of *ekpurōsis* into their eschatologies, without buying into Stoic pantheism or the cyclic aspects of the theory; I see no reason why the author of 2 Peter could not have drawn selectively on Stoic cosmology in a similar way.[73] It is well recognized that in 1.3-11, the writer expresses himself in 'terms that make contact with the ideals and aspirations of contemporary pagan culture',[74] utilizing in vv. 5-7, material from Stoic ethical tradition.[75] It is not unlikely that in defending the hope of the parousia and the end of the world he also makes use of 'pagan' material conducive to his argument. The three features of vv. 5-7 noted above, as I have shown, are best explained on the assumption of Stoic influence.

The author's adoption of these elements of Stoic cosmology is apologetically motivated. Faced with an objection to the parousia promise on the ground of the philosophical doctrine of cosmic indestructibility, he responds by invoking a traditional rival viewpoint. This enables him to offer a scientific defence of his eschatological convictions as well as a biblical one.[76]

Origen, *C. Cels.* 4.11-13. Some are more prepared to see Stoic influence: Kraftchick 2002: 158 (cautiously); Perkins (1995: 190–1); Reicke 1964: 177.

72. One supposed key difference is that for Stoics the conflagration is a naturalistic event, whereas, for our author, the fiery dissolution is brought about by the action of God (so, e.g., Bauckham 1983: 325; Kelly 1969: 367–8). But in orthodox Stoicism, the conflagration is both a 'natural' event and the action of a providential deity (see Chapter 3, pp. 116–7). As was observed at the end of Chapter 3 (pp. 128–9), there was some convergence between Jewish and Stoic 'end of the world' doctrines.

73. He could hardly have subscribed to the biological version of the cosmogonal theory, with its view of God as utterly conjoined with matter, as an impersonal, energizing power operating within, and as the active male component in, the generative process.

74. Bauckham 1997: 926.

75. See Fornberg 1977: 97–101.

76. One may compare the appeal that the second-century Christian apologist Minucius Felix makes, in *Oct.* 11.1-3, to Stoic physical theory in his defence of

6.2.3 *The Arguments of 2 Peter 3.5-7*

These verses contain three interwoven lines of argumentation, though interpreters have often failed to distinguish them clearly. Each is a defence of the principle of cosmic destructibility. The first and most obvious argument directly addresses the opponents' argument about the world's freedom from catastrophe. The writer disputes their premise that the world has continued in an unbroken line from creation to the present day. In making this claim, he points out, the scoffers deliberately leave the flood out of the account. During the flood, the cosmos was destroyed by water. If the universe was undone once before, it can be ruined again. On the final day of judgement, the world will be destroyed by fire. Underlying the author's argument is the notion, which, as we have seen, is well established in Jewish apocalyptic and related literature, that the Noachic flood is a typological precursor of the final judgement.[77]

In *rerum* 5.380-415, Lucretius argues for cosmic destructibility from the fact that the world has been subject to massive catastrophes in the past. In 5.380-415, he specifically mentions Deucalion's flood. In general terms, the writer of 2 Peter follows this reasoning. The specific point made by Lucretius is that past terrestrial catastrophes point to an eventual cosmic disaster. But Aristotle had already provided a response to this argument by insisting that terrestrial calamities even on a global scale affect only the sub-lunar realm and can never threaten the cosmos as a whole. By portraying the Noachic flood as a total *cosmic* catastrophe, the writer of 2 Peter goes beyond Lucretius and effectively obviates this potential objection.

The second line of argument may be discerned from the author's reference to creation and his stress on the divine word. The cosmos was formed by the word of God (τῷ τοῦ θεοῦ λόγῳ, v. 5). By God's word, it was flooded and reduced to water. By the same word (τῷ αὐτῷ λόγῳ), God has ordained that the world will be destroyed by fire (v. 7). The author thus argues for cosmic destruction from belief in the divine creation of the world, a belief to which his opponents also subscribed. Since the world has been *created* by God's command, it can also be *de-created* by it. It was Plato's axiom that only the creator himself can unmake the world he has created;[78] the writer accepts and builds on this principle. He contends that the divine word by which the world was

---

belief in the future destruction of the world by fire, in response to an opponent who rejects it as contrary to the theorem of cosmic indissolubility.

77. E.g., *1 Enoch* 10; *LAB* 3.9-10.
78. Plato, *Tim.* 32C.

made is the very same word by which it was once and will again be destroyed.

The third line of argument develops in three steps, the first two forming the basis for the third,[79] and hinges on the references to water and fire. This is a physical argument for cosmic destructibility which draws specifically on Stoic physics. Underlying the logic is the Stoic physical principle articulated by Seneca: 'Water and fire dominate earthly things. From them is the origin, from them the death.'[80] Verse 5 contains the first stage of the argument. Heaven and earth were formed out of the element water (ἐξ ὕδατος). Water, however, was not the earliest form of this element but the altered condition (δι' ὕδατος) of a more pristine entity – obviously fire (v. 7). Since the ordered world arose from fire and water, it is destined to be resolved into these twin elements.[81] Verse 6 expresses the second point. The cosmos was destroyed by water (ὕδατι) at the time of the flood, when it returned to its primordial aquatic state. Verse 7 draws the conclusion derived from points one and two. The world now awaits a second destruction, this time by fire (πυρί). This destruction will take place at the parousia, when God will intervene decisively to judge the ungodly. The author thus argues for coming cosmic destruction from the physical origins of the world, informed by Stoic cosmogony. The world's emergence from fire and water points to twin cosmic catastrophes by these phenomena. The watery destruction lies in the past; a fiery destiny lies ahead.

The author thus provides in vv. 5-7 a three-line defence of cosmic destructibility. The first line of argumentation contradicts the argument of the opponents that since all things have endured without change from creation they will *always* endure. The second and third lines offer additional support for belief in the future destruction of the cosmos, on theological and physical grounds.

It is noteworthy that the writer's second and third lines of argumentation contain neat replies to the standard Platonic/Aristotelian theological and physical arguments against cosmic destructibility. Plato stressed that only the creator could de-create what he has made. But he insisted that the demiurge could have no possible motivation for destroying the world; therefore the cosmos will endure unceasingly.[82] Aristotle refined this argument, considering then dismissing hypothetical

79. Cf. Horrell 1998: 176.
80. Seneca, *Nat. quaest.* 1.28.
81. On the twin assumptions that generation implies destructibility and that all things dissolve into that out of which they were generated.
82. Plato, *Tim.* 29A.

motives.[83] By emphasizing that the divine word which brought about creation is the *same* word which has decreed its destruction, the writer of 2 Peter meets Plato's requirement. He then supplies a motivation for God's destruction of the world, though not one which Plato or Aristotle would have considered as valid, but which fits with the Stoic perspective.[84] God destroys the world in order to effect judgement on the ungodly who have polluted the world (v. 7; cf. v. 13).

Plato and Aristotle also objected to cosmic destructibility on physical grounds. According to Plato, destruction is caused by external or internal means, but the cosmos is susceptible to neither. Since all existing matter was used up in the construction of the cosmos, there is nothing outside the cosmos that can cause it harm.[85] Since the four elements are combined in perfect harmony, no one element can gain ascendancy over the rest. The argument was reiterated by Aristotle, who made the additional point that destruction from within, through one element (such as fire) usurping the others, would entail the logical impossibility of a part being able to bring down the whole (Philo, *Aet. Mund.* 22). The author of 2 Peter provides a response to this reasoning. By indicating that the world is subject to destruction by water and fire, he shows that the cosmos is susceptible to destruction from within; the universe 'contains the material for its own ruin'.[86] His adoption of Stoic physical theory gives him an answer to Aristotle's objection that the whole cannot be undone by one of its parts.[87] An element may destroy the whole if it was itself *once* the whole and again *becomes* the whole. When the cosmos was destroyed by water, it was resolved into a material condition that presently constitutes a part, but at one time formed the whole (3.5). At the conflagration, it will return to its original state of pure fire.

Verses 5-7 thus form a concentrated defence of the destructibility of the cosmos, which appears to reflect an awareness of the polemics involved in the philosophical debate on the fate of the cosmos, and which exploits Stoic cosmological theory in particular.

---

83. Philo, *Aet. Mund.* 39-43.
84. Neither Plato nor Aristotle considered the punishment of the wicked and obliteration of evil as one of the possible reasons God might have for destroying the world. It is true that the Stoics did not regard the conflagration as a divine judgement on human wickedness, but, some did see it as having a moral effect – as cleansing the world of moral evil (see Chapter 3, pp. 117–8, 121–2).
85. Plato, *Tim.* 33A.
86. Calvin 1963: 362.
87. Cf. Mansfeld 1979: 144–5.

6.3 *The Fiery Destruction of the Existing Cosmos: 2 Peter 3.10-12*

Having provided a Stoically informed justification for belief in cosmic destructibility and having declared that the heavens and earth are 'reserved for fire', in v. 10 and vv. 11-12 the author depicts the coming cosmic catastrophe. Before this, in vv. 8-9, he deals with the issue of delay, addressing the temporal objection of the scoffers. First (v. 8), he argues, on the basis of Ps. 90.4, that God's apprehension of time is very different from that of human beings. From the divine point of view, what seems to humans a long span of time – a thousand years – appears very short – a mere day – to God. Second (v. 9), he insists that God is not slow concerning his promise. He recognizes that there has indeed been a delay in the fulfilment of the promise, but maintains that the postponement of the eschatological parousia is due to God's forbearance, so that people may have an extended opportunity for repentance.

In v. 10, he insists that, though the eschatological intervention has been delayed, it will certainly take place.[88]

> But the day of the Lord will come like a thief, and then the heavens will pass away with a loud noise, and the elements will be dissolved in the heat, and the earth and the works in it will be disclosed.
>
> ἥξει δὲ ἡμέρα κυρίου ὡς κλέπτης, ἐν ᾗ οἱ οὐρανοὶ ῥοιζηδὸν παρελεύσονται στοιχεῖα δὲ καυσούμενα λυθήσεται καὶ γῆ καὶ τὰ ἐν αὐτῇ ἔργα εὑρεθήσεται.

The author speaks in terms of the 'day of the Lord', rather than the 'parousia', but that the two terms refer to the same concept – the eschatological intervention[89] – is clear from their combination in v. 12 (τὴν παρουσίαν τῆς τοῦ θεοῦ ἡμέρας). The day will come with the suddenness and unexpectedness of a burglary. The comparison of the final intervention to a thief seems to reveal an awareness of the use of this image in the traditions of the sayings of Jesus.[90] In three clauses the writer portrays what will happen on that day.

---

88. The position of ἥξει (will come) at the beginning of the sentence is significant in this respect, laying emphasis on the fact it will indeed come. So Bauckham 1983: 314.

89. As noted earlier, the Christological dimension of the final event is not to the fore in this passage.

90. The metaphor of a thief is used of the coming of the Son of man in Mt. 24.43-44 = Lk. 12.39-40, the day of the Lord in 1 Thess. 5.2 and the coming again of Jesus in Rev. 3.3 and 16.15; cf. *Gos. Thom.* 21; *Did.* 16.1.

6.3.1 'The heavens will pass away with a loud noise'

The 'heavens' are the created, material heavens (cf. vv. 5, 7). The verb παρέρχομαι is the verb used for the passing away of heaven and earth in Mk 13.31 + par. and in Mt. 5.18 and Lk. 16.17. The traditions of Jesus' sayings on the dissolution of heaven and earth may well have exercised an influence on the wording of this clause. The adverb ῥοιζηδόν is an onomatopoeic word used for a rushing or crackling sound.[91] The noise could be, as Bauckham suggests, the thunderous roar of God in his eschatological coming.[92] The voice of God is sometimes an element of Old Testament theophanies,[93] and post-biblical Jewish depictions of the catastrophic intervention. One is reminded especially of *1 En*. 102.1 ('when he utters his voice against you with a mighty sound, will you not be shaken and frightened?').[94] The wording, though, more obviously suggests the sound made by the heavens as they dissolve, that is, the noise of the conflagration itself.[95]

6.3.2 'The elements will be dissolved in the heat'

This line speaks of a burning destruction: καυσούμενα λυθήσεται, literally, 'being burned with intense heat will be dissolved'. The meaning of the word στοιχεῖα is debated. The common cosmological sense of the term at the time was 'physical elements', that is, the four elements, earth, water, air and fire.[96] Most commentators, however, are reluctant to accept this meaning. The position generally adopted is that the heavenly bodies – sun, moon and planets – are in view.[97] A reference to the four material elements is deemed unlikely because it seems to entail the absurdity that fire is dissolved by fire. Most interpreters are also swayed by the syntactical position of 'elements' between 'heavens' and 'earth'. The author is thought to be distinguishing three cosmic layers: the outer heavens, the

---

91. Bauckham 1983: 315.
92. So Bauckham 1983: 315.
93. Pss. 18.13-15; 77.18; cf. Joel 3.16.
94. Cf. 1QH 11.34-35.
95. As in *Sib. Or.* 4.175, 'The whole world will hear a bellowing noise and mighty sound.'
96. See G. Delling στοιχέω, etc., *TDNT* 7: 666-87.
97. E.g., Bauckham 1983: 316; Kelly 1969: 364: Horrell 1998: 180; Van der Horst 1994: 246-7. A variation of the second view is that the elements are the heavenly bodies and the spiritual powers connected to them. The word has other lexical senses, but, in the present context, a cosmological sense (the physical elements; stars) is required.

intermediate spheres of the luminaries and the planets, and the earth. Bauckham argues that the words 'the elements will be dissolved in the heat', along with the similar statement in v. 12, allude specifically to Isa. 34.4 LXX B, 'and all the powers of the heavens shall melt' (καὶ τακήσονται πᾶσαι αἱ δυνάμεις τῶν οὐρανῶν),[98] referring to the celestial bodies.

However, the sense, 'heavenly bodies', is doubtful on lexical grounds. It is securely attested from the middle of the second century CE onward, but less certain before that.[99] Also, as noted in connection with Mk 13.24-25 + par., we cannot be sure that the reading of LXX B was known to New Testament writers; indeed, the reading could have been influenced by Mt. 24.19 and 2 Pet. 3.12 (which uses the verb τήκω).

In v. 12, the author refers to οὐρανοί and στοιχεῖα, and says that both will be burned and dissolved, but he makes no mention of the earth. Here, 'the heavens' and 'the elements' appear to comprehend the whole of the created physical universe, with the latter denoting the earthly realm.[100] It would be natural to assume that the term στοιχεῖα has the same application in v. 10. Now this may seem to make the specific mention of the 'earth' in v. 10d redundant, but, as we will see below, this clause develops a different thought to that of the foregoing clauses. In v. 10bc, the focus is on fiery dissolution; in v. 10d, it will be seen, the thought turns to the judgement of human beings, just as in v. 7. In v. 10d, the emphasis is not on the earth as a component of the cosmos but on the earth as the scene of human activity.

The application of the term στοιχεῖα to the realm of the earth, in contradistinction to the heavens, is perfectly in line with Stoic cosmology. In Stoic physics, the four elements of Greek physics, earth, water, air and fire, are seen as the constituents of everything *on earth*. The celestial realm, including the celestial bodies, the Stoics took to be composed of ether, or creative fire.[101] The author's twofold division of the cosmos, into the heavens and the elements, thus fits with the standard Stoic division of material reality.

A reference to the four physical elements, understood along Stoic lines as denoting the physical composition of things on earth, would not involve the contradiction of fire being dissolved with fire. Stoics distinguished between the terrestrial element fire and the designing fire which

---

98. Bauckham 1983: 316.
99. E. Plümacher (στοιχεῖον, *EDNT* 3: 277–8, here p. 278) states that the celestial bodies 'were probably called στοιξεῖα only after the NT'.
100. Cf. Neyrey 1993: 243.
101. Cf. Chapter 3, p. 115.

burns up the cosmos at the conflagration. At the conflagration, terrestrial fire, along with the other terrestrial elements, is dissolved into the primal elemental fire. Within a Stoic physical framework, it would not be nonsensical to speak of the sub-lunar element fire dissolving or 'melting' (as in v. 12) in the heat of celestial fire.

This line thus envisages the burning up and dissolution of the physical elements of which all earthly things are made; it balances the preceding clause which envisages the passing away of the physical heavens.

6.3.3 *'The earth and the works in it will be found'*

This clause presents us with perhaps the most important of all the *cruces interpretum* in the whole passage. An initial problem is a text-critical one: the manuscripts reveal a number of variants for the verb: 'will be burned up',[102] 'will disappear',[103] 'will not be found',[104] 'will be found dissolved'[105] and 'will be found'.[106] The clause is omitted entirely in some manuscripts.[107] In addition to the textual variations, scholars have proposed numerous emendations so as to find a form of wording which fits with the surrounding images of destruction;[108] all such reconstructions, it must be stressed, are scholarly conjectures; none is supported by manuscript evidence. It is now generally accepted that the reading εὑρεθήσεται, 'will be found', has the best claim to authenticity.[109] It has the best manuscript support and, as the *lectio difficilior*, all the other readings can be explained as attempts to correct it.

A greater problem lies is determining what εὑρεθήσεται might mean in the literary context. It is precisely because interpreters have found it difficult to give it a sense that fits the flow of the passage that they have been drawn towards less well-supported readings or have proposed emending the text.[110] The thought of the earth being 'found' clashes with

102. κατακαήσεται (A, Majority Text).
103. ἀφανισθήσονται (C).
104. οὐχ εὑρεθήσεται (the Sahidic version). As Bauckham notes, the reading is unlikely to be original, but represents an early attempt to correct the text (1983: 317).
105. εὑρεθήσεται λυόμενα (P72); supported by Kelly 1969: 366.
106. εὑρεθήσεται (א, B, K, P and others).
107. The clause is omitted entirely in Ψ, Stuttgart Vulgate and others.
108. See Bauckham 1983: 317–18.
109. E.g., Bauckham 1983: 316–21; Horrell 1998: 180–1; Kraftchick 2002: 163; Neyrey 1993: 243–4; Vögtle 1994: 234–5.
110. Metzger (1994: 636) states that it 'seems to be devoid of meaning in the context'.

the previous two images of cosmic dissolution, and seems to run against the statement in v. 7 that the earth along with the heavens is destined for fiery destruction. It seems to indicate that the existing earth is not destroyed but is rather preserved through the eschatological burning.

As was noted at the opening of the present chapter, Wright appeals to this clause as proof that 2 Pet. 3.5-13 cannot be talking about the dissolution of the present creation and the making of a brand new one.[111] He endorses a reading of the passage centred on εὑρεθήσεται in 3.10d, proposed by Wolters, which I will now summarize and critique.

Wolters disputes the common assumption that 2 Pet 3.5-13 envisages 'a complete destruction or abolition of the created order'.[112] In speaking of the coming judgement, the writer draws a parallel with the flood. Just as the destruction effected by water 'did not cause the world to vanish (it continues to be preserved ...), so the "destruction" which will be wrought by the fire will presumably not cause the world to vanish either'.[113] According to Wolters, the author is depicting the day of the Lord in terms of a 'smelting process'. He notes the absence of the verb καίω which means 'burn' in the sense of going up in flames. The verbs employed by the writer, καυσόω (vv. 10, 12) and πυρόω (v. 12), he claims, mean to expose to a great heat, rather than to 'burn up'.[114] In fact, the verb πυρόω is often used of the 'refining' of metals (cf. Zech. 13.9 LXX; Rev. 1.15; 3.18). In vv. 10-12, the heavens and the elements melt, as a result of an intense heat, but they are not consumed and burned up.[115] The background to the imagery, Wolters claims, is Mal. 3.2-4, in which the 'day of his coming' is likened to a refiner's fire (cf. Mal. 4.1). The author of 2 Peter expands Malachi's vision, giving it a cosmic application; what comes out of the refining process is not a purified cult as in Malachi, but 'a purified heaven and earth'.[116] In this context, the verb εὑρεθήσεται means 'to have survived', 'to have stood the test', 'to have proved genuine'. Wolters finds an exact parallel to this sense in 1 Pet. 1.7, which reads:

> so that the genuineness of your faith – being more precious than gold that, though perishable, is tested by fire – may be found (εὑρεθῇ) to result in praise and glory and honour when Jesus Christ is revealed.

---

111. N. T. Wright 2003b: 463.
112. Wolters 1987: 408.
113. Wolters 1987: 408.
114. Wolters 1987: 409.
115. Wolters 1987: 409.
116. Wolters 1987: 409–10.

Here, the passive of the verb εὑρίσκω is used absolutely for 'the surviving of a purifying fire'.[117] Wolters thinks that in 1 Pet. 1.7 and 2 Pet. 3.10 the verb is a technical metallurgical term meaning 'emerging purified (from the crucible)'.[118]

Wolters finds support for his overall interpretation of 2 Pet. 3.10-12 in *2 Clem.* 16.3:

> But you know that the day of judgement is already coming like a burning oven, and some of the heavens will melt, as will the whole earth, like lead melting due to fire, and the hidden and manifest works of men will appear.

In this text, the allusion to Malachi (4.1) is explicit, and there are verbal coincidences with 2 Pet. 3.10-12.

Wolters concludes that 2 Pet. 3.5-13 does not exhibit a 'Gnostic' perspective on the expendability of creation. The key verse, 3.10, stresses, 'the permanence of the created earth, despite the coming judgement'.[119]

It is clear that Wolters's denial that 2 Pet. 3.5-13 teaches the complete destruction of the present created order is based on the assumption that 'destruction' can only mean *absolute* destruction, that is, disappearance from existence. As I have said before, it is inappropriate to use this definition as the criterion for determining whether a New Testament author expresses a destructionist position on the future of the cosmos. The idea of the resolution of the cosmos and its matter into nothing was outside the parameters of serious cosmological speculation of the time. The author's Stoic-influenced depiction of the flood as an event which brought about the reversion of the created world to the watery chaos out of which it arose is consistent with the accepted definition of cosmic destruction during this era.[120] Wolters also seems to think that a destructionist interpretation of the passage automatically and inevitably involves the reading of a 'Gnostic worldview' into it, and this, of course, is another fallacious assumption. (Whether the letter shows evidence of a radical cosmic dualism will be considered in due course.)

It is true, as Wolters claims, that the verb καυσόω means to suffer intense heat rather than to burst into flames.[121] The natural sense of πυρόω, though, is to 'destroy by fire', and the verb is generally used of combustible entities.[122] It does have a specialized use for the refining and

---

117. Wolters (1987: 410-11) finds further support for this reading in *Barn.* 21.6; *2 Clem.* 16.3.
118. Wolters 1987: 412.
119. Wolters 1987: 413.
120. See above, pp. 21-2.
121. *TDNT* 3: 644.
122. LSJ 1558; *TDNT* 6: 948-50.

testing of metals,[123] but since the writer does not draw a metallurgical comparison in 2 Pet. 3.12, which one would expect him to do if he wished to convey this less usual sense (the comparison with metal smelting is explicitly drawn in Zech. 13.9 LXX; Rev. 1.5; 3.18), it is right to assume that he means 'burn up', 'destroy by fire'. The suggestion that our author is depicting only the melting down of the heavens and the elements, not their destruction by fire, is in any case ruled out by the fact that καυσόω in v. 10 and πυρόω in v. 12 are combined with the verb λύω (καυσούμενα λυθήσεται, πυρούμενοι λυθήσονται), which makes quite clear that he imagines the heavens and elements being *dissolved* by the heat and the burning fire. There is no indication that the controlling or underlying picture of vv. 10-12 is that of a smelting process. There are no verbal allusions to Mal. 4.1-5 in these verses. Malachi may well have prompted the author's basic association of the day of the Lord/the divine coming with fire (as acknowledged earlier), but, as we have seen, our author takes that association in a different direction under a different influence. The similarity between 2 Pet. 3.10(-12) and *2 Clem.* 16.3 is noteworthy, but the relationship between these passages and between 2 Peter and *2 Clement* in general is notoriously difficult to assess.[124] There are important differences between the two passages, and one should not read these differences – specifically the allusion to Mal. 4.1 and the comparison with melting lead – into 2 Pet. 3.10-12.

As for Wolters's understanding of εὑρεθήσεται, his suggestion that the verb refers to the outcome of a metallurgical process, as he readily acknowledges, has little lexical support outside 1 Pet. 1.7, and it is not clear that the verb has a metallurgical sense even there.[125] Also, his claim that εὑρίσκω is used 'absolutely' in 1 Pet. 1.7, as in 2 Pet. 3.10, is not really correct; the construction εὑρεθῇ εἰς means 'was found to result in' (cf. Rom. 7.10), the result being indicated by the three nouns that follow ('praise and glory and honour'), so it is not 'exactly comparable', as he puts it,[126] to the unqualified use in 2 Pet. 3.10.

---

123. *TDNT* 6: 949.

124. As Bauckham notes (1983: 150), the relationship between 2 Peter and *2 Clement* is not of the kind which literary dependence could explain. Bauckham thinks that 2 Peter and *2 Clement* draw independently on an otherwise unknown apocalyptic source (283–4), and that *2 Clem.* 16.3 may well be a quotation from that source. But this is pure conjecture. *Second Clement* has proved extremely difficult to date.

125. It occurs in *association* with a smelting image, but this does not give it a metallurgical sense.

126. Wolters 1987: 410.

His contention that 2 Pet. 3.10d emphasizes the 'permanence' of the created earth founders on the fact that, in the very next sentence, the writer, summarizing the foregoing verse, speaks of 'all these things' (τούτων ... πάντων) being dissolved; 'all these things' clearly comprehends both the heavens and the earth.

It does seem likely that the author conceives of the fire as purging or purifying, even though he does not make this thought explicit. But Wolters assumes that destruction and purification are mutually exclusive. In Stoic thought, the cosmic conflagration is both utterly destructive and intensely purifying.[127]

Having rejected Wolters's interpretation of 2 Pet. 3.10d (and the wider reinterpretation of 3.5-13 bound up with it), how, then, should the final clause of v. 10 be understood? There is an emerging consensus that εὑρεθήσεται in v. 10d has to do with discovery at the final judgement.[128] This is plainly the sense of the verb (in the passive) only a few verses later, at v. 14 ('to be found by him at peace', αὐτῷ εὑρεθῆναι ἐν εἰρήνῃ), and, in my view, that is the sense of εὑρεθῇ in 1 Pet. 1.7. This understanding of εὑρεθήσεται accords with a wider pattern of usage of the verb in the New Testament.[129] Generally, it is human beings or human qualities that are 'found' by God; here, though, the subject is 'the earth and the works in it' (γῆ καὶ τὰ ἐν αὐτῇ ἔργα). Despite the wording, most think that human beings and their works are actually in view in this clause, and I share this opinion. The phrase 'the earth and the works in it', in my view, should be taken as a grammatical metaphor for 'the works done (by human beings) upon the earth' (ἐπὶ τῆς γῆς).[130] The point being expressed in this clause is that the eschatological dissolution will expose all the deeds of human beings to divine scrutiny. This breaks from the thought of the preceding lines, but the shift from cosmic destruction to the judgement of human beings is consistent with vv. 5-7.[131] The eschatological exposure of all the works of men and women done upon the earth will bring judgement to the ungodly, but vindication to the faithful.[132]

127. See above, pp. 116–8.
128. Danker 1962; Horrell 1998: 181: Kraftchick 2002: 163; Neyrey 1993: 243–4; Vögtle 1994: 237–8; D. Wenham 1987.
129. E.g., 1 Cor. 4.2; Gal. 2.7; 3.9.
130. Cf. Danker 1962.
131. So Horrell 1998: 181.
132. Bauckham (1983: 320) thinks that the judgement will have a negative outcome. But the unpredicated use of the verb suggests a judicial enquiry which will establish both guilt and innocence.

The author's overall teaching in v. 10 may be summarized thus: the 'day of the Lord' will come suddenly and in an overwhelming manner. The physical heavens will fragment and pass away with a great noise. The elements that make up the earthly world will be dissolved by the extreme heat and consumed by fire. And, at that moment, all the works that have been done upon the earth by human beings will be disclosed; 'nothing will remain hidden, and every wicked undertaking of men ... will receive its just punishment'.[133]

6.3.4 *Recapitulation in 2 Peter 3.11-12*

Verse 10 concludes the author's apologetic argument. In vv. 11-13, he focuses on the ethical implications of the expectation of the end and renewal of the world for his readers. The portrayal of cosmic destruction in v. 10 is recapitulated in vv. 11-12.

> 11) Since all these things are to be dissolved in this way (τούτων ούτως πάντων λυομένων), what sort of people ought you to be in leading lives of holiness and godliness, 12) waiting for and hastening the coming of the day of God, because of which the heavens will be set ablaze and dissolved, and the elements will melt with fire (οὐρανοὶ πυρούμενοι λυθήσονται καὶ στοιχεῖα καυσούμενα τήκεται)?

The opening clause of v. 11, τούτων ούτως πάντων λυομένων, summarizes v. 10.[134] The plural πάντων probably picks up the reference to 'the earth' in v. 10d, as well as 'the heavens' and 'the elements', in v. 10bc, thus indicating that the earth is to be dissolved along with the heavens,[135] which is signalled anyway in v. 10c with the reference to the fiery dissolution of 'the elements'. 'In this way', τούτων, evidently means 'by means of fire'. The clause serves as a summary rebuttal of the scoffers' assertion 'all things remain just as they were from the beginning of creation' (πάντα ούτως διαμένει ἀπ' ἀρχῆς κτίσεως).

The second half of v. 12 restates v. 10bc, with the difference that language of conflagration is applied to the heavens as well as the elements. The author asserts that the heavens being on fire will be dissolved (οὐρανοὶ πυρούμενοι λυθήσονται) and that the elements – the physical constituents of all things in the sub-lunar region – being burned up will melt (στοιχεῖα καυσούμενα τήκεται).[136] As noted above, the wording indicates that total consumption and destruction by fire is in view.

133. Riecke 1964: 180.
134. The present participle λυομένων has a future sense.
135. Bauckham 1983: 324.
136. τήκεται is present tense, but with a future sense.

6.3.5 Concluding Observations

Second Peter 3.10-12 describes the fiery dissolution of the existing heavens and earth. The images of cosmic conflagration are not drawn from the Old Testament. The language of 'melting' is used in LXX theophany accounts, but not with reference to the celestial realm.[137] Isaiah 34.4 LXX B reads: 'all the powers of heaven will melt'; but we cannot be sure that this reading of the Isaianic passage was accessible to our writer. We may note a general similarity between the picture in 2 Pet. 3.10-12 and that in *Sib. Or.* 3.75-92 (cf. 2.196-213), but there is nothing to suggest that the writer was aware of, let alone dependent on, the Sibylline material. The parallels, in particular the shared reference to the 'elements', are best explained on the assumption that the writers of both texts are drawing independently on the Stoic *ekpurōsis* doctrine. We noted apparent points of dependence on Stoic cosmology in 2 Pet. 3.5-7; further echoes of Stoic teaching are evident in 3.10-12: the twofold division of the cosmos into 'the heavens' and 'the elements'; the thought of the terrestrial elements, including the element fire, being dissolved by the fire of the conflagration.

Unlike in Valentinian eschatology, as described by Ptolemy, and in the Nag Hammadi tractate, *The Concept of Our Great Power*, the destructive fire is not said to consume itself after it has devoured all else (so that all matter passes out of existence).[138] In line with Stoic thought, the writer seems to imagine that the eschatological fire is not only an instrument of destruction but also a means of (re)generation.

6.4 Timing and Consequences of the Catastrophic End of the Cosmos

Despite Wright's demurral, then, we can be quite confident in concluding that the author of 2 Peter envisions the catastrophic destruction of the present cosmos on the 'day of the Lord'. What timescale does he attach to this expectation?

6.4.1 Timescale

On the standard interpretation of 2 Pet. 3.4, 8-9, the author is responding in part to a crisis provoked by the fear that with the passing away of the apostolic generation the deadline for Jesus' parousia had passed. I have

---

137. Ps. 97.5; Mic. 1.4; Nah. 1.6; Hab. 3.6; Jdt. 16.15.
138. Irenaeus, *Ad. haer.*, 1.7.1; Nag Hammadi, *Great Pow.* 46.

argued, however, that this is unlikely. The object of the scoffers' ridicule in 3.4, I have suggested, is not belief in Jesus' return as such but the underlying Old Testament 'promise' of an eschatological advent. They scoff at this expectation because of the immensely long period of time that has passed since it was first articulated. The divine advent has been promised for many centuries, they mock, and nothing has happened. When the writer responds to the temporal objection of his opponents in vv. 8-9, he makes no reference to the passing of an alleged deadline. He argues, first, that God's estimation of time is different from that of humans, and, second, that God has delayed the eschatological intervention so that all can come to repentance. He does not in these verses set his own timescale for fulfilment. The day of the Lord will certainly come (v. 10), but whether it will come sooner or later is known only to God. The author seems to imply that God's patience could yet last a very long time ('with the Lord one day is like a thousand years, and a thousand years are like one day', v. 8, appealing to Ps. 90.4).

In vv. 12-14, however, he urges his readers to live in anticipation of the final events. Noticeable here is the language of 'waiting': 'waiting for … the coming of the day of God'; 'we wait for new heavens and a new earth'; 'while you are waiting for these things'. He now seems to be implying that they could be alive to see these things. In v. 12, he indicates that his readers can actually 'hasten' the day of the Lord, through godly living. This is the counter-side to the belief, expressed in v. 9, that God delays his intervention to give time for repentance; holy living may actually bring the day forward.

We thus find in 2 Peter the same creative tension between the unknownness and nearness of the end that we find in Mark 13 + par., generating a sense of expectancy that is not aligned to a timetable.

6.4.2 Consequences

Does the thought of the cosmos coming to an end, and in such a violent way, reflect an anti-creational bias? Is it linked with a non-material view of the final state? Does it discourage action and endeavour?

6.4.2.1 Creational Consequences

Quite evidently, the author has no misgivings about the divine creation of the world. On the interpretation of 2 Pet. 3.5 I have given above, he creatively combines the Genesis creation account with a Stoic view of cosmic origins.

A radical dualism which negates the material creation and views the goal of salvation as escape from materiality has sometimes been detected in 1.4, which reads as follows:

> Thus he has given us, through these things, his precious and very great promises, so that through them you may escape from the corruption that is in the world because of desire (ἀποφυγόντες τῆς ἐν τῷ κόσμῳ ἐν ἐπιθυμίᾳ φθορᾶς), and may become participants of the divine nature.

Ernst Käsemann comments on this verse: 'It would be hard to find in the whole New Testament a sentence which ... more clearly marks the relapse into Hellenistic dualism.'[139]

This is a very hasty verdict. Two things should be noted about this verse. First, the author does not talk about escaping the world as such. The word κόσμος here denotes the created, physical cosmos, but the object of the verb ἀποφεύγω is φθορά, not κόσμος. The distinction is an important one. Redemption is not said to be from the material cosmos itself, but from the 'corruption' – which means, for this author, both physical and moral corruption (cf. 2.12, 19)[140] – that is *in* it (ἐν τῷ κόσμῳ). Second, the writer indicates that 'corruption' is not original or endemic to the κόσμος; rather it has come into the world as a result of ἐπιθυμία, sinful 'desire'. Our author seems to imagine some kind of 'fall', brought about by human sin, affecting the human and natural world, much as Paul does in Rom. 5.12 and 8.20-22. The escape of which the writer speaks in 2 Pet. 1.4 is thus an escape from sin and its effects, not a release from the constraints of created, material existence.

One presumes that the writer expects the world to be purged of the 'corruption' which has entered into and spoiled it when it is dissolved by fire and created anew.[141] This seems to be indicated in 3.13, where he speaks of the new heavens and earth as an environment in which 'righteousness' dwells (implying that corruption has been wiped out). In *4 Ezra* 7.30-32, the 'corruption' that is the hallmark of the present world/age is eradicated when the world returns to the primeval chaos.

In 2 Pet. 2.20, the author speaks of baptism/conversion as an escape from 'the defilements of the world through the knowledge of our Lord and Saviour Jesus Christ'. In this verse, κόσμος refers to the human

---

139. Käsemann 1964: 180. I leave aside the problematic assumptions entailed in the construct 'Hellenistic dualism'.
140. Cf. Neyrey 1993: 157.
141. If so, there is an interesting contrast with what Paul expects in Romans 8. Here, Paul looks for the existing creation to be 'liberated' from its bondage to corruption. For our writer, something more extreme is required: the world must be destroyed and created anew.

world, rather than the physical cosmos, and the 'defilements' or pollutions (μιάσματα) are the immoral and defiling actions of human beings. There is no thought here, therefore, of a contaminated materiality.

6.4.2.2 *Eschatological Consequences*
'New heavens and a new earth' are expected to follow the fiery dissolution of the present created order (3.13). The new creative act of God is not a *creatio ex nihilo* but a *creatio ex vetere*, a creation out of the old. Material continuity between the present outgoing cosmos and the new eschatological creation is presumed, on the analogy of the continuity that existed between the pre-deluge and post-deluge world, and also on the basis of Stoic physics, according to which matter is preserved (in the form of fire) through conflagration and regeneration. The author looks for the world to come to a definite and spectacular end, but he expects a material re-creation, in continuity with this world, to follow. Wright is thus correct when he maintains that 2 Pet. 3.5-13 does not teach that 'creation as a whole is to be thrown away and a new one, freshly made, to take its place',[142] though he errs, of course, in concluding that a scheme of *destruction* and re-creation is not involved at all.

Unlike John the seer, the author of the book of Revelation, the writer of 2 Peter offers no description of the new heavens and earth. The only detail he mentions is that they serve as a fit habitation for righteousness. Presumably, the new creation is for him not just a return to the conditions of the original creation but a surpassing and transformation of them; otherwise, the new order would also be vulnerable to alternating destructions by water and fire. However, it has to be admitted that he does not sufficiently block out this possibility. John the seer, as we will see in the following chapter, stresses the transformed nature of the new heavens and earth and indicates that they are beyond the threat of returning to chaos.

6.4.2.3 *Practical Consequences*
In 3.11-12a, the author makes an ethical appeal precisely on the basis of the world's coming destruction: 'Since all these things are to be dissolved in this way, what sort of people ought you to be in leading lives of holiness and godliness, waiting for and hastening the coming of the day of God ... ?' The writer does not give content to the terms 'holy lifestyles' and 'godlinesses' (the terms are plural); presumably, he imagines that holiness and godliness can be expressed in a variety of ways. In v. 14, he states that as they await the new heavens and new earth, his

---

142. N. T. Wright 2003b: 463.

addressees should 'strive (σπουδάσατε) to be found by God at peace, without spot or blemish'. The verb σπουδάζω points to strenuous endeavour. There is thus no legitimation here of passivity and inactivity during the period of waiting for the end.

6.5 Conclusions

Second Peter 3.5-13 presents in the clearest terms we have yet encountered in the New Testament the catastrophic demise of the cosmos. Attempts to read this passage in non-destructionist terms, I hope to have shown, are exegetically unsustainable. The writer has expressed the conviction that the existing created order will come to a violent end as emphatically as he could.

The author advances his teaching on the catastrophic end of the cosmos in opposition to 'scoffers' who rejected the possibility of cosmic destruction on philosophical grounds. They took the Platonic/Aristotelian line that the cosmos is everlasting. In combating their position, he draws on Stoic cosmology and the theory of *ekpurōsis* in particular, which itself had been formulated in opposition to the Platonic and Aristotelian theorem of cosmic indestructibility. So this was an astute tactical move on his part, even if it poses serious hermeneutical problems for contemporary appropriation.

Second Peter 3.4-13 serves as evidence that belief in the end of the cosmos was held in at least some early Christian circles. The scoffers apparently took for granted that the destruction of the cosmos was entailed in the expectation of God's/Jesus' parousia (is this indirect evidence that Mk 13.24-27 was being understood in 'end of the cosmos' terms at this time?) and attempted to rebut it; the author defended it as a cardinal tenet of the faith (though his expression of it in terms of a fiery destruction may have been his own contribution to the 'Christian' expectation).

The writer does not expect the material cosmos to be destroyed absolutely, that is, wiped out from existence. He teaches that the existing heavens and earth are to be resolved into fire and reconstituted anew. Wright is thus on target when he says that the worldview of the author is 'not that of the dualist who hopes for creation to be abolished'[143] (but off target in maintaining that the existing creation is merely refined by the eschatological fire). The author does not look for a *creatio ex nihilo* after the fiery destruction, but a *creatio ex vetere*.

---

143. N. T. Wright 2003b: 464.

The end is near yet potentially still a long way off, a tension which is left unresolved. There is thus no clearly defined horizon for fulfilment. Intriguingly, the author imagines that the timing of the day of judgement can be manipulated; it can be delayed or brought forward.

The inevitable end of the cosmos is not a cause for pessimism, but a source of hope because a new world of righteousness lies beyond. The end, as the author depicts it, is not a disincentive to productive ethical activity, but a catalyst for it.

Chapter 7

'HEAVEN VANISHED LIKE A SCROLL ROLLED UP':
REVELATION 6.12-17

The book of Revelation is at the same time intensely fascinating and immensely daunting. The document has many affinities with Jewish apocalyptic literature and is normally classed by scholars as an 'apocalypse'. It is introduced as the 'revelation', or 'apocalypse' (ἀποκάλυψις), of Jesus Christ, though it is unlikely that the term is being used as a formal indicator of its genre. The composition is also identified by its author as a 'prophecy' (1.3; 22.7, 10, 19) and has epistolary characteristics. It is addressed 'to the seven churches that are in Asia' (1.4); in chapters 2–3, each of the churches is given a specific message, relating to its particular situation and circumstances. The seer's name is John (1.4, 9; 22.8), and he writes from the island of Patmos (1.9), which appears to have been his place of exile. As early as Justin Martyr (died 165 CE),[1] he was equated with John the apostle, but this identification cannot be proved from the text. Most commentators tend to place the composition of Revelation during the later years of the reign of Domitian (81–96 CE),[2] though some would date it earlier.[3] The author writes to convey to his readers 'what must soon take place' (1.1). He describes through the medium of 'literary visions'[4] a series of disasters and distresses leading up to the climactic intervention. These events are signalled in heaven by the breaking of seals, blowing of trumpets and the pouring out of the contents of bowls (chs 6–16). The unfolding revelation reaches its climax in 19.11–22.5, with the narration of the appearance of Christ and the triumph of God, the millennial reign of Christ and the martyrs, the last assize and the new creation.

With its exuberant and often baffling imagery and symbolism, sudden switches of scene and sequential ambiguities, the book of Revelation has

1. Justin, *Dial.* 81.
2. Following early church tradition: Irenaeus, *Ad. Haer.* 5.30.3.
3. Rowland (1982: 403–13) argues that John was writing around 68 CE.
4. Fiorenza 1991: 29.

been a battlefield of conflicting interpretations.[5] Our key text, Rev. 6.12-17, is not unaffected by these debates. Before dealing with it, though, we look first at 21.1, which speaks of the passing away of the present heaven and earth and the appearance of a new creation.

7.1 *The Dissolution and Re-Creation of the World: Revelation 21.1*

In 21.1–22.5, the seer relates his vision of the new creation and its centrepiece, the new Jerusalem (21.2; 21.9–22.5). He declares in 21.1, 'Then I saw a new heaven and a new earth; for the first heaven and the first earth had passed away' (καὶ εἶδον οὐρανὸν καινὸν καὶ γῆν καινήν. ὁ γὰρ πρῶτος οὐρανὸς καὶ ἡ πρώτη γῆ ἀπῆλθαν). In v. 5, God, who is seated on his throne, announces, 'See, I am making all things new' (ἰδοὺ καινὰ ποιῶ πάντα).

The theme of a new heaven and new earth in 21.1 is of course drawn from Isa. 65.17 and 66.22. In these Old Testament texts, there is no mention of the passing away of the present heaven and earth, though the line, οὐ μὴ μνησθῶσιν τῶν προτέρων, 'the former things shall not be remembered', in Isa. 65.17 LXX could well have motivated the author's contrast between the *first* creation (ὁ ... πρῶτος οὐρανὸς καὶ ἡ πρώτη γῆ) and the new. The wording of Rev. 21.1 is strikingly reminiscent of *1 En.* 91.16: 'The first heaven shall depart and pass away; a new heaven shall appear.' Matthew Black and J. T. Milik think that John the seer may have known this text and been dependent on it.[6] It is also possible that the author was aware of the traditions of Jesus' sayings on the passing of creation, and that Rev. 21.1ab was formed out of Isa. 65.17 and the affirmation that 'heaven and earth will pass away' (Mk 13.31).

The statement, ἰδοὺ καινὰ ποιῶ πάντα, in 21.5 seems to be modelled partly on Isa. 43.19a LXX (ἰδοὺ ποιῶ καινά). The declaration also recalls the words addressed to God earlier in Revelation, at 4.11: 'you created all things' (σὺ ἔκτισας τὰ πάντα) and thus implies that God's eschatological creative activity corresponds to his original creative act.[7]

Much debated is exactly how the future of creation is conceived in 21.1 and 5, and what terminology best captures the writer's thought: for example, 're-creation';[8] 'the eschatological renewal of this creation, not

---

5. On the reception history of Revelation, see now Kovacs and Rowland 2004.
6. Black 1976: 17–18; Milik 1976: 199.
7. Bauckham 1993b: 50.
8. Caird 1966: 265.

its replacement by another';[9] 'not merely ethical renovation but transformation of the fundamental cosmic structure (including physical elements)';[10] 'a qualitatively new world'.[11] According to Bauckham, the thought is of 'a radical renewal of the old creation rather creation from nothing',[12] a view endorsed by Wright.[13] Similarly Greg Beale concludes that the writer envisages 'the transformation of the old creation rather than an outright new creation *ex nihilo*', though he adds that 'renewal does not mean that there will be no literal destruction of the old cosmos'.[14] We can readily agree that the formulation, 'I am making all things new', in 21.5, seems to rule out reduction to and creation out of non-being; as Caird writes, 'This is not an activity of God ... after the old has been cast as rubbish to the void'.[15] But, at the risk of labouring the point, such a notion is unlikely to have been a real cosmological option for writers of this period. As we saw in Chapter 2, Jewish eschatological hope for the renewal of creation found expression in two forms: the non-cataclysmic transformation of the present creation, and the destruction of the world and its creation anew, the latter being the more predominant of the two ideas. Destruction and re-creation meant the reversion of the world to the chaos from which it was first made and its re-formation from this state. These, then, are the alternatives which should be considered when assessing how the cosmic future is portrayed in Rev. 21.1.

The wording of 21.1, in my opinion, makes it quite clear that, as Aune states, 'the author has in view the *complete destruction* of the physical universe'[16] followed by an act of re-creation. The announcement, 'I saw a new heaven and a new earth; *for the first heaven and the first earth had passed away*', indicates that an act of cosmic dissolution precedes the appearance of the new heaven and earth. We do not have here a miraculous transformation of the existing created order. Rather, the first creation is taken back to its pre-created, chaotic state and a new creative act takes place. The picture is indeed that of the renewal of creation, but the renewal is accomplished precisely by destruction and re-creation.[17]

9. Bauckham 1993b: 49.
10. Beale 1999: 1040.
11. Fiorenza 1991: 109.
12. Bauckham 2001: 1303.
13. N. T. Wright 2003b: 473 n. 60.
14. Beale 1999: 1040.
15. Caird 1966: 265.
16. Aune 1998b: 1117.
17. Caird (1966: 265) speaks helpfully of 'the process of re-creation by which the old is transformed into the new'.

In Rev. 21.1, John states that the present heaven and earth *had* passed away, implying that it happened earlier in the narrative. Within the narrative development, the cosmic dissolution seems to take place at the beginning of the great white throne judgement in 20.11: 'the earth and the heaven fled from his face, and no place was found for them'.

The words 'and the sea was no more' (καὶ ἡ θάλασσα οὐκ ἔστιν ἔτι) at the end of v. 1 have sometimes been taken as suggesting destruction by cosmic conflagration (the cosmic fire having consumed all the earth's moisture),[18] but it is highly unlikely that the writer meant for such an inference to be drawn. The sea, in the book of Revelation, is a symbol of the chaotic potential that exists in the present world.[19] Its removal signifies that the new creation is clear of the threat of chaos. I will return to this point later, when discussing the author's conception of the new heaven and earth.

The main thing I want to bring out here is that the writer of Revelation anticipates the end of the world, in a fully cosmic and destructionist sense. He expects the dissolution of the present creation and its remaking as the final act in the story of redemption. With this in mind, we turn now to 6.12-17.

7.2 *The Great Day of Wrath: Revelation 6.12-17*

The breaking of the first of the seven seals (6.1–8.5) signals the onset of the end-time evils, the eschatological woes. The first four seals (6.1-8) unleash the four horsemen of the apocalypse and effectively mark 'the beginning of the birthpangs' (Mk 13.8).[20] With the second and third riders come war and economic upheaval; the fourth rider brings death and Hades, in the form of war, famine, pestilence and invasions of wild animals. As a result of these disasters, the earth is depopulated by a quarter (v. 8). At the breaking of the fifth seal, the souls of the martyrs in heaven pray for vindication (vv. 9-11); they are told to rest a while longer, until their full number is complete. When the sixth seal is broken, there is 'a great earthquake', σεισμὸς μέγας, which triggers catastrophic cosmic events (vv. 12-14).

> the sun became black as sackcloth made of hair,
> the whole moon became like blood,

---

18. Augustine, *City of God* 20.16; cf. Swete 1906: 272.
19. Rev. 12.12; 13.1; 16.3; 20.13.
20. Unlike Mk 13.5-23, it is difficult to equate the predictions of Rev. 6.1-8 with known events.

13) and the stars of heaven fell to the earth as the fig tree drops its late figs when shaken by a great wind.
14) The heaven vanished/split like a scroll rolling up, and every mountain and island was removed from its place.

καὶ ὁ ἥλιος ἐγένετο μέλας ὡς σάκκος τρίχινος
καὶ ἡ σελήνη ὅλη ἐγένετο ὡς αἷμα
13) καὶ οἱ ἀστέρες τοῦ οὐρανοῦ ἔπεσαν εἰς τὴν γῆν, ὡς συκῆ βάλλει τοὺς ὀλύνθους αὐτῆς ὑπὸ ἀνέμου μεγάλου σειομένη,
14) καὶ ὁ οὐρανὸς ἀπεχωρίσθη ὡς βιβλίον ἑλισσόμενον
καὶ πᾶν ὄρος καὶ νῆσος ἐκ τῶν τόπων αὐτῶν ἐκινήθησαν.

These occurrences provoke terror on earth among all ranks of human beings from kings to slaves, who hide in caves and mountains, crying out to the mountains (vv. 15-17), 'Fall on us and hide us from the face of the one seated on the throne and from the wrath of the Lamb; for the great day of their wrath has come, and who is able to stand?'.[21]

7.2.1 *Old Testament Influences*

The catastrophic imagery of 6.12-14 is largely drawn from the Old Testament, with Isa. 34.4 being the dominant influence. The first two lines, about the sun and moon, are based on Joel 2.31 (3.4 LXX) (ὁ ἥλιος μεταστραφήσεται εἰς σκότος καὶ ἡ σελήνη εἰς αἷμα, 'The sun shall be turned into darkness, and the moon to blood'). Joel refers to the darkening of the moon rather than its turning black as sackcloth. The sackcloth image was probably drawn from Isa. 50.3 (LXX καὶ ἐνδύσω τὸν οὐρανὸν σκότος καὶ θήσω ὡς σάκκον τὸ περιβόλαιον αὐτοῦ, 'I will clothe the heaven with darkness, and will make its covering as sackcloth').[22] John speaks of ἡ σελήνη ὅλη, 'the whole moon' becoming like blood.[23] The wording is reminiscent of *T. Mos.* 10.5 which has, 'the moon will entirely be turned into blood' (*et tota convertit se in sanguine*). R. H. Charles has suggested that John knew the *Testament of Moses* and was relying on it at this point,[24] but direct literary dependence is not certain. The motif of the downfall of the stars is clearly derived from Isa. 34.4 LXX (καὶ πάντα τὰ ἄστρα πεσεῖται ὡς φύλλα ἐξ ἀμπέλου καὶ ὡς πίπτει φύλλα ἀπὸ συκῆς, 'all the stars shall fall like leaves from a vine,

---

21. Verses 15-17 reflect several Old Testament passages: Isa. 2.10, 19, 21; Hos. 8.10 (alluded to in Lk. 23.30); Joel 2.11; Nah. 1.6; Mal. 3.2.
22. Sackcloth, σάκκος, was a dark coloured material woven out of camel or goat hair; hence σάκκος τρίχινος, 'sackcloth made of hair'.
23. Some late manuscripts omit ὅλη. See Aune 1998a: 385.
24. Charles 1920a: 180.

and as leaves fall from a fig tree').[25] In Isa. 34.4 LXX, the fall of the stars is likened to the fall of the *leaves* both of the vine and the fig tree; here, the reference to the vine is dropped, and it is the fall of the *fruit* (ὄλυνθος, 'late figs') of the fig tree, to which the plummet of the stars is compared. John extends Isaiah's image by adding, ὑπὸ ἀνέμου μεγάλου σειομένη, 'when shaken by a great wind'; this may indicate that the collapse of the stars is the result of the 'great earthquake', since the verb σείω is the cognate of σεισμός.[26] The next line is also based on Isa. 34.4 (καὶ ἑλιγήσεται ὁ οὐρανὸς ὡς βιβλίον). John embellishes the Isaianic image with the verb ἀποχωρίζω, which normally means 'to separate', 'to split'. The thought could be that of heaven splitting in two as a scroll splitting apart in the middle, and each of its halves being rolled back.[27] Alternatively, the picture could be that of heaven disappearing or receding from sight as the heaven is rolled up like a scroll, in which case ἀπεχωρίσθη would have the sense, 'vanish' (from view, not into nothing). The final line may be dependent on Isa. 54.10 for the thought of all the mountains being removed.[28] The linkage of mountains and islands in this clause may have been suggested by Isa. 42.15.[29]

7.2.2 *Similar Images Elsewhere in Revelation*

Similar motifs are found in other places in the book. Earthquakes occur after the short silence following the breaking of the seventh seal in 8.5; after the resurrection and ascension of the two witnesses in 11.13; at the blowing of the seventh trumpet in 11.19; at the pouring out of the seventh bowl of judgement in 16.18. The sun, moon and stars are darkened at the sounding of the fourth trumpet in 8.12. The light of the sun is concealed when the bottomless pit is opened after the fifth trumpet blown at 9.1-2. A great star, named 'wormwood', falls like a fiery torch from heaven into the waters at the blowing of the third trumpet in 8.10-11. The star poisons the waters, causing many to die. A star falls to earth when the fifth trumpet is blown in 9.1. Here, the star is an angel who is given the task of opening the bottomless pit. A third of the stars are swept from the sky and cast down to earth by the tail of the dragon in the

---

25. The MT speaks of the heavenly host withering like a vine leaf or fruit on a fig tree.
26. This is the only occurrence of the verb σείω in Revelation.
27. Cf. Beale 1999: 397; Charles 1920a: 181.
28. 'For the mountains may depart and the hills be removed.'
29. 'I will lay waste mountains and hills, and dry up all their herbage; I will turn the rivers into islands, and dry up the pools.'

vision of the woman, the child and the dragon in chapter 12.[30] The 'stars' of 12.4 are probably the angels who are cast out of heaven along with Satan (12.9).[31] As noted earlier, heaven and earth are said to flee from God's presence in the narration of the great white throne vision (20.11). The dissolution of mountains and islands is mentioned again in 16.20, as a feature of the pouring out of the seventh bowl of judgement (16.17-21).

7.2.3 Comparison with Mark 13.24-25 + Parallels

There is some similarity with Mk 13.24-25 and Mt. 24.29, but there are also marked differences. Mark (whom Matthew follows almost verbatim) speaks of the sun and moon being darkened, drawing principally on the language of Isa. 13.10. In Rev. 6.12, the sun turns black, and the moon the colour of blood; the Old Testament influence is Joel 2.31, rather than Isa. 13.10. Mark speaks of the stars falling from heaven, taking up the basic image of Isa. 34.4. John has the same image, but likens the fall of the stars to the fall of fruit from the fig tree, alluding more extensively to Isa. 34.4, but developing the analogy in his own way. Mark's line about the shaking of the powers in the heavens has no direct equivalent in Rev. 6.12-14. John does, though, depict seismic activity. The upheavals are initiated by a 'great earthquake', and the dropping figs to which the falling stars are compared are said to have been 'shaken' by a mighty wind. However, in expressing the latter, John uses σείω rather than σαλεύω which is the verb used by Mark. In Mk 13.24-25, there is no parallel to the image of heaven being rolled up in Rev. 6.14a, though, of course, in Mk 13.31, Mark's Jesus declares that heaven (and earth) shall pass away. Mark has nothing corresponding to the removal of islands and mountains in Rev. 6.14b. In Mk 13.24-25, the upheavals are entirely celestial.

Luke's version of Mk 13.24-25 (Lk. 21.25-26) simply refers to 'signs' in the sun, moon and stars. Luke mentions terrestrial upheavals as well as celestial events, but his image of the roaring of the sea and waves does not really match John's image of the removal of mountains and islands.[32] Luke's mention of people fainting with fear and foreboding at what is coming on the world in Lk. 21.26 is, though, in very broad terms a parallel to Rev. 12.15-17.

---

30. Alluding to Dan. 8.10, where the little horn casts down some of the stars to the ground and tramples on them.
31. Stars frequently represent evil angels in *1 Enoch*, e.g. 18.14; 21.3-6.
32. *Contra* D. Wenham 1984: 311.

Revelation 6.12-14 certainly resembles the Synoptic passages and may reflect knowledge of a form of the tradition (or traditions) underlying them, but it does not seem to be literarily reliant on them.

7.2.4 *Socio-political Upheaval, Preliminary Woes or Catastrophic Intervention?*

As is the case with Mk 13.24-25 + par., there is debate as to how the catastrophic imagery of Rev. 6.12-14 is to be interpreted. It seems to be generally accepted that the language has a strongly figurative dimension (this is clear from similes employed), but there is disagreement about what it actually refers to. Four main views can be distinguished: the reference is to: (1) political upheavals;[33] (2) preliminary eschatological woes;[34] (3) catastrophic events, marking the arrival of climactic judgement, but not the end of the cosmos;[35] (4) catastrophic events that signal or constitute the dissolution of the cosmos.[36]

The lack of evidence for a socio-political usage of this kind of language in Jewish apocalyptic and similar writings, in my view, renders unlikely a socio-political reference here. That the seer explicitly narrates the judgement of earthly powers in vv. 15-17 also tells against this reading. There is nothing in the text to signal that vv. 15-17 are a recapitulation of vv. 12-14, or a historical interpretation of the foregoing imagery of upheaval in nature. Indeed, the terror in vv. 15-17 is presented as a *response* to the awesome physical events narrated in vv. 12-14. As Thomas states, 'It may be granted that the physical events result in political and social turmoil, but the first cause of all this is the cosmic and terrestrial disturbances.'[37]

That the natural upheavals of 6.12-14 are preliminary woes rather than expressions of the final intervention might seem to follow from the fact that cosmic darkening and falling stars clearly belong to the preliminary distresses in 8.10-12, 9.1, and 12.4. However, in 8.12, the darkening at the sound of the fourth trumpet is partial: the light of the sun, moon and

---

33. E.g., Caird, who thinks the language symbolizes 'the overthrow of a worldly political order organized in hostility to God' (1966: 90).
34. E.g., Aune 1998a: 413–24; Charles 1920a: 179; Swete 1906: 90.
35. E.g., Thomas 1992: 451
36. E.g., Fiorenza 1991: 64–5; the phenomena are so terrible 'that they can only be understood in apocalyptic terms to mean the final dissolution of the whole world'. Yet she stresses that the language is 'hyperbolic rather than descriptive or predictive of actual events'. Beale (1999: 397) thinks that the author is depicting final cosmic dissolution, but that the portrayal is figurative.
37. Thomas 1992: 451.

stars is diminished by a third. Revelation 6.12, by contrast, envisages the complete darkening of the sun and reddening of the whole of the moon. In 8.10-11 and 9.1, a single star falls, and in 12.4, a third of the stars are cast down. Revelation 6.13, in contrast, seems have to have in view a more comprehensive plummet of the stars.

Whether the convulsions of 6.12-14 are preliminary woes or features of the eschatological intervention is bound up with the question of whether the seal, trumpet and bowl visions of chapters 6–16 follow a linear or cyclic pattern. If the sequence were purely linear, the upheavals would obviously belong to the eschatological woes. Recognition of a cyclic patterning would allow for a more 'final' reference.

With most interpreters, I see the seal, trumpet and bowl judgements as parallel rather than consecutive outpourings of judgement. This reading is consistent with the fact that each series reaches its peak in a scene of climactic judgement and victory (6.12-17; 11.14-19; 16.17-21).

Whereas the first five seals of chapter 6 clearly unleash preliminary disasters, the sixth seal announces the full and unrestrained venting of God's wrath. The scene depicted in 6.12-17 is evidently God's answer to the martyrs' plea in 6.10: 'Sovereign Lord, holy and true, how long will it be before you judge and avenge our blood on the inhabitants of the earth?' With the breaking of the sixth seal, their wait for vindication is over. The significance of what is taking place is made clear at the end of the pericope: 'for the great day of their wrath has come, and who is able to stand?' This is evidently a reference to climactic and universal judgement.[38] The 'great day of ... wrath' is the decisive 'day' of God's triumph (cf. 16.14).

The climactic judgement scene of 6.12-17 is recapitulated and enlarged upon in 11.18; 16.17-21; and 19.11-21. Revelation 11.14-19 describes the celebratory scene at the blowing of the seventh trumpet. The announcement that the wrath of God has come echoes 6.17. The coming of judgement and the opening of the heavenly temple are marked by 'flashes of lightning, rumblings, peals of thunder, an earthquake, and heavy hail' (11.19).

Revelation 16.17-21 describes the seventh and final vial judgement; the words 'it is done', in 16.17, indicate that, with this bowl judgement, the end has been reached. At the pouring out of its contents, there are lightning flashes, peals of thunder and 'a great earthquake, such as had

---

38. The specific phrase 'the great day' (of the Lord) occurs in the Old Testament only in Zeph. 1.14, as a variant of the 'day of the Lord'. *First Enoch* 10.6 refers to 'the great day of judgment'. The words, 'who is able to stand?' characteristically emphasize the universal scope of coming judgement.

not occurred since people were upon the earth, so great was that earthquake' (16.18). The seismic disaster causes the devastation of the 'great city', the 'cities of the nations' and 'great Babylon', as well as the disappearance of the mountains and the islands (16.20). The 'great earthquake' of 16.17 is surely to be identified with the 'great earthquake' of 6.12,[39] even though its effects are global in 16.17-21 rather than fully cosmic as in 6.12-17.[40]

Revelation 19.11-21 portrays the climactic universal judgement in terms of Christ's coming as divine warrior at the head of the celestial army to defeat the beast and the kings of the earth with all their armies. In this passage, there is no mention of a great quake or other dramatic events in nature; the focus is on the eschatological war (anticipated in 16.12-16) and the banquet of human flesh (cf. Ezek. 39.17-20). However, the various groups upon whose flesh the birds of the mid-air are invited to gorge correspond to the groups mentioned in 6.15.

> the kings of the earth and the magnates and the generals and the rich and the powerful, and everyone, slave and free, hid in the caves ... (6.15)

> Come, gather for the great supper of God, to eat the flesh of kings, the flesh of captains, the flesh of the mighty, the flesh of horses and their riders – flesh of all, both free and slave, both small and great. (19.17c-18)

All these passages – 6.12-17, 11.18, 16.17-21 and 19.11-21 – then, in different ways but with recurring features picture the culminating judgement at the end of the tribulation.

Since 6.12-17 is a climactic judgement scene, the convulsions of 6.12-14 are not to be interpreted as preliminary woes, features of the protracted period of tribulation; they belong to the final intervention that brings the tribulation to a close. They do not just signal that the awesome day of divine wrath is 'near' or is 'at hand'. Rather, they make evident that that it *has come* (ὅτι ἦλθεν ἡ ἡμέρα ἡ μεγάλη).[41] In other words, the ruinous events are *constitutive* of the day of wrath.

---

39. Bauckham 1993a: 208. Bauckham notes that in 8.5, 11.19 and 16.18-21 allusion is made to the Sinai theophany.

40. Echoes of the Sinai theophany (thunder, lightning, earthquake) are plainly to be heard.

41. Charles agrees that v. 17 suggests that, with the cosmic uproar, the end has come. But he claims that the words express the alarm of the inhabitants of the earth, not the thought of the author himself (1920a: 183). While the people believe the end has arrived, the author teaches that there are worse woes to come. But there is nothing in the text to indicate such a disjunction between the people's point of view and the author's.

Revelation 6.12-17 fits the 'catastrophic intervention' pattern evident in a number of post-biblical Jewish texts, and which we found to be exhibited in Mk 13.24-27 + par. and Heb. 12.25-29. God comes or intervenes, and nature trembles and breaks down. It is true that God (or Christ) is not said to come or descend, but the divine presence is implied in Rev. 6.16, where the inhabitants of the earth seek to hide 'from the face of the one seated on the throne'. This verse has a parallel in *1 En.* 102.3 which depicts 'all the sons of the earth' seeking 'to hide themselves from the presence of the great glory'. There is also a parallel between Rev. 6.17 and *Apoc. Zeph.* 12.6-7, where the people cry out, 'Who will stand in his presence when he rises in his wrath?'.[42]

One cannot know for sure how John imagined the events narrated in his eschatological visions to play out in 'real history' (they are obviously not literal predictions). It seems reasonable to suppose, though, that, like other apocalypticists before him, he would have expected God's decisive intervention in judgement actually to take a catastrophic form. It is appropriate to conclude that he probably meant the catastrophic imagery of 6.12-14 to convey this prospect.

7.2.5 *The Catastrophic End of the Cosmos?*

We know from Rev. 20.11 and 21.1 that the existing heaven and earth are to be dissolved. Is Rev. 6.12-17 a visionary portrayal of the calamity that brings about the promised dissolution? Or, is the catastrophe depicted in this passage something less than world-ending? According to Charles, the end of the cosmos cannot be in view in these verses, since the earth's inhabitants survive the fall of the stars and rolling up of heaven; they are still there on the earth, hiding in the caves and among the rocks![43] To be sure, the narrative of 6.12-17 does not get us to the point where the cosmos is actually dissolved, but this does not rule out an 'end of the cosmos' interpretation since the portrait could be that of the created universe in *process* of collapse.[44]

---

42. The *Apocalypse of Zephaniah* displays a number of points of contact with Revelation. See *OTP* 1: 504–5.

43. Charles 1920a: 179.

44. The rolling up of the heavenly canopy seems to be a fairly clear image for the dissolution of the material heavens (cf. *Sib. Or.* 3.82-83; *Gos. Thom.* 111). However, in this context, as in Isaiah 34, the idea may be that of the temporary rolling back of the heavenly tent, so that the earth may be totally exposed to the onslaught of the divine wrath (cf. Isa. 63.1).

Whether Rev. 6.12-17 is to be taken as a representation of the onset of the passing away of the first heaven and earth depends on what interpretation is given to the millennium of 20.1-10, and this is the biggest single exegetical problem in the whole book.

Revelation 20.1-10 envisions a thousand-year reign of Christ and his saints, during which time Satan is bound and prevented from deceiving the nations. Is this passage about an intermediate phase of eschatological fulfilment that comes between the parousia of 19.11-21 and the new creation of 21.1–22.5, as the 'premillennial' view has it? Or, is it a symbolic description of the period between Christ's ascension and return, as 'amillenialism' holds?[45] If the premillennial view is taken, the cosmic catastrophe of 6.12-14 could not be identified with the cosmic dissolution of 20.11 and 21.1. On an 'amillennial' reading, the identification could be made.

Revelation 20.1-10 is extremely enigmatic. On the one hand, there is strong evidence to indicate that the passage should be taken as it stands as descriptive of a temporary messianic kingdom between the parousia and the new creation.[46] On the other hand, reading the passage in this way seems to involve a rather unnecessary duplication of 'final' events.[47]

It is significant that the language of 6.12-17 is picked up at 20.11: *heaven* and earth flee (cf. 'heaven vanished like a scroll', 6.14) from the *face of the one sitting on the* great white *throne* (cf. 'from the face of the one sitting on the throne', 6.16) and no *place* is found for them (cf. 'every mountain and island was removed from its place', 6.14). A connection is thereby established between the cosmic catastrophe of 6.12-17 and the dissolution of 20.11 and 21.1.

---

45. For a review of interpretative approaches to Rev. 20.1-10, see Kovacs and Rowland 2004: 201–14; Mealy 1992: 15–58.

46. Satan's confinement in the pit is clearly subsequent to his casting out from heaven in 12.9; that expulsion precedes the rise of the beast and false prophet (ch. 13), whereas his imprisonment follows their destruction (20.10; cf. 19.20). During the thousand years, Satan is rendered impotent, whereas prior to Christ's victory in 19.11-21, he is powerfully active on earth (esp. 12.13–13.4). In the pre-parousia period, the martyrs exist as disembodied souls in heaven and await vindication (6.9-11); at the beginning of the millennium, they are resurrected, and during it they reign victoriously with Christ (20.4-6). For exegesis of the passage along a premillennial line, see Aune 1998b: 1081–1108; Beasley-Murray 1974: 287–92. Bauckham (1993a: 18–21; 1993b: 106–8) takes the millennium as consequent on the parousia, but understands it as a symbol of the messianic victory, not a chronological interval between the parousia and the final, final judgement.

47. A premillennial reading gives us two final wars, two resurrections, two 'final' judgements and two states of eschatological blessing; cf. Aune 1998b: 1108.

The following conclusion seems justified. The cosmic catastrophe of 6.12-14 is to be understood either as a foreshadowing and anticipation of a cosmic destruction that follows later, or as the beginning of the process that ends in the dissolution of the present heaven and earth. Whether it is the former or the latter is dependent on what sense is accorded to 20.1-10, and I am content to leave this an open issue.

7.3 Timing of the Catastrophe and Consequences of the End of the Cosmos

Revelation 6.12-17 envisions a catastrophe which, if not cosmos-ending in itself, prefigures the dissolution of the existing cosmic order to follow on after the millennium (20.11; 21.1). What timescale attaches to the expectation of coming catastrophe?

7.3.1 Timescale

Whether the end of the cosmos and its re-making are expected soon or are viewed as still a long way off is dependent on what interpretation is given to Rev. 20.1-10. The risen Jesus indicates that his coming will be 'soon' (2.6; 3.11; 22.7, 12, 20). But again, the nearness of the event is not put within a particular time frame. In 'amillennial' readings of Rev. 20.1-10 that stand in the tradition of Augustine, the reference to a 'thousand years' is sometimes taken to indicate that, from John's vantage point, the parousia lies in the far distant future.

7.3.2 Consequences

What are the associations and implications of John's expectation of the passing away of heaven and earth?

7.3.2.1 Creational Consequences
The book of Revelation expresses a strong belief in God as creator of the world. In the hymn of 4.11, God is honoured as the one who 'created all things', and by whose will 'they existed and were created'. That God is the maker of heaven, earth and sea is stressed in 10.6 and 14.7.[48] There is no attempt in the book to alienate God from the material cosmos. It is said in 11.18, that at the coming judgement, God will destroy the

---

48. In 3.14, Christ is identified as the 'beginning', or perhaps 'originating principle', of creation (ἡ ἀρχὴ τῆς κτίσεως τοῦ θεοῦ). Beale (1999: 300–1) thinks that 'creation' here is the new created order, not the present creation.

destroyers of the earth. As Bauckham notes, this is a clear indication of God's faithfulness to his creation.[49] John's expectation that the existing heavens and earth will be dissolved, therefore, is not part of a dualistic outlook that rejects the material order.

7.3.2.2 Eschatological Consequences
Quite obviously the notion of the end of the cosmos does not involve for John a purely heavenly and non-material view of the final state of blessedness. John looks for a new heavens and earth after the present world has passed away. The new creation of 21.1, 5, as we have already observed, is not a creation *ex nihilo*, but a creation from the material resources of the old. John is the only New Testament writer to give a description of the final blessedness. How does he conceive of the new heavens and earth in relation to the present world?

In 21.1-8, the new creation is largely defined by negation.[50] In vv. 1 and 4, John specifies five features of the present creation and life in it which are 'no more' in the new created order: sea, death, mourning, crying and pain. The absence of the sea is particularly significant. For John, the sea is one of the primary constituents of the present cosmos; the whole universe can be defined as 'heaven, earth and sea' (10.6; 12.12; 14.7).[51] The sea also represents for John, as within the Old Testament, the primeval chaos (compare 13.1 with 11.7), the principle of disorder present within creation from the beginning. It symbolizes, as Bauckham states, the 'destructive potential which remains to threaten the created universe'.[52] The removal of the sea thus 'implies that creation is established eternally, beyond any threat of reverting to chaos'.[53] The fivefold 'no more' signifies the absence of physical evil from the new created order; the absence of moral evil is indicated by the list of excluded groups in v. 8 (the cowardly, faithless, polluted, etc.).

In 21.9–22.5, the vision concentrates on the new Jerusalem. A general vista of the city, in 21.9-14, paves the way for a more detailed description of it in 21.15–22.5. Verses 15-21 outline its architectural features: its dimensions, walls, foundations, gates and street. Verses 22-

49. Bauckham 1993b: 53.
50. D. M. Russell (1996: 207) notes the correspondences between Isa. 65.17-25 and Rev. 21.1-15, while stressing that 'the differences between the two passages clearly reflect that John recognizes a transcendent aspect to the new world not evident in Isaiah'.
51. Cf. 5.13, where the universe is divided into heaven, earth, the underside of the earth, and sea. See 7.1-3 and 10.2 for the basic division of earth and sea.
52. Bauckham 1993b: 53.
53. Bauckham 2001: 1303.

27 focus on the glory of the city, the glory of God and the lamb, and the glory brought into the city by those who populate it, including the nations and their kings; anything that defiles has no place in it. The glory of the Lord removes the need for sun and moon (v. 23). Revelation 22.1-5 depicts the new Jerusalem as paradise restored. Running through the middle of the main street of the city is 'the river of the water of life', a feature drawn from the Edenic depictions of the restored Jerusalem in Ezek. 47.1-12 and Zech. 14.8, but with a further biblical antecedent in the river that flowed out of Eden (cf. Gen. 2.10). On either side of the river grows 'the tree of life' (cf. 22.14, 19), referring to the tree in the garden in Eden to which access was forbidden after the expulsion of Adam and Eve (Gen. 3.22-24). In the new Jerusalem/new creation open access is restored.[54] Nothing accursed is found; the curse of Gen. 3.17 is withdrawn.[55] Revelation 22.5 adds to the fivefold 'no more' of 21.1-4, with the statement, 'there will be no more night' (cf. 21.23).

The new heavens and earth are both continuous and discontinuous with the present world. The continuity is most evident in the description of the new Jerusalem in 21.9-27. The city is recognizably patterned on this-earthly models. The materials of which it is constructed and with which it is adorned are this-worldly commodities. Boring states: 'The beauty of this world ... becomes the vehicle of expressing the beauty of the Eternal City.'[56] Progression from this world to the next is vividly expressed in 21.24-26 in the images of nations and kings bringing their glory into the great city. The discontinuity is apparent in the things which are said to be absent from it.

The new creation is both a restoration of the original scheme of creation (22.1-3) but also a transcendence of it.

7.3.2.3 *Practical Consequences*
John does not draw practical implications from the thought of the passing away of the existing heavens and earth. It is clear, though, that waiting for the soon-coming Lord is no reason for inactivity. In the messages to the seven churches, John, speaking for the risen Jesus, commends toil,

---

54. The curious thought of a singular tree on both sides of the river suggests a twin reference to the tree of life from which people were excluded after the expulsion of Adam and Eve in Gen. 3.22-24 (the Genesis tree is clearly in view in Rev. 22.14, 19) and to the multiple 'trees' on both banks of the rivers in Ezekiel's vision (Ezek. 47.7, 12).

55. Boring 1989: 218. There could also be an allusion to Zech. 14.11 (so Aune 1998b: 1178–9). In Zechariah, the point is that Jerusalem shall never again be subject to the ban of destruction (the *herem*).

56. Boring 1989: 222.

commitment and persistent endurance (2.2, 19, 26; 3.1-2). Particularly noteworthy is the stress on the doing of appropriate 'works' (2.2, 5, 6, 19, 22, 23, 26; 3.1, 2, 8, 15).

7.4 Conclusions

In Rev. 6.12-17, John the seer envisages a great shaking with cosmic repercussions. The scenario fits the 'catastrophic intervention' pattern well established in Jewish eschatological texts. The catastrophic irruption anticipates the end of the cosmos narrated in 20.11; 21.1; it may perhaps initiate the final dissolution.

The notion of the passing away of the present creation in 21.1 is not an expression of an anti-creational perspective in Revelation. In various ways, creation is affirmed in the book. The passing of the first heaven and earth is followed by the appearance of a new creation, which is understood, albeit symbolically, in quite materialist terms. The new created order is both a restoration of the original and a transformation of it; it is the fulfilment of the creation's design. John expects the time of waiting for the Lord's return to be characterized by faithful activity.

CONCLUSIONS

This enquiry has focused on New Testament texts employing language of cosmic catastrophe: Mk 13.24-25 + par.; Heb. 12.25-29; 2 Pet. 3.5-13; Rev. 6.12-17. I have sought to examine these texts in their immediate and wider textual contexts and in the light of relevant Jewish and Graeco-Roman comparative material. The study was carried out with two main aims in view: first, to determine whether a 'real' catastrophe is in view, and whether this amounts to or leads to the complete destruction of the cosmos (as the ancients defined cosmic destruction); second, to establish the timescale which attaches to the catastrophic intervention and also to assess the theological and practical consequences of belief in the end of the cosmos for the writers concerned. The discussion has been conducted in critical interaction with the claims of N. T. Wright: in particular, his contentions that the early Christians, like first-century Jews, did not contemplate, as he puts it, 'the end of the space-time universe'; that such a notion is inherently dualistic and anti-materialist; that language of cosmic breakdown and collapse, as we find it in Mk 13.24-25 + par., was standard first-century Jewish language for referring to a major crisis in the socio-political realm.

In presenting now my conclusions, I first summarize the main findings of the foregoing investigation in relation to the aims with which I set out. I next highlight the significance of this work for our broader understanding of New Testament cosmic eschatology. I then consider whether the catastrophe texts, as I have interpreted them, present intractable problems for a biblically informed Christian response to the environmental crisis.

1 *Summary of Main Findings*

That the created universe is destined to be dissolved is clearly expressed in the Old Testament (along with other views of creation's future); it is also a common conviction in Jewish apocalyptic and related writings. The idea of the material cosmos coming to an end goes right back to the very beginnings of Greek natural philosophy in the sixth century BCE.

Plato and Aristotle rejected the idea, maintaining that the cosmos is indestructible. Epicureans and Stoics firmly believed in the ultimate destruction of the cosmos and their teachings on the matter seem to have had some influence at a popular level in New Testament times. Neither in Old Testament and Jewish sources nor in Epicurean and Stoic sources is the end of the cosmos part of a negative, dualistic cosmology. Old Testament writers and later Jewish writers had little difficulty in affirming the end of the present created order while maintaining a robust creational monotheism.[1]

Jewish language of global or cosmic catastrophe, which has its origins in Old Testament prophecy, is deployed in an eschatological context in a large range of pseudepigraphal and other texts spanning a period from the third century BCE to the early second century CE. In none of these texts is the reference to the downfall of a city or nation. The imagery is largely traditional, and the mode of employment imaginative, but a 'real' catastrophe on a global or cosmic scale is in view none the less. In some texts (especially the *Sibylline Oracles*), the catastrophe plainly issues in total cosmic destruction. Language of cosmic catastrophe also figures in Stoic sources; again it is imaginatively deployed, but the reference is quite clearly to the catastrophic end of the cosmos.

In the light of the comparative evidence, language of cosmic catastrophe such as we find in the New Testament simply cannot be regarded as conventional, first-century language for referring symbolically to sociopolitical change. In the key New Testament passages employing this language, a catastrophe of cosmic dimensions (within an ancient cosmological framework) is genuinely in view. This is not only suggested by the parallel data but is evident from a close reading of the texts themselves in their literary contexts.

Hebrews 12.25-29 and 2 Pet. 3.5-13 definitely envisage the catastrophic demise of the present cosmos. The author of Hebrews, having already made clear that creation will perish (1.10-12), indicates with his

---

1. It is somewhat ironic, given his keenness to dissociate ancient Jewish theology from Platonism, that in insisting on the incompatibility of the thought of the created cosmos coming to an end with Jewish creational monotheism, Wright himself exhibits a Platonic logic. For Plato, the demiurge was bound by his own nature to create an everlasting cosmos; a good god could not have done otherwise. By ascribing immortality and other perfections to the cosmos, Plato blurs the distinction between it and 'god' (*Tim.* 34B; 68E; 92C). In Old Testament and early Jewish thought (generally speaking), there is more emphasis on the freedom and sovereignty of God vis-à-vis the created world. According to Ps. 102.25-27, the distinction between creator and creation is evident precisely in the fact that God is eternal, whereas heaven and earth will wear out and perish.

own explanatory comment in 12.27 that the future shaking of heaven and earth of which he speaks in 12.26 entails their destruction. The writer of 2 Peter has expressed as clearly as he could that the existing cosmos is to be destroyed by fire. Attempts to argue that what is pictured is a radical but essentially non-destructive purification of the cosmos come to grief on the exegetical evidence. The author presents his eschatological teaching in opposition to 'scoffers' who rejected the notion of God's eschatological coming, which they took to imply a cosmos-ending catastrophe. They adhered to the Platonic line that the cosmos is everlasting. In combating their position, the author draws on the resources of Stoic cosmology.

It is reasonable to regard the catastrophic convulsions of Mk 13.24-27 as belonging to a process that leads to cosmic dissolution, when these verses are read in the light of the declaration just a few verses later, that 'heaven and earth will pass away' (13.31). An 'end of the cosmos' interpretation can be sustained on similar grounds for Mt. 24.29-31 and Lk. 21.25-27. The catastrophic occurrences of Rev. 6.12-17 either prefigure the dissolution of the present heaven and earth spoken of in 21.1 or constitute the beginnings of that process (depending on whether a premillennial or amillennial view is taken of 20.1-10).

Our study has brought to prominence a significant number of New Testament texts which envisage the present created cosmos coming to an actual end: Mk 13.31 + par.; Heb. 1.10-12; 12.25-28; 2 Pet. 3.5-13; Rev. 20.11; 21.1. This evidence contradicts Wright's claim that early Christians never contemplated such a thing. To be sure, none of these texts speak of a cosmic destruction that extends to the point of the annihilation of matter itself, but, as I emphasized at the beginning of the study, this was not a genuine option available to writers of the New Testament period (and so should not be used as the criterion for assessing whether total cosmic dissolution is in mind in these passages). What is anticipated is the winding up of the existing cosmos (as perceived from an ancient perspective) none the less, not merely a transformation of social-political conditions, a change in heaven and earth, or a non-destructive refining of creation, but the 'real' end of the cosmos by the cosmological standards of the day.

According to Wright, an 'end of the cosmos' interpretation of Mk 13.24-27 + par. would undermine the credibility of Jesus and the evangelists, since the upheavals and the coming of the Son of man are set within the lifetimes of the first Christian generation. However, none of the Synoptists ties the catastrophic intervention in a definitive way to the time frame of a generation, and so they were not proved wrong when it failed to happen within this delimited period. As to when the end will occur, what we find in each of these writers is a tension between its nearness and its unknown timing. For the author of 2 Peter, the catastrophic end of the cosmos may be soon, within the lifetime of his addressees, or it may belong to the far-distant future. The question of John's position on the timing of the catastrophic intervention is complicated by the millennial issue; leaving this aside, what we get is an emphasis on the closeness of Christ's return, but without any precise indication as to 'when'.[2]

The expectation of the end of the cosmos, whether expressed in the catastrophe texts or in other passages we have examined (Mk 13.31 + par.; Heb 1.10-12; Rev. 20.11, 21.1) generally does not carry for our writers the adverse associations which some deem to be bound up with it: radical dualism; heavenism; ethical passivity.

For none of the authors concerned does it entail a radical cosmic dualism, that is, the kind of dualism that denigrates creation and materiality. All of these writers were heirs to the positive valuation of the created world in Jewish scriptural and theological tradition; nothing is said by them to contravene that estimation, and various statements are made that support and express it. The author of Hebrews has sometimes been thought to be unenthusiastic about creation, but there is clear evidence that shows otherwise. His contrast between the destructibility of heaven and earth and the eternity of God/the Son is entirely drawn from the Old Testament; it does not betray an allegedly 'Gnostic' dualism.

It is extremely doubtful that any of the writers concerned look for a purely heavenly, non-material state of final blessedness. The writers of 2 Peter and the book of Revelation explicitly speak of a new heavens and earth. Matthew and Luke evidently look for a cosmic restoration (Mt.19.28; Acts 3.21); Mark probably does so too. Hebrews has often been thought to anticipate a wholly spiritual and heavenly salvation, but there are good grounds for assuming that its author, like the other writers, expects a re-creation of the cosmos after its dissolution.

2. These observations do not, of course, remove the credibility problem arising from the temporal perspective of the writers; they simply address that issue as Wright has framed it. For modern critics, the issue of credibility arises from the fact that nearly two millennia have passed since these texts were penned. Though they did not set any deadlines for the catastrophic intervention, the New Testament writers could hardly have expected such a lengthy time of waiting to transpire. Modern-day critics could echo the complaint of the scoffers of 2 Pet. 3.4, that the long time of non-fulfilment makes it difficult to take the 'promise' of a potentially imminent final irruption very seriously. One might reply, as the writer of 2 Peter did, that God's timescale is totally different from that of human beings, but this is unlikely to be found wholly satisfactory. Many Christians, of course, are happy to acknowledge the imminent expectation of the earliest believers and do not find the long period of non-fulfilment particularly troubling.

None of our authors reasons that since the cosmos is to be dissolved there is nothing to be done except wait inertly for the end. Each makes clear that the time of waiting is to be marked by productive activity and moral endeavour, and that sluggishness, indolence or apathy will bring serious judgement. Living in the expectation of the end of the world or the coming intervention, for these writers, promotes action rather than discourages it.

2 Significance for An Understanding of New Testament Cosmic Eschatology

The findings of this study contribute to a fuller understanding of New Testament cosmic eschatology (or perhaps eschatologies). This investigation has shown that the expectation of the end of creation is an important strand of New Testament cosmic-eschatological thought. The 'end' is not an absolute end but belongs to a pattern of end followed by new beginning. In 2 Peter and Revelation, it is clear that the new heavens and new earth are not a new creation *ex nihilo*, but a re-creation *ex vetere*. In Revelation, the new heavens and earth exhibit striking continuities, as well as discontinuities, with the present order and pattern of the world (chs 21–22). What is brought by the unmaking and remaking of the world, as John visualizes it, is a redemptive recovery and transformation of the 'first' creation, which both restores primordial conditions and also surpasses them. In this new creative work, God brings about what he has always intended for this creation.

There is another strand of New Testament cosmic eschatology, represented above all by Rom. 8.18-25, which has not been the subject of this investigation but has been more fully treated in other work,[3] that envisions the cosmic future in a different way. In Rom. 8.18-25, Paul speaks of creation waiting with eager anticipation for the eschatological revelation (v. 19). He declares that creation will be released from the corruption, decay and frustration to which it has been subjected and will share in the liberation to be enjoyed by God's children (v. 21). This passage seems to anticipate a non-destructive (yet radical) transformation of the existing creation (note especially the formulation, 'creation *itself* will be set free', αὐτὴ ἡ κτίσις ἐλευθερωθήσεται, v. 21), rather than its dissolution and creation afresh.[4] The redemptive outcome is perhaps not

---

3. Esp. D. M. Russell 1996.
4. Cf. Adams 2000: 181–2. Paul, though, does not take a consistent position on the fate of the created order. His formulation, 'this form of this world is passing away', in 1 Cor. 7.31, strongly suggests a scheme of cosmic destruction followed by

altogether dissimilar to what is pictured in Revelation 21–22 – a repristinized and perfected world which actualizes God's goals for creation from the beginning – but the redemptive activity itself is conceived differently: as an act of transformation rather than de-creation and re-creation.

We thus find in the New Testament two distinct cosmic-eschatological schemes. Both schemes – destruction and creation anew and non-destructive transformation – are attested in Jewish apocalyptic and related writings, though the former is the more dominant idea. In exhibiting both conceptions, the New Testament reflects the Jewish eschatological milieu of the time.[5]

That the New Testament has different perspectives on the cosmic future, or more precisely, how the cosmic future is brought about, should not be found surprising. As Craig Hill has warned, we must not come to the Bible assuming that there is a 'uniform biblical eschatology';[6] this applies to the New Testament as much as the Old Testament. Hill contends, quite rightly, that we must resist the temptation to harmonize disparate viewpoints; rather we should treat them fairly and with integrity. Despite the difference, which is quite a fundamental one, it still makes sense to speak of a general New Testament hope for the 'ultimate redemption' of the created order.[7] This general hope can appropriately be labelled a hope for cosmic 'renewal' (so on this terminological point I agree with Wright). The terminology of renewing and renewal has a background in Jewish eschatological literature and captures both the concept of non-violent transformation and that of destruction and creation anew, and conveys the point that the latter involves a re-creation of what exists, not an annihilation (reduction to nothing) and new creation *ex nihilo*.[8]

3 *Significance for Environmental Ethics*

New Testament 'cosmic catastrophe' and other destructionist texts seem to create difficulties for a biblically informed Christian response to the

re-creation. See further the discussion in Adams 2000: 130–6. Van Kooten (2003) detects a debate on the issue of the destiny of the cosmos in the Pauline School.

5. Both ideas arise from the Old Testament: cf. Chapter 1, p. 50.
6. Hill 2002: 28.
7. So D. M. Russell 1996: 7.
8. According to contemporary natural science, the physical universe will either keep on expanding until it eventually evanesces or collapse in a 'big crunch' (cf. Stoeger 2000: 26–7). The timescale involved is in the region of trillions of years. On the relationship between biblical/theological and scientific accounts of the cosmic future, see further Benz 2000; the relevant essays in Polkinghorne and Welker 2000; Polkinghorne 2002.

environmental crisis. If the present creation is destined for destruction, one might reason, there is little point in bothering with it. Why try to preserve and protect the earth if it is going to perish and dissolve?[9] Passages such as 2 Pet. 3.5-13 seem at best to provide little incentive for environmental action, and at worst actively to discourage it. It is for this reason that those who have sought to develop a biblical basis for Christian environmentalism have tended to concentrate on passages that speak of creation's destiny in more positive terms; Rom. 8.18-25 has received particular attention, and has been treated as the definitive biblical statement on creation's future. Certainly, this passage, with its emphasis on the coming liberation of creation, offers a vision of hope that can more easily support environmental interest and action. Paul indicates here that it is *this* creation – not another – that will serve as the eschatological environment of the people of God. Though he anticipates a radical transformation, his portrayal implies an 'organic' continuity between creation as it is now and creation as it will be. On the basis of this passage, one could perhaps argue that present-day attempts to free the environment from oppression anticipate its eschatological liberation.[10] But as was stressed in the Introduction, in constructing a biblically informed ecological theology or framework for environmental care, it is necessary to engage with the full range of biblical material that may be relevant to the environment, including texts that may seem to encourage its neglect or even its outright exploitation. It is important, at least, to acknowledge that the New Testament has other ways of talking about the cosmic future, and that Romans 8 is not the only statement on the matter.

I do not think that the presence of 'cosmic catastrophe' texts in the New Testament is an obstacle to the development of a positive environmental ethic, when one keeps in mind the general New Testament perspective on cosmic redemption and renewal. Also, there are factors that mitigate the seemingly 'Ruin of Earth'[11] perspective. I will pursue this point with regard to 2 Pet. 3.5-13, which seems to be the most resistant of our texts to retrieval for a Christian response to the environmental crisis.

First, there is the observation that cosmic destruction here does not entail the judgement that the earth or the physical world is bad or

---

9. This is really a fallacious line of argument. All sorts of things that are not long lasting (buildings, possessions, physical bodies) are deemed to be worthy of care and protection.

10. Though this is not a line of reasoning that would have entered into Paul's mind. It would be going too far to argue from Romans 8 that specific actions done on behalf of the environment actually carry over into the transformed creation.

11. To take up Dyer's (2002: 53) phrase.

worthless. Without doubt, the writer agrees with the verdict of Genesis 1, that creation is *intrinsically* good (he alludes to the Genesis creation account in v. 5). Second, and most crucially, there is the fact that dissolution of the earth is understood here not as an end in itself, but as the prelude to a new *earthly* future. The destructive process is part of the process of renewal and renovation (conceived along the lines of the Stoic *ekpurōsis*), which leads to a new heavens and new earth which stand in material continuity with the present heavens and earth. The author does not reduce the present earth 'to a ball of corrupted matter about to be thrown onto the corrupted waste dump of eternity'.[12] His perspective is not annihilationist. The new earth is regenerated out of the old; in the process, cosmic matter is not dumped but *recycled*. Third, we note that living in expectancy of the end, for this author, does not mean the forsaking of moral responsibility; he issues a moral appeal precisely on the basis of the coming end and renewal (vv. 11-12). Now this writer would never have considered environmental care as part of Christian ethical responsibility, but these days we might consider it to be so. His exhortation to 'hasten' the coming of the day of God could admittedly be taken as an invitation to participate in activities that lead to the ruination of the earth,[13] but it would be perverse indeed to argue that by using up the earth's resources Christians may actually expedite the Lord's coming.[14] There is no note of *schadenfreude* here, no malicious glee at the thought of the earth's burning-up. The author eagerly desires to see the coming of the day of God because it brings about, via a process of destruction, the just world order that God has promised. This is the real object of his longing, not the end of the world as an end in its own right.

I am not suggesting that 2 Pet. 3.5-13 or the other catastrophe and/or destructionist texts can be embraced and re-branded as 'eco-friendly' texts, but there are elements in these passages which are retrievable for a Christian response to the environmental crisis.

The catastrophic expectation we find in the New Testament is not ultimately a pessimistic one; it is part of an eschatology of hope. In 2 Peter and Revelation, that hope is for a new heavens and earth, brought about by God's redemptive action. This hope is one that can inspire action for change and justice and in a world and society where God is not yet 'all in all'.

---

12. N. C. Habel, as cited in Dyer 2002: 46.
13. So Dyer 2002: 55–6.
14. Though Hill (2002: 197) cites the example of a senior American politician in the Reagan administration who did in fact make this very argument.

BIBLIOGRAPHY

Primary Sources

Bible

Biblia Hebraica Stuttgartensia (Stuttgart: Deutsche Bibelgesellschaft, 5th edn, 1997).
The Holy Bible Containing the Old and New Testaments with the Apocryphal/Deuterocanonical Books, New Revised Standard Version, 1995.
Novum Testamentum Graece (Stuttgart: Deutsche Bibelgesellschaft, 27th edn, 1993).
Septuaginta (ed. A. Rahlfs; 2 vols; Stuttgart: Deutsche Bibelgesellschaft, 1935).

Other Ancient Sources

For Graeco-Roman sources (and the writings of Josephus and Philo), the Loeb Classical Library has generally been used; some citations of ancient philosophical sources have been taken from KRS and LS (as indicated in the footnotes).

Black, M.
    1970   *Apocalypsis Henochi Graece* (Leiden: Brill).
    1985   *The Book of Enoch, or, 1 Enoch: a New English Edition with Commentary and Textual Notes* (in consultation with James C. VanderKam; SVTP 7; Leiden: Brill).
Brock, S.
    1967   *Testamentum Iobi* (Leiden: Brill).
Charles, R. H.
    1897   *The Assumption of Moses: Translated from the Latin Sixth century MS* (London: A. & C. Black).
    1912   *The Book of Enoch: or 1 Enoch Translated from the Editor's Ethiopic Text* (Oxford: Clarendon, 2nd edn).
Charlesworth, J. H. (ed.)
    1983, 1985   *The Old Testament Pseudepigrapha* (2 vols; London: Darton, Longman and Todd).
Feldman, H., and M. Simon
    1977   *The Midrash Rabbah* (5 vols; London, Jerusalem and New York: Soncino).
García Martínez, F.
    1994   *The Dead Sea Scrolls Translated: the Qumran Texts in English* (Leiden: Brill).

Geffken, J.
    1902   *Die Oracula Sibyllina* (Leipzig: Hinrichs).

Hayward, R.
    1987   *The Targum of Jeremiah* (The Aramaic Bible 12; Edinburgh: T&T Clark).

Kirk, G. S., J. E. Raven and M. Schofield
    1983   *The Presocratic Philosophers: A Critical History with a Selection of Texts* (Cambridge: Cambridge University Press, 2nd edn).

Knibb, M. A.
    1978   *The Ethiopic Book of Enoch: a New Edition in the Light of the Aramaic Dead Sea Fragments* (Oxford: Clarendon Press).

Kraft, R. A, et al. (eds)
    1974   *The Testament of Job According to the SV Text: Greek Text and English Translation* (Texts and Translations 5; Pseudepigrapha Series 4; Missoula, Montana: Society of Biblical Literature and Scholars Press).

Long. A. A., and D. N. Sedley
    1987   *The Hellenistic Philosophers: Translations of the Principal Sources with Philosophical Commentary* (Cambridge: Cambridge University Press).

Milik, J. T.
    1976   *The Books of Enoch: Aramaic Fragments* (Oxford: Clarendon Press).

Robertson, A., J. Donaldson, et al. (eds)
    1887   *The Ante-Nicene Fathers* (10 vols; Buffalo: The Christian Literature Publishing Company).

Robinson, J. M. (ed.)
    1988   *The Nag Hammadi Library in English* (Leiden: Brill, 3rd edn).

Schaff, P., et al. (eds)
    1896–8   *The Nicene and Post-Nicene Fathers* (1st series 14 vols; 2nd series 13 vols; Buffalo: The Christian Literature Publishing Company).

Schneemelcher, W. (ed.)
    1991–2   *New Testament Apocrypha* (ed. and trans. R. McL. Wilson; 2 vols; Cambridge: James Clarke).

Stählin, O.
    1905–9   *Clemens Alexandrinus* (GCS; Leipzig: Hinrichs).

Tromp, J.
    1993   *The Assumption of Moses: A Critical Edition with Commentary* (SVTP 10; Leiden: Brill).

Usener, H.
    1887   *Epicurea* (Leipzig: B. G. Teubner).

Violet, B.
    1910   *Die Esra-Apokalypse (IV Ezra), Erster Teil, Die Überlieferung* (GCS 18; Leipzig: Hinrichs).

Von Armin, H.
    1903–24   *Stoicorum Veterum Fragmenta* (4 vols; Leipzig: B. G. Teubner).

Waterfield, R.
    2000   *The First Philosophers: The Presocratics and Sophists* (Oxford: Oxford University Press).

Secondary Sources

Adams, E.
    1997   'Historical Crisis and Cosmic Crisis in Mark 13 and Lucan's *Civil War*', *TynBul* 48.2: 329–44.
    2000   *Constructing the World: A Study in Paul's Cosmological Language* (SNTW; Edinburgh: T&T Clark).
    2005a   'Creation "out of" and "through" Water in 2 Peter 3:4', in Van Kooten 2005: 21–30.
    2005b   'The Coming of the Son of Man in Mark's Gospel', *TynBul* 56.2: 39–61.
    2005c   '"Where is the Promise of his Coming?" The Complaint of the Scoffers in 2 Peter 3.4', *NTS* 51: 106–22.
    2006   'The Coming of God Tradition and its Influence on New Testament Parousia texts', in C. Hempel and J. M. Lieu (eds), *Biblical Traditions in Transmission: Essays in Honour of Michael A. Knibb* (JSJSup 111; Leiden: Brill): 1–19.

Allison, D. C.
    1985   *The End of the Ages has Come: An Early Interpretation of the Passion and Resurrection of Jesus* (Philadelphia: Fortress Press).
    1998   *Jesus of Nazareth: Millenarian Prophet* (Minneapolis: Augsburg-Fortress).
    1999   'Jesus and the Victory of Apocalyptic', in Newman 1999: 126–41.

Andersen, F. I.
    2001   *Habakkuk: A New Translation with Introduction and Commentary* (AB 25; New York: Doubleday).

Andersen, F. I., and D. N. Freedman
    2000   *Micah: A New Translation with Introduction and Commentary* (AB 24E; New York: Doubleday).

Anderson, A. A.
    1972   *The Book of Psalms* (NCB; London: Oliphants).

Anderson, B. W. (ed.)
    1984   *Creation in the Old Testament* (Issues in Religion and Theology 6; London: SPCK; Philadelphia: Fortress Press).

Anderson, H.
    1976   *The Gospel of Mark* (London: Oliphants).

Attridge, H.
    1989   *A Commentary on the Epistle to the Hebrews* (Hermeneia; Philadelphia: Fortress Press).

Aune, D. E.
    1997   *Revelation 1–5* (WBC 52; Dallas: Word Books).
    1998a   *Revelation 6–16* (WBC 52B; Nashville: Nelson).
    1998b   *Revelation 17 to 22* (WBC 52C; Nashville: Nelson).

Aune, D. E., T. J. Geddert and C. A. Evans
    2000   'Apocalypticism', in C. A. Evans and S. E. Porter (eds), *Dictionary of New Testament Background* (Leicester: IVP): 45–58.

Bailey, C.
    1947   *De rerum natura. Edited with Prolegomena, Critical Apparatus, Translation and Commentary* (Oxford: Clarendon Press).

Barclay, J. M. G.
    1987   'Mirror-Reading a Polemical Letter: Galatians as a Test Case', *JSNT* 31: 73–93.
    1996   *Jews in the Mediterranean Diaspora: From Alexander to Trajan (323 BCE to 117 CE)* (Edinburgh: T&T Clark).

Barrett, C. K.
    1994   *A Critical and Exegetical Commentary on the Acts of the Apostles* (Vol. 1; ICC; Edinburgh: T&T Clark).

Barton, J.
    2001   *Joel and Obadiah*: *A Commentary* (OTL; Louisville, Kentucky: Westminster John Knox Press).

Bauckham, R.
    1983   *Jude, 2 Peter* (WBC 50; Waco, Texas: Word Books).
    1993a   *The Climax of Prophecy: Studies on the Book of Revelation* (Edinburgh: T&T Clark).
    1993b   *The Theology of the Book of Revelation* (New Testament Theology; Cambridge: Cambridge University Press).
    1997   '2 Peter', in R. P. Martin and P. H. Davids (eds), *Dictionary of the Later New Testament and Its Developments* (Leicester: IVP): 923–27.
    1999   'The Millennium', in R. Bauckham (ed.), *God will be All in All: The Eschatology of Jürgen Moltmann* (Edinburgh: T&T Clark): 123–47.
    2001   'Revelation', in J. Barton and J. Muddiman (eds), *The Oxford Bible Commentary* (Oxford: Oxford University Press): 1287–1306.

Beale, G. K.
    1999   *The Book of Revelation: A Commentary on the Greek Text* (NIGTC; Grand Rapids: Eerdmans).

Beasley-Murray, G. R.
    1954   *Jesus and the Future* (London and New York: St. Martin's Press).
    1974   *The Book of Revelation* (NCB; London: Oliphants).
    1993   *Jesus and the Last Days: The Interpretation of the Olivet Discourse* (Peabody, Massachusetts: Hendrickson).

Benz, A.
    2000   *The Future of the Universe: Chance, Chaos or God* (New York and London: Continuum Books).

Berkouwer, G. C.
    1972   *The Return of Christ* (Grand Rapids: Eerdmans).

Bigg, C.
    1910   *A Critical and Exegetical Commentary on the Epistles of St. Peter and St. Jude* (ICC; Edinburgh: T&T Clark).

Black, M.
    1973   'The Maranatha Invocation and Jude 14, 15 (1 Enoch 1:9)', in B. Lindars and S. S. Smalley (eds), *Christ and Spirit in the New Testament: in Honour of Charles Francis Digby Moule* (Cambridge: Cambridge University Press): 189–96.
    1976   'The New Creation in 1 Enoch', in R. W. A. McKinney (ed.), *Creation, Christ and Culture* (Edinburgh: T&T Clark): 13–21.

Blomberg, C.
 1999 'The Wright Stuff: A Critical Overview of Jesus and the Victory of God', in Newman 1999: 19–39.

Bolt, P. G.
 2004 *The Cross from A Distance: Atonement in Mark's Gospel* (NSBT 18; Leicester: Apollos).

Borg, M. J.
 1984 *Conflict, Holiness and Politics in the Teaching of Jesus* (Studies in the Bible and Early Christianity 5; Lewiston, Queenston and Lampeter: Edwin Mellen).
 1987 'An Orthodoxy Reconsidered: The "End-of-the-World Jesus"', in L. D. Hurst and N. T. Wright (eds), *The Glory of Christ in the New Testament: Studies in Christology* (Oxford: Clarendon Press): 207–17.

Boring, E. M.
 1989 *Revelation* (Interpretation; Louisville: John Knox Press).

Box, G. H.
 1912 *The Ezra-Apocalypse, Being Chapters 3–14 of the Book Commonly Known as 4 Ezra (or II Esdras)* (London: Pitman).

Bridge, S. L.
 2003 *Where Eagles are Gathered: The Deliverance of the Elect in Lukan Eschatology* (JSNTSup 240; London: Sheffield Academic Press).

Bruce, F. F.
 1964 *The Epistle to the Hebrews. The English Text with Introduction, Exposition and Notes* (New London Commentaries; London: Marshall, Morgan and Scott).

Brueggemann, W.
 1998 *Isaiah 40–66* (Westminster Bible Companion; Louisville: Westminster).

Bullmore, M. A.
 1998 'The Four Most Important Passages for a Christian Environmentalism', *Trinity Journal* 19NS: 139–62.

Bultmann, R.
 1952 *Theology of the New Testament* (trans. K. Grobel; London: SCM Press).
 1960 *Jesus Christ and Mythology* (London: SCM Press).

Burnett, F.W.
 1983 'Παλιγγενεσία in Matt. 19:28: A Window on the Matthean Community', *JSNT* 17: 60–72.

Byrne, B.
 2000 'Creation Groaning: An Earth Bible Reading of Romans 8.18-22', in Habel 2000b: 193–203.

Cadwallader, A. H.
 2002 'Earth as Host or Stranger?: Reading Hebrews 11 from Diasporan Experience', in Habel and Balabanski 2002: 148–65.

Caird, G. B.
 1966 *A Commentary on the Revelation of St. John the Divine* (BNTC; London: Black).
 1980 *The Language and Imagery of the Bible* (London: Duckworth).
 1994 *New Testament Theology* (Completed and edited by L. D. Hurst; New York: Clarendon Press; Oxford: Oxford University Press).

Calvin, J.
    1963   *The Epistle of Paul the Apostle to the Hebrews and the First and Second Epistles of St Peter* (trans. W. B. Johnston; Calvin's commentaries; Edinburgh: Oliver & Boyd).

Carrington, P.
    1960   *According to Mark: A Running Commentary on the Oldest Gospel* (Cambridge: Cambridge University Press).

Carroll, R. P.
    1986   *Jeremiah: A Commentary* (OTL; London: SCM Press).

Casey, M.
    1979   *Son of Man: The Interpretation and Influence of Daniel 7* (London: SPCK).

Chaine, J.
    1937   'Cosmogonie aquatique et conflagration finale d'après la *secunda Petri*', *RB* 46: 207–16.

Charles. R. H.
    1920a   *A Critical and Exegetical Commentary on the Revelation of St. John* (Vol. 1; ICC; Edinburgh: T&T Clark).
    1920b   *A Critical and Exegetical Commentary on the Revelation of St. John* (Vol. 2; ICC; Edinburgh: T&T Clark).

Childs, B. S.
    1959   'The Enemy from the North and the Chaos Tradition', *JBL* 78: 187–98.

Chroust, A.-H.
    1973   'The "Great Deluge" in Aristotle's On Philosophy', *AC* 42: 113–22.

Clements, R. E.
    1980   *Isaiah 1–39* (NCB; Grand Rapids: Eerdmans).

Clines, D.J.
    1989   *Job 1–20* (WBC 17; Dallas: Word Books).

Coggins, R. J.
    2000   *Joel and Amos* (NCB; Sheffield: Sheffield Academic Press).

Cole, R. A.
    1989   *The Gospel According to Mark: An Introduction and Commentary* (TNTC; Leicester: IVP, 2nd edn).

Collins, J. J.
    1974a   *The Sibylline Oracles of Egyptian Judaism* (SBLDS 13; Missoula, Montana: Scholars Press).
    1974b   'The Place of the Fourth Sibyl in the Development of the Jewish Sibiyllina', *JJS* 25: 365–80.
    1974c   'Structure and Meaning in the Testament of Job,' *SBL 1974 Seminar Papers* 1: 35–52.
    1990   'Old Testament Apocalypticism and Eschatology', in R. E. Brown (ed.), *The New Jerome Bible Commentary* (London: G. Chapman, 2nd edn): 298–304.
    1993   *Daniel: A Commentary on the Book of Daniel* (Hermeneia; Minneapolis: Fortress Press).
    1998   *The Apocalyptic Imagination. An Introduction to Jewish Apocalyptic Literature* (Grand Rapids: Eerdmans, 2nd edn).

    2000a   'From Prophecy to Apocalypticism: The Expectation of the End', in Collins 2000b: 129–61.
    2002   'Temporality and Politics in Jewish Apocalyptic Literature', in C. Rowland and J. Barton (eds), *Apocalyptic in History and Tradition* (JSPSup 43; Sheffield: Sheffield Academic Press).

Collins, J. J. (ed.)
    1979   *Apocalypse: The Morphology of a Genre* (Semeia 14; Missoula, Montana: Scholars Press).
    2000b   *The Encyclopedia of Apocalypticism* (London: Continuum).

Conzelmann, H.
    1960   *The Theology of Saint Luke* (London: Faber).

Cotterell, P., and M. Turner
    1989   *Linguistics and Biblical Interpretation* (London: SPCK).

Craddock, F. B.
    1995   *First and Second Peter and Jude* (Westminster Bible Companion; Louisville: Westminster John Knox).

Cranfield, C.E.B.
    1959   *The Gospel According to Saint Mark: An Introduction and Commentary* (CGTC; Cambridge: Cambridge University Press).

Crenshaw, J. L.
    1988   *Ecclesiastes: a Commentary* (OTL; London: SCM Press).
    1995   *Joel: A New Translation and Commentary* (AB 24C; New York: Doubleday).

Cross, F. M.
    1973   *Canaanite Myth and Hebrew Epic: Essays in the History and Religion of Israel* (Cambridge: Harvard University Press).

Crossley, J.
    2004   *The Date of Mark's Gospel: Insight from Law in Earliest Christianity* (JSNTSup 266; London: T&T Clark).

Danker, F. W.
    1962   'II Peter 3:10 and Psalm of Solomon 17:10', *ZNW* 53: 82–6.

Davies, W. D., and D. C. Allison
    1988   *The Gospel According to Saint Matthew* (Vol. 1; ICC; Edinburgh: T&T Clark).
    1997   *The Gospel According to Saint Matthew* (Vol. 3; ICC; Edinburgh: T&T Clark).

Day, J.
    1985   *God's Conflict with the Dragon and the Sea: Echoes of a Canaanite Myth in the Old Testament* (University of Cambridge Oriental Publications 35; Cambridge: Cambridge University Press).

Dillon, J.
    1996   *The Middle Platonists: A Study of Platonism 80 B.C. to A.D. 220* (London: Duckworth, rev. edn).

Donahue, J. R., and D. J. Harrington
    2002   *The Gospel of Mark* (SP; Collegeville, Minnesota: Liturgical Press).

Downing, F. G.
    1995a   'Common Strands in Pagan, Jewish and Christian Eschatologies in the First Century', *TZ* 51.3: 197–211.

1995b   'Cosmic Eschatology in the First Century: "Pagan", Jewish and Christian', *AC* 64: 99–109.

Dyer, K.
1998   *The Prophecy on the Mount: Mark 13 and the Gathering of the New Community* (International Theological Studies 2; Berne: Lang).
2002   'When Is the End Not the End? The Fate of Earth in Biblical Eschatology (Mark 13)', in Habel and Balabanski 2002: 44–56.

Earth Bible Team
2000   'Guiding Ecojustice Principles', in Habel 2000b: 38–53.
2002   'Ecojustic Hermeneutics: Reflections and Challenges', in Habel and Balabanski 2002: 1–14.

Eddy, P. R.
1999   'The (W)Right Jesus: Eschatological Prophet, Israel's Messiah, Yahweh Embodied', in Newman 1999: 46–60.

Eichrodt, W.
1967   *Theology of the Old Testament* (Vol. 2; OTL; London: SCM Press).

Ellingworth, P.
1993   *The Epistle to the Hebrews: A Commentary on the Greek Text* (NIGTC; Eerdmans: Grand Rapids; Paternoster: Carlisle).

Ellis, E. E.
1999   *The Making of the New Testament Documents* (Biblical Interpretation 39; Leiden: Brill).

Elsdon, R.
1992   *Greenhouse Theology: Biblical Perspectives on Caring for Creation* (Tunbridge Wells: Monarch).

Endres, J. C.
1987   *Biblical Interpretation in the Book of Jubilees* (CBQMS 18; Washington, DC: Catholic Biblical Association of America).

Evans, C. A.
2001   *Mark 8:27–16:20* (WBC 34B; Nashville: Thomas Nelson).

Evans, C. F.
1990   *Saint Luke* (London: SCM Press; TPI: Philadelphia).

Everson, A. J.
1974   'The Days of Yahweh', *JBL* 93: 329–37.

Fiorenza, E.S.
1991   *Revelation: Vision of a Just World* (Proclamation Commentaries; Minneapolis: Fortress Press).

Fletcher-Louis, C.
1997   'The Destruction of the Temple and the Relativization of the Old Covenant: Mark 13:31 and Matthew 5:18', in K. E. Brower and M. W. Elliot (eds), *'The reader must understand': Eschatology in Bible and Theology* (Leicester: Apollos): 145–69.
2002   'Jesus, the Temple and the Dissolution of Heaven and Earth', in C. Rowland and J. Barton (eds), *Apocalyptic in History and Tradition* (JSPSup 43; Sheffield: Sheffield Academic Press): 117–41.

Fornberg. T.
1977   *An Early Church in a Pluralistic Society: A Study of 2 Peter* (ConBNT 9; Lund: Gleerup).

France, R. T.
  1971   *Jesus and the Old Testament: His Application of Old Testament Passages to Himself and His Mission* (London: Tyndale).
  2002   *The Gospel of Mark: A Commentary on the Greek Text* (NIGTC; Grand Rapids: Eerdmans; Carlisle: Paternoster Press).
Furley, D. J.
  1987   *The Greek Cosmologists. Volume 1: The Formation of the Atomic Theory and its Earliest Critics* (Cambridge: Cambridge University Press).
Gamble, H. Y.
  1995   *Books and Readers in the Early Church: A History of Early Christian Texts* (New Haven and London: Yale University Press).
García Martínez, F.
  2005   'Creation in the Dead Sea Scrolls', in Van Kooten 2005: 49–70.
Gardner, A.
  2001   'Ecojustice or Anthropological Justice? A Study of the New Heavens and the New Earth in Isaiah 65:17', in N. Habel and S. Wurst (eds), *The Earth Story in Psalms and Prophets* (Earth Bible 2; Sheffield: Sheffield Academic Press): 204–18.
Gathercole, S. J.
  2000   'The Critical and Dogmatic Agenda of Albert Schweitzer's *The Quest of the Historical Jesus*', *TynBul* 51.2: 261–83.
  2002   *Where Is Boasting? Early Jewish Soteriology and Paul's Response in Romans 1–5* (Grand Rapids and Cambridge, UK: Eerdmans).
Geddert, T. J.
  1989   *Watchwords: Mark 13 in Markan Eschatology* (JSNTSup 26; Sheffield: Sheffield Academic Press).
Gleason, R. C.
  2002   'The Eschatology of the Warning in Hebrews 10:26–31', *TynBul* 53.1: 97–120.
Gnilka, J.
  1979   *Das Evangelium nach Markus* (EKKNT; Neukirchen–Vluyn: Neukirchener Verlag).
Goldingay, J.
  1987   *Theological Diversity and the Authority of the Old Testament* (Grand Rapids: Eerdmans).
Gould, E. P.
  1896   *A Critical and Exegetical Commentary on the Gospel According to St Mark* (ICC; Edinburgh: T&T Clark).
Gowan, D. E.
  1985   'Fall and Redemption of the Material World in Apocalyptic Literature', *HBT* 7: 83–103.
  1987   *Eschatology in the Old Testament* (Edinburgh: T&T Clark, 2nd edn).
Green, M.
  1987   *The Second Epistle General of Peter and the General Epistle of Jude* (TNTC; Leicester: IVP, rev. edn).
Green, W. M.
  1942   'The Dying World of Lucretius', *AJP* 63: 51–60.

Gundry, R. H.
> 1993   *Mark: A Commentary on His Apology for the Cross* (Grand Rapids: Eerdmans).

Gunkel, H.
> 1895   *Schöpfung und Chaos in Urzeit und Endzeit: eine religionsgeschichtliche Untersuchung über Gen 1 und Ap Joh 12* (Göttingen: Vandenhoeck und Ruprecht).

Haas, C.
> 1989   'Job's Perseverance in the Testament of Job', in M. A. Knibb and P. W. van der Horst (eds), *Studies on the Testament of Job* (SNTSMS 66; Cambridge: Cambridge University Press): 117-54.

Habel, N. C.
> 2000a   'Introducing the Earth Bible', in Habel 2000b: 25-37.

Habel, N. C. (ed.)
> 2000b   *Reading from the Perspective of the Earth* (Earth Bible 1; Sheffield: Sheffield Academic Press).

Habel, N. C., and V. Balabanski (eds),
> 2002   *The Earth Story in the New Testament* (Earth Bible 5; Sheffield: Sheffield Academic Press).

Haenchen, E.
> 1971   *The Acts of the Apostles: A Commentary* (Oxford: Blackwell).

Hagner, D. A.
> 1995   *Matthew 14-28* (WBC 33B; Dallas: Word Books).

Hahm, D.
> 1977   *The Origins of Stoic Cosmology* (Columbus: Ohio State Press).

Hahn, F.
> 1975   'Die Rede von der Parusie des Menschensohnes Markus 13', in R. Pesch and R. Schnackenburg (eds), *Jesus und der Menschensohn* (Festschrift A. Vögtle; Freiburg: Herder): 240-66.

Hamilton, V. P.
> 1990   *The Book of Genesis: Chapters 1-17* (NICOT; Grand Rapids: Eerdmans).

Hanson, P. D.
> 1975   *The Dawn of Apocalyptic* (Philadelphia: Fortress Press).

Hare, D. R. A.
> 1996   *Mark* (Westminster Bible Companion; Louisville: Westminster John Knox).

Harrington, W. J.
> 1993   *Revelation* (SP 16; Collegeville, Minnesota: Liturgical Press).

Hartman, L.
> 1966   *Prophecy Interpreted: The Formation of Some Jewish Apocalyptic Texts and of the Eschatological Discourse Mark 13 par.* (Gleerup, Lund).
> 1979   *Asking for a Meaning: A Study of 1 Enoch 1-5* (ConBNT 12; Lund: Gleerup).

Harvey, A. E.
> 1982   *Jesus and the Constraints of History* (London: Duckworth).

Hatina, T. R.
> 1996   'The Focus of Mark 13:24-27: The Parousia, or the Destruction of the Temple', *BBR* 6: 43-66.

2002 *In Search of a Context: The Function of Scripture in Mark's Narrative* (JSNTSup 232; Studies in Scripture in Early Judaism and Christianity 8; Sheffield: Sheffield Academic Press).

Hayes, K. M.
2002 *'The Earth Mourns': Prophetic Metaphor and Oral Aesthetic* (Society of Biblical Literature Academia Biblica 8; Atlanta, Georgia: Society of Biblical Literature).

Hengel, M.
1985 *Studies in Mark's Gospel* (London: SCM Press).

Hill, C. C.
2002 *In God's Time: The Bible and the Future* (Grand Rapids: Eerdmans).

Hinnells, J. R.
1973 'The Zoroastrian Doctrine of Salvation in the Roman World: A Study of the Oracle of Hystaspes', in E. J. Sharpe and J. R. Hinnells (eds), *Man and His Salvation: Studies in Memory of S. G. F. Brandon* (Manchester: Manchester University Press): 125–48.

Hoffmann, Y.
1981 'The Day of the Lord as a Concept and a Term in the Prophetic Literature', *ZAW* 93: 37–50.

Hooker, M. D.
1991 *The Gospel According to St Mark* (BNTC; London: A. & C. Black).

Horrell, D. G.
1998 *The Epistles of Peter and Jude* (Epworth Commentaries; Peterborough: Epworth).

Houtman, C.
1993 *Der Himmel im Alten Testament: Israels Weltbild und Weltanschauung* (Oudtestamentische Studiën d. 30; Leiden: Brill).

Hughes, P. E.
1977 *A Commentary on the Epistle to the Hebrews* (Grand Rapids: Eerdmans).

Hultgard, A.
2000 'Persian Apocalypticism', in Collins 2000b: 39–83.

Hurst, L. D.
1990 *The Epistle to the Hebrews: Its Background of Thought* (SNTSMS 65; Cambridge: Cambridge University Press).

Hurtado, L. W.
1989 *Mark* (NIBC; Peabody, Massachusetts: Hendrickson).

James, M. R.
1971 *The Biblical Antiquities of Philo* (Translations of Early Documents Series 1; London: Macmillan; New York: SPCK).

Jeremias, J.
1965 *Theophanie: die Geschichte einer alttestamentlichen Gattung* (WMANT 10; Neukirchen-Vluyn: Neukirchener Verlag).

Johnson, D. G.
1988 *From Chaos to Restoration: an Integrative Reading of Isaiah 24–27* (JSOTSSup 61; Sheffield: JSOT Press).

Johnson, S. E.
1960 *A Commentary on the Gospel According to St. Mark* (BNTC; London: A. & C. Black).

Juel, D. H.
　1991　*The Gospel of Mark* (Interpreting Biblical Texts; Nashville: Abingdon Press).

Käsemann, E.
　1964　'An Apologia for Primitive Christian Eschatology', in E. Käsemann, *Essays on New Testament Themes* (London: SCM Press): 69–95.

Kee, H. C.
　1974　'Satan, Magic, and Salvation in the Testament of Job', *SBL 1974 Seminar Papers* 1: 53–76.

Kelly, J. N. D.
　1969　*A Commentary on the Epistles of Peter and Jude* (BNTC; London: A. & C. Black).

Kidner, D.
　1973　*Psalms 1–72: An Introduction and Commentary on Books I and II of the Psalms* (TOTC; London: Inter-Varsity Press).

King, K.
　2003　*What Is Gnosticism?* (Cambridge, Massachusetts and London: Harvard University Press).

Kittel, B. P.
　1981　*The Hymns of Qumran: Translation and Commentary* (SBLDS; Chico, California: Scholars Press).

Knibb, M. A.
　1979　*1 Esdras*, in R. J. Coggins and M. A. Knibb, *The First and Second Books of Esdras* (The Cambridge Bible Commentary: New English Bible; Cambridge: Cambridge University Press).
　1987　*The Qumran Community* (Cambridge Commentaries on Writings of the Jewish and Christian World, 200 BC to AD 200, Vol. 2; Cambridge: Cambridge University Press).

Knight, J.
　1995　*2 Peter and Jude* (New Testament Guides; Sheffield: Sheffield Academic Press).

Koester, C. R.
　2001　*Hebrews: A New Translation with Introduction and Commentary* (AB 36; New York: Doubleday).

Kovacs, J., and C. Rowland
　2004　*Revelation* (Blackwell Bible Commentaries; Malden, Massachusetts, Oxford, UK, and Carlton, Australia: Blackwell).

Kraftchick, S. J.
　2002　*Jude, 2 Peter* (ANTC; Nashville: Abingdon).

Ladd, G. E.
　1994　*A Theology of the New Testament* (Cambridge: Lutterworth, rev. edn).

Lane, W. L.
　1991a　*Hebrews 1–8* (WBC; Dallas: Word Books).
　1991b　*Hebrews 9–13* (WBC; Dallas: Word Books).

Lapidge, M.
　1978　'Stoic Cosmology', in J. M. Rist (ed.), *The Stoics* (Berkeley, Los Angeles and London: University of California Press): 160–85.
　1979　'Lucan's Imagery of Cosmic Dissolution', *Hermes* 107: 344–70.

1989 'Stoic Cosmology and Roman Literature, First to Third Centuries A.D.', *ANRW* 36.3: 1379–1429.

Lawson, J. M.
    1994 'Romans 8:18–25: The Hope of Creation', *RevExp* 91: 559–65.

Lenski, R. C. H.
    1961 *The Interpretation of St Mark's Gospel* (originally published 1946, Wartburg Press; Minneapolis: Augsburg Publishing House).

Levenson, J. D.
    1994 *Creation and the Persistence of Evil: The Jewish Drama of Divine Omnipotence* (Mythos Series; Princeton: Princeton University Press).

Licht, J.
    1961 'Taxo, or the Apocalyptic Doctrine of Vengeance', *JJS* 12: 95–103.

Lieu, J.
    1997 *The Gospel of Luke* (Epworth Commentaries; Peterborough: Epworth).

Lincoln, A. T.
    2006 *Hebrews: A Guide* (London and New York: T&T Clark/Continuum).

Lindars, B.
    1991 *The Theology of the Letter to the Hebrews* (Cambridge: Cambridge University Press).

Long, A. A.
    1985 'The Stoics on World-Conflagration', *The Southern Journal of Philosophy* 23: 13–37.

Luce, J. V.
    1992 *An Introduction to Greek Philosophy* (London: Thames and Hudson).

Luz, U.
    1989 *Matthew 1–7: A Commentary* (trans. W. C. Linss; Minneapolis: Augsburg).

Mack, B. L.
    1988 *A Myth of Innocence: Mark and Christian Origins* (Philadelphia: Fortress Press).

MacRae, G.
    1983 'Apocalyptic Eschatology in Gnosticism', in D. Hellholm (ed.), *Apocalypticism in the Mediterranean World and the Near East: Proceedings of the International Colloquium on Apocalypticisim, Uppsala, Aug 12–17 1979* (Tübingen: Mohr): 317–25.

Mann, C. S.
    1986 *Mark: A New Translation with Introduction and Commentary* (AB 27; Garden City, New York: Doubleday).

Mansfeld, J.
    1979 'Providence and the Destruction of the Universe in Early Stoic Thought', in M. J. Vermaseren (ed.), *Studies in Hellenistic Religion* (Leiden: Brill): 129–88.
    1981 'Bad World and Demiurge: A Gnostic Motif from Parmenides and Empedocles to Lucretius and Philo', in R. van den Broek and M. J. Vermaseren (eds), *Studies in Gnosticism and Hellenistic Religions* (Leiden: Brill): 261–314.
    1983 'Resurrection Added: The Interpretatio Christiana of a Stoic Doctrine', *VC* 37: 218–33.

Marcus, J.
    1992   'The Jewish War and the Sitz im Leben of Mark', *JBL* 107: 663–75.
    1993   *The Way of the Lord: Christological Exegesis of the Old Testament in the Gospel of Mark* (SNTW; Edinburgh: T&T Clark).
    2000   *Mark 1–8: A New Translation with Introduction and Commentary* (AB 27; New York: Doubleday).
Marshall, I. H.
    1978   *The Gospel of Luke* (NIGTC; Exeter: Paternoster).
    1992   'The Parousia in the New Testament – and Today', in M. J. Wilkins and T. Paige (eds), *Worship, Theology and Ministry in the Early Church: Essays in Honor of Ralph P. Martin* (JSNTSup 87; Sheffield: JSOT Press): 194–211.
May, G.
    1994   *Creatio Ex Nihilo. The Doctrine of 'Creation out of Nothing' in Early Christian Thought* (Edinburgh: T&T Clark).
Mayor, J. B.
    1907   *The Epistle of St. Jude and the Second Epistle of St. Peter* (London: Macmillan).
McKenzie, J. L.
    1974   *A Theology of the Old Testament* (London: Geoffrey Chapman).
Mealy, J. W.
    1992   *After the Thousand Years: Resurrection and Judgment in Revelation 20* (JSNTSup 70; Sheffield: JSOT Press).
Meier, J. P.
    1976   *Law and History in Matthew's Gospel* (AnBib 71; Rome: Biblical Institute Press).
Meier, S.
    1988   '2 Peter 3:3–7 – An Early Jewish and Christian Response to Eschatological Skepticism', *BZ* 32: 255–7.
Metzger, B. M.
    1994   *A Textual Commentary on the Greek New Testament* (Stuttgart: Deutsche Bibelgesellschaft, 2nd edn).
Moffatt, J.
    1924   *A Critical and Exegetical Commentary on the Epistle to the Hebrews* (ICC; Edinburgh: T&T Clark).
Moloney, F. I.
    2002   *The Gospel of Mark: A Commentary* (Peabody, Massachusetts: Hendrickson).
Moltmann, J.
    1979   *The Future of Creation* (trans. M. Kohl; London: SCM Press)
    1985   *God in Creation: An Ecological Doctrine of Creation* (trans. M. Kohl; The Gifford Lectures 1984–5; London: SCM Press).
    1996   *The Coming of God: Christian Eschatology* (trans. M. Kohl; London: SCM Press).
Morris, L.
    1987   *The Book of Revelation: An Introduction and Commentary* (TNTC 20; Leicester: Inter-Varsity, 2nd edn).

Moule, C. F. D
    1965   *The Gospel According to Mark* (The Cambridge Bible Commentary: New English Bible; Cambridge: Cambridge University Press).
Murphy, F. J.
    1993   *Pseudo-Philo: Rewriting the Bible* (New York: Oxford University Press).
Newman, C. C. (ed.)
    1999   *Jesus and the Restoration of Israel: A Critical Assessment of N. T. Wright's* Jesus and the Victory of God (Downers Grove: IVP; Carlisle: Paternoster).
Neyrey, J. H.
    1980   'The Form and Background of the Polemic in 2 Peter', *JBL* 99: 407–31.
    1993   *2 Peter, Jude: A New Translation with Introduction and Commentary* (AB 37C; New York: Doubleday).
Nickelsburg, G. W. E.
    1981   *Jewish Literature between the Bible and the Mishnah: A Historical and Literary Introduction* (Philadelphia: Fortress Press).
    2001   *1 Enoch 1: A Commentary on the Book of 1 Enoch, Chapters 1–36; 81–108* (ed. Klaus Baltzer; Hermeneia; Minneapolis: Fortress Press).
Nineham, D. E.
    1968   *The Gospel of St Mark* (The Pelican Gospel Commentaries; London: A. & C. Black, rev. edn).
Nolland, J.
    1993   *Luke 18:35–24:53* (WBC 35C; Dallas: Word Books).
Painter, J.
    1997   *Mark's Gospel* (New Testament Readings; London and New York: Routledge).
Paley, F. A.
    1883   *The Epics of Hesiod: With An English Commentary* (Bibliotheca Classica, ed. George Long; London: Whittaker & Co./George Bell & Sons).
Paul, S. M.
    1972   'Psalm 72:5 – A Traditional Blessing for the Long Life of the King', *JNES* 31.4: 351–5.
Pearson, B.
    2001   'Indo-European Eschatology in 2 Peter 3', in M. Stausberg (ed.), *Kontinuitäten und Brüche in der Religionsgeschichte* (Fest. A. Hulgard; RGA-E 31; Berlin and New York: W. de Gruyter): 536–45.
Perkins, P.
    1980   'On the Origin of the World (CG II, 5): A Gnostic Physics', *VC* 34: 36–46.
    1995   *First and Second Peter, James, and Jude* (Interpretation; Louisville: Westminster John Knox).
Pesch, R.
    1968   *Nahwewartungen, Tradition und Redaktion in Mk 13* (Düsseldorf: Patmos Verlag).
    1977   *Das Markusevangelium* (Vol. 2; HTKNT; Freiburg: Herder).
Plevnik, J.
    1997   *Paul and the Parousia: An Exegetical and Theological Investigation* (Peabody, Massachusetts: Hendrickson).

Polkinghorne, J.
    2000   'Eschatology: Some Questions and Some Insights from Science', in Polkinghorne and Welker 2000: 29–41.
    2002   *The God of Hope and the End of the World* (New Haven: Yale University Press).

Polkinghorne, J., and M. Welker (eds.)
    2000   *The End of the World and the Ends of God: Science and Theology on Eschatology* (Harrisburg, Pennsylvania: Trinity Press International).

Porter, S. E.
    2000   *The Criteria for Authenticity in Historical-Jesus Research: Previous Discussion and New Proposals* (JSNTSup 191; Sheffield: Sheffield Academic Press).

Raabe, P.
    2002   'The Particularizing of Universal Judgment in Prophetic Discourse', *CBQ* 64: 652–74.

Reicke, B.
    1964   *The Epistles of James, Peter, and Jude: Introduction, Translation and Notes* (AB 37; New York: Doubleday).

Ringgren, H.
    1995   *The Faith of Qumran: Theology of the Dead Sea Scrolls* (New York: Crossroad, expanded edn).

Roberts, J. J. M.
    1991   *Nahum, Habakkuk, and Zephaniah: A Commentary* (OTL; Louisville: Westminster John Knox).

Rowland, C.
    1982   *The Open Heaven: A Study of Apocalyptic in Judaism and Early Christianity* (London: SPCK).
    2002   *Christian Origins: An Account of the Setting and Character of the Most Important Messianic Sect of Judaism* (London: SPCK, 2nd edn).

Rowley, H. H.
    1947   *The Relevance of Apocalyptic: A Study of Jewish and Christian Apocalypses from Daniel to the Revelation* (London: Lutterworth, 2nd edn).

Runia, D. T.
    1981   'Philo's *De Aeternitate Mundi:* The Problem of Its Interpretation', *VC* 35: 105–51.
    1986   *Philo of Alexandria and the Timaeus of Plato* (Philosophia Antiqua 44: Leiden: Brill).

Russell, D. M.
    1996   *The 'New Heavens and New Earth': Hope for Creation in Jewish Apocalyptic and the New Testament* (Philadelphia: Visionary Press).

Russell, J. S.
    1887   *The Parousia: A Critical Inquiry into the New Testament Doctrine of our Lord's Second Coming* (London: T. Fisher Unwin, new edn).

Sanders, E. P.
    1993   *The Historical Figure of Jesus* (London: Penguin).

Schnutenhaus, F.
    1964   'Das Kommen und Erscheinen Gottes im Alten Testament', *ZAW* 76: 1–22.

Schweitzer, A.
   2000   *The Quest of the Historical Jesus* (London: SCM Press, First Complete Edition).

Scott, J. M.
   2005   *On Earth as in Heaven: The Restoration of Sacred Time and Space in the Book of Jubilees* (JSJSup 91; Leiden: Brill).

Seow, C. L.
   1997   *Ecclesiastes: A New Translation with Introduction and Commentary* (AB 18c; New York: Doubleday).

Sidebottom, E. M.
   1967   *James, Jude and 2 Peter* (NCB; London: Nelson).

Sim, D.
   1993   'The Meaning of παλιγγενεσία in Matthew 19:28', *JSNT* 50: 3–12.
   1996   *Apocalyptic Eschatology in the Gospel of Matthew* (SNTSMS 88; Cambridge: Cambridge University Press).

Simkins, R.
   1994   *Creator and Creation: Nature in the Worldview of Ancient Israel* (Peabody, Massachusetts: Hendrickson).

Skinner, J.
   1929   *The Book of the Prophet Isaiah Chapters XL–LXVI* (Cambridge: Cambridge University Press).

Solmsen, F.
   1951   'Epicurus and Cosmological Heresies', *AJP* 72: 1–23.
   1953   'Epicurus on the Growth and Decline of the Cosmos', *AJP* 74: 34–51.

Stacey, D.
   1993   *Isaiah: Chapters 1–39* (Epworth Commentaries; London: Epworth Press).

Stewart, R. A.
   1965–6   'Creation and Matter in the Epistle to the Hebrews', *NTS* 12: 284–93.

Stoeger, W. R.
   2000   'Scientific Accounts of Ultimate Catastrophes in Our Life-Bearing Universe', in Polkinghorne and Welker 2000: 19–28.

Stone, M. E.
   1983   'Coherence and Inconsistency in the Apocalypses: The Case of "the End" in 4 Ezra', *JBL* 102: 229–43.
   1989   *Features of the Eschatology of IV Ezra* (Harvard Semitic Studies 35; Atlanta, Georgia: Scholars Press).
   1990   *Fourth Ezra: A Commentary on the Book of Fourth Ezra* (Hermeneia; Minneapolis: Fortress Press).

Suter, D. W.
   1979   *Tradition and Composition in the Parables of Enoch* (SBLDS 47; Missoula, Montana: Scholars Press).

Swete, H. B.
   1906   *The Apocalypse of St. John* (London: Macmillan).
   1909   *The Gospel According to St. Mark: The Greek Text* (London: Macmillan, 3rd edn).

Szeles, M. E.
    1987   *Wrath and Mercy: A Commentary on the Books of Habakkuk and Zephaniah* (International theological commentary; Grand Rapids: Eerdmans; Edinburgh: Handsel).

Talbert, C. H.
    1966   'II Peter and the Delay of the Parousia', *VC* 20: 137-45.

Taylor, N. H.
    1996   'Palestinian Christianity and the Caligula Crisis Part II: The Markan Eschatological Discourse', *JSNT* 62: 13-41.

Taylor, V.
    1952   *The Gospel according to St. Mark* (London: Macmillan; New York: St. Martin's Press).

Theissen, G.
    1992   *The Gospels in Context: Social and Political History in the Synoptic Tradition* (trans. L. M. Maloney; Edinburgh: T&T Clark).

Thiede, C. P.
    1986   'A Pagan Reader of 2 Peter: Cosmic Conflagration in 2 Peter 3 and the *Octavius* of Minucius Felix', *JSNT* 26: 79-96.

Thomas, R. L.
    1992   *Revelation 1-7: An Exegetical Commentary* (Chicago: Moody Press).
    1995   *Revelation 8-22: An Exegetical Commentary* (Chicago: Moody Press).

Thompson, J. W.
    1982   *The Beginnings of Christian Philosophy: The Epistle to the Hebrews* (CBQMS 13; Washington, DC: The Catholic Biblical Association of America).

Tödt, H. E.
    1963   *The Son of Man in the Synoptic Tradition* (London: SCM Press).

Tuckett, C. M.
    1996   *Luke* (New Testament Guides; Sheffield: Sheffield Academic Press).
    2001   'Mark', in J. Barton and J. Muddiman (eds), *The Oxford Bible Commentary* (Oxford: Oxford University Press): 886-922.

Van der Horst, P. W.
    1989   'Images of Women in the Testament of Job', in M. A. Knibb and P. W. Van der Horst (eds), *Studies on the Testament of Job* (SNTS; Cambridge: Cambridge University Press): 93-116.
    1994   '"The Elements Will Be Dissolved with Fire": The Idea of Cosmic Conflagration in Hellenism, Ancient Judaism, and Early Christianity', in P. W. Van der Horst, *Hellenism, Judaism, Christianity: Essays on Their Interaction* (Kampen: Kok Pharos): 227-51.

VanderKam, J. C.
    1973   'The Theophany of Enoch 1:3b-7, 9', *VT* 23: 129-50.
    1977   *Textual and Historical Studies in the Book of Jubilees* (HSM 14; Missoula, Montana: Scholars Press).
    1984   *Enoch and the Growth of an Apocalyptic Tradition* (CBQMS 16; Washington, DC: Catholic Biblical Association of America).
    1992   'Righteous One, Messiah, Chosen One, and Son of Man in 1 Enoch 37-71', in J. H. Charlesworth (ed.), *The Messiah* (Minneapolis: Fortress Press): 169-91.

Vanhoye, A.
    1964   'L'οἰκουμένη dans l'épître aux Hébreux', *Bib* 45: 248–53.

Van Iersel, B. M. F.
    1996   'The Sun, Moon, and Stars of Mark 13, 24-25 in a Greco-Roman Reading', *Bib* 77: 84–92.
    1998   *Mark: A Reader-Response Commentary* (trans. W. H. Bisscheroux; JSNTSup 164; Sheffield: Sheffield Academic Press).

Van Kooten, G. H.
    2003   *Cosmic Christology in Paul and the Pauline School: Colossians and Ephesians in the Context of Graeco-Roman Cosmology, with a New Synopsis of the Greek Texts* (WUNT 171; Tübingen: Mohr Sibeck).

Van Kooten, G. H. (ed.)
    2005   *The Creation of Heaven and Earth: Re-interpretations of Genesis 1 in the Context of Judaism, Ancient Philosophy, Christianity, and Modern Physics* (Themes in Biblical Narrative 8; Leiden: Brill).

Van Ruitten, J. T. A. G. M.
    1989   'The Influence and Development of Is 65, 17 in 1 En 91.16', in J. Vermeylen (ed.), *The Book of Isaiah* (Leuven: Leuven University Press): 161–6.
    2005   'Back to Chaos: The Relationship between Jeremiah 4:23-26 and Genesis 1', in Van Kooten 2005: 21–30.

Verheyden, J.
    1997   'Describing the Parousia: The Cosmic Phenomena in Mk 13,24-25', in C. M. Tuckett (ed.), *The Scriptures in the Gospels* (BETL 131; Leuven: Leuven University Press, 1997): 525–50.

Vögtle, A.
    1970   *Das Neue Testament und Die Zukunft des Kosmos* (KBNT; Düsseldorf: Patmos-Verlag).
    1994   *Der Judasbrief /Der zweite Petrusbrief* (EKKNT 22; Neukirchen-Vluyn: Neukirchener Verlag).

Volz, P.
    1966   *Die Eschatologie der Jüdischen Gemeinde im neutestamentlichen Zeitalter nach den Quellen der rabbinischen, apokalyptischen und apokryphen Literatur* (Hildesheim: Georg Olms).

Von Rad, G.
    1959   'The Origin of the Concept of the Day of Yahweh', *JJS* 4: 97–108.
    1972   *Genesis: A Commentary* (OTL; London: SCM Press, rev. edn).

Watts, J. D.
    1987   *Isaiah 34–66* (WBC 25; Waco, Texas: Word Books).

Weiss, J.
    1971   *Jesus' Proclamation of the Kingdom of God* (Lives of Jesus Series; Philadelphia: Fortress Press).

Wenham, D.
    1984   *The Rediscovery of Jesus' Eschatological Discourse* (Gospel Perspectives 4; Sheffield: JSOT Press).
    1987   'Being "Found" on the Last Day: New Light on 2 Peter 3.10 and 2 Corinthians 5.3', *NTS* 33: 477–9.

Wenham, G. J.
    1987   *Genesis 1–15* (WBC 1; Waco, Texas: Word Books).
Westermann, C.
    1969   *Isaiah 40–66: A Commentary* (trans. D. M. H. Stalker; OTL; London: SCM Press).
    1984   *Genesis 1–11: A Commentary* (London: SPCK).
Whybray, R. N.
    1975   *Isaiah 40–66* (NCB; London: Oliphants).
Wildberger, H.
    1997   *Isaiah Vol. 2: A Commentary* (Continental Commentaries; Minneapolis: Fortress Press).
Wilder, A. N.
    1950   *Eschatology and Ethics in the Teaching of Jesus* (New York: Harper & Brothers, rev. edn).
Williams, C. J. F.
    1966   'Aristotle and Corruptibility', *RelS* 1: 95–107, 203–15.
Williams, M. A.
    1996   *Rethinking 'Gnosticism': An Argument for Dismantling a Dubious Category* (Princeton: Princeton University Press).
Williamson, H. G. M.
    1999   'Gnats, Glosses and Eternity: Isaiah 51:6 Reconsidered', in P. J. Harland and C. T. R. Hayward (eds), *New Heaven and New Earth – Prophecy and the Millennium: Essays in Honour of Anthony Gelston* (VTSup 77; Leiden: Brill).
Wilson, R. McL.
    1987   *Hebrews* (NCB; Grand Rapids: Eerdmans; Basingstoke: Marshall, Morgan and Scott).
Winter, B. W.
    2001   *After Paul Left Corinth: The Influence of Secular Ethics and Social Change* (Grand Rapids and Cambridge, UK: Eerdmans).
Witherington, B.
    1998   *The Acts of the Apostles: A Socio-Rhetorical Commentary* (Grand Rapids: Eerdmans).
    2001   *The Gospel of Mark: A Socio-Rhetorical Commentary* (Grand Rapids: Eerdmans).
Wolters, A.
    1987   'Worldview and Textual Criticism in 2 Peter 3:10', *WTJ* 40: 405–13.
Wright, M. R.
    1981   *Empedocles: The Extant Fragments* (New Haven: Yale University Press).
    1995   *Cosmology in Antiquity* (London: Routledge).
Wright, N. T.
    1992   *The New Testament and the People of God* (Christian Origins and the Question of God 1; London: SPCK).
    1996   *Jesus and the Victory of God* (Christian Origins and the Question of God 2; London: SPCK).
    1999a   'In Grateful Dialogue: A Response', in Newman 1999: 244–77.
    1999b   *New Heavens, New Earth: The Biblical Picture of the Christian Hope* (Cambridge: Grove).

	2001	*Mark for Everyone* (London: SPCK).
	2002	*Matthew for Everyone, Part 2 Chapters 16–28* (London: SPCK).
	2003a	*Hebrews for Everyone* (London: SPCK).
	2003b	*The Resurrection of the Son of God* (Christian Origins and the Question of God 3; London: SPCK).

Young, E. J.
    1965–72   *The Book of Isaiah: Volume 1 Chapters 1–18* (NICOT; Grand Rapids: Eerdmans).

Zuntz, G.
    1944   'The Greek Text of Enoch 102:1–3', *JBL* 61: 193–204.

INDEXES

INDEX OF REFERENCES

HEBREW BIBLE		6.5-8	25	8.21	26, 28
Genesis		6.5	26	8.22	28, 33, 60,
1–11	25	6.7	26, 42		77, 78, 80,
1–2	4, 28	6.9-22	25		91
1	26, 86–7,	6.11-12	26	9.1-17	25, 27
	210–12,	6.13	26	9.8-17	4, 26, 45
	259	6.17	56	9.11	27
1.1–2.4	34, 39	7.1-7	25	9.15	27
1.1	34	7.8-9	25	9.16	45
1.2	26, 39, 87,	7.10	25	11.1-9	58
	213	7.11	25, 26, 45,	11.10-25	57
1.3	39		214	17.7	45
1.4	28	7.12	25	17.13	45
1.6-10	26	7.13-16	25	17.19	45
1.6	211	7.14	26	19.24-25	49
1.10	28	7.16-20	25		
1.11	39	7.17-24	214	*Exodus*	
1.12	28	7.19	26	7–10	49
1.18	28	7.21	25, 26	10.14	145
1.20-28	42	7.22-23	25	11.6	145
1.20-26	26	7.24	25, 26	14.26-31	49
1.20	39	8.1-2	25	19.9	151
1.21	28	8.2-3	25	19.11	36
1.25	28	8.2	45	19.12-13	186
1.26	26, 39	8.3-5	25	19.16-25	40, 56
1.31	28	8.4	26	19.16	186
2.1	34	8.6	25	19.18	187
2.4	34	8.7	25	34.5	151
2.5	211	8.8-12	25		
2.10	250	8.13	25	*Leviticus*	
3.17	28, 250	8.14-19	25	26.34	144
3.22-24	250	8.17	26	26.35	144
6–9	25	8.20-22	25, 27		
6.3	57	8.21-22	77		

Numbers		*Job*		68.7-8	36, 40
11.25	151	9.6	30, 159	68.8	187
12.5	151	13.28	30	68.17	151
		14.12	33	72.5-7	32
Deuteronomy		26.11	30, 47	72.7	33
4.11-12	186	38.6	30	74.12-17	28
4.24	191			75.3	30
5.22-26	186	*Psalms*		76.9	159
8.4	30	2	88	76.19 LXX	159
9.19	186	2.7	185	77.16-20	40
11.21	32, 33	8.4-6	197	77.18	159, 187, 222
13.7	151	8.6	198		
28.12	67	9.27 LXX	190	78.69	32
29.5	30	14.5 LXX	190	82.5	30
30.4	151	15.8 LXX	190	89.9-10	28
32.22	98	17.8 LXX	159	89.29	32
32.43	183	17.12 LXX	151	89.36-37	32
33.2	36, 56, 150, 151	18	36, 41	90.2	29
		18.6-19	40	90.4	221, 231
		18.7-19	151	90.10	33
Judges		18.11-12	151	93.1	32
5.4-5	36, 40, 151	18.11	151	94.7	36
5.4	187	18.13-15	222	95.9 LXX	159
5.5	159	18.13-14	36	95.10 LXX	190
		18.15	30, 73	95.13 LXX	150
1 Samuel		20.8 LXX	190	96.4 LXX	159
2.8	30	21.13	151	96.10	32
		29.7 LXX	190	96.11-13	40, 176
2 Samuel		32.3	30	96.11	29
7.14	183	37.9	57	96.13	36
22.8-20	151	37.11	57	97.1-5	40
22.12	151	37.20	31	97.2-5	151
		37.22	57	97.2	151
2 Kings		37.29	57	97.4	159
17.16	155	45.6-7	183	97.5	230
18.13–19.36	29	46.1-3	29	97.7 LXX	159, 183
21.3	155	46.1	30, 47, 151	97.9 LXX	150
21.5	155	46.2-3	30	98.7-9	40, 176
23.4	155	46.4-7	29	98.7	29, 159
23.5	155	46.6	47	101.23	183
		46.7	29	101.24 LXX	183
2 Chronicles		46.8-11	29	101.26-28 LXX	183
18.18	155	46.11	29	102.2-12	30
		59.16	151	102.3	31
Ezra		65.7	29	102.13-23	30
9.7	174	66.3	151	102.24-25	30

Index of References

102.25-29	30	13.6-8	43	24.19	56, 57, 160
102.25-27	16, 30, 31, 33, 50, 162, 183–5, 190, 196, 197, 199, 253	13.9-16	43	25–27	46
		13.9-13	37, 203	25.8	46
		13.10	37, 40, 47, 61, 73, 138, 154, 157, 159, 160, 242	26.19	46
				26.20	194
				27.1	45
				27.12-13	46, 151
102.25	185			29.6	97
102.26-27	184, 185	13.11	37	30.26	34, 61, 64
104	4	13.13	40, 61, 155	30.27	97, 150
104.4	183	13.14	37	30.30	97
104.5	32	13.15-16	37	34	5, 11, 18, 37, 43, 44, 46, 48, 50, 123, 157, 246
110.1	152, 183	13.17-22	43		
113.6	34	13.17	37		
113.7 LXX	159	13.19-22	37		
114.7	159	13.19	5, 36		
119.90	32	14	46	34.1-4	157
135.7	67	14.12-15	154	34.2-3	38
148.6	32	14.12	154	34.2	37
		17.12	29	34.4	37, 91, 97, 138, 154, 155, 157, 159, 169, 183, 223, 230, 240–2
Proverbs		19.1	36, 150, 151		
8.25	29				
8.29	30	19.2	142		
		24–27	44		
Ecclesiastes		24	12, 27, 44–6, 47–50, 56, 156		
1.4	32, 33			34.5-17	38
				34.5-7	5, 38
Isaiah		24.1-6	44	34.8-17	203
2.10	240	24.1	44, 45	35.1	34
2.19	240	24.2	45	35.4	150
2.21	240	24.3	45	35.6	34
5.30	29	24.4-13	45	40–55	32
10.33	62, 86	24.4-12	45	40.8	161, 162
11.6-9	34	24.4	45	40.10	150, 205
11.6-8	89	24.5	27, 45, 46, 50	40.12	29, 32
11.11	151			40.31	72
13–26	36	24.6	45	41.5	56
13	5, 9, 11, 18, 36, 40, 42–4, 48, 50, 123, 157	24.7-9	45	41.19	34
		24.10-12	45	42.5	32
		24.13	45	42.15	241
		24.14-16	45	43.6	151
		24.17-18	176	43.18-19	35
13.1	36	24.17	45, 175	43.19	237
13.2-5	36	24.18	30, 45, 46, 50	45.18	32
13.2-3	36			48.13	32
13.6-13	36, 157	24.19-20	45	50.3	240

Isaiah (cont.)		4.23	39	11.31	143
51.1-8	31	5.22	29	12	140
51.1	31	6.1-30	38	12.1	72, 140, 142
51.4-6	31	6.23	29		
51.4	31	7.34	144	12.2	74
51.5	31	10.11	34	12.3	74
51.6	31, 33, 35, 50, 161, 162, 196	10.13	67	12.6-7	140
		20.4-6	174	12.7	140
		22.5	144	12.11	143
51.7	31	25.18	144		
51.9-10	28	31.35-36	33, 161, 162	*Hosea*	
51.15	29			2.18	34
54.9-10	161, 162	31.37	30	8.10	240
54.9	27	33.20-21	161, 162	13.3	31
54.10	27, 31, 162, 241	40.4	97		
		44.6	144	*Joel*	
59.19-20	150	44.22	144	1	39
59.19	151	50.42	29	1.1–2.27	39
60.1-9	151	51.16	67	1.15	39, 203
60.11	89	51.55	29	1.19	97
60.20	34			1.20	97
61.2	174	*Ezekiel*		2	44
63.1	246	32.1-16	35	2.1-11	39
63.18	174	32.7	35, 154	2.1-2	39, 203
64.1-2	155	32.9	174	2.1	205
64.1	40	32.20	174	2.2	145
65.17-25	50, 57, 58, 68, 249	38–39	35	2.3	97
		38.19-20	89	2.7-9	39
65.17	34, 35, 59, 63, 203, 237	38.22	97	2.10-12	39
		39.17-20	245	2.10	47, 73, 154, 155, 159, 160, 176
		47.1-12	250		
65.18-25	34	47.7	250		
65.25	35	47.12	250		
66.15-16	36, 97			2.11	39, 240
66.18	36, 150, 151	*Daniel*		2.12-27	40
		7.1-8	147	2.20-31	203
66.22	34, 59, 203, 237	7.9-14	147–9	2.28–3.21	46–9
		7.9-10	147	2.28-32	176, 177
		7.11-12	147	2.28-29	47
Jeremiah		7.13-14	147	2.30-32	47
4	44	7.13	148–52, 168	2.30-31	16, 46, 98, 177
4.5–6.30	38				
4.5	38	7.14	180	2.30	47, 176
4.6-31	38	8.10	242	2.31	73, 159, 160, 240, 242
4.6	38	8.13	144, 174		
4.7	144	9.18	144		
4.16	38	9.26-27	144	3–4	89
4.23-28	38	9.27	143	3.2-17	46

Index of References

3.3 LXX	176	1.5	41, 62, 97, 159	14	34, 88, 149, 150
3.14-16	47	1.6	230, 240	14.1-5	89, 169
3.14	203	1.9	41	14.2	174
3.15	47, 157, 205			14.4-5	139
3.16	65, 222	*Habakkuk*		14.5	36, 56, 139, 149–51, 180
4.15-16	154	2.3	194, 205		
4.15	154	2.11	83		
4.16	155	3	48	14.6-8	34
		3.3-15	203	14.6-7	80, 91
Amos		3.3	151	14.8	250
1.4	97	3.6-12	49	14.11	250
1.7	97	3.6	155, 159, 230		
1.10	97			*Malachi*	
1.12	97			3.1-4	36
4.13	29	*Zephaniah*		3.1	215
5.18-20	36, 203	1	43, 44	3.2-4	225
5.18	37	1.1	41	3.2-3	98
5.20	37	1.2	41	3.2	240
7.4	70, 97	1.3	41	4.1-5	227
8.9	37, 47	1.4-6	42	4.1	98, 215, 225–7
9.5	40, 159	1.4	42		
9.13-14	34	1.7-18	203		
		1.7	205	*1 Esdras*	
Micah		1.14	205, 244	1.58	144
1	43, 44	1.18	42, 97		
1.2-4	203, 205	3.8	97	*2 Esdras*	
1.2	40			3–14	78
1.3-4	39, 41, 55–7	*Haggai*			
		2	48, 49	*Judith*	
1.3	40	2.1-9	188	8.22	144
1.4	40, 62, 73, 97, 155, 230	2.6-7	48	16.15	159, 230
		2.6	84, 188, 189, 192, 198	*Wisdom of Solomon*	
				5.14	31
1.5	41	2.7-9	48, 188	10.4	214
6.2	30	2.7	193		
7.6	143	2.21-22	48	*Sirach*	
		2.21	84, 189	16.18	155, 159
Nahum				43.14	67
1	43, 44	*Zechariah*		43.16	159
1.2-8	41	2.6	151		
1.3-5	151, 203, 205	9.14-15	151, 169	*1 Maccabees*	
		9.14	169	1.54	144
1.3	41, 151	12.2-3	174	1.59	144
1.4-5	41	12.10-14	168		
1.4	41, 73	13.9	225, 227		
1.5-6	155				

New Testament

Matthew

2.2	169
2.7	169
2.9	169
2.10	169
3.11	200
3.12	172
5.5	172
5.18	4, 170, 178, 222
5.22	172
5.45	169, 171
6.20	171
6.25-33	171
7.19	172
8.24	169
10.17-21	168
10.32	149
11.25	171
12.32	172
13.6	169
13.39	167, 170
13.40	167, 170
13.43	169
13.49	167, 170
16.27	148
17.2	169
19.28	172, 181, 255
23.30	204
23.32	204
24.2	167
24.3	167
24.4–25.46	166
24.4-36	166
24.4-28	168
24.4-25	171
24.5	168
24.6-7	168
24.7	168, 169
24.9-14	168
24.9	168
24.10-12	168
24.14	168, 198
24.15-20	168
24.15	143, 168
24.19	223
24.21-22	168
24.21	171
24.23-24	168
24.26-28	168
24.27	167, 168
24.29-31	16, 133, 168, 169, 254
24.29	97, 155, 169, 170, 171, 242
24.30	167, 168
24.32-36	170
24.33	171
24.34	170, 171
24.35	170–2, 178
24.36	171
24.37-44	166
24.37	167
24.38-39	170
24.39	167
24.43-44	221
24.44	167
24.45–25.30	167, 171, 172
24.48	171
25.5	171
25.26-30	172
25.31-46	167
25.31	150, 167
25.34	171
27.45	169
27.51	193
27.54	169
28.2	169
28.20	168

Mark

1.11	149
1.16-20	140
2.10	149
2.28	149
3.11	149
4.1-34	134
4.10	134, 140
5.7	149
7.17	140
8.12	164
8.34-38	148
8.38	139, 148–52, 164, 180, 204
9.7	149
9.19	164
9.28	140
10.6	166
10.10	140
10.30	164, 166, 172
11.25	155
11.27	139
12.25	166
13	8, 134–6, 139, 157, 160, 163, 172, 180, 231
13.1-23	133, 139
13.1-4	140, 141
13.1	139
13.2	8, 134, 139, 140, 146, 155, 158, 163
13.3-23	168
13.3	139
13.4	140, 141, 146, 155
13.5-37	135
13.5-31	163, 166
13.5-27	160, 180
13.5-24	173
13.5-23	134, 141, 146, 165, 239
13.5-6	146
13.5	141, 142, 165
13.6	142, 146
13.7-8	142, 165

13.7	141, 143		175, 176,	13.32	137, 141,
13.8	142, 143,		180, 181,		165
	160, 239		189, 223,	13.33-37	165, 175
13.9-13	143, 168		242, 243,	13.34-36	134
13.9	141, 165		252	13.34	175
13.10	143, 151	13.24	139, 146,	13.35	166
13.11	141, 165		158, 160,	13.36	175
13.12	143		165, 174	13.37	134, 135,
13.13-14	147	13.25	154, 155,		157, 166
13.13	141, 143,		175	14.62	152
	165	13.26-27	8, 133,	15.33	139
13.14-18	143, 174		138, 147,	15.39	149
13.14	141, 143–		148, 151–		
	6, 165, 174		3, 155,	Luke	
13.15-16	143		156, 159,	1.17	204
13.17	143, 145,		180, 204	1.55	204
	174	13.26	133, 138,	1.72	204
13.18	141, 143		139, 147,	2.1	198
13.19-20	145, 165,		148, 150,	4.2	140
	174		151, 152,	4.5	198
13.19	142, 160,		153, 158,	4.13	140
	166		160, 175,	6.23	204
13.21-23	146, 173		180	6.43	179
13.21-22	146, 165	13.27	147, 151,	8.49	173
13.21	141		157, 158,	9.38	173
13.22-23	142		161, 163	9.58	179
13.23	141, 146,	13.28-32	170	10.21	179
	165	13.28-31	134, 175	10.25	173
13.24-30	5, 203	13.28-29	164	11.45	173
13.24-27	2-5, 8–10,	13.28	164	11.50	179
	15–17, 19,	13.29-30	165	12.6	179
	133, 134,	13.29	165	12.8	149
	146, 157,	13.30	8, 134,	12.34-37	179
	159, 160,		136, 161,	12.35-48	173
	163–5,		164, 171,	12.38	175
	168–70,		178	12.39-40	179, 221
	180, 181,	13.31-37	157	12.42-46	179
	234, 246,	13.31	4, 16, 133,	13.6-9	179
	254		134, 159–	13.19	179
13.24-25	5, 6, 8, 10,		66, 170,	13.34	179
	15–18,		178, 179,	16.17	162, 178,
	133, 137–		180, 181,		222
	9, 147,		193, 222,	16.19-31	179
	152–61,		237, 242,	17.6	179
	163-5,		254, 255	17.20-37	173, 175
	169, 170,	13.32-37	134, 166	17.23-24	168

Luke (cont.)		4.20	204	8.18-23	4
17.37	168	6.31	204	8.19	256
18.25	178			8.20-22	232
19.12-13	175	Acts		8.21	256
19.41-44	174	1.1	173	9.5	204
21	173	1.4	203	15.19	143
21.5-38	172	1.6	180	15.23	143
21.5-11	173	1.7	179		
21.5	173	1.9-11	175	*1 Corinthians*	
21.6	173	1.11	179	3.13	200
21.7	173	2.16-21	177	4.2	228
21.8-24	173	2.17-21	176	7.31	4, 75, 256
21.11	173, 177	2.17	177	15	14
21.16	143	2.19-20	16, 177	15.52	169
21.20-24	174, 176	2.33	203	16.17	167
21.20-22	178	2.39	203		
21.20	174	3.13	204	*2 Corinthians*	
21.21	173	3.19-21	179	7.6	167
21.22	174, 178	3.21	179, 181,	7.7	167
21.23	173, 176		255	10.10	167
21.24	174	3.25	204		
21.25-28	174–7	4.24	179	*Galatians*	
21.25-27	16, 133,	7.17	203	2.7	228
	177, 178,	7.56	179	3.9	228
	254	11.28	142	3.14	203
21.25-26	16, 175–9,	12.1-2	143	3.16	203
	242	13.15	182	3.17	203
21.25	176, 177	13.23	203	3.18	203
21.26	176, 198,	14.15-17	179	3.21	203
	242	16.23	143	3.22	203
21.27	173	17.1-5	143	3.29	203
21.28	175	17.22-31	179		
21.29-33	173, 175	21.27	140	*Philippians*	
21.32	178	22.19	143	1.26	167
21.33	178, 179	24–26	143	2.12	167
21.34-36	175, 179				
21.34-35	177	*Romans*		*Colossians*	
21.34	175	2.5	215	1.17	211
21.35	175, 176	4.13	203	1.23	143
21.36	175, 179	4.14	203		
21.37-38	173	4.16	203	*1 Thessalonians*	
22.28	208	4.20	203	3.13	150
23.30	240	5.12	232	4.13-18	147
23.43	179	7.10	227	4.15-17	16, 169
24.36	180	8	232, 258	5.2	221
24.49	203	8.18-28	4		
John		8.18-25	256, 258		

2 Thessalonians		6.1-8	182	11.26	196
1.6-10	16	6.2	197	11.28	196
1.7-8	150	6.4-6	182	11.32-37	196
1.8	200	6.4	197	11.35	197
2.7	16	6.5	197	11.38	196
		6.7-8	191	11.39-40	196
Titus		6.8	200	12.1	182
2.12	75	6.12	203	12.4-12	196
		7.3	191	12.9	186
Hebrews		7.12	190	12.14-17	182
1.1	204	7.24	191	12.18-24	185, 187
1.2	185, 190,	7.26	187	12.18-21	189
	195, 197	8–10	182	12.18-19	185, 187
1.4	183	8–9	195	12.18	185
1.5-13	183	8.5	187, 195	12.19-20	187
1.5	183	8.13	184	12.20	186
1.7	183	9.1-14	186	12.22	185, 197
1.10-12	4, 16, 183,	9.9	197	12.23-24	186
	185, 190,	9.11	195, 197	12.23	187
	196, 198,	9.13-14	186	12.25-29	4, 5, 16,
	208, 253–5	9.23-24	195		20, 182,
1.10	187, 188,	9.24	187		183, 185,
	191, 195	9.26	189, 197		186, 194,
1.11-12	184, 185	9.27	189		197, 198,
1.11	183, 184,	9.28	189, 194,		246, 252,
	190		197		253
1.12	183	10.1-10	186	12.25-28	17, 254
1.13	183	10.1	195, 197	12.25	186–8, 191
2.1-4	182	10.2	189	12.26-27	15, 18,
2.5	197	10.25	194		183, 187,
2.6-8	198	10.26-31	182		190–4
2.7-8	197	10.28-29	186	12.26	186–89,
2.10	185, 195	10.32-34	196		194, 254
3.1	197	10.34	191	12.27	189, 192,
3.4	185, 195	10.36	182		254
3.5	190	10.37	194, 197	12.28-29	187
3.6	190	11	196	12.28	191
3.7–4.14	182	11.1	185, 196	12.29	191
3.9	204	11.3	185, 191,	13.1	191
3.14	182		195	13.13	182, 196
3.16	186	11.5	190	13.14	191, 197
3.18	186	11.7	187, 196	13.18-25	182
4.1	203	11.12	187	13.20	197
4.3-4	185, 195	11.13-16	196	13.22	182
4.10	195	11.13	196	13.24	182
4.14	182, 187	11.16	196, 197		

James			216–19,	*Jude*	
5.3	215		220, 228, 230	14-15	150
1 Peter		3.5	211, 212,	*Revelation*	
1.7	225, 226		213, 214, 218, 220, 222, 231	1.1	236
				1.3	236
2 Peter				1.4	236
1.3-11	217	3.6-7	214	1.5	227
1.4	203, 213, 232	3.6	26, 213, 214, 219	1.7	148, 168
				1.9	236
1.14-15	201	3.7	213–15, 218–20, 222, 223, 225	1.15	225
1.15-21	201			2–3	236
1.16-22	203			2.2	251
1.16-18	203			2.5	251
1.16	203	3.8-9	205, 209, 221, 230	2.6	248, 251
1.20-22	203			2.19	251
1.20-21	206	3.8	205, 221	2.22	251
2.1	202, 202	3.9	203, 205, 221, 231	2.23	251
2.2	201			2.26	251
2.3	207, 210	3.10-13	10, 207	3.1-2	251
2.5	213	3.10-12	201, 202, 214, 221, 225–7, 230	3.1	251
2.6	213			3.2	251
2.7	213			3.3	221
2.9	207	3.10	16, 204, 209, 221, 223, 225–31	3.8	251
2.12	232			3.11	248
2.13	201			3.14	248
2.19	232			3.15	251
2.20	232	3.11-13	229	3.18	225, 227
3.3	201, 202	3.11-12	221, 229, 233	4.11	237, 248
3.4-13	204, 234			5.13	249
3.4-10	201	3.11	229	6–16	236, 244
3.4-7	207	3.12-14	231	6.1–8.5	239
3.4	201–3, 208–10, 230, 255	3.12	16, 204, 221, 223–5, 227, 229, 231	6.1-8	239
				6.8	239
				6.9-11	239, 247
				6.10	244
3.5-13	4, 5, 15, 17, 19, 20, 200–2, 204, 225, 226, 228, 233, 234, 252–4, 258, 259	3.13	4, 203, 220, 228, 232, 233	6.12-17	4, 16–18, 20, 237, 239, 244, 246–8, 251, 252, 254
		3.14	233		
		3.16	210		
		1 John		6.12-14	239, 242–8
3.5-10	209	2.14	204	6.12	241, 242, 244, 245
3.5-7	201, 202, 207, 209,	2.17	75	6.13	244

Index of References

6.14	242, 247	20.4-6	247	1	159
6.15-17	240, 243	20.10	247	1.3-9	52, 55, 57,
6.15	245	20.11	239, 242,		65, 66, 74,
6.16	246, 247		246–8,		86, 96, 97,
6.17	244, 246		251, 254,		150, 159,
7.1-3	249		255		189
8.5	241, 245	20.13	239	1.4	57
8.10-12	243	21–22	256, 257	1.5-7	56
8.10-11	241, 244	21.1–22.5	237, 247	1.5	56
8.12	16, 241,	21.1-15	249	1.6	56
	243	21.1-8	249	1.7	56
9.1-2	16, 241	21.1-4	250	1.9	151
9.1	241, 243	21.1	16, 237–	5.7	57
10.2	249		39, 246–	5.8-9	57
10.6	248		49, 251,	6–11	55, 57
11.7	249		254, 255	10	218
11.13	241	21.2	237	10.2–11.1	57
11.14-19	244	21.4	249	10.2	57
11.18	244, 245,	21.5	237, 238,	10.6	244
	248		249	10.16–11.2	57
11.19	241, 244	21.8	250	10.17	57
12	242	21.9–22.5	197, 237,	10.21	58
12.4	242, 243		249	17–36	55
12.9	242, 247	21.9-27	250	18.14	242
12.12	239, 249	21.9-14	249	21.3-6	242
12.13–13.4	247	21.12	240	31.7	88
12.15-17	242	21.15–22.5	249	37–71	54, 153
13	247	21.15-21	249	38–44	58
13.1	239, 249	21.22-27	249	38.2	58
14.7	248	21.23	250	45–57	58
16.3	239	21.24-26	250	45.4-5	52, 58, 69,
16.12-16	245	22.1-5	250		78, 99
16.14	244	22.1-3	250	46.3	58
16.15	221	22.5	250	46.4	58
16.17-21	242, 244	22.7	236, 248	48.2	58
16.17	244, 245	22.8	236	48.6	58
16.18-21	245	22.10	236	48.10	58
16.18	241, 245	22.12	248	51.4-5	58
16.20	242, 245	22.14	250	52.4	58
19.11–22.5	163, 236	22.19	236, 250	52.6	58
19.11-21	244, 245,	22.20	248	52.7-9	58
	247			53.6	58
19.17-18	245	Pseudepigrapha		54.7	67
19.20	247	*1 Enoch*		58–69	58
20.1-10	247, 248,	1–36	54, 55	58.6	58
	254	1–5	55	69.29	58

1 Enoch (cont.)		102.1-3	52, 65, 74,	78.3	85
70	58		91, 96, 97,	82.2	85
71	58		159, 177,	85.10	52, 85, 98,
72–82	54, 59,		189		99
	127, 128	102.1	222		
72.1	35, 52, 59,	102.2	65, 159	*4 Ezra*	
	60, 94, 99,			3.1–5.20	79
	141	*2 Enoch*		3.4	84
72.32	59	3–37	86	3.18	188
80.2-8	59, 60, 98,	24–33	86	4.26	82
	141	24.1	87, 191	4.27	84
80.4-8	52, 83, 83,	24.2	87	4.28	84
	98, 158,	38–66	86	4.29	84
	159	47.3-6	88	5.1-13	82, 83, 141
80.4	98	50.2	87	5.4-5	52, 82, 98,
80.5	98	50.5	87		158
80.6-8	98	51.3	87	5.21–6.34	79
82	78	65.6-11	52, 99	5.42-45	84
82.2-8	78	65.6-10	87	5.50-55	52, 81, 98,
83–90	54, 61				99, 109
83–84	54, 61, 99,	*2 Baruch*		5.50	81
	127, 128	3.7	80, 85	5.54-55	81
83.2-5	52	3.8	85	6.1-6	80, 84
83.3-5	61–2, 96,	14.17	85	6.13-25	141
	97, 99, 214	14.18	85	6.15-16	82
83.3	61	15.7	85	6.20-24	82
83.4	61, 86	15.8	85	6.20	82
83.5	61	19.2	85	6.24	143
83.11	62	21.4-5	85	6.35–9.25	79
84.2-3	62	21.19	85	6.38-55	84
84.2	62	21.24	85	6.38-54	80
84.5	62	26–30	141	6.39	80
85–90	54	30.1	84	7.11-13	80
90.15-19	141	32.1	52, 84, 97,	7.11-12	84
91–107	64		159, 189	7.26-44	79, 99
91–105	54	32.6	84	7.26	197
91.7	141, 150	40.3	84, 85	7.29	79
91.11-17	54, 62	44.9	85	7.30-44	80
91.16	35, 52, 63,	48.50	85	7.30-42	52, 99
	64, 99, 237	49.3	85	7.30-32	79–80, 82,
91.17	63	51.14	85		98, 99,
92.1	64	54.13	85		166, 232
93.1-10	54, 62	56.3	85	7.30	80
94.6–104.8	65	57.2	85	7.31	80
100.1-2	143	59.3	52, 84, 97,	7.32	80, 84
100.4	141, 150		188, 189	7.39-43	80, 82
100.7-102.3	65	70.3-4	84	7.39-42	80, 98

Index of References

7.39	164	1.15	69	2	63, 90
7.43	80	1.23-29	69	2.196-213	90, 91, 230
7.50	84	1.26	69	3–5	54, 96
7.70	80	1.27-29	150	3	88, 93, 128
7.75	82	1.29	35, 52, 68,	3.1-96	88
7.77	215		78, 94, 99	3.75-92	91, 99,
7.83-84	215	4.26	35, 52, 69,		127, 230
7.113-114	80		78, 94, 99	3.80-92	52, 90, 164
8.47	84	8.19	68	3.82-83	246
8.50-52	84	23.13-23	141	3.88-92	80
8.50	82	23.19	143	3.97-161	88
8.52	80	23.26-31	69	3.162-195	88
9.3-12	82	23.26	69	3.196-294	88
9.26–10.59	79			3.350-380	90
11.1–12.51	79	*Liber Antiquitatum*		3.545-656	88
13	79, 153	*Biblicarum*		3.657-808	88
13.31	142	3.9-10	218	3.657-662	88
13.36	197	3.10	52, 76, 77,	3.669-701	88, 141
14	79		98, 99, 166	3.669-681	88
14.10-18	99	9.3	78, 99	3.673-681	89
14.10	81	10.9	78	3.675-681	52, 97, 159
14.12	84	11.5	77, 188	3.682-701	88
14.16	81	11.8	78	3.741-95	89
14.17	81	15.5-6	78	3.767	89
14.18	52, 98	16.2-3	78	3.772-5	89
15.15	142	16.6-7	78	3.777-95	89
		16.13	78	3.796-808	89, 90
Apocalypse of Elijah		19.12-13	150	3.796-804	52, 98, 158
2.1	54	19.13	52, 77, 83,	3.796	90
			98, 158,	3.798	89
Apocalypse of Zephaniah			159	3.801-3	90
12.5-8	52, 97,	23.10	77, 188	4	63, 88,
	159, 160,	26.3-4	78		100, 127
	177, 208	32.7-8	78, 188	4.100-1	92
12.5	86	32.13-17	78	4.130-5	92
12.6-8	86	32.17	78	4.171-8	92
12.6-7	246	44.10	77	4.175-92	52, 99
		60.2	78, 80	4.175-8	96
Ascension of Isaiah				4.175	222
4.5	83	*Life of Adam and Eve*		4.178-9	99
		49.3–50.3	66, 97	4.179-83	92
Greek Apocalypse of Ezra				4.179-82	166
3.38	54	*Psalms of Solomon*		4.187	93
		9.5	215	5	54, 88, 93,
Jubilees					126
1.1	68	*Sibylline Oracles*		5.1-51	93
1.15-18	69	1	63, 90	5.52-110	93

Sibylline Oracles (cont.)					
5.93-110	93	*Testament of Job*		10.10	72, 74
5.111-78	93	2.4	76	10.12	71
5.137-54	93	4.6	76		
5.155-61	52, 93	33.3-9	75, 99	QUMRAN	
5.168-78	93	33.3-5	75	*1QH*	
5.179-285	93, 94, 99, 127	33.4	75	11.19-36	52, 66, 69, 74, 96, 159
5.179-99	94	33.8	75	11.19-28	70, 71
5.200-5	94	36.3-6	75	11.28-36	66
5.206-13	94, 99	36.3	75	11.29-36	54, 71, 91, 97
5.211-13	52, 94	38.5	75		
5.211-12	94	39.12	76	11.34-35	222
5.213	94	47.11	76		
5.214-27	93	48.3	75	*1QS*	
5.214-19	94	49.1	75	4.25	52
5.228-37	94	49.2-3	76		
5.238-85	94	50.2	75	*4Q225*	
5.249-55	94	52–53	76	1.6-7	52
5.273	94				
5.277	96	*Testament of Levi*		TARGUMS	
5.281-3	94	4.1	54	*Targum Jeremiah*	
5.285	96			33.25	100
5.286-434	93, 95	*Testament of Moses*			
5.328	96	1.15	71	MIDRASH	
5.346-52	94, 98	3.3	71	*Genesis Rabbah*	
5.346-9	52, 98, 158	6.5-6	72	13.11	151
5.360	96	7–10	160		
5.361-85	93	8	72	PHILO	
5.406	96	8.1	72, 141, 160	*De aeternitate mundi*	
5.420-7	95	10	72, 159	5-6	21
5.420-1	95	10.1-10	11, 73, 150	8	122, 125
5.435-531	93, 95, 99, 127	10.1-7	141	10	195
5.447-83	95	10.1	74	17-18	103
5.476-83	99	10.2	72, 73	20-44	108
5.476	95	10.3-10	72	20-24	108
5.477-80	95, 164	10.3-6	52, 72, 97, 159	20	195
5.477-8	52			22	220
5.478	96	10.3	73	39-44	108
5.482-483	95	10.4-6	73, 177	39-43	220
5.499	96	10.4	73	39	108
5.512-51	52, 94, 95, 164	10.5	73, 159, 240	41-43	109
		10.6	73	47	118
5.513-31	90, 99	10.7	72, 74, 160	61	208
5.514	95	10.8-10	160	62-65	208
5.528-31	95	10.9	72, 73	76-77	125
				76	118

Index of References

85	118	CLASSICAL AND EARLY		16.3	226, 227
90	120	CHRISTIAN TEXTS			
117-150	120	Aristotle		*Didache*	
117-149	208	*De Caelo*		16.1	221
132	125	1.10-12	108	16.7	150
143-144	112	1.10	105, 119		
		1.12	108	Dio Chrysostom	
Quod Deus sit immutabilis		279b17-		*Discourses*	
31	195	280a10	108	36.47-49	119, 125
		280a22	108	36.51-54	119, 125
Legatio ad Gaium		280a11-23	119	36.56-57	116, 213
197-337	136	280a23-27	108	36.58-60	121
JOSEPHUS		*Metaphysics*		Diodorus Siculus	
Antiquities of the Jews		983b6-14	104	*History*	
1.70	66, 97			1.6.3	125
3.320	142	*Meteorologica*			
18.96-104	142	351b8-352b18	113	Diogenes Laertius	
18.109-119	142			7.136	116, 213
18.256-309	136	Augustine		7.142	115, 213
20.97-98	142	*City of God*		10.39	113
20.101	142	20.16	239	10.45	110
				10.73	110
The Jewish War		*Barnabas*		10.74	110
2.17.433-34	142	21.6	226	10.88-90	110
2.184-203	136			10.90	110
4.150-157	145	Cicero			
4.286-287	142	*De finibus*		Empedocles	
6.288-316	174	1.21	110	Frag.17.1-13	106
6.316	145				
7.29-31	142	*De natura deorum*		Epictetus	
		1.67	110	*Discourses*	
NAG HAMMADI TEXTS		2.118	117	3.13.4	125
Concept of Our Great					
Power		Clement of Alexandria		Epicurus	
46	21, 230	*Stromata*		*Epistle to Herodotus*	
		5.14	66	39	113
On the Origin of the		5.121-2	66	45	110
World				73	110
99	14	Clement of Rome		74	110
126-7	21	*1 Clement*			
126	14	23.3	204	*Epistle to Pythocles*	
127.1	14			88-90	110
127.3	14	*2 Clement*		90	110
		5.5	203		
		11.2	204		

Eusebius
Historia ecclesiastica
3.5.3   145

Praeparatio evangelica
1.7   105
13.13.48   66

Gospel of Thomas
21   221
111   246

Hesiod
Theogony
116-135   102
116   102
678-81   102
693-705   102
847-52   102
861-8   103

Hippolytus
Refutatio omnium haeresium
9.27   71
9.30   71

Homer
Iliad
14.201   104
14.246   104

Irenaeus
Adversus haereseis
1.7.1   21, 230
5.30.3   236

Justin Martyr
1 Apology
20.1-4   200, 216
20.1   19
60.8-9   200, 216

2 Apology
7.2-3   200, 216

Dialogue with Trypho
81   236

Lactantius
Institutes
7.1.10   110

Lucan
Pharsalia
1.72-81   124
2.289-92   124
7.135-138   124

Lucretius
De rerum natura
1.248-9   113
1.556   111
2.1105-75   110
2.1105-72   110
2.1118-9   110
2.1136   110
2.1144-45   111
2.1150-52   81
2.1160-70   111
2.1173-4   111
5.65-6   111
5.91-109   110
5.92-6   111
5.104-9   112
5.195-234   113
5.235-415   110, 113
5.235-323   112
5.324-50   112
5.330-1   112
5.345-50   113
5.351-79   113
5.380-415   113, 218
5.828-30   207

Malalas
Chronicle
243.10   142

Minucius Felix
Octavius
11.1-3   217

11.1   200
11.34   200

Origen
Contra Celsum
4.11-13   217
4.64   118
7.29   75

Ovid
Metamorphoses
2.1-400   113

Plato
Critias
109B   112
111A-B   112
112A   112

Leges
677A   112

Republic
378E-283A   107

Timaeus
22C-23A   112
22C-E   66
29A-D   107
29A   219
29E-30A   107
32C   107, 218
33A   107, 220
34B   253
68E   253
92C   253

Pliny the Elder
Naturalis Historia
2.1-2   111
2.84   142
2.236   111, 126
7.73   81, 111

Pliny the Younger
6.20   126

Index of References

Plutarch
De communibus
1075   122

De defectu oraculorum
415F   103

De Stoicorum repugnantiis
1052c   117
1053a   115, 116
1053b   116

Pseudo-Justin
De monarchia
3   66

Pseudo-Seneca
Octavia
391-394   123

Pseudo-Sophocles
Frag.2   52, 66-8, 91, 96

Seneca
De beneficiis
6.22   95, 122

De consolatione ad Marciam
26.6-7   95, 122
26.6   94, 118

Hercules Oetaeus
1102-1117   94, 123

Naturales quaestiones
1.28   219
3.13   213
3.27   122
3.28.7   117, 118, 121, 214
3.29.1   66, 120
3.30.8   82, 122

Thyestes
835-884   123
844-874   95

Tacitus
Annals
6.31-44   142
6.31-37   142

Histories
5.13   174

Tertullian
Against Hermogenes
34   21

Theophilus
Ad Autolycum
2.37-38   200

INDEX OF AUTHORS

Adams, E. 36, 53, 123, 153, 180, 195, 204, 256, 257
Allison, D. C. 1, 2, 10, 16, 52, 69, 138, 141, 147, 170, 200
Andersen, F. I. 40, 41, 86, 87
Anderson, A. A. 29, 33
Anderson, H. 137, 161
Attridge, H. 67, 68, 184, 187, 190, 193, 195
Aune, D. E. 13, 238, 240, 243, 247, 250

Bailey, C. 111, 112
Barclay, J. M. G. 88, 93, 202
Barrett, C. K. 177
Barton, J. 39, 42, 46, 47
Bauckham, R. 150, 201–6, 208, 210–16, 221–4, 227–9, 237, 238, 245, 247, 249
Beale, G. K. 238, 241, 243, 248
Beasley-Murray, G. R. 8, 134, 135, 138, 144, 159, 161, 165, 247
Benz, A. 257
Berkouwer, G. C. 10
Bigg, C. 202, 207, 211
Black, M. 59, 64, 65, 150, 237
Blomberg, C. 10, 164
Bolt, P. G. 139, 152, 153
Borg, M. J. 1
Boring, E. M. 250
Box, G. H. 80, 83
Bridge, S. L. 72
Bruce, F. F. 191, 198
Brueggemann, W. 31
Bullmore, M. A. 4
Bultmann, R. 2, 3
Burnett, F. W. 172
Byrne, B. 4

Cadwallader, A. H. 196
Caird, G. B. 9, 12, 15, 21, 34, 43, 237, 238, 243
Calvin, J. 220
Carrington, P. 8

Carroll, R. P. 39
Casey, M. 152
Chaine, J. 211
Charles, R. H. 71, 72, 74, 240, 243, 245
Childs, B. S. 29
Chroust, A.-H. 112
Clements, R. E. 43, 44
Clines, D. J. 33
Coggins, R. J. 47
Cole, R. A. 138, 157
Collins, J. J. 11, 12, 19, 44, 53, 58, 61, 71, 86, 88–95, 147
Conzelmann, H. 172
Cotterell, P. 156
Craddock, F. B. 206
Cranfield, C. E. B. 15
Crenshaw, J. L. 33, 40
Cross, F. M. 36, 40
Crossley, J. 134, 136, 147, 151, 153

Danker, F. W. 228
Davies, W. D. 170
Day, J. 28, 45
Dillon, J. 195
Donahue, J. R. 137
Downing, F. G. 19, 81, 120, 126, 137, 158
Dyer, K. 5, 17, 138, 144, 145, 153, 158, 166, 258, 259

Earth Bible Team 18
Eddy, P. R. 10
Ellingworth, P. 183, 184, 187, 190, 191, 197
Ellis, E. E. 201
Elsdon, R. 4, 18
Evans, C. A. 135, 136, 138, 140, 145, 161
Evans, C. F. 175, 176
Everson, A. J. 36

Fiorenza, E. S. 236, 238, 243
Fletcher-Louis, C. 9, 161–4, 170, 193
Fornberg, T. 211, 217

Index of Authors

France, R. T. 8, 9, 11, 133, 137–42, 144–9, 152, 156, 158, 162, 167, 180
Freedman, D. N. 40, 41
Furley, D. J. 21, 103–6

Gamble, H. Y. 182
García Martínez, F. 52, 54
Gardner, A. 34, 38
Gathercole, S. J. 2, 74
Geddert, T. J. 12, 141
Gleason, R. C. 193, 194
Gnilka, J. 15
Goldingay, J. 32
Gould, E. P. 8, 136, 161
Gowan, D. E. 64, 87, 88
Green, M. 206, 208, 211, 216
Green, W. M. 110, 111
Gundry, R. H. 138, 158
Gunkel, H. 29

Haas, C. 74
Habel, N. C. 5
Haenchen, E. 177, 180
Hahm, D. 108, 114, 119
Hahn, F. 137
Hamilton, V. P. 27
Hare, D. R. A. 15
Harrington, D. J. 76, 137
Hartman, L. 52, 57, 88, 89, 135, 140, 176
Harvey, A. E. 1
Hatina, T. R. 8, 136, 140, 152, 153, 155, 156, 157
Hayes, K. M. 39, 45, 46
Hayward, R. 100
Hengel, M. 136
Hill, C. C. 257, 259
Hinnells, J. R. 19
Hoffmann, Y. 36
Hooker, M. D. 15, 135, 158, 161
Horrell, D. G. 202, 206, 216, 219, 222, 224, 228
Houtman, C. 32
Hughes, P. E. 191
Hultgard, A. 19
Hurst, L. D. 195, 197
Hurtado, L. W. 15

James, M.R. 76
Jeremias, J. 40

Johnson, D. G. 46
Juel, D. H. 137

Käsemann, E. 204, 232
Kee, H. C. 75, 76
Kelly, J. N. D. 210–12, 214, 216, 222, 224
Kidner, D. 31
King, K. 14
Kittel, B. P. 71
Knibb, M. A. 56, 65, 70, 84
Knight, J. 206
Koester, C. R. 184, 191
Kovacs, J. 237, 247
Kraftchick, S. J. 206, 210, 214, 215, 224, 228

Ladd, G. E. 15
Lane, W. L. 182, 184–89, 192, 193, 198
Lapidge, M. 115, 117, 119, 123, 124, 125
Lawson, J. M. 4
Lenski, R. C. H. 137
Levenson, J. D. 27
Licht, J. 72
Lieu, J. 174
Lincoln, A. T. 182, 190, 192
Long, A. A. 108, 114, 116, 118, 119–22
Luce, J. V. 106, 109, 114
Luz, U. 170

Mack, B. 1
MacRae, G. 14
Mann, C. S. 139, 152, 153
Mansfeld, J. 105, 108, 110, 117, 118, 120, 121, 125, 220
Marcus, J. 136, 142, 145, 148
Marshall, I. H. 147, 173, 175, 176
May, G. 87
Mayor, J. B. 211
McKenzie, J. L. 149
Mealy, J. W. 247
Meier, J. P. 170
Meier, S. 206
Metzger, B. M. 224
Milik, J. T. 237
Moffatt, J. 187, 191
Moloney, F. I. 137, 145, 146, 161
Moltmann, J. 10
Moule, C. F. D. 15
Murphy, F. J. 77

Neyrey, J. H. 206, 207, 223, 224, 228, 232
Nickelsburg, G. W. E. 54–9, 61–6, 75
Nineham, D. E. 137, 161
Nolland, J. 173, 177

Painter, J. 137
Paley, F. A. 103
Paul, S. M. 32
Pearson, B. 91, 215
Perkins, P. 14, 216
Plevnik, J. 169
Polkinghorne, J. 257
Porter, S. E. 136

Raabe, P. 42-44
Reicke, B. 212, 216, 229
Ringgren, H. 52
Rowland, C. 11–12, 53, 57, 64, 65, 68, 135, 141, 236, 237, 247
Rowley, H. H. 74
Runia, D. T. 102, 107, 108
Russell, D. M. 4, 35, 58, 172, 180, 213, 249, 256, 257
Russell, J. S. 8, 200

Sanders, E. P. 1
Schnutenhaus, F. 36
Schweitzer, A. 2
Scott, J. M. 68, 69
Seow, C. L. 33
Sidebottom, E. M. 207
Sim, D. 52, 53, 142, 162, 167, 168, 170, 172
Simkins, R. 25, 26, 28, 49, 52
Skinner, J. 34, 35
Solmsen, F. 110
Stacey, D. 37
Stählin, O. 67
Stewart, R. A. 185
Stoeger, W. R. 257
Stone, M. E. 78, 79, 80–2, 83, 84
Suter, D. W. 58
Swete, H. B. 138, 157, 239, 243
Szeles, M. E. 42

Taylor, N. H. 136
Taylor, V. 137
Theissen, G. 134, 136
Thiede, C. P. 200

Thomas, R. L. 243
Thompson, J. W. 184, 185, 195–7
Tödt, H. E. 137
Tromp, J. 54, 71, 72, 73–4
Tuckett, C. M. 137, 173, 179
Turner, M. 156

Van der Horst, P. W. 27, 67, 71, 75, 91, 97, 98, 100, 121, 222
VanderKam, J. C. 55, 60, 68, 148
Vanhoye, A. 190
Van Iersel, B. M. F. 139, 153, 154
Van Kooten, G. H. 257
Van Ruitten, J. T. A. G. M. 35, 39, 63
Verheyden, 15, 153, 154, 159
Vögtle, A. 3, 4, 138, 189, 192, 206, 215, 216, 224, 228
Volz, P. 13
Von Rad, G. 27, 36

Waterfield, R. 104, 105
Watts, J. D. 34, 35
Weiss, J. 2
Welker, M. 257
Wenham, D. 134, 153, 242
Wenham, G. J. 25–8
Westermann, C. 28, 35, 152
Whybray, R. N. 35
Wildberger, H. 42
Williams, C. J. F. 108
Williams, M. A. 14
Williamson, H. G. M 31
Wilson, R. McL. 191
Winter, B. W. 125, 142
Witherington, B. 15, 145, 161, 177, 180
Wolters, A. 201, 225–8
Wright, M. R. 22, 106, 120
Wright, N. T. 1–18, 20, 21, 53, 73, 74, 99, 100, 133, 136–41, 144, 147–9, 153–6, 161, 162, 167, 180, 181, 192, 193, 200, 201, 225, 230, 233, 234, 238, 252–5, 257

Young, E. J. 43

Zuntz, G. 65

Lightning Source UK Ltd.
Milton Keynes UK
UKHW022017240123
415904UK00005B/190